Christianity and the
Mass Media in America

Rhetoric and Public Affairs Series

Christianity and the Mass Media in America

Toward a Democratic Accommodation

◩ ◩ ◩

Quentin J. Schultze

Michigan State University Press
East Lansing

© 2003 by Quentin J. Schultze

⊗ The paper used in this publication meets the minimum requirements of ANSI/NISO
Z39.48-1992 (R 1997) (Permanence of Paper).

Michigan State University Press
East Lansing, Michigan 48823-5245

Printed and bound in the United States of America.

10 09 08 07 06 05   1 2 3 4 5 6 7 8 9 10
First paperback edition 0-87013-774-3

The Library of Congress catalogued the original hardcover edition of this book as follows:

LIBRARY OF CONGRESS CATALOGING-IN-PUBLICATION DATA
Schultze, Quentin J. (Quentin James), 1952–
Christianity and the mass media in America : toward a democratic accomodation /
Quentin J. Schultze.
p. cm.— (Rhetoric and public affairs series) Includes bibliographical references and index.
ISBN 0-87013-696-8 (alk. paper)
1. Mass media in religion—United States. 2. Mass media—Religious aspects—Christianity.
I. Title. II. Series.
BV652.97.U6S38 2003
261.5'2'0973—dc22
2003020164

Cover design by Julia Herzog
Book design by Sans Serif, Inc.

green press Michigan State University Press is a member of the Green Press Initiative and is
INITIATIVE committed to developing and encouraging ecologically responsible publishing
practices. For more information about the Green Press Initiative and the use of recycled paper in
book publishing, please visit *www.greenpressinitiative.org.*

Visit Michigan State University Press on the World Wide Web at *www.msupress.msu.edu*

Acknowledgments

The debts I incurred while working on this book over the last twenty years extend far beyond my memory. Unable to reconstruct in detail the history of this project, I shall do my best to mention those whose efforts were so obvious that I could not forget them.

I owe special gratitude to former students Jeff Febus, Ernie Stetenfeld III, Sara Jane Toering, Stacey Wieland and Mark Schemper. The McGregor Fund's Fellowship Program supported Ms. Toering's and Mr. Schemper's efforts while both were students at Calvin College. Drake University's graduate school funded Mr. Stetenfeld's work.

The Calvin Center for Christian Scholarship (CCCU) at Calvin College provided support that was crucially important for the completion of this project in the fall of 2001 and the winter of 2002. Jim Bratt and Donna Romanowski of the CCCU staff were especially helpful both conceptually and practically.

A sabbatical leave from Calvin College during the 2000/2001 academic year enabled me to spend nine months in Florida, where I worked with few interruptions under some glorious winter sunshine. The study time enabled me to address some of the more complex aspects of the relationship between religion and the mass media in liberal democracies, making this a significantly better book.

My colleagues in Communication Arts and Sciences at Calvin College were sources of delight and wisdom. Thanks especially to Bob Fortner, Bill Romanowski, and Randy Bytwerk.

The staff of Calvin College's Hekman Library has served me admirably over the years, but I especially want to thank Conrad Bult and Kathy Struck, who gave me more personal attention than I deserved.

Annette K. Tanner, Robert Burchfield, and Jessica Miller of Michigan State University Press deserve special thanks for seeing this through both the production and the editorial processes.

My friend Bob Banning collaborated on the fine points of style and proofing, while Jan Ortiz ably created the excellent index.

Marty Medhurst has been a wonderful colleague and friend on this and other projects. I am honored that my book is part of his excellent series on rhetoric and public affairs with Michigan State University Press.

All errors are mine. Any grace is a gift for which I am eternally grateful.

Contents

Introduction

I address in this book the relationship between the mass media and Christian "tribes" in America. At its core this relationship is a dynamic tension between civil generality, on the one hand, and a sectarian particularity, on the other. The Christian metanarrative of transcendence assumes a theistic perspective where God acts in real human history; this God-oriented view of human affairs is never fully in accord with the mainstream media's own subnarratives of immanence, which morally assume that human action is the beginning and end of history. Nevertheless, religious groups and the media borrow each other's rhetoric both to embrace and to criticize one another. They come together harmoniously during media coverage of emotionally charged events such as the funeral of President John F. Kennedy, the landing of an American spaceship on the moon, and terrorists' destruction of the World Trade Center in New York City.[1] During such historic moments talk of prayer and God in public life seems appropriate. At other times the media and Christian groups fire salvos at each other over issues like political bias in news reporting, the morality of television programming and films, and religious stereotyping. As the studies in this book indicate, the tension between Christianity and the media helps Americans to rediscover their shared public life and gives religious tribes an opportunity to assert their own individualities. Thus the interaction between tribal faith and the mainstream media can contribute positively to public and private life in democratic America.

Although the impact of the media on society has been studied nearly to death, the influence of Christianity on Americans' understanding of the media barely enters contemporary scholarship. The influence of Christianity on the media extends to the depths of public imaging about technology, community, and progress. James W. Carey shows compellingly that American rhetoric about media technology often is quasi-religious.[2] He persuasively argues that the dominant paradigm of mass communication, the "transmission view," emerged from American Protestants' hopes to fashion the New World into the biblical City upon a Hill.[3] Protestants largely controlled mass communication in early America, creating a seductive rhetoric of the "technological sublime" that associated developments in transportation and media technologies with the progressive movement of God in

1

history.[4] For some Protestants, America was the arena in which God was equipping Christians to evangelize the rest of the world.

Mainstream American media became the cultural stage on which Americans eventually expressed secular versions of this utopian rhetoric. Religious rhetoric shaped how America as a nation conversed about the media and how the nation institutionalized media technologies in public and private life. Perhaps the most important dimension of this rhetoric during the twentieth century was the way that it seamlessly equated the marketplace with the New Jerusalem. Popularity became a form of public praise in the United States, a means of implicitly and uncritically discerning culture's intrinsic value for society. No matter how much the media and religion in America appear to be at odds with one another, they borrow from each other cultural forms, rhetorical styles, and message strategies that reflect shared modes of understanding the world.

As Carey argues, new media technologies have elicited both utopian and dystopian American rhetoric.[5] I suggest throughout this book that Americans' rhetoric about new media technologies parallels the hopes and fears expressed in popular Christian theology, particularly evangelical theology. Americans' utopian rhetoric regarding the mass media reflects an evangelistic imagination. Their dystopian rhetoric reflects a moralistic imagination. Most Americans use such evangelistic and moralistic rhetorics to make sense of mass communication, regardless of their religious or secular backgrounds; taken together, these two forms of rhetorical imagining represent a popular theology of the media. This popular theology in turn both influences and is shaped by secular storytelling in society, from television programs and films to the literature of science fiction. Americans often talk about the media alternately as a kind of heaven or hell, Second Coming or Armageddon, Jerusalem or Babylon.[6]

Perhaps only in America could Ray Kurzweil, author of *The Age of Spiritual Machines*, be dubbed a "technopioneer and businessman." And maybe only in the United States would a reviewer write seriously about Kurzweil's prediction that "humans themselves will be sorely tempted to give up their physical bodies entirely in favor of an immortal 'life' as software."[7] By 2029, says Kurzweil, "we'll be able to match the flexibility and intelligence of the human brain, in part by actually reverse-engineering the brain. . . . We'll also be able to plug in to the World Wide Web directly through our brains, without any external equipment."[8] Is this the language of philosophy, science fiction, or theology—or all three? In any case it is distinctly American language formed out of a rhetoric of a popular theology that Kurzweil inherited from both Christianity and the market.

In this book, then, I aim to extend and deepen the scholarly thinking about the connections between Christianity and the media in the United States. I focus on Christianity both because it is the dominant religious expression in America and because among all of the major faiths it has most influenced the nation's rhetoric about the media as well as the media's rhetoric about religion. Along the way I distinguish among various Roman Catholic, mainline Protestant, and evangelical rhetorics about the media. This book is an integrated series of case studies of the rhetorical relationships between Christianity and the media in "one nation under God."

Chapter 1 outlines the five major rhetorical topoi that implicitly guide American sentiments and thought about the mass media: conversion, discernment, communion, exile, and praise. I locate these rhetorical motifs in American cultural history, using the intellectual insights and case studies of the Chicago School of Social Thought and its influential proponents— Charles Horton Cooley, Robert E. Park, Louis Wirth, and, most recently, Carey. I rely extensively on their theoretical insights about communication and culture in order to frame my arguments in distinctly American terms.

The second chapter addresses the historical continuities between popular Christian theology, on the one hand, and American popular rhetoric about the positive social benefits of new media technologies, on the other. My historical inquiry supports Carey's thesis about the "mythos of the electronic revolution."[9] As Protestants imagined the role of new media in God's kingdom, they "baptized" the latest technologies as tools for converting heathens to faith in God. Their distinctly religious rhetoric in turn increasingly shaped the popular American imagination, creating various quasi-religious understandings of communication technologies. Although this rhetoric of the technological sublime is deeply appealing to Americans, it is also challenged by religious criticism that emerges from particular Christian tribes. Park and one of his colleagues, Ernest W. Burgess, capture the reason for tribal criticism of the media: "Every new mechanical device, every advance in business organization or in science, which makes the world more tolerable for most of us, makes it impossible for others."[10] The very media that would supposedly usher in the kingdom of God on earth became the domain of mammon.

Chapter 3 analyzes some of the nuances in Christian responses to the rise of broadcasting in America. I review every article on the subject of radio and television broadcasting in five periodicals—three Roman Catholic

(*America, Commonweal,* and *Catholic World*), one evangelical (*Christianity Today*), and one mainline Protestant (*Christian Century*). The subtleties of media criticism characteristic of different Christian traditions suggest that tribal criticism is one source for some profound and provocative ideas about the role of the media in democratic society, not just in religious communities. Tribal media can engage in media criticism that transcends tribal self-interest with a genuine concern for the public good.

Chapter 4 addresses the role of Christianity in the development of American radio. I explain how evangelicals and fringe sects, in particular, were deeply involved in this medium from the beginning. They not only imagined this medium in evangelistic terms; they also took their messages of salvation to their own religious communities and to the public airways. In the 1920s the Federal Radio Commission (FRC) shut down nearly all of these religious broadcasters by appealing to the "public interest." The commission had the difficult task of distinguishing between tribal interests and the broader public good. In effect, the FRC concluded that the consumer-oriented rhetoric of conversion (advertising) took precedence over all "sectarian" rhetorics of conversion. The FRC's policies forced evangelicals to learn how to operate successfully in a market system by buying airtime, cultivating financial contributors, and crafting engaging programming. The FRC's and later the Federal Communication Commission's dependence on the market, rather than extensive regulation, eventually gave evangelicals an upper hand over the other Christian groups in radio and television broadcasting. As evangelicals championed radio in a market system, however, they also forged a religious consumerism for their tribes. Their rhetoric of conversion backfired.

Chapter 5 addresses the implications of America's "free-market" policy for the rise of national media. In a market system the mainstream commercial media strive for general narratives that will attract large audiences for advertisers. Television, in particular, becomes a priestly social institution organized by managerial experts for the purpose of garnering mass audiences to its broadly mythological fare. In the United States network television became a mythopoetic behemoth, a quasi-religious TV "altar" for the nation.[11] In response to such generic tales, tribal media critics helped their religious communities use tribal metanarratives to critique the mass-mediated subnarratives. I review the media criticism of four tribal critics— Protestants William F. Fore, Edward J. Carnell, and John Wiley Nelson and Roman Catholic Andrew M. Greeley. Once again I discover that some of the best tribal criticism addresses public interests, not just the penchants of the tribes.

Chapter 6 closely examines the quasi-religious mythology of mainstream television programming. Although the centripetal forces of television tend to homogenize religious faith, mainstream programming still must address mythologically some of the most fundamental questions answered by all major religions. Probably the most compelling question is the origin and nature of evil. The secular "gospel" of television implicitly limits evil to particular kinds of people and to specific types of evil action, thereby affirming the myth that Americans might be able to reduce the hurt and hardship around the globe by eliminating these evil people. American television's gospel of hope depends on a limited view of human evil that I call civil sin. This nontribal concept of sin is a linchpin of mainstream media's own rhetoric of communion that seeks to affirm the beliefs of the mass market.

Chapter 7 considers the role of the news media in the relationship between American Christianity and the mass media. The two major news media in the history of early American society were probably the pulpit and the religious press. In the seventeenth century colonial Americans used the "Good News" of the Christian Gospel to frame the "bad news" of the day, thereby interpreting "daily occurrences" in the light of "divine providence." As commercial, secular news media replaced the distinctly religious press during the eighteenth and especially the early nineteenth centuries, the prophetic role of the reporter was increasingly separated from religious communities of interpretation. By 1900 the secular newspaper greatly overshadowed the power of the tribal press, thrusting mainstream journalists into the role of prophet for the increasingly national society. This is partly why the Chicago School in the early years of the twentieth century looked to the newspaper as an organ of "intelligence" that would supposedly ameliorate urban problems and usher in the Great Community.[12] Early-twentieth-century journalists organized their new professional ideology loosely around objectivity and accuracy, essentially adopting the fundamentalist epistemology of Scottish realism. Twentieth-century American reporters thereby used a rhetoric of discernment to claim superior powers of description, but their underlying hermeneutic had much in common with Protestant fundamentalism as well as with scientism. This reductionistic hermeneutic tends to pit the secular news reporters against most Christian tribes' more theistic and metanarrational hermeneutic.

The last chapter draws some conclusions about the interaction of mass media and religions in twentieth-century America, especially the responsibilities of media and religious tribes. How might religious traditions and the media serve each other in democratic America? What is the larger public good that they both need to affirm? By stepping back from the self-interested rhetoric that influences both tribal and media rhetoric, we can discover some reasonable affinities between the media and religion, some areas for healthy conflict, and even some directions for religious sustenance in an increasingly high-tech world. Four healthy tensions are crucial for the future of tribal religion and mass communication in democracy: (1) balancing space-binding and time-binding culture and communication, (2) balancing tribal and public interests, (3) balancing secular and religious culture, and (4) balancing technology and culture. The particularities of religious traditions challenge Americans' communal desire to embrace everyone democratically in public life, but they also open up insightful media criticism and foster habits of the heart that leaven our otherwise overly instrumental and pecuniary culture. As Martin E. Marty once said of denominations, we cannot live with them and we cannot live without them.[13] In a similar fashion the mainstream mass media in America cannot live with religion and cannot live without it. Meanwhile Christian tribes cannot live with or without the secular media. A healthy tension between the media and Christianity is ultimately a good thing for democracy in America, as long as both sides are civil even when they disagree.

1

Conversing about Faith and Media in America

◪ ◪ ◪

Alexis de Tocqueville recalled reading a news story during his visit to the United States in the 1830s about a court in New York where a witness declared that he did not believe in the existence of God or the immortality of the soul. As a result of the witness's confession, the judge refused "to accept his oath, given, he said, that the witness had destroyed in advance all the faith that could have been put in his words." Apparently astonished by the story, Tocqueville added to his report the fact that the newspaper offered no commentary about the judge's decision.[1] Tocqueville wondered how a witness's account of an event could be disregarded simply because the witness did not believe in God. The whole matter astonished Tocqueville but apparently caused little amazement to the reporter who covered the trial.

American democracy depends on religion, but not on any particular religious institutions. Religion in the United States is not fundamentally about church-building programs and theological education, although it certainly includes these kinds of endeavors. Nor is religion largely the pronouncements of Rome, the synodical meetings of Presbyterians, or the conventions of Baptists. As Tocqueville concludes, religion in America includes dynamic cultural activities anchored deeply in the practices of the people. New World Christianity, writes Tocqueville, is "democratic and republican." Each sect, he observes, "adores God in its manner, but all sects preach the same morality in the name of God." As a result, Tocqueville concludes, "America is . . . the place in the world where the Christian religion has most preserved genuine powers over souls; and nothing shows better how useful and natural to man it is in our day, since the country in which it exercises the greatest empire is at the same time the most enlightened and most free."[2]

American religious life is like an ongoing discussion, intimate but open-ended and regulated by social propriety. Sharing what Tocqueville calls "an ostensible respect for Christian morality and equity," Americans join together in religious conversations about who they are and where they are headed as a nation.[3] The American future is wide open, just like the outcome of a rich and meaningful conversation among friends. Without the burden of the particularity of one tradition, Americans are nor inclined to pay full obeisance to the past. Instead they imagine together a future that is possible, even if not probable. Sometimes such imagining is deeply religious, as within a tribe, whereas other times it is more broadly nonsectarian. In both cases Americans frequently have perceived the hoped-for future in religious metaphors and language. Americans have always seen their collective future partly in the sermons and postworship discussions across the land, in the daily prayer of millions of individuals, and especially in the heart-felt religious enthusiasms of citizens. Religion is still a major part of the unregulated conversation that makes America democratic and republican.

American Christianity, too, is not like a scripted sermon or carefully crafted lecture but rather like a conversation played out on the public stages of porch, pew, and religious periodical. The conversation occurs in all types of media, from pulpits to newspapers and from electronic media to cyberspace. Whereas in many countries peoples' religious life is purely personal, private, and traditional—anchored largely in the ossified rituals of the past—in the United States matters of faith have always been part of the ongoing discourse of public as well as private life. James W. Carey, one of the most astute communication theorists and historians in America, argues that the freedoms mentioned in the First Amendment—religion, speech, press, and assembly—are together a "compact way of describing a political economy." The amendment, according to Carey, says "that people are free to gather together without the intrusion of the state or its representatives. Once gathered, they are free to speak openly and fully. They are further free to write down what they have to say and to share it beyond the immediate place of utterance." Freedom of religion, he adds, was absolutely crucial for maintaining this open process of organizing, speaking, and recording Americans' thoughts: "Of all the freedoms of public life in the eighteenth century, freedom of religion was, perhaps, the most difficult liberty for Americans to adjust to. . . . No one could be excluded from the public realm on the basis of religion, the one basis upon which people were likely to exclude one another."[4] If Carey is correct, the founders built religious conversation into the symbolic fabric of American society. America's freedom of religion is nothing short of the liberty to gather religiously, to talk religiously, and to publicize religiously.

This chapter describes the major rhetorical topoi that Americans use to interpret the relationships between mass media and Christianity. Along the way, it also accomplishes four purposes behind the entire volume: (1) to offer a rationale for documenting American religious history culturally in the mediated conversations of the people rather than institutionally in the official documents of churches, denominations, and parachurch organizations; (2) to reconstruct some of these American conversations about Christianity and the media as Christians and the general public have expressed them in and through the mass media primarily during the twentieth century; (3) to use the theory of communication developed by the Chicago School of Social Thought to illuminate the dynamic interplay of religion and the media in American life; and (4) to establish the importance of rhetorical imagination in the history of the relationship of media and Christianity in America.[5] This history, representing national as well as local and parochial conversations, occurs as an ongoing dialogue about Americans' hopes and fears, not just about the media and religion.

The main focus of this chapter, however, is to describe the five major rhetorical topoi that serve as doors to the public arenas in which Americans imaginatively discussed the media and faith. These rhetorical topoi are conversion, discernment, communion, exile, and praise. Each of the subsequent chapters examines how the media and Christian tribes used the topoi in particular contexts. By "rhetoric" I do not mean empty verbiage or purely self-interested persuasion; nor do I mean false talk or ideological jargon. I simply mean the ways that people used meaningful verbal and nonverbal symbols to interpret their world, to build and share those interpretations with others, and sometimes to persuade outsiders to agree with tribal or mainstream beliefs. In this sense, rhetoric is essentially an intentional form of persuasive communication in which participants pay attention to their public discourse, including how that discourse relates to their own self-identities, to others' identities, and to their private as well as other public interests. As Martin J. Medhurst and Thomas W. Benson suggest, the study and practice of rhetoric have a long and distinguished history in Western culture and certainly include the study of mass-mediated forms of communication.[6] As a land of ongoing conversations, America is a lively symbolic arena in which tribal and mainstream rhetorics interact partly in and through the media.

The Rhetoric of Conversion

During the twentieth century mainstream American media and the church—by "church" I mean all Christian groups—created contrasting versions of the same vocational rhetoric: a calling to build media organizations that would attract, engage, and convert people to faith. As strange as it might seem today, the mass media in America were grounded in the particularly Protestant notion that communication, including the press, had the power to change people, to beneficially alter their perspective, and to usher them into a new community of shared hope. Tocqueville was amazed at the fact that in America "there is almost no small town that does not have its own newspaper." He was also surprised at the amount of space in the press allocated to advertising, probably the most characteristically American form of public communication. The press, he recognized, extended to "all opinions of men. It modifies not only laws, but mores."[7] Americans negotiated and maintained culture partly through innovative public media, not just through ritualistic obedience to tradition. In other words, the constant process of cultural conversion, of cultural movement toward something new and potentially better, kept America afloat in the turbulent seas caused by the ongoing arrival of new and different people to the land of opportunity. As Alvin W. Gouldner points out, American Puritanism largely replaced the ritual of the Mass with the exhortation of the sermon. "In the sermon," he writes, "the age of ideology could find a paradigm of righteous and energetic persuasion, the paradigm of a rhetoric that could mobilize men to deeds."[8] The advertiser and the preacher were two sides of the same rhetorical strategy—conversion. No matter how much they disagreed about the message, they shared a rhetoric of conversion.

By the time of Tocqueville's arrival in the 1830s, America was a land of open persuasion, propaganda, and presentations of all kinds—a country of largely unrestricted attempts and wide-open means to convert others to one cause or another. Born out of hope in the future, America embraced a rhetoric of conversion that included both faith and commerce. Modern advertising, which is essentially an American invention, is particularly important as a form of nonreligious conversion. Indeed consumerism itself is a type of evangelization, a means of transforming people into dedicated buyers and then encouraging them to live faithfully in what Daniel Boorstin calls "consumption communities."[9] The ways that Americans imaginatively think of the media as means for improving society—whether through public-service campaigns, regulating media content, or winning the nation to Jesus Christ—are formed out of the nation's strongly Protestant and deeply evangelical roots in a sermonic rhetoric of conversion. Some American Christians complain about the ways that the media try to entertain, inform, and persuade, but they rarely question whether the media should even try to influence citizens; the presumed propaganda function of the media is an accepted part of the mass-media's evangelistic calling in the United States. Even national disasters become special media events in which Americans claim shared sentiments and call the country to become more of what it claims to be, a place of happiness and compassion, justice and peace. Governmental regulators believe that by shaping how the media are used they can socially engineer a better society—just as their opponents plead persuasively that the free market of unbridled liberty will create a better nation.

The rhetoric of conversion is a crucial aspect of the Protestant impulse in American culture, partly an outgrowth of the country's legacy of revivalism. Television, of all of the mass media, has most captured the imaginations of Protestants who eagerly hope to use it to ameliorate social and psychological ills. Religious television is largely the product of conversionary-minded American Protestantism.[10] Roman Catholic television, apart from the amazing popularity of Bishop Fulton J. Sheen in the 1950s, is largely imitative and derivative of Protestant programming.[11] Even the satellite network of Mother Angelica, one of the most striking Catholic television personalities, is grounded in a tribal call for conversion that beckons Catholic Christians back to the one true faith.[12] Judaism has produced only one moderately popular television celebrity, Jan Bresky; even he shares the conversionary rhetoric.[13] American Protestants created a powerful rhetoric of conversion that shapes practically every excursion into religious broadcasting. Protestants have long imagined mass-media technologies as powerful tools for transforming culture, building churches, and teaching society moral lessons. American media endeavors almost inevitably take on a sermonic quality.

Historically speaking, this Protestant enthusiasm for religious television in the United States is hardly surprising. From the printing press to early radio and eventually satellites, Protestants dominated religious mass communication in America. American Catholics and Jews were less interested in evangelization and far more preoccupied with maintaining their religio-ethnic identities across generations or simply assimilating into the largely Protestant nation. In other words, Protestant communication tended toward cultural conversion, while Catholic and Jewish communication tended toward cultural conservation. Of course there have been Protestant pockets of resistance, such as some North American Anabaptist communities and Midwestern enclaves of ethnic Lutheranism and Calvinism.[14] In spite of such countervailing religious sentiments, however, the rhetoric of conversion is so strong in American Protestantism and so deeply entrenched in the public imagination that few religious groups are able to resist the lure of the imagery or to deny the aesthetic delight that such rhetoric elicits. The overall exploitation of mass communication by Americans is stunning. But the story of religious media in the United States is unparalleled around the world. Beginning with Puritan book publishing, continuing with the Bible and tract societies' revolution in mass printing and distribution during the 1830s, and culminating today in Protestant excursions into cyberspace, Protestant mass communication is a crucial element in the story of American cultural history, not just religious history.[15] American history is partly the tale of a heterogeneous people balancing their conversionary desires to change each other with their communal hope to be a cohesive nation. To be American has meant to be both tribal and American, to pursue tribal interests but also those of the public good—both with conversionary zeal.[16]

The history of American media reflects the myriad ways that the nation and especially its Protestant tribes have tried to grow through conversion. Historians Harry S. Stout and Nathan O. Hatch address the significance of Protestant communication in early America. Stout's work on early American preaching documents the influential role of the sermon as a public act of cultural formation, not just religious expression.[17] Hatch shows how preaching, music, and later printing generated a multimedia explosion of popular Protestantism.[18] Long before the rise of American fundamentalism and well before the development of broadcast evangelism, American Protestantism was anchored in public persuasion as much as in personal piety. In this sense, American Protestant culture has always had its evangelistic impulses, and the distinctions between evangelical and mainline groups have often reflected contrasting rhetoric about conversion more than widely different commitments to conversion.[19]

As Perry Miller argued, nineteenth-century Protestant thought about the predicted benefits of mass communication largely drove the nation's rapid industrial expansion and paved the way for the twentieth-century explosion in religious media in America. From the mid-nineteenth century to the present, American Protestants became the champions of religiously inspired technological rhetoric. Their evangelistic hopes blended powerfully with the nation's technological dreams and its ongoing industrial progress. Faith *and* technology became faith *in* technology, and eventually it was hard to distinguish between missionary activity and technological innovation.[20] Missionary endeavors, more than other religious activities, became matters of technique and causes for technological development and celebration. American Protestants did not just use technology; they thought in terms of technology. In Jacques Ellul's language, they became "technologically minded" religious entrepreneurs.[21] The rhetoric of conversion drove America's technological imagination.

Of all of the metaphors used by American Protestants to describe earthly paradise, perhaps the most lasting and evocative is the City upon a Hill. New England Puritans such as Massachusetts governor John Winthrop, who used the phrase to coalesce the Puritanical imagination, dreamed of that city. If the Church of England was unredeemable, perhaps America, the virgin wilderness, could become God's new community—a beacon of spiritual light for the world, a truly holy city, the New Jerusalem. Three centuries later, Republican president Ronald Reagan saw the same city. Hardly a Puritan, Reagan was a movie star-turned-political-orator who preached the metaphor, but with a combination of jeremiad and apocalypse. His hilltop city was a providential place of freedom and prosperity, God's chosen beacon of liberty to the rest of the world. But it was also a city of villains, including Democrats and Communists. The Puritans had dreamed of the New Jerusalem in sermons and books. America's president, dubbed the Great Communicator, dreamed on television. His pulpit was the Oval Office of the White House, and his national congregation was a remarkably heterogeneous collection of residents of the New World, including converted Democrats who helped elect him in 1980.

The rhetorical idea of a place for the American Dream—however defined—came alive in this nation's discourse about the media during the

twentieth century. The media came to represent the general hope that society could be improved through the power of mass communication. This
rhetoric was an ode to persuasion or, to put it more religiously, an aria to
the power of symbols to foster social progress as well as to save souls. This
quasi-religious calling appears in virtually every form of mass communication in the United States: when a televangelist gets on the airways to win
people to Jesus Christ; when an advertiser pays $8 million for a handful of
thirty-second spots during the Super Bowl; when political candidates try to
control the ways that news organizations will present their case to the
American people; or when bookstores fill their shelves with the newest
round of self-help books. If Americans share any ideas in common, says sociologist Allan Nevins, surely one of them is a hope in the future.[22] The future is a source of hope precisely because of the presumed malleability of
the human condition through communication, from therapy sessions to
self-help literature and workout videos. "A new day is dawning," say thousands of commercials and preach hundreds of Christian radio and television broadcasts; the City upon a Hill is under construction.

In the first half of the twentieth century, Louis Wirth and his colleagues
in Chicago expressed this evangelistic optimism in the midst of the city's
rapid industrialization and the resulting decline in social solidarity among
traditional ethnic groups. Wirth wondered whether the growing "mass" of
people could become an "organized group," a people of shared sentiment
and common values rather than just a collection of disparate egos and personalities. The mass, he wrote, "has no common customs or traditions, no
institutions, and no rules governing the action of the individuals." It is made
up of "unattached individuals or, at best, individuals who for the time being
behave not as members of a group, playing specific roles representative of
their position in that group, but rather as discrete entities." He perceived
that mass communication was "rapidly becoming, if it is not already, the
main framework of the web of social life." In the midst of the apparent fragmentation of society, Wirth and his colleagues remained hopeful that the
media could "hold together" the "human race."[23] If mass media were the
problem because they challenged tribal traditions, perhaps they were also
the solution that could rebind the nation to a new consensus. If mass communication could break apart relationships and weaken cultural customs,
perhaps it could also rebuild new, better American communities of shared
values and beliefs.[24] After all, argued Wirth, Hitler "and his cohorts" recognized that the media "instrumentalities" were the "principal means for
moving great masses of men into at least temporary adherence to their

objectives and in using them for their own purpose. That they almost succeeded and that the rest of the world had to pay a terrible price in blood and treasure at the last moment to avert their domination might serve as a warning to those who minimize the importance of mass communication."[25] The media were two-edged swords; they could cut swaths of freedom or of oppression. It was up to democratic America to use communication technologies wisely to build consensus for the future of liberty.

Americans' hopes and fears about the media are two sides of the same rhetoric of conversion. As conversations within American churches and denominations increasingly addressed the growth of the modern mass media, they alternately focused on the perceived problems, especially secularization, and on the opportunities, particularly evangelizing the masses. But in both cases Americans tended to think hopefully about the kind of society and even the type of world that they might be able to produce through judicious use of media technologies. From congregational multimedia systems to the use of computers and the Internet in public schools, Americans still imagine the potential for social and cultural progress as primarily a technical issue.

The evangelistic metaphor of conquering evil gives American rhetoric about the media a moral-spiritual cast. The editors of the official periodical of the United Methodist Church wrote in 1948 about movies, "We believe the support of good pictures by good people is a wider method of winning quality than is censorship. To that end we direct our Board of Education to examine the motion pictures, and to inform our people weekly in *The Christian Advocate* whether these pictures meet our standards of the true, the good and the beautiful, and which are proper for children, youth and adults." The medium is a "powerful persuader," the magazine warned, that "has lured thousands . . . into evil habits," but it can "just as easily turn more thousands against immorality and crime, if it will portray sin in its sordidness."[26] The belief that bad can be converted into good resonates deeply with American sentiments about hard work and the promises of the future. "In mass communication we have unlocked a new social force of as yet incalculable magnitude," writes Wirth. "In comparison with all previous social means for building or destroying the world this new force looms as a gigantic instrument of infinite possibilities for good or evil."[27] Wirth imagined not just like a humanistic sociologist, but also like an optimistic and pragmatic American.

Americans feel a sense of evangelistic calling to use the media to usher in a better world. No matter how disillusioned they become about particular misuses of mass communication, Americans remain sanguine about the future, which will presumably introduce even better technologies and more efficient ways of creating a veritable heaven on earth. This kind of optimistic rhetoric may be the most important strain of thought in the interaction of Christianity and the media in the twentieth century. Americans planted secular versions of the rhetoric of the City upon a Hill in virtually every social institution that uses communication technologies. As the nation moved into the twenty-first century, the rhetoric of evangelistic calling was as strong as ever, although its contemporary expressions frequently were disconnected from its religious roots. If nothing else, the media symbolized the potential for transforming a nation of disparate people into one land of shared hope. Nothing held together this rhetoric more powerfully than the fear that America was becoming too diverse. "Today the myth of an intractably divided people—a polyglot people divvied up by race, class, sex, language," writes columnist Paul Greenberg, "is celebrated as diversity. And sure enough, we become more diverse. For we become what we celebrate. Myths still make reality. And the integrity, the oneness of civil life breaks up. From out of the one, we become many."[28] The evangelistic calling of Americans is to remake the many as one, to forge unity even while promoting liberty. The problem is that Americans often cannot agree on who or what that "one" is. Meanwhile the mainstream media implicitly take up the cause of consensus, offering the market system as the process for unifying Americans under the creed of consumption. In response Christian tribes often clamor for a rhetoric of discernment to help them keep their cultural distance from the perceived evils of the wider world, including the media.

The Rhetoric of Discernment

If Americans think about using the media to convert everyone to a world of peace and harmony, they also imagine the media as sources of differentiation, diversity, and competing dominions. Religion, as Carey points out, was a crucial part of the U.S. Constitution's First Amendment precisely because religion is a source of tension and disagreement in any multicultural society.[29] The nation's competing religions are a crucial dimension of American self-identity. During the twentieth century the United States became a nation of a myriad of international and local faiths, of cults and denominations, parachurch groups and religious movements. When Wirth and Robert E. Park looked at Chicago in the early decades of the twentieth century, they saw growing diversity represented largely by the influx of

Roman Catholics and the public visibility of Protestant denominations that tended to attract different social classes, from upscale Presbyterians and Episcopalians to middle-class Baptists and Methodists, and from working-class Pentecostals to the inner-city black churches that Park fondly studied. "We are forced," Park wrote in "Missions and the Modern World," "to realize that a society whose intellectual direction consists only of unrelated specialisms must drift and that we dare not drift any longer." The task of missions, he argued, is "to create from the existing social and cultural units a common culture and a moral solidarity in which all can share."[30]

In the American imagination the differences among people are simultaneously the bases for intertribal division and the sources of strength. Taken too far, diversity destroys the common sentiments that hold the nation together culturally. American diversity has come to include special-interest groups based on gender, sexual orientation, leisure activities, political issues such as gun control and abortion, and probably thousands of others. The mass media, as agents of social change, are right in the middle of the fray of competing cultural tribes. As an alternative to forging a society of superficial homogeneity, Americans create, discern, and celebrate differences among themselves—as long as those differences do not fundamentally challenge the "sacred" nonnegotiables of what it means to be an American, such as freedom and hope. The intersection of religion and the media is one of the most cherished and contested public arenas in which Americans discern the many competing self-identities.

Mass media, as agents of diversification and differentiation, enable new religious groups and quasi-religious movements to form across the boundaries of geographic space and even across traditional religious groups. These new groups and parachurch movements are usually grounded in such things as shared moral standards, ideological beliefs, missionary causes, and self-help philosophies. Most of these organizations encourage members to take their faith seriously by participating financially if not symbolically in social movements that transcend American individualism. Evangelicals may be the major media participants, but mainline Protestants and Roman Catholics are involved as well. These diverse groups and movements enliven local churches while contributing to what Robert Wuthnow cogently calls the "restructuring of American religion" into ideologically polarized, cross-denominational categories.[31] American public conversation during the twentieth century increasingly addressed the growing differences among citizens rather than their shared beliefs and collective actions—the same trends that troubled the Chicago School decades earlier. The line between healthy cultural differentiation and destructive social conflict is not always clear in America. Rhetorics of discernment enable a cultural group to identify itself as a distinct tribe and to strengthen its cohesiveness across space, but they can also challenge the common cultural threads of cross-tribal national identity.

For their limited experience with electronic media, members of the Chicago School captured an amazingly persuasive snapshot of how mass media fostered cultural fragmentation in America. "The characteristic feature of public opinion in our society," writes Wirth, "lies both in the fact that so many human beings are affiliated with a variety of organized groups, each of which represents only a segment of their interest, and that another large proportion of our fellow men is unattached to any stable group."[32] Public consensus, he realizes, depends on agreement among diverse individuals and groups. If the concept of "public opinion" is to mean anything more than a statistical rendering of how people in such a heterogeneous society feel about a given issue or problem, then such consensus somehow has to help reconnect the various competing groups that make up the nation. But if public opinion replaces all tribalism it will also destroy the cultural distinctions necessary for strong tribes. "In modern society," says Wirth, "men exercise their influence and voice their aspirations through delegated powers, operating through functionaries and leaders, through lobbies, party organizations, religious denominations, and a variety of other organized groups."[33] In other words, the mass media depend on other mediating bodies in society for democracy to work well; "organized groups," in particular, can participate through such media in the wider social world. If an American is no longer comfortable in one or another group, he or she can simply move along to other voluntary associations. Without such mediating organizations, Americans might only be able to participate in society as lone individuals or as an incoherent mass.

The interaction of the media and Christianity in America is part of this massive shift from relatively small rural towns and local geographies of shared culture to a heterogeneous nation of many identity-forming groups with their own speech communities and their distinct modes of cultural discernment. Carey, relying extensively on the work of Canadian scholar Harold Adams Innis as well as that of the Chicago School, uses the term "centrifugal" to describe this process of social and cultural fragmentation and diversification.[34] Mass-media technologies, he argues, help facilitate the development of "specialized media of communication located in ethnic, occupational, class, regional, religious and other 'special interest' segments of society." These segmented groups, formerly dependent upon "face-to-face contact," are increasingly organized into new, national groups held together by mass-mediated symbols that "transcend space, time, and culture."[35] In the early twentieth century, while mainstream American media were evangelistically gathering up massive national audiences for advertisers of consumer goods, tribal media were helping subcultures to stake out their own symbolic terrain within the national landscape. In the early years of the century, religious groups did this almost entirely through in-house publishing, but by the 1920s the centrifugal energy moved partly to radio, then to television in the 1950s and 1960s, and eventually to the Internet in the 1990s. Thus, while national media enabled the formation of relatively homogeneous consumer cultures, they also facilitated the creation and expansion of all kinds of specialized national tribes. Indeed the cultural threats of secular media elicited flurries of tribal responses through their own media. Rhetorics of conversion led to opposing rhetorics of discernment.

American Christian groups, from denominations to parachurch ministries, used media to build their distinctive identities and to differentiate themselves from others in the expanding nation. In fact, the tribal call to conversion was often not so much a reaching out to the unsaved as it was a means for Christian movements and institutions to assert their own beliefs to themselves, on the one hand, and to legitimize their particular beliefs to the rest of society, on the other. Christian tribes immediately began using radio in the 1920s to express publicly their distinctive beliefs and to discern the differences between themselves and what they imagined as apostate mainstream culture. Of course the people who operated these early radio stations claimed that they were evangelizing the nation, but there is not much evidence that most of them were very successful. Clearly, however, a public presence on the radio helped such tribes convince themselves that they were a group to be reckoned with in American society—that they had a distinct message and the God-given authority to express themselves. One after another, dozens of Protestant denominations started radio ministries largely to show their own group that they were important in the expanding national culture. Mass communication became the major public means for a kind of self-referencing legitimacy among American religious groups, especially Protestants. They perceived broadcasting as a vehicle to help them step out of the parochialism of the religio-ethnic tribe and into the cosmopolitan world of the new, expanding

America. Religious groups could thereby articulate their own rhetorical voice across geographic space. Christian journals of comment and opinion, for instance, became public but also tribal voices of discernment for particular Roman Catholic and Protestant traditions. Like organizations that today launch public ministries on the Internet, thereby circumventing the older, established media, these organizations that operated radio and later television ministries took their distinct messages directly to American listeners and viewers.

The growth of the mass media in twentieth-century America, then, did not simply homogenize Christianity within the expanding industrial nation—although it did diminish the importance of some demarcations among Christian groups—but instead facilitated forms of religious discernment already begun by print media in the nineteenth century. Throughout the book the word "tribe" refers to each of the Christian groups and movements in America. I mean no disrespect by that term. Rather I hope to encourage discussion about the ongoing "tribalization" of American Christianity. Christianity in the United States is remarkably dynamic and diverse, with a plethora of different groups claiming dominion over their own, distinctive versions of the faith. Often these tribes differ as much in their cultural sensibilities and styles of rhetoric as they do in their official beliefs. They cultivate distinct habits of the heart and modes of expression, not just opposing worldviews or theological and biblical doctrines. Some of these are independent local congregations, for instance, while others are relatively small but amazingly cohesive associations and parachurch ministries that exist in and through their own specialized media, from magazines to broadcast programs and Web sites. Carey argues that beginning in the 1970s such cultural fragmentation exploded under the pressures of new media, from cable TV to the VCR and eventually cyberspace.[36] But American Christianity has been tremendously diverse at least from the early years of the twentieth century forward. For all of the apparent standardization and homogenization among so-called megachurches during the 1980s and 1990s, and in spite of the weakening of some denominational allegiances, American Christianity is still a smorgasbord of tribes.

Using rhetorics of discernment, the various Christian groups in America formed their own social institutions, including specialized mass media, partly to shore up support for their local groups grounded in familial, ethnic, and community ties. Religious tribes engaged print and electronic media as rhetorical mediating structures between the mainstream media institutions and the individual members of their tribes.[37] No reading of the history of the relationships between Christianity and the media would make sense without recognizing that the social interactions among religious and nonreligious groups, including between the media and local churches, often are influenced by other social institutions, from schools to denominations and religious media. In his early sociology textbook, *Social Organization: A Study of the Larger Mind* (1909), Charles Horton Cooley identified the crucial importance of the "primary group" in shaping individual self-identity. Primary groups, in his view, included "the family, the playgroup of children, and the neighborhood or community of elders."[38] Church communities often provided religion-based primary groups that somewhat insulated the local tribe from the mainstream mass media.

But Cooley also argued that the "existing creeds" of the churches, "formulated in a previous state of thought, have lost that relative truth that they once had and are now, for most of us, not creeds at all, since they are incredible." "We need to believe," he wrote, but "we shall believe what we can."[39] So what could people believe in twentieth-century America? Could traditional religious and orthodox creeds, often expressed in printed media, meaningfully differentiate among religious groups in America? "Without some regular and common service of the ideal, something in the way of prayer and worship," wrote Cooley, "pessimism and selfishness are almost sure to encroach upon us."[40] Cooley could not shake off his own intellectual pretensions in order to see more lucidly the grassroots dynamism of populist Christianity. He hoped for a new, rational faith anchored in basic principles that everyone, including the well-educated person, could believe. Like later Progressives, Cooley wanted to overcome the nation's competing rhetorics of discernment with a rational rhetoric of communion, but the new mass-mediated alternatives to the primary group would make such national consensus increasingly unlikely. Tribes often generated their own personality cults and in-house experts who depended on strong rhetorics of discernment to maintain tribal status and authority.

Cooley and the other members of the Chicago School believed that the mainstream national media could serve a "quasi-religious" purpose by fostering rational substitutes for the primary group and local tribes. John Dewey thought, for instance, that the newspaper could help to usher in "'one world' of intelligence and understanding."[41] Faith no longer needed to be expressed with parochial particularity because, as Cooley put it, "Jesus himself had no system: he felt and taught the human sentiments that underlie religion and the conduct that expresses them. . . . The perennial truth of what Christ taught comes precisely from the fact that it was not a system, but an intuition and expression of higher sentiments the need of which is a central and enduring element in our best experience." Cooley even argued that the "less intellectual a religious symbol is the better, because it less confines the mind." He concluded that the church is "possibly moving toward a differentiated unity, in which the common element will be mainly sentiment—such sentiments as justice, kindness, liberty and service. These are sufficient for goodwill and cooperation, and leave room for all the differentiation of ideas and methods that the diversity of life requires."[42] Cooley's Social Gospel essentially rejected the tribalization of faith in favor of a more generic and unified religion that would rise above the clatter of denominations and squelch the cacophony of sects and cults. Cooley saw the importance of local primary groups, but he also perceived the need for new groups that would reach beyond parochial mythology for a more scientific, cultured, and universal approach to the religious life. Cooley and his colleagues discerned a fundamental difference between formal, rational forms of knowledge and more informal, personal ways of knowing.[43] They sought a new type of nonreligious knowing that would somehow combine science and religion. In other words, they hungered for a national rhetoric of discernment that would have the power to distinguish between knowledge and superstition, between mere custom or habit and rational thought and action.

Of course in hindsight Cooley and his colleagues misread the times. First, the mainstream media never were able to provide the kind of public enlightenment that would make parochial religious belief unnecessary. Walter Lippmann, who shared many of the Chicago School's sentiments about merging faith and science, later argued in *Public Opinion* that American society should have the equivalent of Plato's philosopher-kings who would use the national media to spread truth and wisdom.[44] As Carey has suggested, Lippmann rejected the need for a public; the news experts would somehow be able to know truth and to act upon that truth without the vagaries of public sentiment or the traditionalism and parochialism of the tribe. Lippmann's own rhetoric of discernment distinguished between experts and common citizens, between the intelligentsia and the less-discerning citizens. He created a new tribe of reporter-kings while rejecting the possibility for a cross-tribal public. The "public," argues Carey, was actually the "God term of the press, the term without which the press does not make any sense. In so far as the press is grounded, it is grounded in the public."[45] Under Lippmann's scenario, the religious tribes in America are part of the problem rather than part of the solution to the nation's need for unity; religious groups foster special-interest rhetoric, unenlightened discernment, and eclectic dominion.

The Chicago School was wrong, secondly, in its hope that a new Social Gospel would replace sectarian religion. The so-called liberal church movement gained momentum early in the twentieth century, but the real story of American Christianity, in terms of growth and impact, was the uncanny ability of traditional denominations to more or less keep their spiritual and theological moorings in the midst of the turbulent storms occurring in the surrounding culture.[46] The United States was created largely by Europeans seeking religious and other freedoms; since then one religious group after another has taken its own rhetorical place in the nation's conversations about what it means to be American. As a result, America is about as religiously tribalized as one can imagine in a unified land, with new religious groups born every year and older ones transforming themselves into new and varied institutions—a stunning array of religious variety maintained partly in and through tribal media. If anything, the rhetoric of the Social Gospel was subsumed by liberal democratic thought and increasingly disappeared as a distinct theology with its own public conversation. At least this is what happened at formerly religious American universities that tried to hang on to the ethos of the Social Gospel without maintaining the particularity of Christian tradition and the close ties to sponsoring denominations.[47] When a cultural group fails to discern its differences with the wider culture, it is often assimilated and ceases to exist as a separate tribe with its own conversations. As Raymond Williams posits, a religion is a distinctive zone of signification that simultaneously exists within a wider culture and society.[48] Although a religious tribe's membership may be relatively small, usually its rhetorical claims are broader and deeper than those of the wider culture. This is partly why in America religious rhetorics of discernment will always represent a threat to democracy even as they foster the moral backdrop necessary for civil discourse. There can be no democracy without the freedom to discern. Religion and public opinion, in particular, are both expressions of the social will, as Ferdinand Tönnies suggests, and therefore will always more or less conflict.[49]

The Rhetoric of Communion

Cooley and his compatriots in Chicago recognized that emerging centripetal media were increasingly shaping the cultural contours of American life. Citizens willingly consumed these mainstream media, presumably because they enjoyed the narratives, sentiments, and personalities of popular culture. In addition, Americans desired to be "one," to find a common culture in the midst of their cultural and ethnic diversity. Most American Christians were not only tribal but also patriotic; they loved the land of the free and wanted the best for those who identified with other tribes. John Locke believed that to be a member of the public was to accept a calling.[50] If he was right, members of the Christian tribes heard two callings and resided in two worlds, which Augustine called the "City of Man" and the "City of God."[51] Members of the tribes had dual allegiances, two masters. National freedom made it possible for tribes both to cultivate their own subcultures and to participate in the cross-tribal culture disseminated through mainstream mass media. These national media gave Americans an opportunity to participate in this supratribal world of shared national sentiment and belief. The telegraph launched electronic national communication in the 1830s, eventually creating the national news services and national news media. National magazines also contributed to coast-to-coast consumer cultures beginning in the 1890s. By the 1930s the new medium of radio was part of the national system of communication. As Carey puts it, "Modern communications media allowed individuals to be linked, for the first time, directly to a national community without the mediating influence of regional and other local affiliations."[52] Wirth observed that the new mass media "transcend the peculiar interests and preoccupations of the special and segmental organized groups and direct their appeal to the mass."[53] Mass media symbolized a new American unity, a national communion of all people from every tribe.

The interaction of Christianity and the media occurs in the midst of the rise of increasingly visible and powerful national media. By and large these mainstream media had little interest in distinctly religious issues and institutions throughout the twentieth century. The major nationally syndicated newspaper columnists and radio and television networks generally overlooked the proliferation of religious tribes. Mainstream news media historically ignored religion unless it was directly related to events that were politically or economically newsworthy. Similarly, network television, arguably the major American storyteller of the 1950s through the 1990s, only occasionally paid attention to Christianity. Christian individuals consumed large quantities of mainstream media, but mainstream media were interested primarily in garnering heterogeneous audiences for advertisers, not in addressing the specialized interests of religious groups. Indeed the various sections of any contemporary issue of *USA Today*—sports, money, life, and news—reflect which secular groups were granted rhetorical space in the emerging, national media already in the 1930s. As Wirth put it, "Mass communication is rapidly becoming, if it is not already, the main framework of the web of social life." Striving to garner larger audiences, these media "tend furthermore to be as near everything to everybody and hence nothing to anybody as it is possible to be."[54] In other words, visible national media yoked themselves abstractly to national markets instead of to existing tribal cultures, creating new means for Americans to create rhetorics of communion across geographic space.

Without a state church and with a largely free-market approach to media regulation, the United States was a fertile ground for the interaction of the Christian metanarrative with the mainstream media's own subnarratives— those mediated stories not linked explicitly to any particular worldview or to a political philosophy. Indeed a major part of the story of church-media interaction is the rhetorical tensions and continuities between the Christian Gospel and the everyday stories of mainstream news, drama, comedy, sports, and advertising. Within each of the Christian tribes, Christianity's core narrative—the Gospel, or the Christian metanarrative—interacts with the more general and contingent narratives of mainstream media. Instead of eclipsing tribal culture, the large mass-media empires found themselves increasingly at odds with the various tribes' own public spokespersons, from media critics to lobbyists and media boycotters. The deeper that the mainstream media were able to penetrate American mass audiences, the more feisty and in some cases resilient many religious tribes seemed to become. Intratribal communion was often much more powerful than nationalistic, consumer-oriented, and market-driven communion. As Chapter 3 shows, religious periodicals' responses to the rise of television were sometimes finely tuned and deeply penetrating critiques of the media, but such critiques were almost entirely for tribal rather than general consumption. If religious journals wanted to maintain their own tribal audiences, clearly they had to address subjects and concerns that their readers shared. A large measure of the interaction of media and Christianity in the twentieth century was the creative ways that Christian tribes and their media critics assessed and evaluated mainstream media. Tribes often assumed that the nation's mainstream media and broader culture were one and the same. By discerning the difference between themselves and the mainstream culture, the tribes unified their own ranks and built national communities of resistance. Tribes often were far more interested in internal rhetorics of communion that directly served the cohesiveness of the tribe than they were in

supratribal rhetorics of communion that seemingly threatened tribal autonomy and integrity.

Nevertheless, the growth of mainstream media put Christian tribes on
the defensive with respect to both social control and social status. For good
or for bad, the mass media became enormously important agents of social
control that tended to serve the interests of mass markets and advertisers
more than the needs of either the general public or any of the special-
interest tribes. American communication companies became experts at
identifying markets and producing media products and programming that
would attract economically viable audiences and readerships. The systems
of public polling and market research, as Carey says, became substitutes for
the public. "Public life started to evaporate with the emergence of the public opinion industry and the apparatus of polling," writes Carey. "In political theory, the public was replaced by the interest group as the key political
actor. But interest groups, by definition, operate in the private sector, behind the scenes, and their relationship to public life is essentially propagandistic and manipulative."[55] Polling, market research, and all kinds of
consumer- and political-oriented research gave the mainstream media and
their allied agencies an influential role as seemingly legitimate agents of
social control. The national media became the real evangelists, the main
tag team that carried the mantle of social control directly into the various
tribes that made up "mass society." Meanwhile religious tribes responded
both defensively and proactively through their own centrifugal media and
somewhat through the mainstream media to assert their particular interests and to express their sentiments in order to protect their stake in the
American Dream.

The mainstream media's rhetoric of communion entered the cultural
contest for social status as well, creating a phenomenal national system of
fame, celebrity, and popularity. Although the secular media pay attention
occasionally to national religious figures such as Billy Graham, they focus
primarily on entertainers, newsmakers, and experts. Americans were inclined to identify themselves with particular consumption communities as
much as with religious, ethnic, or other traditionally defined groups. By
the end of the twentieth century there was essentially no difference between Christians' and non-Christians' rates of adoption of new media technologies, while the older technologies such as television and radio had
saturated the Christian tribes. Interpreting some of the most revealing data
of all, researcher George Barna says that it "is possible to argue persuasively that many Christians have been seduced by the power of the tools

they have acquired. Born again adults spend an average of seven times more hours each week watching television than they do participating in spiritual pursuits such as Bible reading, prayer, and worship."[56] Certainly tribes continued to develop their own media and to create tribal rhetorics of communion. Mainstream national media never fully eclipsed alternative, centrifugal media and their tribal cultures. Park defined the word "communication" in the context of "self interest" or ego. Communication, he said, is "a form of interaction or a process that takes place between persons—that is to say, individuals with an ego, individuals with a point of view, conscious of themselves and more or less oriented in a moral world."[57] But national news and entertainment media seemed to offer American tribes an attractive means of celebrating shared culture. Such national culture looked more cosmopolitan and sophisticated, if not simply more interesting and more fun, than tribal cultures.

As personal communication is a means for individuals to express their independent egos, the media are means for people to create, maintain, and change common cultures—shared ways of life, collective egos. "Culture includes," writes Park, "all that is communicable. . . . Communication creates, or makes possible at least, that consensus and understanding among the individual components of a social group which eventually gives it and them the character not merely of society but of a cultural unit. It spins a web of custom and mutual expectation which binds together social entities as diverse as the family group, a labor organization, or the haggling participants in a village market." Park summarizes this cultural process as "transmitting tradition" and argues that communication can maintain traditions in two dimensions, space and time—that is, across geographic space and through generational time. He makes his case with one of the most-quoted sentences from Dewey's writings: "Society not only continues to exist by transmission, by communication, but may fairly be said to exist in transmission, in communication."[58] Communication is a form of communion— literally a way of cocreating culture and maintaining shared ways of life in time and space. Although communication can drive people apart through argument and antipathy, it can also bring them together through empathy and consensus. In the twentieth century, national entertainment and news media became enormous arenas in and through which individuals could transcend their tribal affiliations to participate in national rhetorics of communion.

Already in the early years of the twentieth century the rituals of the commercial media were substituting for the more organic and historic traditions of particular American tribes. In short, the escalating power and authority of the mainstream mass media reflected largely the interests of the behemoths of advertising, public relations, marketing, and audience research. The national, commercial media had little or no interest in transmitting cultural tradition, let alone religious tradition. The media were busily creating new, consumer-driven rituals such as nightly television viewing, daily newspaper reading, and especially regular shopping—first at downtown department stores and eventually at suburban malls, which by and large substituted for the pub in American culture. Moreover, the national media companies became increasingly sophisticated at carving out national niche markets for various groups, especially American youth. The music industry and radio stations collaborated to transform much of the radio business into a fairly national and highly standardized system of musical "hits" and personalities.[59] Radio "stood at the very center of American society," argues Daniel Czitrom, "an integral part of economic, political and cultural processes. In its mature state radio succeeded not in fulfilling the utopian visions first aroused by wireless technology, but in appropriating those urges for advertising interests."[60] Later the media added MTV to the mix—the most researched television channel in the history of America. MTV was a marketing machine that transformed commercials for rock music recordings and concerts into a popular entertainment form.[61] Mainstream media were uninterested, at best, in tradition, let alone religious traditions. If anything, the American mass media helped to transform established religious traditions such as Christmas into consumer events.[62] Shopping became a ritual of communion in consumer society—a means symbolically of connecting with others and affirming a collective identity. Consumer markets replaced much local community and religious tradition.

Of course the subnarratives of the media, anchored in their own mythology of consumerism and secular hope, could not eclipse all religious traditions built on the Christian metanarrative. The interaction of the subnarratives of mainstream media with the metanarrative of Christianity, interpreted by the faith's own communities of interpretation, is an enormous part of the story of the interaction of Christianity and the media in the twentieth century. Using their own centripetally organized media, Christian groups established distinct national identities and fostered communities of resistance against mainstream culture. They also used their own communication channels to critique the wider cultural world in which they lived and in so doing reminded themselves who they were and what they believed and felt. In this sense, tribal leaders used media in a priestly way to maintain rhetorics of communion and thereby to confirm and maintain their own, distinct tribal subcultures in the face of perceived threats from mass culture. As the mainstream media coalesce national consumer cultures, they also elicit moralistic tribal responses that reinforce unity within the tribe. Park perceptively suggests that Dewey's definition of communication as the "transmission of culture" seems to "identify the social with the moral order and limit the term 'social' to those relations of individuals that are personal, customary, and moral."[63] Tribal media in America helped religious subcultures to keep their own culture "close to home," both morally and theologically. In spite of the threats of mainstream national media to the ways of life of distinct Christian groups, tribal media continued to play a crucial role in maintaining separate and often critical communities of cultural resistance. Americans juggled their national and tribal commitments in order to maintain religious diversity in the midst of their growing communion within the wider consumer culture. With few exceptions, they simultaneously broke bread at two communion tables—the nation and the tribe.

The Rhetoric of Exile

No matter how deeply American Christians dug themselves into the growing national consumer culture, many of them simply did not feel at home there. Throughout the twentieth century even some of the most financially successful Christians criticized the wider culture. The tribes have always felt uneasy about the media's self-serving representations of truth, happiness, and security.[64] Theologian Donald B. Rogers suggests, "Today the people of faith find themselves once again the minority in a mildly hostile cultural environment. The environment is hostile in that it presents patterns, values and symbols that are in significant dissonance with those envisioned and put forth by the faith community." The automobile, he writes, transformed parish life, enabling people of faith to cut their ties to the neighborhood in which they worshiped and to "ignore that neighborhood's problems."[65] Similarly, television is transforming the context in which the church lives and ministers. The church in twentieth-century America is in exile, he concludes, walking a "tight-rope in a foreign culture" and trying to keep from losing its "cultural/faith identity." And as with the exile of the Old Testament Jews, the contemporary exile is a "time of humble yet determined waiting for a future that would become the reality only for subsequent generations. . . . Exile called for a strategy of quixotic character rather than heroic, a strategy of comedic tendencies rather than tragic." He urges this exiled people "to maintain tenaciously the ritual and educational activities that communicated the richest parts of their past to the next generations."[66] In both Hebrew and Christian history the exiled community became self-consciously aware of its need to reassert its uniqueness for fear the tribe would otherwise lose its own role in redemptive history.

The interaction of the media and Christianity in the last century is partly the story of religious tribes finding themselves in exile and then re-creating their distinct ways of life in a new rhetorical vernacular. American Christians today are in a cultural situation oddly similar to that of minority faiths in ancient Greece. There was no single Greek religious tradition any more than there is *an* American religious tradition. The Greek polis had no "priests of the gods" or even "priests of a god."[67] Instead the Greeks used individual priests in order to address specific gods at particular temples. Myth was local and particular. Poets, on the other hand, were the "theologians" who made mention of gods and endeavored "to support a religious ethic by the sanctions of deities singularly ill fitted to the task." Greek philosophy, not the local Greek cult, advised "the more articulate Greek on the way life should be lived."[68] In addition, the tension in Greek society was not between myth and philosophy, but rather between *mythos* and *logos*. Just as philosophy dominated public life in Greece, the mainstream media dominate public life in the United States. Christian "mythology," like Greek *mythos*, seems particular, local, parochial, and exclusive—certainly nothing to inform the public square and to shape public philosophy. To the extent that the United States now has a working public philosophy as a basis for national discourse, the philosophy is formed not among the many religious tribes but rather out of the philosophy of life implicitly enacted like a national ritual in the mainstream media.

American Christians are fully able to participate, like other religious believers, in the life of the nation, but the vernacular of participation frighteningly seems to require them to shed their distinctive beliefs. Richard J. Neuhaus refers to this religiously compromised society as the "naked public square," a public place, both geographically and intellectually, without a strong sense of the presence of God or even the presence of people who believe in God.[69] Faith commitments are relegated to private space, so that anyone who enters the public square with a religious interest is likely to be dismissed as a fanatic or criticized as an interloper. Just as reporters do not normally admit their personal political biases, people of faith should be careful not to reveal publicly their religious commitments unless they can express them generically in a way that will overcome the appearance of parochialism. Similarly, mainstream television programming shies away from explicit and particular expressions of religious commitment in dramatic and comedic programming. When the networks do offer expressions of faith, it is usually newsworthy and a cause for comments and criticisms from secular and religious observers alike. The mainstream music industry has been so inhospitable to explicitly Christian recordings that in the 1970s evangelicals formed a separate industry for producing and marketing religious recordings.[70] Similarly, the Christian book-publishing industry operates largely independent from the American Booksellers Association and its distribution systems. As David Paul Nord argues, religious publishers and reform organizations "are usually overlooked by business historians because they stood apart from the main current of market capitalism in nineteenth-century America. But precisely because they operated against the marketplace, they were very early forced to gather their entire business enterprise within the purview of administrations."[71] Across the spectrum of media in America, Christian tribes have acted like exiles that are deeply concerned with maintaining their own subcultures in the face of large, hostile social forces that threaten to take them completely captive. Rhetorics of exile enable tribes to share their concerns and fears, to discern their captors, and to encourage themselves to reclaim and reassert their tribal culture in the face of perceived threats.

Exilic Christian tribes feel vulnerable, beleaguered, and even exploited—just like other special-interest groups in American society. R. Laurence Moore uses the term "religious outsiders" to describe how some Christian groups perceive their position in the broader culture.[72] But outsiders are also often the most cognizant of their situation and the most likely to take extraordinary efforts to counter external threats. Less taken in by mainstream culture, outsiders are more open to meeting God, recognizing their distinctive identity, and searching for a mission. In American popular culture, from Hollywood films to prime-time television and popular novels, outsiders are likely to speak with a purpose and act with conviction. Americans often feel trapped by a national culture seemingly created by people who disrespect their tribes' particular beliefs and sentiments—perhaps even disrespect the tribes' freedom to express their own rhetorics of discernment and communion. Over the last few decades, some of the most distraught and agitated religious outsiders have fought for their own piece of the public square. From Rev. Jerry Falwell's Moral Majority to Rev. M. G. "Pat" Robertson's Christian Coalition, evangelicals have led tribal

attacks on mainstream politics, Hollywood, the Supreme Court, and beyond.[73] Sometimes these right-wing religious attacks elicit left-wing religious counterattacks, such as those led by Norman Lear's People for the
American Way. One could argue that the American Christian groups that
were pushed the farthest to the perimeter of mainstream American culture
have worked the hardest to build strong self-identities. They taught themselves how to use tribal media effectively to build their own constituencies,
raise funds, and launch cultural attacks on their foes. As insiders to American society during the first half of the twentieth century, mainline Protestant tribes were much less likely to perceive and to act upon the cultural
gap between themselves and mainstream culture. By contrast, an evangelical such as author and radio personality James Dobson organized strong
and influential lobbying efforts through his Focus on the Family organization and the more directly political Family Research Council.[74] A rhetoric
of exile identifies the enemies, coalesces the tribe, and directs tribal action
toward a "reclamation" of American life.

Clearly Wirth and his colleagues in Chicago could not have predicted
that subcultures of exile would develop their own mass-mediated opposition. Wirth wrote that modern society has two essential types of groups:
(1) organized groups, ranging from "informally constituted intimate groups
to highly formalized organizations such as the modern corporation, the
union, the church, and the state," and (2) the "detached masses held together, if at all, by the mass media of communication."[75] In fact, parachurch organizations and Christian special-interest groups combine
elements of both of these types of groups in order to use mass-media technologies and informal networks of churches and nondenominational
groups to build elaborate fund-raising apparatuses, launch political-action
groups, and enter the culture wars. These organizations sometimes feel little "consensus" with the broader society.[76] American Christianity begins to
look more and more like the rest of society as a collection of special-
interest and even single-issue groups with short-term goals and largely
pragmatic, political agendas. When religious tribes enter the public arena
as special-interest movements, they too often identify the public interest
with their own penchants. In some cases they even use pollsters and public relations specialists to make their cases as persuasively and professionally as possible. Religious tribes then resemble corporations and
governments that also act privately with communication plans and marketing strategies, relying on propagandistic and manipulative strategies to
conform society to their own interests. A tribe in exile can begin to look

and act like its captors as it fights for freedom. Anabaptists have taken a much tougher stand than most other Christian groups on this issue, arguing that the primary obligation of the tribe under exile is to maintain its distinctive self-identity as a community of faith.[77] In general, however, the proliferation of tribal rhetorics of exile reflects the politicization and cultural diminution of tribal culture, not just the rebirth of religiously informed cultures of discernment.

But one crucial difference between the Christian tribes and many of the other self-interest groups working under their own rhetoric of exile is the authenticity of the rhetoric. Whereas politicians and pundits often play for the audience, changing their symbolic colors like chameleons, Christian tribes in America tend to be much more difficult to mold from the outside and much more committed to their own principles. If American religious tribes bow to priestly forms of propaganda, it is usually because their leaders are trying to appeal primarily to in-house groups, not because they realistically expect to conquer American public opinion. Tribal priests tend to restrict most of their rhetoric to their own tents, telling the tribe more or less what it wants to hear. With few exceptions—such as highly polarizing issues like gun control and abortion—exilic rhetoric is largely intratribal and therefore politically impotent in the broader public sphere. Evangelicals, in particular, may claim to be able to vote or act as a bloc in society, but the truth is that all of the different Christian tribes in America are relatively diverse and diffuse, held together more by the metanarrative of the faith than by every jot and tittle of theology, politics, and culture. They operate as much from a sense of divine order and tribal allegiance as from political or specifically cultural viewpoints. The more respected Christian media critics are amazingly cogent and forthright about the particular ways that their biblical and theological convictions direct their own critiques of mainstream media. Clever tribal leaders can use rhetorics of exile to build tribal cohesion and to enhance their own standing in the tribe, but they rarely are able to leverage exilic rhetoric outside of the tribe as part of a broadly appealing public philosophy. This is an unfortunate aspect of exilic rhetoric because, as Michael Sandel suggests, religious beliefs often are matters of conscience rather than merely matters of choice; at their best religious beliefs can "promote the habits and dispositions that make good citizens."[78]

Strangely enough, the biggest threat to such tribal cultures in exile might be their willingness to sell their own traditional culture in the broader marketplace in order to earn a voice that the mainstream culture will find attractive and persuasive. Typically exile is a time for a tribe to build its idiosyncratic rhetorics of discernment and communion. As Rogers argues, the tribe must focus on its differences with the captors' culture, becoming sure about what it believes and being able to articulate those beliefs first of all to itself.[79] But in a kind of Faustian bargain, some tribal leaders point the tribe to the easy way out of exile, the back door out of their predicament; they steer the tribe to the doorway that opens onto the media stage, where the tribe learns the value of celebrity status, the power of imitating the dominant culture, even the apparent joy of defining success in worldly terms. In Jean Bethke Elshtain's language, the exilic tribe gravitates toward "pride and forgetfulness."[80] The so-called electronic church, for instance, has tried to mimic Hollywood and successful network-television programs, from talk to variety, while mainline Protestant broadcasting has generally failed to get beyond talking heads and pedantic presentations of theology and cultural analysis.[81] The mainline tribes might not have garnered large audiences or captured the imagination of the news media, but neither have they simply appropriated cultural styles of presentation from the marketplace. Evangelicals, on the other hand, frequently have managed to move from the tribal subcultures to the mainstream media stage, but in the process usually weakening their own distinctive self-identity with its particular rituals and forms of public and private life. Religious radio, for instance, increasingly adopted the programming strategies, personality-driven formats, and commercial revenue formulas that mark mainstream radio. When these stations and networks manage to climb out of the "religious radio ghetto," as some in the industry call it, they dive into the quagmire of market-driven media. Along the way they lose the distinction between marketing and ministry. The tribal journey out of exile frequently leads pridefully to a mainstream cultural co-optation in which the tribe forgets who it is.

Finally, tribal attitudes toward technology frequently lead to a mythological exile in which tribes perceive their cultural bondage as the result of a lack of technological power and authority. American Protestants historically saw this nation potentially as the City upon a Hill, the bucolic land where believers could build the New Jerusalem. Secular variations on that metaphor have so captivated mainstream American culture that it is nearly impossible to have serious public conversations about the benefits and drawbacks of media technologies and their accompanying social arrangements. Americans as a whole tend to be held captive by a nearly unquestionable enthusiasm for new technologies, to the point where any criticism raises cries of "Luddite" and draws blank stares from everyone else.[82] Without any dominant tradition-conserving elements in American society, we seem unable to know exactly who we are and whether any new idea or technology is really good for both the individual and the broader society. In the words of historian John Lukacs, tribes are losing their capacity to be "reactionary"—to deny the "immutable idea of immutable progress: the idea that we are capable not only of improving our material conditions but our very nature, including our mental and spiritual nature."[83] Tribes tend to lack a reasonable public rhetoric of dissent that places important issues into public discourse, engenders insightful debates in the light of history, and illuminates the shadows of contemporary America. The liberal legacy, which admits few traditional perspectives into public discourse, affects tribal rhetoric and culture as well.

If tribes see their problem as exile, they often perceive the solution as more technology—the very thing that threatens the tribe in the first place. Both the nation and the tribe are so unswervingly committed to progress and so favorably disposed toward the latest media technologies that they wrongly assume that being technologically "backward" will lead them into a negative form of cultural exile. A rhetoric of exile offers tribes an opportunity to question mainstream culture, nuture deeper discernment and establish greater internal consensus, but in the United States such rhetoric also can lead tribes to place their hope in the same technologies and techniques that oppress them. A tribe does not gain freedom by becoming like its captors. Instead it has to remember who it is and then react wisely and civilly to its oppression with a public voice that invites those outside the clan to join the discussion. After all, tribes have a stake in how well the nation articulates the common good, not just how much it supports voluntary tribal liberties.

The Rhetoric of Praise

The interaction of the media and Christianity in the United States is also a struggle between conflicting and shared rhetorics of praise. Rhetorics of conversion often lead both religious and mainstream media to produce popular culture, the major medium of symbolic exchange in market economies. To be "popular" in American society, rhetorically speaking, is to be successful, important, and legitimate. Although some citizens in the twentieth century looked unfavorably upon all kinds of popular culture, most Americans tended to view positively any culture that attends to

widespread interests, whether measured by the box office, audience ratings, or circulation data.[84] Many of the conversations between religious
tribes and the media address implicitly the value of cultural popularity. In
fact, some rhetorics of discernment contrast popularity with quality, truthfulness, and authenticity. The conflicts between tribes and mainstream culture often are struggles over popularity as a form of cultural legitimacy.
Evangelistic rhetoric, too, sometimes equates mere popularity with success
in the marketplace. As one manager of recording artists in the Christian
music industry told an industry gathering, the goals of ministry and marketing are "exactly the same—market share."[85] Popularity becomes a public vehicle for establishing the praiseworthiness of people, artifacts, and
organizations. American rhetoric about the media turns pundits and
celebrities into icons of praise. Popular culture in a market system offers a
widely shared arena for expressions of public praise.

Although some academic critics assume that popular culture is inferior to
fine art and insignificant in civilization, history tells a very different story
about its value and impact. The idolization of fine art in modern society is
based on a number of false assumptions about the nature of art and its historical role in society, including that fine and popular art are mutually exclusive categories of artifacts and that fine art challenges existing human
beliefs while popular art merely confirms them. Cultural elitists frequently
invoke these assumptions as defenses for elitist views of storytelling and culture. But such elitists wrongly assume that popular narrative is culturally
ineffective, aesthetically inferior, and hence unworthy of serious study.
They undervalue the mythopoetic functions of most art throughout the
ages. In effect, they want to classify and categorize art in secular terms and
according to the political, cultural, or economic interests of particular people. No doubt much popular art is merely the product of markets rather
than part of the ways of life of particular tribes. But such simplistic di-
chotomies between fine and popular art obfuscate the significance of popular forms of tribal expression. Moreover, they fail to capture the evangelistic
thrust of so much tribal popular culture. Finally, they wrongly apply one
narrow standard of cultural praise across all forms of culture.

Categorizing works as fine or popular art ignores the history of human
culture and the social nature of human action. Over the centuries the uses
of and ideas about particular artifacts changed as cultures and artistic communities redefined the significance and purpose of art. The most important
development has been the "museumization" of art—its separation from
daily life, including the life of the church. Much historic Christian art today

is recontextualized in galleries without its original social setting of cathedral or palace. Such separation defines the function of the art narrowly as aesthetic contemplation, when in fact the original social function might have been closer to community worship and collective confirmation of belief. Simplistic categories, such as fine and popular art, obscure real similarities and differences among cultural artifacts, stereotype their social uses, and overlook their influences on each other.[86] Moreover, such typologies typically confuse the intended purpose behind the creation of a work of art with how the various artifacts are actually used. Park, for instance, discusses scholars' persistent tendency to distinguish between referential and didactic art, on the one hand, and expressive art, on the other. The former was supposedly the communication of ideas, and the latter was "where sentiments and attitudes are manifested."[87] Although such a distinction is quite helpful for categorizing art, it hardly helps people to evaluate it.

In order to make sense of tribes' normative judgments about popular media, we need a theory of communication that also embraces a theory of culture. We especially require a theory of rhetorical praise that illuminates, exegetes, and critiques tribal rhetorics of praise in particular social and cultural contexts. We need to know how narratives host cultures and how society maintains multiple and competing subcultures, each with its own signifying system and sometimes with its own metanarrative. Although it has become fashionable for communication scholars to assume that popular stories are sociologically important and therefore worthy of careful analysis and interpretation, most mass-media research is not grounded in any explicit theory of narrative or even in any theory of communication or culture.[88] Popular-culture research tends to be sociologically and epistemologically thin, driven more by an abstracted methodology—such as content analysis—than by a theory that actually takes into account how people use popular culture in everyday life. This is especially true, for example, of television criticism, which, even when insightful and cogent, rarely elucidates the assumptions undergirding its methods of interpretation and critique.[89]

When examining religious as well as mainstream popular culture, scholars have tended to assume that popular narratives can be dissected scientifically and abstracted like chemical reactions in a test tube. Such quasi-scientific approaches are bound to fail because they ignore the subjective nature of popular culture. As Wirth put it in his presidential address to the American Sociological Association, "The scientific study of social phenomena is not yet institutionalized like the study of physical and biological phenomena. The student of society will be plagued by the difficulties of achieving 'objectivity,' by the existence of social values, by the competition with common-sense knowledge, by the limits of his freedom and capacity to experiment, and by other serious and peculiar handicaps which trouble the natural scientist less or not at all." Nevertheless, continued Wirth, the social scientist can "avoid studying the processes and problems of man in society only by pretending to be something he is not, or by lapsing into such a remote degree of abstraction or triviality as to make the resemblance between what he does and what he professes to be doing purely coincidental."[90]

Park and his cohorts tentatively resolved this dilemma of objectivity in the social sciences by defining and interpreting culture ethnographically. They studied cultures from within, as participant observers, rather than merely from outside, as dispassionate assessors. This methodology led them to take cultural expressions very seriously as embodiments of particular groups' values, beliefs, and especially sentiments. Park writes that culture is "attitudes and sentiments, folkways and mores," which are "the warp and woof of that web of understanding we call 'culture.'"[91] Instead of anchoring their research in positivistic theories and purely quantitative methods, the Chicago School looked to the humanities for their theories, concepts, and methods. In so doing they created an approach to understanding culture, including popular culture, that is carved distinctively out of the American quest for unity amid diversity.[92] Park, Wirth, and their colleagues assumed that humans desire consensus more than conflict, whereas contemporary British and Continental philosophers such as Walter Benjamin and Jürgen Habermas emphasized class conflict.[93]

These Americans' research was anthropologically sensitive to the varieties of cultural discernment and the striving for communion that always influenced American social life. Moreover, when Dewey and the others defined culture more or less as the understanding and practice of a "moral order," they implicitly moved popular culture to the domain of ethics and religion and, conversely, moved religion to the domain of culture, including popular culture.[94] To put it differently, the Chicago School perceived the crucial role of values and morality in all human culture and thereby kept distinctly religious culture on the intellectual agenda and in the national conversation about culture and society. Moreover, their approach viewed both traditional and mass-mediated culture as serving essentially the same overall functions in society, namely, providing meaningful rituals and elaborate webs of shared meaning in geographical space and across generational time.

Rhetorics of praise often challenge all forms of cultural elitism that embrace the criteria of a select academic group or social class over those of other people. Tönnies rightly argued that public opinion emerges in society as a replacement for the church and its "priestly" leaders.[95] But if the alternative to religious priests is scientific priests, rationalistic epistemologies are hardly an improvement in the social process of mass communication. Americans want a means to regulate popular sentiment, not a priestly class of religious or scientific judges presiding over national or tribal culture. The rhetoric of praise in America is occasionally only tribal, but it tends to look much more broadly to the consensus that forms out of widespread belief and open inquiry. This is why popularity is the most common form of cultural affirmation in the United States. Popularity invariably tends to disenfranchise elitists, although it can be co-opted by a market-driven rhetoric of praise. American religious belief and practice generally support popular culture per se as praiseworthy; tribes frequently criticize the content of popular culture but rarely the merits of its broad appeal. And tribal elites who do criticize popular culture per se typically have acquired that cultural attitude from other elites outside of the tribe.

Popularity as a form of praiseworthy merit is anchored deeply in American Protestant sentiment. "In the early republic," writes historian Leonard I. Sweet, "a tidal wave of democratic principles and populist sentiments washed away the old hierarchical information flow in American Christianity."[96] Tocqueville wrote that immigrants brought to America "a Christianity that I cannot depict better than to call it democratic and republican." Tocqueville also suggested that American Roman Catholics formed the most "democratic class" in the nation.[97] Although the Reformational concept of the "priesthood of all believers" extends back to the heart of the Protestant revolt against ecclesiastical hierarchies, the broad cultural power of such grassroots faith was not unleashed until Protestants began refashioning the faith in the context of American democratic principles. In one sense, American Protestantism became highly individualistic, with each person interpreting the Scriptures and deciding what to believe. In the broader context of the nation's popular sentiments, however, religion joined all other cultural arenas as a vehicle for converting people through popular messages that appealed to wide ranges of people.

The democratic impulse in American Christianity was a way not just of protecting people from a state church but even more a means of letting the people decide for themselves in the court of popular sentiment who or what was praiseworthy. That cultural idea, which linked value with popularity, is at the center of the interaction of Christianity and the media in the United States throughout the twentieth century. American religion, like American culture more generally, became a deeply bardic discourse tied to commonsense experience and integral to the identity of the church tribe as well as to the national popular culture.[98] Popularity created tribal love-hate relationships with mainstream culture. Who could discount the apparent praiseworthiness of a hit TV show or Hollywood box-office smash? As William D. Romanowski suggests in *Pop Culture Wars*, religious tribes, the entertainment industry, and secular critics often battled over whether the market was a means of adjudicating the value of cultural products in America.[99] Popularity became a kind of proof of value that tribes had to address if they expected to be taken seriously by the wider society. Either they had to question the real popularity of cultural artifacts out of tune with the tribal rhetoric of praise or they were not likely to be accepted in public discourse. Praise and popularity are still difficult to untangle in American rhetoric about the quality or value of culture.

As long as the study of communication and culture attends to the need for moral order in society, it remains open to humans' corresponding desire to find things that are worthy of praise. Humankind's relationship to culture is like the religious believer's association with the local church—a communal avenue to discerning and sharing what is praiseworthy. This impulse to praise something outside of one's self is not simply an Arnoldian quest for fine art or high civilization; it can also be a recognition of the sheer joy of everyday life, such as the satisfaction of conversation and the enjoyment of reading the newspaper. The drive to praise is part of a fundamentally human need to find value beyond the limits of the self, to recognize that as human beings we are neither islands nor gods. The interaction of the media and Christianity in America is partly a conversation about what is or should be praiseworthy in a democratic nation that nearly enshrines the "priesthood" of all makers of truly popular culture.

Conclusion

Christian tribes in the United States entered the twentieth century calling variously for conversion, discernment, communion, exile, and praise. Like all of the other subcultures in America, Christian groups alternately were enchanted by and disgusted with the mainstream media. Driving for market share and advertising revenues, the mainstream commercial media, to paraphrase Wirth, seemed to be creating media content for everyone in general and no one in particular.[100] As the century ended, consumerism shaped the arenas of the daily news media and local radio. Although few tribes cut themselves off completely from mainstream culture, neither did most religious groups feel completely comfortable with the surrounding culture represented in even some of the most popular media fare.

Modern media waxed and waned in two, often contradictory directions. The new centripetal media enabled all geographic and demographic parts of the nation to be linked together as one complex web of news, entertainment, and persuasion. Driving these centripetal developments was a distinctly American, religiously shaped "mythos of the electronic revolution," to use Carey's term.[101] Under the spell of this public rhetoric about the benefits of media technologies, Americans often felt like they were living in a new Eden, although tribal dissidents warned that an apocalypse might be just around the corner. As the next chapter suggests, religious tribes championed technological innovation and delighted in the apparent power of new media to serve the church as praiseworthy agents of conversion and communion.

Such tribal optimism, however, was somewhat naive, maybe even a sign of Americans' Pollyannaish attitudes toward technology and mass communication. As Flannery O'Connor writes, "The fleas come with the dog."[102] Technology enables, but it also disables; in the process of making some worthwhile things happen, it prohibits other good things from taking place—even things that are primarily matters of the spirit or habits of the heart. Moreover, the unexpected consequences of new media are sometimes more powerful than the carefully planned ones. Many Christian tribes were similarly unconvinced of the sublimity of the new media; their rhetoric of discernment led them away from mainstream culture and into cultural exile. Some of the more liberal groups attacked the media for their commercialism and for their unwillingness to give public voices to the poor and alienated in society. Serving a prophetic role, these salvos from mainstream Roman Catholic and Protestant tribes often echoed the concerns of nonreligious groups in society. Occasionally mainline Christian churches and denominations directly entered public discussion about the media, especially in matters of governmental regulation of the broadcast industry. United Methodists, Presbyterians, Episcopalians, and other mainline groups worked though the National Council of Churches to enter collectively the public policy debates and to influence how the federal agencies allocated radio and television frequencies as well as how the agency would require broadcasters to serve all members of society.[103] The media were not always praiseworthy, even in the hands of technical experts and political masters who supposedly should know better.

Evangelicals during the same period spent far less time criticizing the media and much more time building the kinds of in-house media empires that would give them a national tribal voice and might even enhance their social status in the expanding industrial nation. Evangelicals criticized the media, but typically for immoral content in Hollywood movies, television programs, music, and comic books.[104] If mainline Christian organizations served a prophetic role in criticizing the mainstream media, evangelicals served much more of a priestly role within their own tribes, encouraging members to keep the faith. By the end of the twentieth century, evangelicals were the champions in America at using the media for building religious organizations. But as leaders they also seemed to be mimicking the ways and means of the mainstream media, especially the commercialization and the technological wizardry. They were just as apt as other Americans to equate success in the media marketplace with popularity as a sign of conversionary power. Praising technology, evangelicals seemed to lose some of their critical, prophetic voice amid the awe and wonder of the latest media fad. Theologian Eugene H. Peterson suggests that some Christians end up "hauling in truckloads of rationalism and technology from the world" in order to "be more spiritual!" In the process, they take on life more as a "problem to be solved" than a "mystery to be explored." Moreover, says Peterson, we "live in jerky times, assaulted by 'urgent' demands. For most of our ancestors in the Christian way, Scripture and prayer were embedded in routine and validated by social structures. Today those routines have been replaced by fax and telephone."[105] Evangelicals are spreading among their own ranks the very consumer culture that the mainline Christian tribes have repeatedly criticized in popular media. Such a state of affairs challenges the stereotypical categories of "liberal" and "conservative" faith.

There is little serious public discourse about the interaction of media and religion. The topic is not usually a major part of Americans' own conversation about their society. Christian tribes, like the rest of society, are consumers, first, and critics and dissenters, second. The First Amendment encourages public dialogue and guarantees that people will not be excluded because of their faith. That amendment, Carey says, was designed to "create a conversational society, a society of people who speak to one another, who converse. . . . While people often dry up and shy away from the fierceness of argument, disputation, and debate, and while those forms of talk often bring to the surface the meanness and aggressiveness that is our second nature, conversation implies the most natural and unforced, unthreatening, and most satisfying of arrangements."[106] The early church was countercultural partly because it was so decentralized, dynamic, and discourse driven. People sometimes talk about Christianity as a religion of the "Book," when in fact it has always been a faith primarily of the Word—both in the sense of the Word of God in scripture and the Word-made-flesh in Jesus Christ. The vibrancy of Christian tribes even in twentieth-century America depends significantly on how well they cultivate conversation. If it lacks strong tribal cultures anchored in orality and community, Christianity will follow the ways of the wider society toward amorphous consumerism and weak public participation. Strong religious tribes are much more likely to challenge mainstream media. As the case studies in this book suggest, such tribal challenges nevertheless can transcend parochial interests and enliven public discourse about the good life that we all seek.

2

Praising Technology:
Evangelical Populism Embraces
American Futurism

◩ ◩ ◩

In 1995 Americans witnessed a remarkable technological feat as the Hubble space telescope captured images of the planet Mars and broadcast them via satellites and cable to viewers around the world. As the photographs were shown on television and printed in newspapers, journalists began reporting that Americans saw meaningful images in them—like the interpretations of inkblot designs. "Pictures taken by the . . . telescope have created a phenomenon of sorts," said CNN television news anchor Lou Waters, "with folks calling in, saying that they see something in these pictures that perhaps others of us do not see. Maybe it's becoming clearer to you now." Waters and CNN anchor Bobbie Battista then took phone calls from viewers who wanted to share their interpretations of the photos. The live television conversation went like this:

> WATERS: We have someone on the line from Texas. Texas?
> CALLER: Yes?
> WATERS: Are you seeing something here?

CALLER: Yes, I do. I noticed it last night. I saw it on CNN as I was about to go to bed, and I thought to myself, "That appears to be Jesus Christ in that, but I will wait till tomorrow and see if anyone else sees what I see, because to me it just looks like him."

WATERS: Well, we have been getting a lot of calls who agree with what you see in this picture, but why do you see that?

CALLER: Well—why?

WATERS: Yeah, why?

CALLER: I don't know. It just—I just—what appears to be a picture of Jesus Christ. Let me say first of all I believe in probably a supreme being, not necessarily god, quote. I do not go to church regularly. I try to live a decent, good life, just plain, good life, so I'm not a religious fanatic that, you know, sees Jesus Christ in everything I look at.

WATERS: Right.

CALLER: But when I walked by the TV and looked at that, I thought, "My God, they say this is the birthplace of stars and things, and that appears to be Jesus Christ, and I thought, wait a minute. Just see if anyone else sees this. Wait till tomorrow." So when I heard this, I couldn't believe it.

Waters soon takes a phone call from Florida:

CALLER: What I'm seeing is, last night when I looked at it, I saw a portrayal of what I read about as being a portrayal of what looks like Jesus Christ—the big hair, the skin, the mustache, the nose, the eyes. I saw it last night, and his face very prominent coming through. I'm not, like the lady from Texas, not a—I don't attend a denominational church, but I believe in the Word and I clearly see that face, as we've painted a human face in the reflection of Jesus, and the description as it is in the Word is clearly there. I'm a commercial artist and that's what I see—the dimensions are there and the shadows and that type of thing is there for that face there.

Then a caller from New Jersey claims to see the Statue of Liberty in the Hubble photos, followed by a caller from Toronto who says that the photos look a little bit like Gene Shalit, a network film critic. Finally, Waters wraps up the live conversation with callers, "We've cleared that up, haven't we? Seven-thousand light-years away—Gene Shalit." Battista responds, "Which we might add is 5,000 years before the birth of Christ." Waters concludes, "Well, I guess that doesn't mean anything if you're into the trinity and spirit and all that."[1]

What are we to make of the callers' seemingly preposterous interpretations of the images from Mars? Maybe some CNN viewers decided to have a bit of fun with Waters and Battista. But print media from around the country were already reporting similar interpretations, so the calls to CNN were probably authentic. Perhaps the power of mass-mediated suggestion was strong enough to influence what many individuals saw in the otherwise ambiguous photos. Could it be that the real images of a planet so far away created a special sense of transcendence—similar to the national reactions to live television coverage of the landing of a U.S. space vehicle on the moon in 1969? If so, some Americans might have been trying to make spiritual sense of the images from the space telescope—to infuse the new technology with religious significance as a way of understanding it.

Rhetorical theorist Kenneth Burke suggests that through the use of language human beings enact a "kind of magic of attitudes, choices, values, feelings, and stances."[2] As we "name" the world around us, says Burke, we decree the way things supposedly are, and we call into being a particular picture of reality. Moreover, we use language to "fit experience together into a unified whole," thereby creating fairly coherent, even if greatly oversimplified, maps of reality.[3] Our past experiences enable us to interpret the current world. According to Burke, humans create a sense of piety that dictates symbolically "what properly goes with what."[4] We view even the future through the lens of such piety, projecting our past and current understandings of reality into an unknown and largely ambiguous future. Some of the CNN callers interpreted images of Mars in light of their religious experiences, investing a kind of populist spirituality into their interpretations of a completely new and otherwise highly ambiguous phenomenon. In short, CNN viewers, like all of us, tried to make sense out of new events that lacked any established frame of reference and begged for pietistic interpretations.

This chapter argues that Americans have always tended to interpret the meaning and significance of new technologies partly in spiritual if not in distinctly religious terms. James W. Carey and John J. Quirk document a long and significant history of popular American futurism that identifies electricity and electronic technologies with "a new birth of community, decentralization, ecological balance, and social harmony." American Protestants, in particular, have created one of the clearest contemporary expressions of what Carey and Quirk call the "mythos of the electronic revolution."[5] Americans frequently forge their understandings of media technologies out of implicitly salvific and apocalyptic rhetoric—opposite ends of the same spectrum of pietistic understanding. The salvific language typically captures rhetorics of conversion, communion, and praise, whereas the apocalyptic language expresses rhetorics of discernment and exile.

The first section of this chapter suggests that Americans' optimism about the role and impact of new media technologies stems partly from the Judeo-Christian concept of progress. The idea that human history is progressive, teleological, and thus inherently meaningful reflects an understanding of the role of God in history that is commensurate with an understanding of God's role as reflected in biblical narrative. Just as early American colonists tended to interpret the news of the day in the context of God's providence, twentieth-century reporters and journalists associated new media technologies with a quasi-religious notion of progress. To paraphrase Burke, the dominant reading of technological developments in America is a ritualistic form of symbolic piety. Americans implicitly embrace a national will that insists on the praiseworthiness and conversionary power of new media. Moreover, this collective optimism is essentially a secular version of the Christian Gospel of divine providence. Under this scenario, mass media supposedly will rebuild human community and usher in a time of peace and prosperity. The media are deemed agents of progress that reflect the goodness of human invention if not the divine creativity of God.

The second part considers the close affinity between evangelical theology and American understandings of the missionary role of the mass media. American evangelicals championed a rhetoric of the media that emphasized the power of such technologies to change people, especially to convert them to the evangelical faith. This missionary impulse gives virtually all major American media initiatives a conversionary significance; Americans still think of mass communication moralistically as an agent either of life or death, good or bad. Although evangelical interpretations of the media demonstrate this most clearly, the same type of missionary zeal and conversionary rhetoric guides mainstream American thinking about the media. In a sense, Americans borrow their understanding of mass communication not just from the Judeo-Christian notion of historical progress but even more closely from American evangelicals' faith in the power of media technologies to usher in the Second Coming of Jesus Christ. Evangelical rhetoric about mass communication is probably the most characteristically American form of technological piety.

The third section explores the mythos of the electronic church, the largely evangelical rhetoric that imagines both the media and the church in technological terms. This salvific rhetoric links the church as community to the media as agents of spiritual renewal. Influenced strongly by premillennial theology, late-nineteenth- and early-twentieth-century evangelicals created a pious language that views mass media technologies as humanly devised instruments of God and frames the predicted impact of such media in terms of both conversion and communion. They envisioned a future world where new media technologies will supposedly create heaven on earth by overcoming the problems of human conflict, confusion, and chaos. The mythos of the electronic church is grounded in the idea of Christian progress, grafted to American optimism about technology, and formed by twentieth-century evangelical theology.

The last part of this chapter examines the remarkable continuities of idea and expression found in the literary genre of science fiction and the popular evangelical thinking about the media. Science fiction, as a style of apocalyptic and salvific storytelling, often expresses religious imagery and quasi-theological ideas without requiring the audience to commit to any particular religious tradition. Science fiction thereby serves as a mythos of secular prophecy, coalescing and refining vaguely held American beliefs about the technological future. The genre enables Americans to explore different technological ideas and effects through a common language of quasi-religious hope and fear. In fact, some popular forms of science fiction storytelling are remarkably similar to particular expressions of evangelical theology, while various types of popular evangelical theology are imaginary scenarios seemingly borrowed from American science fiction. Science fiction tends to be more critical about media technologies than does popular theology, but they both offer apocalyptic warnings about the potential negative impacts of the media on the individual and the community. Contemporary science fiction storytelling thereby provides Americans with symbolic space to imagine different technological futures, serving as a kind of secular prophecy of doom as well as hope.

Americans are populist pietists who imagine the future in both technological and religious terms. They use religious ideas to understand mass communication; those understandings in turn shape how they actually use the media in church and society. Of course this process of cultivating a quasi-religious understanding of media technologies is neither fully rational nor a completely conscious process. As Robert E. Park and Ernest W. Burgess suggest, human beings "act as they do elsewhere from motives they do not fully comprehend, in order to fulfill aims of which they are but dimly or not at all conscious." Moreover, the "same social forces, which are found organized in public opinion, in religious symbols, in social convention . . . are constantly re-creating the old order, making new heroes, overthrowing old gods, creating new myths, and imposing new ideals."[6]

Christian Optimism and Technology

When Thomas More created the word "utopia," he drew upon the meanings of two possible Greek prefixes associated with the root word for "place" (*topos*). One prefix would create the meaning "no-place," while the other one would establish a seemingly opposite meaning, "good-place."[7] By selecting a root word that could be interpreted in either way, More captured the dual role of utopian thought. In one sense, a utopia is a human search for a good society that is better than the existing state of affairs. But in another sense there is no such perfect place, no particular time and specific location that entirely embody the human quest for communal perfection. Utopian society is always an archetype and never a living reality. To put it in distinctly religious terms, human beings cannot create heaven on earth even though people will always desire to do so. "Human beings are utopian," writes Darrell J. Fasching, "in so far as they move along the vector of their hopes to create a new world; and they remain utopian only in so far as they are able, ever and again, to transcend the given horizon of the present world to imagine a new one."[8] Utopian rhetoric assumes the possibility of a better world and posits that it is possible for human beings to make significant progress toward that world.

Utopias are often the product of religious beliefs and directed toward the establishment of religious community. As Park argues, most attempts to establish planned societies have failed, but those that "lasted longer" usually rested on a religious foundation. Park suggests that the success of even a Communist community depends "more upon its ability to propagate and establish a new and essentially religious faith—than upon the merits of its economic Program."[9] Utopian thought is most powerful when it is anchored in and inspired by broadly religious sentiment that expresses the anticipated community in terms of the deepest human desires for intimacy and hope. Futuristic mythology becomes utopian when it blends rhetorics of conversion, communion, and praise in order to show a tribe the ways out of exile and into the Promised Land. The future then becomes a site in which the antagonisms and uncertainties of the present evaporate;

everyone will supposedly be led from the oppressive culture of exile and converted to the same communion of praise.

Americans owe their modern concept of progress largely to the Judeo-Christian doctrine of messianic intervention and salvation. The classical view of history as an endless series of cycles, each with the same pattern of recovery and degeneration, offered no ultimate hope beyond repetition and encouraged a reverence of the past. In response to such pessimism the Hebrews and especially the Christians held a view of history as a cosmic drama in which all humans played their predestined part and in which all who believed would have eternal life. In historian Carl L. Becker's words, Christianity transferred "the golden age from the past to the future [and] . . . substituted an optimistic for a disillusioned view of human destiny."[10] From the fourteenth to the nineteenth centuries, the Western revolt against ecclesiastical and secular authority, along with the development of experimental science, transformed the Christian doctrine of salvation into the modern idea of progress.[11] "When man conceives of himself in a way that links him to the Creator in a relationship of mutuality and common purpose," writes Kenneth Vaux, "and when that unity is found in dominion over the world, a powerful impulse is released that generates high technological accomplishment. . . . Frequently the press toward the future has taken the form of striving for a technological utopia."[12] Protestant thought, in particular, fostered the idea of historical progress and engendered a hope that technology could be the route out of exile and into the Promised Land.

The roots of such Christian utopian thought are deeply planted in specific interpretations of the biblical narrative. In the biblical book of Genesis, human beings are created to be coworkers with the Creator.[13] God tells Adam and Eve to plant and care for the garden that God made for them. God then blesses humankind and gives people the power to act upon their God-created role in the world as caretakers of Creation. As one observer puts it, the "power of the Creator's blessings enables [human beings] to grow up and grow into technical and technological activities. It is both the gift of God and the fruit of human work and thought. Humankind is empowered by God to work with the world and to create."[14] In addition, the technical work that humankind begins in the Garden of Eden will end in the city, the New Jerusalem. "The life of humankind through fall and redemption . . . involves shaping and forming the earth, moving from the garden to the city."[15] According to this perspective, by cocreating technology with God human beings presumably have the power and ability to imitate God's original creative work, to become minicreators that help call into being the City upon a Hill. Of course this human vocation can go tragically wrong, as it does at the Tower of Babel, where the city becomes a godless reflection of the passions of arrogant and apostate people who care more about making a name for themselves than about cultivating the Creation responsibly in the name of God.[16] Nevertheless, the fundamental assumption that humankind has a privileged role in working with God to spread creative progress on earth is deeply anchored in interpretations of the biblical metanarrative. When it fails to recognize the human tendency to turn technology into a form of idolatry, however, the Christian view of God's redemptive plan in history can easily become a religious form of technological utopianism. Failing to heed to the biblical account of the Fall from grace, Christians can transform "the glory and service of the Lord" into "a means of proud domination."[17] Technology in turn becomes a vehicle for exercising self-interest and oppressing the weak in society. The utopian turns dystopian.

During the thirteenth and fourteenth centuries radical Franciscan advocates of the arts fused Christianity's prophetic tradition with human cultural activity, especially artistic endeavors. They saw art increasingly as a means of converting all races to Christianity. Such worldwide evangelization of all people to the Christian faith "was a necessary precondition for, and unmistakable indication of, the coming of the millennium." Franciscans carried this kind of millennial message beyond the cloister through their public preaching and writing, formulating "what would become an enormously influential and enduring eschatology of technology, a perception of the advancing useful arts as at once an approximate anticipation of, an apocalyptic sign of, and practical preparation for the prophesied restoration of perfection."[18] These religious believers reached beyond the mystery of tradition to practical and instrumental eschatology, framing utopian ideas within the work of artisans who could presumably hasten the future through their sustained efforts. Their own eschatological convictions, equated with divine providence, encouraged human exploration in geography, astronomy, navigation, shipbuilding, metallurgy, and weaponry.[19] The apocalypticism of that age of exploration was inseparable from the explorers' own cosmology; religious faith both inspired invention and directed it toward particular religious ends. For Christopher Columbus, the journey to North America was a matter of divine inspiration, a means of reconquering the Holy Land, and an eschatological pilgrimage to link all people together in the world before the final climax of history.[20]

Howard P. Segal locates the European roots of distinctly American technological utopianism in the writings of the pansophists, influential six-
teenth- and seventeenth-century visionaries whose religious orientation
sharply differentiated their ideas from nontechnological forms of Western
utopianism.[21] Seeking to harmonize science and Christianity, as well as to
combat the secularism of Renaissance thinkers, they projected an image of
a utopian New World civilization called "Pansophia," meaning universal
knowledge or wisdom. Their utopias boasted such technologies as mechan-
ically propelled ships, lighting systems, clocks, and agricultural machines,
all of which presumably would enable humankind better to serve God on
earth. Johann Andreae's *Christianopolis* (1619) and Francis Bacon's *The New
Atlantis* (1627) even envisioned scientific think tanks invested with spiritual significance; Andreae's place of techno-intellectual truth was the "in-
nermost shrine of the city," and Bacon called his the "very eye of this
kingdom."[22] Like later technological utopians, the pansophists were motivated by a belief that faithful human effort could usher in a better world.
Looking back at earlier inventions, they concluded that God had given
human beings this role to build such utopian societies. The inventions of
the lateen (or triangular sail), the swinging rudder, deeper boat hulls, and
the advent of the compass had led earlier Europeans to expand trade, increase material abundance, and reduce the time required to traverse great
geographic spaces.[23] God seemed to be directing history, working providentially through faithful people to create a new world. Perhaps most interesting of all, these utopians defined progress primarily in terms of
innovations in transportation and communication technologies. Humans'
enhanced ability to overcome geographic space seemed to be elevating the
species toward the omnipresence of God.

The literary and philosophical works of the pansophists typified European technological utopianism throughout the late nineteenth century,
when Americans created a popular genre of their own. Unlike their earlier
European counterparts, visionaries in the United States saw their country
as a probable, not merely a potential, utopia. The American brand of
utopia was to be realized through technological changes rather than
through a purely religious commitment or even via a complex combination
of political, economic, social, and technological innovations.[24] Americans
made technological progress equivalent to progress itself, modeling their
quasi-religious utopia after the machines and structures that made such
technological progress probable. Under the spell of the predicted New
World, unfettered by the past, cognizant of the seemingly miraculous

developments in transportation technologies, Americans built their own concept of technological optimism out of the Hebraic-Christian doctrine of messianic intervention and salvation. American Protestants saw the New World as the God-given location for reestablishing the pre-Fall, golden age of God's reign on earth. Just as Italian humanists once "turned to the study of classical writers" and as Protestant reformers "appealed from current theologians to the beliefs and practices of the primitive church," American Christians combined the basic optimism of humanism with both early church primitivism and advanced technological invention.[25] Technical control of the social and natural environments became a particularly American means of building the "City of God" on earth.

Many Americans adopted the New World metaphor for progress, believing their land to be the New Atlantis idealized by European writers.[26] Immigrants often viewed America as a Promised Land, a "place of new beginnings."[27] Various types of utopian communities and styles of utopian thought, all based on the dream of a better, God-ordained world, sprang up throughout the country.[28] What began in Europe as a literary strategy to explore the possible benefits of technological development and to challenge Renaissance humanism was soon transformed by pragmatic and optimistic Americans into a popular faith in technology itself. Adopting the appropriate religious metaphors, Americans viewed their land as the "garden of the world" and their technology as the "machine in the garden."[29] America was the "symbol of a fresh start."[30] "We may perhaps learn to deprive large masses of their gravity, and give them absolute levity, for the sake of easy transport," wrote Benjamin Franklin. "Agriculture may diminish its labor and double its produce; all diseases may be . . . cured . . . and our lives lengthened at pleasure. . . . O that men would cease to be wolves to one another."[31] Within American Christianity, this impulse toward social regeneration sometimes took the form of a nationalistic theology that identified the United States itself with God's redemptive plan for the nations of the world, a "Redeemer Nation."[32] "Perhaps nowhere is the intimate connection between religion and technology more manifest than in the United States," writes David F. Noble, "where an unrivaled popular enchantment with technological advance is matched by an equally earnest popular expectation of Jesus Christ's return."[33] American revivalism was a "sibling to the technological."[34]

Americans essentially transformed the biblical metaphors of agriculture and stewardship into new language of machinery, technology, and control. The agricultural metaphor, argues Wendell Berry, preserved the "natural cycles of birth, growth, death, and decay," whereas the machine metaphor placed human beings in charge of Creation, doing away with "mystery on the one hand and multiplicity on the other." Warns Berry, "By means of the machine metaphor we have eliminated any fear or awe or reverence or humility or delight or joy that might have restrained us in our use of the world. We have indeed learned to act as if our sovereignty were unlimited and as if our intelligence were equal to the universe." Driven by an almost "occult yearning for the future," modernists turned to technical experts for advice: "The future has been envisioned, dreamed, projected, painted for us by prophets of every kind: scientists, comic-book writers, novelists, philosophers, politicians, industrialists, professors."[35] Historian Perry Miller suggests that by the 1850s the American missionary effort was associated metaphorically with the nation's "titanic entrance into the world of steam and electricity," fusing the secular mission of America—as a land where mechanization and industrialization would overcome European misfortune—with the sacred mission of American Christians to save humankind.[36] Popular futurologist Edward Bellamy warned in the late nineteenth century that America was the "great experiment, on which the last hopes of the race depends [sic]. . . . If it be a failure, it will be a final failure. There can be no new worlds to be discovered, no fresh continents to offer virgin fields for new ventures."[37]

Americans found in this rhetoric of conversion a way of harmonizing their adventurous technological dreams with their conservative religious convictions. Citizens of the New World were not just God's chosen people; Americans were also the almighty Creator's ordained social and cultural engineers, the people who would usher in the New Jerusalem that had previously slipped through the hands of Europeans. One minister captured this kind of sublimely nationalistic optimism in 1839, hailing the era of steam power as the period that would "bring mankind into a common brotherhood; annihilate space and time in the intercourse of human life; increase social relations; draw close ties between philanthropy and benevolence; multiply common benefits . . . and religion into an empire which they have all but nominally possessed in the conduct of mankind." The nineteenth century became an "age of optimistic swagger."[38] Preachers might still insist that the moral and spiritual missionary endeavors were more important than canals and railways, but, says Miller, by "1848 the mind had become so adjusted to the technological revolution that pious language was changed from contrast to analogy. . . . Over and over again, to the point of tedium, but never to satiety, orators identified missions with the industrial 'scene of astonishing activity.'"[39]

By the beginning of the twentieth century in America the new inventions of electricity and electrical forms of communication were eliciting some of the same hopes and fears that had challenged Christian thinking about technological changes in earlier eras of Western history. The public and the experts alike saw electricity as a "set of concrete opportunities or threats to be weighed and figured into the pursuit of ongoing social objectives such as preserving class stability or moving upward socially." The "life-giving and -destroying potential of the ether," writes Carolyn Marvin, "made it ideally suited to carry the freight of social fantasy."[40] In addition to wondering about the impact of electricity on the human body, Americans also imagined the meaning of electricity for the immediate family and for the wider community outside the home. People were "confidently and proudly prophesying utopian accomplishments" that would occur as a result of the human mastery of the new technology, but they were also "anxious . . . about the possible social catastrophes of electrical metamorphosis."[41] Nineteenth-century Americans effortlessly attached spiritual meaning to new modes of transportation and communication, including steamships, locomotives, the telegraph, and eventually the wireless.[42] In 1951, as engineers linked the television networks across the continent, viewers tuned in to watch an amazing broadcast that included the Brooklyn Bridge and the Golden Gate Bridge on the same screen. Commentator Edward R. Murrow optimistically pronounced, "For the first time in the history of man we are able to look at both the Atlantic and Pacific coasts of this great country at the same time. [No] age was ever given a weapon for truth with quite the scope of this fledgling television."[43] Murrow voiced a traditional American hope for the future, an expectation generated through and about communication technologies, and a utopian rhetoric that shaped both Christian and more generally American imaginations throughout the twentieth century.

Americans figured out how to maintain remarkable optimism and severe pessimism about the media technologies—to define the electronic sublime in terms of a rhetoric of conversion that would capture both the spread of evil and the creation of good. By championing mass-mediated conversion Americans were able to catch a ride on the symbolic energies created long ago in the Western traditions of popular theology and scientific progress. Evangelicals proved by their thoughts and actions that rational, scientific inquiry had not wholly replaced religion as the guiding force of American culture. Theologian H. Richard Niebuhr observed in 1937, "Christianity, democracy, Americanism, the English language and culture, the growth of industry and science, American institutions—these are all confounded and confused. The contemplation of their own right-eousness filled Americans with such lofty and enthusiastic sentiments that they readily identified it with the righteousness of God. . . . [T]he Kingdom of the Lord . . . is in particular the kingdom of the Anglo-Saxon race, which is destined to bring light to the gentiles by means of lamps manufac-tured in America."[44] The stage was set for modern American evangelicals to become the primary Christian champions of communication technology and the major religious advocates of the technological sublime.

Evangelical Theology and Mass Communication

The 1830s in America witnessed the incredible growth of two competing developments: the penny newspaper, which expanded the market for non-political, secular news, and the Bible and tract societies, which launched evangelistic Protestants into the business of mass printing and distribution. Both developments sought to garner large audiences with inexpensive products mass-produced through newer technologies for heterogeneous audiences. The so-called penny press was remarkably cheap—a mere penny for a few pages of readable news about politics, crime, economics, and people. But the Bible societies were not to be outdone. They produced staggering numbers of religious tracts and distributed them across the country for free, thereby hoping to avoid the corrupting nature of popular demand for mediated products and achieving a "purer and grander vision for mass media in America."[45] Historian David Paul Nord suggests that the "missionary impulse" was the foundation for the popularization of print in nineteenth-century America.[46] William Cogswell, secretary of the Ameri-can Education Society, captured American Protestants' enthusiasm for these mass-produced materials distributed without cost to the reader: "The Bible Society is often and appropriately compared to the sun. But if the Bible society is the sun, the Tract society is the atmospheric medium that reflects the glorious rays, and throws them into every dark corner of the earth." Moreover, wrote Cogswell in *Harbinger of the Millennium*, "[t]racts impart pious instruction in a perspicuous, concise, and interesting manner. They must, therefore, be productive of the happiest effects," offering read-ers "a word in season, for the intemperate, the profane, and the Sabbath-breaker; for parents and children; for the high and the low, the rich and

the poor, the righteous, and unrighteous, the civilized and uncivilized. . . .
Are not these things a sign of the Millennium's approach?"[47]

Millennial theology, which Protestants strongly advocated in several different forms, integrated popular theology and technological utopianism
during the nineteenth century. As Nord's revealing studies of early-
nineteenth-century Bible and tract societies document, evangelicals were
leaders in both printing technology and the organization of national distribution networks.[48] Dedicated evangelicals indefatigably launched technological initiatives with tremendous zeal and unfailing optimism. Although
they focused on printing, they also spoke gloriously of railroads,
steamships, and the telegraph.[49] Indeed the more visible and popular the
secular media, the more likely that these Protestants would establish paradigms of mass communication that rivaled the best-funded, entrepreneur-
ial efforts of mainstream publishing. The expansion of newspapers, novels,
and political tracts worried traditional religious elites, who connected such
new media to a decline in public morality and to a growing lack of respect
for authority in society.[50] Evangelicals were not to be outdone by godless
people and an increasingly corrupt culture, for in their view the very souls
of Americans were at stake. Managers of the American Tract Society, for
instance, believed that they could supplant the "satanic press" with the
"sanctified press."[51] The conversionary thrust of nineteenth-century American evangelicalism fueled the nation's technological dynamism. If unconverted souls were doomed to hell, as many foreign and domestic
missionaries apparently believed, all possible communication and transportation technologies must be launched into evangelistic service as
quickly as possible. America would serve God and humanity by ushering in
the "second creation," which would be patterned after God's original Creation but established on earth by faithful human hearts and dedicated
Christian toil. Popular postmillennial and eventually premillennial theology interpreted technological development in America through biblical
frameworks.

Postmillennialism, the dominant Protestant eschatology before the Civil
War, was spread throughout the nation through the religious press as well
as through conversation and the pulpit. Based on the idea that Jesus
Christ would return after God's millennial reign on earth, postmillennialism tended to view improvements in printing and religious literature
distribution as marks of the progressive and inevitable expansion of the
kingdom of God in America. Postmillennialism was ripe for a kind of scientific and technological progressivism because it assumed that human

beings could be part of the gradual redemption of society.[52] Progressive thinkers such as John Dewey combined modern science and liberal Protestantism, creating a mainline alternative to evangelicals' openly religious rhetoric of conversion. Dewey argued that "the biblical notion of the kingdom of God eventually come to earth was a valuable truth which had been largely lost to the world because history had not been ready to turn it from an idea into a reality." Dewey and many mainline Protestant clergy "lent to reform thought much of its optimism, its perfectionism and its faith in the ability of brotherhood, united to the modern scientific spirit, to conquer all the evils of the world."[53] In the end, however, such a "this-worldly utopia" was not nearly as compelling as evangelicals' stirring emphasis on premillennial theology.

Premillennialism, which became the major eschatology of American evangelicals in the antebellum period and grew throughout the twentieth century, imagined new technologies less as a mere sign of the kingdom of God on earth and more as "instruments by which the church could inaugurate the millennium."[54] This eschatology, well developed and eagerly spread in America, assumed that Christ's imminent return would be followed immediately by God's thousand-year reign on earth. Once the gospel of Jesus Christ had been proclaimed around the world, presumably through all available media, Christ would return to reign supreme on earth. In this seductive theological narrative, new developments in communication technologies prefigured the imminent entry of Christ into the world. George Duffield, a popular proponent of premillennial theology after the Civil War, wrote, "Never was there a day so marked with advancement in science, improvement in the arts, and the diffusion of general intelligence, by the pulpit, the press, and the public lecturers as the present."[55] He and other premillennialists believed that the same technology that could foster evil would also inevitably distribute the Gospel ever more quickly across the country and throughout the world. New communication technologies were human opportunities to hasten the return of Jesus Christ and to usher in the new millennium foretold in the Scriptures.[56] This popular eschatology gave evangelicals a biblical basis for seizing every new mass medium as a means of converting many people to faith in Jesus Christ. It also gave American technological optimism a religious home and provided evangelicals with a rhetoric of technological praise throughout the twentieth century.

Millennial theology drove evangelical Protestants' imaginative uses of the mass media throughout the nineteenth and twentieth centuries.

Protestants first viewed the printed word in the early nineteenth century as the indispensable "lever of social reform."[57] Evangelicals, in particular, usually justified their mastery of the mass media in communal and apocalyptic terms; human beings could both build a new Edenic community and hasten the return of Jesus Christ by appropriating new technologies. All they needed to do, evangelicals believed, was to develop distinctly religious versions of every new medium instituted by "secular" society. As one Texas Baptist wrote in 1856, "The periodical press is the body, life and spirit of the nineteenth century."[58] The telegraph, some evangelicals believed by midcentury, could communally unite prayer across the country and even eventually across the ocean with the laying of the Atlantic cable.[59] The telegraph would usher in peace and unity as a divine "Oracle of Peace," the "great invention of the century [that] impresses upon the mind and heart of the religious world the ideas of UNITY, and thus aids in creating a power antagonistic to the injurious separation and alienation, too long prevalent in the church. A better era is at hand. Unity is the familiar message among the religious demonstrations of Providence. Unity is the loving truth of Gospel grace."[60]

By the turn of the century evangelicals used the same kinds of rhetorics of conversion and communion to define publicly the crucial role of wireless technology in ushering in social unity and generating religious enthusiasms from coast to coast. Robert S. Fortner concludes that Protestants celebrated "the ability of radio to cross the demographic boundaries and bind people together" as well as "the ecstasy that would come from the particularity of the Christian evangelistic message."[61] Millennial thought established the framework for conservative Protestant understandings of the mass media in America. In the process, popular theologizing both shaped and reflected the ways that people tried publicly to make sense of the new technologies, even in the nonreligious media.

American evangelicalism was not a revolt against modernization as much as an attempt to steer the new industrial world in a millennial direction, to co-opt the rational use of technology for the goals of the kingdom of God and especially for the salvation of individual souls before the return of Jesus Christ.[62] While Roman Catholics generally displayed a "profound ambivalence" toward the new media, evangelicals embraced communication technologies enthusiastically, filled with hope that mass communication was the solution to the need for worldwide evangelization.[63] This kind of premillennially focused modernization essentially connoted "self satisfaction and an easy identification of God's ways with the ways of his fallen creatures." Evangelicals used modernistic rhetoric, including terms such as "progress," "universal," "power," and "perfect," which punctuated evangelical speech "in a bizarre mixture of Enlightenment idealism and traditional theological language." Phrases such as "conquest of the whole world for Christ," "all is Progress," and "the conversion and sanctifying of the world," says Douglas Frank, reflected "a people drunk on their own power—and confusing it with the power of God."[64] Premillennial evangelical theology tended to view mass communication in precisely the same kinds of mechanistic and rationalistic terms that business and science used to express their powerful mastery of technology. These Protestants supported a "transmission" view of communication as a "process whereby messages are transmitted and distributed in space for the control of distance and people."[65] Evangelicals embraced a manipulative concept *of* communication that eventually led them to manipulative concepts *for* communication. To the extent that American evangelicals adopted this control-oriented view of communication, they, too, probably contributed to the "chaos of modern culture."[66]

Popular evangelical rhetoric of conversion also persuasively embraced modern individualism in America by imagining the recipients of print and electronic messages as "mass audiences" comprised of isolated persons. Indeed the tradition of itinerant preaching and mass revivals is anchored in a kind of rhetoric of atomistic anonymity; the preacher assumes that he or she can connect quickly with individual listeners whom he or she has never met and likely will never get to know personally. The audience in this scenario is composed of lone souls waiting to be converted to personal salvation. A religious communicator does not need a community to engage in such hit-or-miss evangelism; he or she needs merely an audience, whether readers, listeners, or viewers. Moreover, even churches can focus on the opportunities for numerical growth in local "markets." This individualistic concept of communication meshed perfectly with evangelical broadcast efforts in the twentieth century. Ben Armstrong, executive director of the National Religious Broadcasters (NRB), suggested in a 1988 article in the association's magazine, *Religious Broadcasting*, that "the fastest growing churches use radio or television broadcasting." He called such congregations "super churches" and provided a chart of numerical growth for "America's Fastest Growing Churches."[67] Such evangelicals saw the church itself as made up of individual converts, not as a community. These optimistic believers often were so "filled with zeal to proclaim the gospel that they felt compelled to move beyond ponderous denominational structures" in order to set up their own extradenominational agencies and "to promote the cause more efficiently."[68] In this way evangelicals tended to institutionalize individualism first within parachurch movements and later within the church, usually in the name of greater communicative power and evangelistic impact. They increasingly borrowed the ideology of market research and consumer behavior to rationalize their evangelistic efforts.[69] Ironically, individualism thereby provided some of the rhetorical basis for mass-media evangelism as a prelude to the new community.

Twentieth-century evangelical Protestants were unequivocally the major advocates of religious uses of the mass media, particularly of evangelistic efforts to convert the unsaved. The development of radio broadcasting in the 1920s gave evangelicals their first opportunity since mass printing to master a new medium of mass persuasion. Premillennial theology and technological utopianism merged powerfully in early-twentieth-century evangelical thought and have been strongly integrated ever since. Evangelicals championed the broadcast media, believing once again that God ordained the new technology for the salvation of the world. While mainline Protestants pontificated about the ethical and theological ramifications of the new medium, individualistic evangelical entrepreneurs were busily expanding their broadcast activities from coast to coast.[70] Evangelicals took to the radio with few concerns or second thoughts, believing that it was ordained by God as a medium for mass conversion. Charles E. Fuller's *Old-Fashioned Revival Hour* elicited thousands of letters weekly from listeners in the 1940s and may have been the most popular American radio program of all time.[71] Largely because of their theological commitments, especially their millennial eschatology and their emphasis on individual conversion, evangelicals frequently attributed great spiritual significance to broadcasting technologies. If the Second Coming of Jesus Christ was imminent, as conservative Protestants increasingly believed, there was no time to waste and no technology to overlook in the task of global evangelism. Unrighteous people had to be brought to Salvation.[72] Evangelicals projected American technological optimism onto their views of radio and later television. For them, broadcasting represented an old religious hope in a new cultural setting.

Many evangelical leaders believed that radio was the most powerful God-given technology for proclaiming the Gospel and saving souls. Eugene Bertermann of *The Lutheran Hour*, sponsored by the Lutheran Church—Missouri Synod, was one of the major evangelicals writing on behalf of religious broadcasting. He traced the history of God's use of the media from the apostles' "primitive" and "laborious" proclamation by "word of mouth" to "the mighty . . . miracle of radio." "Radio has several remarkable advantages," he said. "First of all there is its spread, in that it reaches out over tremendous territories in a single moment. There is its speed, since radio waves travel with a speed of 186,000 miles a second. There is also its penetration, since it can leap over boundaries, penetrate through walls of steel and bars or iron to bring the Gospel to people whom, humanly speaking, one could hardly reach by any other medium. We who are Christians know that in God's design the radio has been invented particularly for the use of His Church and the upbuilding of His kingdom."[73] Added Bertermann, "Christians who maintain the Christ-centered view of history, properly hold that our Heavenly Father permitted radio and television to be invented or discovered, first and foremost, for the dissemination of His saving Gospel."[74] Few evangelicals made the case for missionary radio any more directly or strongly. Given Bertermann's association with one of the largest Lutheran denominations, his rhetoric of conversion is even more telling.

This rhetoric of conversion led evangelicals to identify the development of electronic communication technologies with the actions of God. They frequently criticized the medium's nonreligious programming, while unequivocally accepting the idea that radio and later television were a necessary and foreordained part of God's historical plan. Either broadcasting glorified God, which usually meant it proclaimed the Gospel, or it was being used to advance the kingdom of darkness, which typically implied it was promoting cultural worldliness.[75] In other words, new media always converted; the real issues were who converted people and to what message. Fortunately, said Bertermann, the vast majority of Protestant broadcasters are "dedicated servants of Christ, earnestly determined to utilize effectively the twentieth-century miracles of radio and television for the proclamation of the Gospel. . . . An abundant measure of the Holy Spirit's power accompanying the broadcasting of the Word will prove it to be 'the power unto salvation to everyone that believeth.'"[76] Media evangelist Jerry Falwell and his associate Elmer Towns similarly concluded years later that "the most effective medium for reaching people . . . is television."[77] They said that they "would like to preach the gospel on every TV station in the free world. That would be carrying out the command of Christ . . . to build the greatest church since Pentecost."[78] Evangelicals' rhetoric of conversion expressed a vision of the power of the Holy Spirit to conquer space and time on behalf of the kingdom of God. Evangelist William H. Foulkes wrote, "There is something so uncanny and far-reaching in the persuasive-ness of the radio waves that to the Christian it might well become another Pentecost—a potential Pentecost at least. . . . Will the Christian church once again demonstrate its short-sightedness, and permit this swift-winged messenger to become the permanent possession of forces hostile to the gospel?"[79] American evangelicals praised the conversionary power of elec-tronic media over and over again. The mass media, they believed, would lead evangelicals out of cultural exile and inaugurate a new era of evangel-icals' cultural dominance in America—a prelude to the return of Jesus Christ.

In the eyes of many evangelicals the impending return of Jesus Christ de-manded the immediate mobilization of technology workers for a spiritual harvest. Preparing for the Second Coming, they would act on the faith that individuals and even entire nations would repent and turn to God—and in the hope that the media were the divinely granted technologies for accom-plishing this worldwide salvation. The Gospel must be preached to "every available person at every available time by every available means. . . . Satu-ration is demanded [because] . . . the imminent return of the Lord Jesus Christ demands that we reach every man with the gospel—soon. We do not have much time. . . . People are dying every day. . . . The church will stand accountable at the judgment seat of Christ for its failure to utilize every means available to us to reach every creature."[80] Similarly, Jimmy Swaggart Ministries stated that its mission was to "reach every person, in every nation . . . using every available means." Swaggart writes, "When I realize that nearly forty million people in forty countries will tune this week to our tele-cast, the immensity of the audience is almost beyond my human compre-hension. And parallel with this unprecedented ability to appear before people is the opportunity to influence them: We can redirect a nation to the paths of righteousness; we can introduce (often for the first time) masses to the gospel of Jesus Christ."[81] Rev. M. G. "Pat" Robertson, then founder and president of the Christian Broadcasting Network, said, "I believe that there is going to be a tremendous move of God in missions. We would use the technology, the wealth, the wisdom, the spiritual implementations that God is giving to reach out to a hungry-hearted world that is prepared now for the knowledge of Jesus and to participate in this harvest process in these last days."[82] The evangelical publication *Christianity Today* praised television in 1968 as "the most effective means of penetrating closed doors and closed minds that the Church has ever had. . . . If we fail, the world will never find the only solution to its desperate need."[83]

Popular evangelical theology, especially premillenialism, embraced the American faith in the conversionary power of communication technologies to save souls in preparation for Second Coming of Jesus Christ. Committed to what evangelicals often called God's "Great Commission" to spread the Gospel, these conservative Protestants charged American technological optimism with particularly religious significance.[84] They adapted their theological convictions to the times, establishing by the 1920s a view of God's work in redemptive history that required faithful followers of Jesus Christ to use every new medium to spread the Gospel. Such biblical interpretations and their accompanying theological commitments supported a strong version of technological utopianism. Unlike the Progressive hope that marked the thought of early-twentieth-century mainline clergy and of scholars such as Dewey, evangelical theology essentially grafted premillennial hopes and fears into the existing technological optimism, thereby establishing a rationale for using modern methods to spread the old-fashioned Gospel. America thereby became the home for the resulting mythos of the electronic church.

The Mythos of the Electronic Church

In 1986 American TV evangelist Jimmy Swaggart unveiled a plan to spread his old-fashioned Gospel to all nations on earth. The plan was not based on traditional evangelistic methods of recruiting, training, and sending missionaries around the world. Instead Swaggart proposed packaging his top-rated weekly religious broadcast for every culture, transmitting it directly to the human race without the inefficiencies of time-intensive local evangelism and stifling quagmires of denominational bureaucracies. Like the communication theorist Marshall McLuhan, Swaggart envisioned an impending global village founded not merely on McLuhan's notion of instantaneous worldwide communication but also on a kind of electronic evangelism that would supposedly transmit the Gospel through geographic space and across diverse cultures, directly and powerfully to the hearts of humankind. Swaggart's evangelist son, Donnie, informed the ministry's "world outreach partners" that it was "D-Day or Delay," depending upon the extent of financial contributions forthcoming from the program's two million viewers.[85] Either viewers would support the ministry financially and quicken the spread of the Gospel around the world, or they would delay the spiritual harvest and stall the Second Coming of Jesus Christ.[86] It was time, the Swaggarts argued, for the church in the United States to embrace the technological revolution and to hasten the salvation of souls around the globe before the imminent return of Jesus Christ.

Swaggart's sanguine expectations for global media evangelism might be dismissed merely as a fund-raising strategy if the sentiments that he expressed were not so widespread among American evangelicals. These conservative Protestants frequently invoked the hope that electronic communication could overcome cultural and political obstacles to worldwide evangelization. Like the predictions of McLuhan and the other media futurists, the hopeful prognostications of American media evangelists found many receptive hearts and minds by tapping a rich reservoir of popular American mythology about technology and the future of humankind—a reservoir of hope and imagination that both reflected and shaped how the nation conceived of new technologies. "Historians looking at the twentieth Century [sic] from the next millennium will likely pinpoint 1945 as the most pivotal year since the voyage of Columbus," wrote a *Los Angeles Times* reporter in 1992. Television has, "for better or for worse, led a modern Crusade, spreading pop culture over the Earth as medieval knights once spread Christendom. In fact, nearly thirty years after Canadian philosopher Marshall McLuhan coined the phrase 'global village' to describe how the electronics revolution was shrinking the world and shortening the time between thought and action, the Media Millennium is at hand."[87] Combining such secular American rhetoric about technological triumphs with popular theology, evangelical broadcasters created a "mythos of the electronic church" that rivaled the nonreligious forms of technological utopianism. During the 1960s and 1970s, in particular, American evangelicals created their own version of what Carey and Quirk appropriately call the "mythos of the electronic revolution."[88] This mythos fused the evangelical rhetorics of communion, conversion, and praise.

The mythos of the electronic church helps explain the broad evangelical support for media evangelism in the face of scant evidence for its domestic ineffectiveness.[89] It also sheds light on the rapid growth of evangelical broadcasting and cable in recent years. Evangelicals by the 1980s owned and operated major broadcast properties, including satellite uplinks, television and radio stations, and state-of-the-art production facilities. Although evangelicalism has had its articulate critics of media evangelism, the members of the movement quickly used the new technologies, from cable to home video.[90] By 1986 there were 1,134 religious radio stations in the United States, an increase of about 10 percent over 1985 alone. Even more impressive was the 100 percent growth in the number of religious television stations during the same one-year period, resulting in 200 such stations nationwide. The NRB also reported conservatively that there were 755 radio and 1,047 television programs and films produced in 1985 by Christian organizations; some of these radio and television programs ran daily throughout the country, and many were repeated over various cable networks. Including the local programs that are not tallied in such data, it is likely that the total number of individual religious broadcasts in America per year by the 1980s was easily in the tens of thousands. From 1968 to 1985 the roster of organizations affiliated with the NRB increased more than tenfold, from 104 to 1,050. Major religious cable television networks in 1985 included CBN Cable Network (30 million subscribers), PTL Television Network (13 million), Trinity Broadcasting Network (6 million), and the Southern Baptist's ACTS Satellite Network (3.5 million).[91]

Christianity Today's special issue, "New Era for Christian Communication," captured the style and beliefs of the mythos. Published just prior to a World Congress on Evangelism held in Berlin, the issue included a revealing editorial that pleaded with evangelicals to "strip away any vestige of suspicion about the technology or intelligence employed in God's service." An editorial argued that "Christians are swept up in the third great revolution of human history," the previous two being the "transition from nomadic hunting to settled agricultural economies" and the industrialization of the West. This third, "breathless epoch of atom and automation . . . computer control and space racing . . . offers worldwide information networks for presenting our Lord to a needy audience of billions." The editorial continued, "These methods of mass proclamation are providentially available at the very time the population is . . . exploding." The magazine also cited the formation of DATA, a Christian organization exchanging information between missionaries and technical experts that, in the editorial's words, was preparing "a worldwide scientific model for evangelism." Finally, the editors praised a global evangelism project established by World Vision and Fuller Theological Seminary and based on the idea of a "brain trust" used by Robert McNamara to design machines of military destruction and scientific exploration.[92]

A missionary expressed this futuristic ode to communication technologies in *Christianity Today* in 1968. "The Communications Revolution has begun—and few Christians are aware of its arrival or importance," he announced. "What the revolution means, in a sentence is: Every person can now communicate with any other person on the face of the globe." Quoting David Sarnoff, chair of the board of Radio Corporation of America, the evangelical writer hailed the expected launching of the first high-power communication satellite that was to accommodate "as many as a dozen television channels, and thousands of telephone-voice, facsimile, and computer-data channels simultaneously. These satellites will evolve into huge orbiting 'switchboards,' automatically relaying electronic signals of every kind from and to any place on earth." The communications revolution presented "an exciting and wholly satisfying way of communicating the Christian Gospel in all its fullness to all peoples and all classes in our own generation." He concluded with a prophetic challenge for the Christian church: "To reach everyone in a country within ten years with everything from education to salvation for $100,000."[93] Exactly how this was to be accomplished was left to the reader's own prophetic imagination—especially given the fact that the majority of the people on the face of the globe still do not have access to such technology.

While advanced by dozens of evangelical authors and clergy, the mythos of the electronic church found its clearest and most forceful expression in the NRB, which had represented the interests of evangelical broadcasters since the 1940s.[94] By the early 1980s the denominationally independent NRB represented over 1,000 member organizations producing or broadcasting religious programs for radio, television, cable, and satellite. According to the NRB, the organization's members were involved in three-quarters of the religious programming in the United States.[95] NRB president Bertermann told members at the 1967 annual convention in Chicago that it was "becoming increasingly apparent that radio and TV are uniquely suited in this century to overcome obstacles and hindrances to missionary outreach." The seven obstacles that Bertermann believed would be overcome included "the worldwide population explosion, poverty, automation, leisure, the shrinking of time and space, rising nationalism, and the resurgent world religions." Citing the relative advantages of the "two giants of radio and television" for spreading the gospel, he concluded that "not one of these obstacles can capably shut out the gospel when [they] are wisely used to their maximum potential."[96] "No pastor today should build a church without building the chancel for television or radio," editorialized Armstrong in *Religious Broadcasting*. "Gospel broadcasting represents the growing edge of Christendom . . . [t]he best methodology of evangelizing the world with the good news of the gospel." He cited the first religious broadcast over Pittsburgh radio station KDKA in 1921 as a "historic event—the birth of the electric church."[97] Armstrong's NRB fostered and disseminated this kind of rhetoric at its conferences and in its publications. As a religious trade group, it translated deeply American sentiments about communication technology into the vernacular of popular, nondenominational evangelicalism.

Journalists cited Armstrong's book, *The Electric Church*, as evidence in the 1980s for the growing role of evangelical broadcasting in the American presidential campaign. It might be the most revealing expression of the mythos of the electronic church ever published. Calling the "awesome technology of broadcasting" one of the "major miracles of modern times," Armstrong compares the foreshadowed world of Christian broadcasting with a nostalgic, preindustrialized era when humankind lived in peace and harmony. "Radio and television have broken through the walls of tradition we have built up around the church," rhapsodizes Armstrong, "and have restored conditions remarkably similar to the early church." According to a vision Armstrong had on an evening flight landing in Chicago, the "electric church" would become "a revolutionary new form of the worshiping, witnessing church that existed twenty centuries ago. . . . Members of the church gathered in homes, shared the Scriptures, prayed together, praised God for the gift of His Son Jesus Christ, and testified to His presence in their lives. They were on fire for the Lord, and their lives had been changed by Him. As a result, they changed the world."[98] Armstrong powerfully fuses rhetorics of conversion and communion, portraying new technologies as the God-ordained means of saving the souls of all people and simultaneously transforming the world into the equivalent of the local, primitive church.

According to the mythos, electronic media eventually would convert the world, build an international community of believers, and lead evangelicals from cultural exile into the Promised Land. Armstrong's prophecies culminate in a picture of a New World created by Christians who were spiritually energized by a Holy Ghost who presumably works through communication technologies. Calling the electric church a "revolution as dramatic as the revolution that began when Martin Luther nailed his ninety-five theses to the cathedral door at Wittenberg," Armstrong predicts that God will use the "electric church to revitalize the older forms of churches, empowering them to keep up with the twentieth-century challenges of a rapidly expanding population and a rapidly diminishing time span before the return of Jesus Christ." Citing repeatedly McLuhan's concept of the "global village," he concludes that religious broadcasting has "changed the church from a collection of isolated groups of believers joined together over an entire continent. . . . Not bound by the limits of geography, these believers grow within their home environments, providing new

depth, insights, and leadership to their home churches."[99] This future
world is so close at hand, predicts Armstrong, that the angel referred to in
the Book of Revelation might actually be a communication satellite used
by God to fulfill prophecy of the last days: "And I saw another angel fly in
the midst of heaven, having the everlasting gospel to preach unto them
that dwell in the earth, and to every nation, and kindred, and tongue, and
people."[100] McLuhan's ideas intellectually justified such metaphysical
claims about the power of the media, although many religious broadcasters
apparently understood little of what McLuhan said in his 1970 presentation to the NRB.[101] "The most important thing he told us," wrote Armstrong about McLuhan's appearance, "was that the only perfect union of
the medium and the message had occurred in the person of Jesus Christ.
His words brought us full circle, back to the origin of what we have to
communicate, back to the Biblical presentation of the divinity of Jesus
Christ."[102] Using McLuhan's theoretical ideas, Armstrong and other evangelicals combined technological futurism with religious communalism. The
electrical machines would return humankind to its bucolic roots in the
Garden of Eden.

In its strongest formulations the mythos of the electronic church sancti-
fies modern communication technologies, reflecting a faith not just in God
but also in the contemporary machinery and electronics used by religious
broadcasters. Evangelicals adopted McLuhan's claim that the "medium is
the message," baptizing the electronic media as God-ordained vehicles for
ushering in tribal community on a global scale. The mythos became the
message of the medium, to play on McLuhan's rhetoric. In one sense,
evangelicals' apparent veneration of technology was simply part of the
American rhetoric of progress. In spite of its sectarian cast the mythos affirms the hope that the future will usher in a better place and time.[103]
Evangelicals shared this hope and were able to give it particular rhetorical
expression through the language of premillennial theology and popular
theories such as those of McLuhan. They situated new technology within
evangelical culture as an object of praise and as a tool for cultivating both
community and conversion.

In their public paeans to the new communication technologies, broadcast evangelists often combined the biblical Second Coming and the historical hope for an Atlantis. Robertson, for instance, in the 1980s equated the
prophetic proclamations of the Book of Joel with social and spiritual conditions in the United States. For him, decreasing interest rates, a rising gross
national product, and a renewed interest in religious matters were clear

signs that the United States was being prepared for the great revival proph-
esied by Joel and facilitated by Robertson's own Christian Broadcasting
Network and other religious programs.[104] Other media evangelists, such as
Falwell and Tim LaHaye, simply identified Americans as the people whom
God had chosen to bring about worldwide justice and spiritual salvation.[105]
Evangelicals preached not only the gospel of Jesus Christ but also a tribal
rhetoric of technological utopia anchored in the idea of progress and in the
notion of Americans as God's chosen people for carrying out the divine
plan of worldwide evangelization.

Although their rhetoric was deeply populist, the proponents of the electronic church created a class of prophetic clergy who sometimes claimed
special knowledge and spiritual insight into the power of modern communication technologies. Their mythos established a rhetorical context in
which influential religious celebrities could gain public stature and tribal
influence. Leaders of the electronic church, including celebrities such as
Falwell and Robertson, gained enormous secular media exposure and became public symbols of conservative values and contemporary evangelicalism. They also gained political power by virtue of the leverage that they
supposedly had with their large constituencies of donors and followers.[106]
In addition, these evangelical leaders became best-selling authors of auto-
hagiographic books and prophetic treatises on the work of God in the contemporary world.[107] No matter how popular its appeal, however, the
mythos of the electronic church simply rearranged some of the power
structures within evangelicalism, creating a new class of influential broadcast celebrities who represented the evangelical movement to itself as well
as to the wider world. They each could develop their own rhetorics of discernment that supposedly offered evangelicalism special insight into the
mysteries of God's work in the world today.

The mythos of the electronic church simply reformulated in the twentieth century the types of millennial eschatology that had influenced evangelical rhetoric about the printing press and telegraph in the nineteenth
century. Perhaps the only novel aspect of the mythos was the appeal to
popular academicians such as McLuhan to legitimize their arguments.
Evangelical pronouncements in the 1970s through the 1990s about the
power of satellites and cyberspace used imagery and metaphors identical to
those mythological predications expressed in the previous century. They
also relied upon the same kinds of fears about the secular media's negative
effects on society to help justify their own major investments in conversionary media campaigns. Perhaps twentieth-century evangelical broadcast

celebrities were no more popular in America than the most celebrated re-
vivalists of earlier times, such as George Whitefield and Dwight Moody.
Some of these earlier evangelists generated tremendous publicity through
newspaper coverage and by word-of-mouth.[108] The more recent versions
of this rhetoric of conversion reflected the same utopianism and communalism of the versions that emerged with mass printing.

From a different angle, however, the mythos of the electronic church may
have anchored evangelical media activity even more deeply in modern rationality and organizational culture. Clearly print-based evangelistic efforts
had already developed systematic management techniques. The American
Tract Society had bureaucratized and rationalized its evangelistic efforts in the
middle of the nineteenth century.[109] With the development of an association
such as the NRB, essentially a trade association for evangelical broadcasters
and allied businesses, however, evangelicals collectively expressed the mythic
rhetoric and standardized some of the media strategies and tactics used in
mass-media evangelism. Evangelical celebrities still used their charisma to
garner large audiences and to elicit contributions as in Whitefield's day, but
behind the scenes late in the nineteenth century a host of fund-raising specialists, professional publicists, and advertising agencies began working hard
to maximize the impact of evangelistic endeavors. The mythos itself was
emotionally and spiritually charged, but the underlying organizational
processes were increasingly bureaucratic, rational, and even managerial.
Thus the mythos of the electronic church separated the public aspects of
media evangelism from the private methods and procedures that conversionary mass-media campaigns depended on to become financially viable. In this
sense, too, evangelistically inspired futurism reflected the broader American
culture's reliance on communication professionals who knew how to formulate effective promotional campaigns and persuasive message strategies. The
mythos of the electronic church fused ethical pragmatism with religious al-
truism, thereby justifying even the most business-like methods in the name
of worldwide salvation and the Second Coming of Jesus Christ. Nevertheless,
the scope of such rhetorics of conversion and communion transcended
American evangelicalism and even North American Christianity to the far
reaches of popular culture, including science fiction.

Prophetic Mythos As Science Fiction

In her fascinating science fiction novel titled *The Long Tomorrow*, Leigh
Brackett pits the traditional concept of primitive Mennonite community

against the kind of societies created through advanced technologies.[110] The novel's setting is a rather dismal future nearly a century after an apocalyptic "Great Destruction" that devastated major cities and destroyed most technologies in an atomic holocaust. Leaders amend the Constitution to forbid any communities of more than 1,000 people or 200 buildings per square mile. In this reversal of technological fortune, the Mennonites now are among the most successful and powerful social groups in the country, controlling the government and ensuring that the nation will not once again become too dependent on destructive technologies. Two Mennonites, curious about the preapocalyptic world of high technology and having heard about the existence of a predestruction culture, set out to find the lost world of technological culture. Their subsequent dilemma, whether to identify personally with the low-tech communalism of the Mennonites or with the high-tech cosmopolitanism of the surviving technologists, shapes the theme of the story.[111]

Just as Brackett's novel explores through science fiction the value of religious community in a technological society, popular evangelical theology addresses the relationship between technology and community. "Popular theology" is theological discourse that is produced in and through the media marketplace, not a traditional theology anchored in a particular faith community over time. American science fiction and popular theology are two expressions of symbolic worlds that address essentially the same issues often with similar motifs and shared concerns—both the utopian and the dystopian. Evangelical rhetoric about the future frequently sounds like science fiction. Moreover, science fiction often critically explores various technological scenarios, serving as a form of secular prophecy that warns people of the likely impact of technology. The hero in Kurt Vonnegut's *God Bless You, Mr. Rosewater* announces at a convention for science fiction writers, "You're all I read any more. You're the only ones who'll talk about the really terrific changes going on, the only ones crazy enough to know that life is a space voyage. . . . You're the only ones with guts enough to really care about the future, who really notice what machines do to us. . . . You're the only ones zany enough to agonize over time and distances without limit, over mysteries that will never die."[112] One science fiction writer suggests that the genre has become the "tale that wags the god."[113] Science fiction and popular evangelical theology celebrate and condemn communication technologies, make claims about the technological future, and address humans as tool-using creatures who dream about conquering space and time. Only history offers a means retrospectively to evaluate the validity of their various predictions, but regardless of whether these two ways of knowing are accurate indices of the human condition, they often reflect real human sentiments that influence how people might act in the present and future.

In the case of evangelical rhetoric, the technological prelates who champion the mythos of the electronic church can always announce that the predicted future has not yet arrived. After all, people continue to develop potentially powerful communication technologies. There is always one more technology to try, one more broadcast station to purchase, another cable system to access, or a million more dollars to raise for online evangelism. By investing communication technologies with futuristic significance, popular theology is able to situate the media as forces outside of human history and therefore unavailable for a historical accounting. Although studies suggest that the electronic media may be rather inefficient and ineffective tools for religious conversion, there are always new media and novel techniques on the horizon.[114] Theology, like science fiction, is always somewhat speculative and invariably conjoined to contemporary human interests, passions, and fears. Theologians and science fiction writers tend over time to shift to newer issues and frames of reference, with little or no historical accountability.

Science fiction and popular theology offer promises and assertions that ought to be verified—especially their futuristic claims about social worlds that have yet to arrive. In spite of all of the evangelical radio and television programs transmitted throughout the United States and around the globe to save humankind, for instance, the spiritual condition of even evangelicals apparently continues to decline. Historian Nathan O. Hatch writes that "within their own walls, evangelicals have never seemed stronger; yet outside those walls the Juggernaut of secularism rolls on."[115] Although their use of the mass media has earned evangelicals' national status as a cultural group and to some extent granted them currency as a political movement, evangelical media have not turned the entire nation to Christ or led to the great prosperity predicted by Robertson.[116] In fact, assessing the overall impact of religious broadcasting in America is akin to evaluating the effects of science fiction writing on the national understanding of technology and its future implications. The mythos of the electronic church, like science fiction stories, offers a gnostic (secret and privileged) form of knowing, not a scientific means of explanation and control. As Robert Galbreath argues about "fantastic literature," gnosis is "religious, mythological, or transcendental knowledge, not scientific or abstractly philosophical knowledge."[117] Gnosis is more of a received revelation, a type of "secret" or exclusive knowledge, not a rational and verifiable epistemology. Both science fiction and popular theology often step beyond the here and now to speculate about the "other"—about other times, other worlds, other beings, and other states of affairs.[118] In the process, they claim to "reveal" previously unknown knowledge of the relationship between humankind and technology.

Within both forms of knowing is a common tendency toward prophetic discourse based on self-evident determinism and unreflective optimism. The self-evident determinism of secular prophecy is meant to guarantee a triumphant future that technology supposedly will bring into existence.[119] Like much science fiction, popular theology asserts a particular state of affairs and invites people to adopt it as their own, to believe in it. Such mythological reasoning is fictional—at least partly a work of human imagination—and invitational, not realistic and verifiable. Proponents of the mythos of the electronic church, for example, simply assert that sacred scriptures and recent technological advances invariably point toward an optimistic future, toward a time in the near future when humans will be able to use technology to save millions of people from sin, misery, and despair. According to this mythological scenario, the power of God working through the media cannot be stopped—if human beings are faithful to God and obedient to God's call to evangelize the world. As Falwell says, we are "living in an age" when God has made it possible "through the broadcast media" to "go into all the world and preach the Gospel to every living creature."[120] The possibility of such a technological future is more or less self-evident, while the optimism that such a future state of affairs will actually occur is largely outside of the biblical narrative and even theological reflection. Science fiction is a "literature of our inner and outer frontiers, and it has always been impossible to subdue the mythic and spiritual imaginations on our frontiers."[121] The same could be claimed about popular apocalyptic theology, which envisions a seemingly incontestable but nevertheless imaginable future.

Behind such self-evident determinism is what Arend Theodoor Van Leeuwen calls the "ought" of silent optimism.[122] Self-evident determinism in all prophetic rhetoric depends on an unreflective optimism that expresses as empirical fact the mere hope of the prophets and their followers. The future seems self-evident because the predicted scenario is precisely what the prophets and their supporters want to occur—what they think should take place. Much of the "faith" within the mythos of the electronic church is really the hope that technology magically will fulfill the Great

Commission by communicating the Gospel to all people and ushering in the Second Coming.[123] This optimism is sustained not by an actual historical record that documents the spiritual accomplishments of communication technologies—assuming such a record could be culled—but rather by the audience's hope in the future of the nation and the world. The rhetoric of the electronic church functions like all other utopian rhetoric to confirm what a tribe wishes to believe is possible. Carey and Quirk write, "Unlike the mere revisionist or clairvoyant, the futurist has the advantage that the future can always be rewritten for there is no record to compare it with, no systematic verification of prophecy. The futurist can keep extending the day of consummation or rely on the forgetfulness of the public when the appointed but unfulfilled day arrives."[124] As long as the symbolic leaders affirm what the tribe wants to believe about the future, there may never be a historical accounting of past predictions. For the tribe, the shared optimism does not even need to be spoken; it already undergirds the group's prophetic imagination.

As with all human communication, the meaning of particular symbols in religious or science fiction discourse is cocreated by the participants. If participants fail to agree on the meaning of the messages, the rhetorics of conversion, communion, and praise lose their power. Often participants' own tribal loyalties influence their openness to specific interpretations of mass-mediated messages. Science fiction author Theodore Sturgeon, for instance, suggests that the literary genre suffers elitist persecution in America because of the public's unreflective faith in the scientific method and in scientific progress. Science, he argues, is "a god-thing: omniscient, omnipotent, omnipresent, master of that terrible trinity of hope, fear and power." He adds that uncritical readers of science fiction bring to the stories a sense that science-the-god is "incomprehensible, unpredictable, and reasonable only in its own mysterious ways." Sturgeon laments the "lack of discrimination amongst the reading-viewing public" and declares that science fiction is "the victim of religious persecution, not from the heretics, but from the devout." After reviewing a stunning array of religiously oriented science fiction, including C. S. Lewis's Narnia series, Sturgeon concludes that religion and science fiction are "no strangers to one another."[125] He contends that religious tribes and devotees of science fiction share a distrust of the totalizing tendencies of scientific thought and the narrow epistemology of the scientific method. The best science fiction films "provide their audiences at least temporary mythic satiation, and also lend implicit support for the assumptional underpinnings of those *mythoi.*"[126]

As mass communication enters the American marketplace of ideas, it finds some tribal adherents who will make its message their own precisely because they are able to interpret the message in support of their existing hopes and dreams. Science fiction and popular theology similarly find and affirm a tribe. Just as science fiction depends on readers who are willing to accept particular nonscientific understandings of the world, the mythos of the electronic church depends on audiences who are willing to accept fashionable religious understandings of the impact of mass communication, namely, the secular version of the rhetorics of technological conversion, communion, and praise. Futuristic rhetoric, whether expressed in science fiction or popular theology, communicates most powerfully, however, when it resonates with the wishful thinking of a tribe. Carol Murphy laments the fact that most science fiction writers "use their imagination in the service of wishful thinking instead of disciplining it in the light of reality which must be shown underlying the fantasy." Science fiction is a "negative witness," she argues, because it "merely points to the mystery of life without giving a Christian answer."[127] But the same criticism could be leveled at popular evangelical eschatology, which cannot really provide an answer as to how and when God will end the world any more than the fictional author can accurately predict the technological future and its implications. Polak tries to solve this problem by defining "utopian" futurism as made by humans and "eschatological" futurism as God-given, but even evangelical eschatology blurs the distinction by implicating Christian believers in the process of "making" the Second Coming.[128] In both religious and nonreligious tribes the relevant community of interpretation sanctions or rejects futuristic appeals. Particularly in the United States, where religious tradition tends to be weak, the marketplace often adjudicates the veracity of both utopian and eschatological claims.

Technological futurism within American evangelicalism is often disconnected from the traditional beliefs and practices of the historic Christian church, leaving the devout more and more susceptible to theological fads and science-fiction-like interpretations of the world to come. As evangelicalism moves from tradition to the market, it joins science fiction as an increasingly time-based mode of understanding. The market can facilitate communication as media writers and producers seek relevance for their stories, but it cannot guarantee a veracity tied to a historic tradition, to a long-standing community of interpretation. The whims of the market for religious hope change, whereas tradition is much more stable. American evangelicalism, like American science fiction, is largely uninterested in cultural let alone religious tradition.[129] Evangelicalism often focuses rather uncritically on pragmatic uses for technologies, on currently fashionable theological ideas, and even on strongly articulated morality campaigns that offer easy solutions to complex social problems. Although premillennial theology is a relatively new way of framing the history and future of the Christian church, most evangelicals probably have little understanding of the alternative traditions of hermeneutical interpretation. To an evangelical, the Christian church's historical wisdom about the amillennial character of eschatology might be little more than science fiction. As "science fiction and the mainstream increasingly merge," the "artificial dichotomy between science fiction and 'Literature,' with a capital 'L' will fade."[130]

Both popular theology and science fiction, then, provide a futuristic means of understanding the meaning of new communication technologies. They imagine implicitly real states of affairs that ask the reader or viewer to accept the plausibility, if not the probability, of a particular kind of technological future. In his essay "Theology, Science Fiction and Man's Future Orientation," J. Norman King suggests that "as the past recedes from proximity and enduring power, man turns his attention more and more to an undetermined future, increasingly divergent from that past. Man's current existential orientation is focused upon that future."[131] He believes that the apparent irrelevance of tradition and historical ways of understanding in America invariably transfers humankind's "existential anxieties" from the past to the future. In this cultural climate, "science fiction, at least in principle, is a peculiarly apt form of literature to speak both of and to our contemporary experience." Humans in this temporal orientation tend to project their tribal self-understandings into an imagined future rather than to situate themselves in the context of age-old ideas or formerly meaningful communities of interpretation. Science fiction, concludes King, "poses to theology the challenge of discovering and articulating ways to affirm that the quest of man is not in vain, that human enterprise is of worth and value."[132]

In other words, popular theology must compete rhetorically with science fiction and other futuristic modes of interpreting the meaning and significance of modern life for contemporary audiences. Science fiction, as a "secular apocalyptic," does not have the "same meaning, the same message, the same content as the Apocalypse of John," but it serves today a similar function by comforting those who are "disillusioned by the failure of science and technology to deliver the world from its miseries."[133]

Meanwhile some of the most provocative science fiction narratives confront issues and questions typically associated with metaphysics and theology.[134] Lacking a historical understanding of their own faith, religious people may find more compelling mythological tales from fiction than from sacred stories or from dry theological excursions into the human condition.

Yet both sacred and secular versions of the rhetorics of technological conversion and communion always depend on the existence of a favorable cultural context. Futuristic versions of the rhetoric seem to come and go with perceived threats to believers' understanding of the contemporary world. The rise of new media forms raises the threat that other social groups and religious movements will gain an upper hand in the culture wars by being the first to exploit new technologies effectively. Just as the penny press elicited an explosion in religious periodicals during the 1830s and 1940s, the rise of the Internet in the 1990s resulted in an amazing array of evangelical initiatives in cyberspace. Futuristic rhetoric waxes and wanes with the concerns and anxieties of a tribe's present cultural situation. Evangelicals, in particular, often view American society as a battleground for competing value systems, incompatible cultural practices, and divergent ways of life—with Christians frequently on the losing side. As sociologist C. Wright Mills once wrote, "The more the antagonisms of the present must be suffered, the more the future is drawn upon as a source of pseudo-unity and synthetic morale."[135] Historian R. Laurence Moore argues that American "religious struggles engage people in elaborate strategies that on each side entail affirmation and denial, advancement and repression, of a set of cultural options." He concludes that "outsiderhood," similar to what I call a "rhetoric of exile," is a characteristic way of "inventing one's Americanness."[136] Evangelicals' own apocalyptic rhetoric situates believers outside of mainstream society by forging the mythos of the technological sublime to their own biblical prophecy. Like science fiction literature, such futuristic theology can have a life of its own apart from any religious tradition or theological paradigm. Science fiction sometimes develops apocalyptic themes and even addresses biblical symbols, but it normally argues its own state of affairs independent of any sacred texts, including the Bible. Since it is not tied to a self-identifiable tribe or community of interpretation, science fiction cannot easily help its audiences to situate themselves as a people in exile from mainstream culture. In fact, science fiction writer Sturgeon's criticism of Americans as too scientific is partly a rhetorical means of locating the science fiction community as cultural outsiders, as literarily or intellectually persecuted people. Like the mythos, science fiction can try to use literary devices to imagine a contemporary context for its futuristic tales.

The mass-mediated use of optimistic futurism in American culture accelerates historically during periods of rapid technological development and social change, beckoning believers to an alternative, typically Edenic past that will somehow be recreated in the future by faithful adherents to the mythos. Both the late-nineteenth- and early-twentieth-century utopians longed for simplicity, unity, and order in the midst of the chaos of the times. Late-nineteenth-century utopian writings were hope-filled responses to various social, economic, and cultural traumas.[137] Like some of today's popular religious broadcasts, they offered hope for the New World contingent upon divine providence and the actions of individual citizens who must simply do their part, whether it be joining an organization or contributing funds. In spite of all of the differences of opinion in America on public issues and regardless of the amazing variety of theological and cultural commitments among evangelicals, the belief that the nation and world are worth saving from evil and destruction is virtually unarguable. The electronic church, largely through its incantations of the mythos of the electronic church, coalesces tribal support around the hope that the world will indeed become a better place because more people will receive the message of the Gospel. Because the mythos of the electronic church says what many people wish to hear, its prophets often are able to attract followers and to garner financial supporters. And because the future predicted by the televangelist is yet to occur, there is no way to prove the televangelist wrong. Indeed it is possible that popular Bible prophecy is accurate in spite of all of its relatively recent hermeneutical turns and its general lack of historical and theological perspective. Perhaps this possibility alone is enough to give hope to audiences and to create constituencies ready and willing to support media evangelists in their ongoing efforts to preach the Gospel to more nations around the globe using new technologies.

Contemporary science fiction and twentieth-century evangelical futurism likely meet some of the same human needs for mystery, insight, and aesthetic joy. Certainly they can both be prophetic when they ask tough questions about the human condition and warn adherents about dystopian versions of the future. So, too, can they both be ideological, as when a particular political movement or party co-opts its futuristic rhetoric for ideological purposes. But the fact that American evangelical futurism has often been used by political conservatives to sanction particular American policies in the Middle East or to condone particular forms of governmental regulation of the media should not blind us to the cross-ideological character of technologically oriented mythologies. Both the political left and the political right tend to seek salvation in worldly enterprises, whether capitalist or Communist rhetoric, individualistic or collectivistic. The "technic civilization," writes Irving Hexham, is a "synthesis created by new technologies which make old social models obsolete."[138] Religious tribes seemingly are stranded between traditionalism, which fails to motivate believers and appears increasingly irrelevant in a high-tech world, and populism, which makes tribal language relevant but also corrupts the tribe's own religious history and dilutes the tribe's integrity. "Radical theologians," admits Hexham, "deplore technology, environmental pollution, and multinational corporations," but they also "fly to simple lifestyle conferences on technologically sophisticated aircraft which consume resources and pollute the atmosphere." Meanwhile fundamentalist churches "rage about evolution and show overt hostility to science" but are "in the forefront of computer use by religious groups and leaders in the use of modern communications for proclaiming their religious message."[139] Futurism helps secular and religious groups alike to focus on everything except the discontinuities of history and the rhetorical inconsistencies of the present.

Futuristic mythology takes many forms and seizes the human imagination through a wide range of different media and technologies. From within the evangelical tribe, current eschatology might not be defined as mythology, but from the perspective of the wider culture such popular religious futurism often seems far-fetched. Historically speaking, religious creeds and confessions translated biblical narratives into propositional language and facilitated systematic theologies that attempted to respond to the human need for rational understandings of belief. On a popular level, however, from at least the late nineteenth century forward in America, evangelicalism loosely wandered from the certainty of tradition to the vagaries of the marketplace of tribal opinion. In addition, such tribal opinion is cast through the dynamics of the marketplace for popular religious eschatology that increasingly resembles science fiction. Meanwhile, evangelical communication professionals finance such science-fiction-like prognostications with increasingly modernistic means of doing business in the media marketplace.

Twentieth-century popular American theology became increasingly like science fiction, while the literary genre of science fiction, both in films and novels, reflected a growing interest in spiritual issues and religious questions that cannot be answered empirically. Perhaps both science fiction writers and contemporary Christians feel discomfort with "a word or will driven cosmos" and perceive the world "with a sense of monkey curious awe and a desire to 'improve' the known world."[140] The idea of improving the world is at the heart of especially American experiments with religious and quasi-religious futurism, which rhetorically integrates technology and hope—both in the Anabaptist-style hope to reclaim an Edenic past through low-tech ways of life and the evangelical-style hope to usher in the New Jerusalem with the latest communication technologies. Harvey Cox and Anne Foerst suggest that we are entering a new historical stage in the "lover's quarrel" between faith and science. Scholars who "write about the frontiers of robotics, cyberspace, artificial intelligence and virtual reality are beginning to appropriate what has normally been thought of as religious language to describe what they believe these new technologies promise for the human future." This new rhetoric, they believe, "transforms humanity into divinity, quests for eternity, seeks the 'Beloved Community.'"[141] At the same time, religious tribes are appropriating the language of science and especially technology for similar ends. Popular evangelical theology and mainstream science fiction are increasingly difficult to distinguish as they co-opt each other's rhetorics of communion, conversion and praise.

Conclusion

The efficacy of mass communication is one of the great myths of contemporary American culture. Practically no right-minded American would question the power of mass communication to shape culture and influence society. In all of its many forms and expressions, futuristic thinking about the media usually assumes that communication technologies will somehow alter the course of human history. Christian optimism generally contends that communication frames cultural beliefs and forms the heart of community life. Communication is the linchpin of history and the gear that drives the engines of faith and commerce. Thus the future depends on who controls the means of communication and especially who has the authority to establish the media's symbols of belief. This belief in the power of mass communication is itself an act of faith and, ironically, a deeply humanistic concept that emphasizes human effort over divine intervention. To put it differently, modern evangelical belief in the power of the media rests on an Enlightenment concept of society as comprised of malleable

individuals who are more or less the product of their symbolic environment. Premillennial eschatology emphasizes the human ability to carry out
divine intention and thereby reinforces modernist thought in the midst of
what otherwise appears to be purely religious mythology.

Contemporary American evangelicalism borrowed the idea of historical
progress largely from the traditional Christian worldview, revised its futuristic rhetoric in the light of popular premillennial theology, adopted Americans' strongly pragmatic faith in the efficacy of technology, and eventually
formulated its own science-fiction-like rhetoric with strongly biblical language and deeply eschatological themes. As the world has been splintered
increasingly into what Louis Wirth called "countless fragments of atomized
individuals and groups," new evangelical tribes coalesced in the United
States around futuristic campaigns of mass evangelism.[142] The tribe's evangelistic rhetoric seemed to mainline Christian groups to be too sectarian.
But of course mainstream popular culture carries similar quasi-religious
themes—what one theologian calls "Hollywood's New Mythology."[143]
Ironically, evangelism in twentieth-century evangelical futurism focused
on America while the Christian church was actually growing most quickly
in other areas of the world, especially Latin America.[144] Given all of the
media clutter and all of the media fragmentation in the United States, domestic mass-media evangelism was increasingly problematic as the nation
entered the twenty-first century. The rhetoric of mass-media conversion
seemed to be increasingly distant from reality. *Christianity Today* editorialized already in 1992 that on the eve of the third millennium of the Christian era "the church is again beset by apocalyptic speculators. . . . American
evangelicals seem to have an insatiable appetite for end-time best sellers."
The periodical admonished evangelicals to remember the "mystery about
the Second Coming that we must respect if are to honor the One we eagerly await."[145]

In both its religious and secular forms the mythos of the electronic sublime is a form of futurism that can be debunked or verified only when the
future becomes history. While today communication signals span the globe
in record time, seemingly devouring geography, the world is not a more
humane, more peaceful, or even more God-fearing place than it was prior
to the adoption of the telegraph by American society in the 1830s. Each
new technology, moreover, eventually has been employed more widely
and probably more successfully in the name of industry and commerce
than in the name of Jesus Christ. And the most recent technologies, such
as satellites and the Internet, like their predecessors, increasingly are

acquired and operated by major media conglomerates. When AOL merges with Time-Warner to form a massive corporation, many other mass media seem comparatively like mom-and-pop endeavors.[146] In the years ahead it is likely that even more of the control of and authority over worldwide mass communication will be in the hands of a few large organizations run by professional management teams whose primary goals are corporate acquisitions, new-market development, and increased profits. Even the major evangelical broadcasting operations, particularly the large cable and satellite networks, are turning to Madison Avenue and Hollywood for advice on how to be successful in the competitive religious and secular markets. "The biggest mistake that pastors make," Robertson told an interviewer, "is to superimpose their 'thing' on the media. They should discover what the media are doing and then adapt to the media format."[147] He did so by transforming the Christian Broadcasting Network into the more secular Family Channel and then selling the latter to Rupert Murdoch's media empire, News Corporation—which renamed the channel Fox Family before selling it to the Walt Disney Company.[148]

Even though they often express the mythos of the electronic church in highly emotional and spiritual terms, religious broadcasters increasingly are part of the trend in international communications toward centralized control and rational decision-making. Perhaps religious broadcasting, as it expands and adopts the latest marketing strategies, computerized methods, large-scale fund-raising techniques, and advanced audience analysis, will follow in the footsteps of its commercial counterparts, becoming part of the trend toward the incorporation of America.[149] "I believe God wants us to be professional broadcasters," said Robertson, complimenting his staff because they "think 'major market television.'"[150] John Kasson contends that the utopian impulse in American culture has kept the nation historically from dealing directly with the crises of industrial society, converting republicanism "from an animating ideology to a static buttress of the conservative industrial order."[151] While religious broadcasting might at first glance appear to place the electronic media democratically in the hands of "the people," a closer inspection reveals that national and international programs often reflect many of the same business values found in commercial American broadcasting.[152]

Ironically, probably the most obvious sign of such centralization and rationalization is the growing notoriety and influence of the major television evangelists, whose style and message are beamed from satellites around the world. Jimmy Swaggart celebrated the fact that "for the first time in history God has given a handful of men the opportunity to reach tens of millions with the gospel of Jesus Christ."[153] But his personal preaching was really only the publicly visible part of an elaborate system of corporate-like planning and production by many businesspersons and technicians. Behind the scenes at such large religious broadcasting organizations today are hundreds of professional employees carrying out specialized duties such as financial planning and market research. This is a far cry from the local worshiping households of the early church that some evangelical leaders romanticize and much more like the bureaucratic apparatus of many mainline Protestant denominations. The mythos of the electronic church expresses the ideal of a worldwide community, a kind of tribal version of the global village, when in fact it seems to be emulating corporate culture rather than early Christian primitivism.

The impact of large-scale religious broadcasting on local and regional cultures also has never been assessed adequately, since the issue is usually framed too narrowly as the effects of such broadcasts on church attendance and financial support.[154] Perhaps the worldwide dissemination of religious programs, like the global transmission of American secular programming, is slowly eroding the vitality and variety of regional and local ways of life, many of which are Christian. Even historian Daniel Boorstin, an optimistic observer of American culture, admits that the "electronic technology that reaches out instantaneously over the continents does very little to help us cross the centuries."[155] The shallowness and fluidity of religious belief today likely are fueled by international, evangelistic broadcasts that are not anchored in the ethnic and religious traditions of the people to whom they are directed. Many broadcasters assume that religion can exist independent of culture, but it may be that the popular culture of religious media is replacing indigenous cultures rooted historically in Christian traditions. As Harold Adams Innis argues, the electronic media might rapidly traverse geographic space at the expense of cultural permanence.[156] A few major evangelists, most notably Billy Graham, recognized this problem and sought to identify itinerant preachers who would develop evangelistic techniques for their native lands.[157] Overall, however, popular evangelical futurism clouds the issues of historical continuity and cultural permanence in a rhetoric of technological praise.

The mythos of the electronic church also assumes that the Gospel can be disseminated throughout the world like the latest consumer product, when even some of the largest American advertising agencies have made major blunders in attempting to communicate with consumers only a few hundred miles north in French-speaking Quebec.[158] The export of American television programs overseas, particularly to developing countries, meets hostile reception from some nations, peoples, and religious tribes that seek freedom from foreign cultural influences, including American religiosity.[159] In Canada the legal ownership of satellite receivers and the religious programming of broadcast stations were stalled in part because of widespread public sentiment that American evangelists, who dominated the satellite signals, were propagating an Americanized gospel—just as mainstream American media content takes little account of Canadian culture.[160] Many Canadians and developing nations view American religious broadcasting as a challenge to cultural autonomy similar to Great Britain's attempts to colonize the world. Indeed the technologies that broadcast the Gospel to the world already are disseminating American commercials, soap operas, and situation comedies. The mythos of the electronic church might be transforming the Gospel into a religious commodity. If so, some evangelical broadcasters could be selling the modern equivalent of indulgences.

Because the mythos of the electronic church so readily confuses information with understanding, its advocates generally overlook the complexity of human communication, a problem that has dogged the American study of mass communication since its development after World War II. Park began his essay "Reflections on Communication and Culture" with the following sober admission: "Communication is so obvious and pervasive a factor in social life that I have often wondered why so little had been said or written about it. Now that I have attempted to write something on the subject, I no longer wonder, I know."[161] John G. Cawelti appropriately calls the widespread scholarly belief in the power of the media one of the "dogmas of the mass communication gospel."[162] The transmission of data can be a simple task, but the communication of spiritual knowledge, the creation of shared religious understanding, and the building of local faith communities are difficult to achieve even within North America, let alone across diverse cultures. The mythos of the electronic church, with all of its futuristic mythology, frequently attempts to solve this problem simply by labeling the so-called communications revolution as another Pentecost. But in the Bible Pentecost was wholly the work of God, not the stratagem of orators, the hard work of business-like organizations, or the product of technologically savvy persons. Pentecostal interpretations of communication assume that the media easily will convert the world to Christianity, regardless of how they are funded, regulated, and operated. Even in regards to evangelization, questions of strategy and tactics are crucial to success.

The models of communication that religious communicators rely upon become their models for communication. In other words, the church as an institution is more or less created in the image of the types of communication and community envisioned by its members.

The church's use of advanced communication technologies in America does not ensure that its religious communication will be authentic. All media technologies require particular institutional arrangements that specify how the technologies will be used, by whom, and for what purpose. Media evangelists must grapple with these institutional problems just as foreign missionaries have for hundreds of years. And no matter how hard they tackle such pragmatic concerns, they will not be able to control fully the impact of their own messages. Reinhold Niebuhr says in *Faith and History* that the growth of human freedom and power always fosters both creative and destructive tendencies, both progress and regress.[163] O. B. Hardison Jr. even argues that traditional understandings of culture are "disappearing through the skylight" of modern culture, and he speculates that computers and other machines might eventually supersede human beings.[164] Although his futuristic speculations might be far-fetched, they imagine a world that is made essentially in the image of the technological sublime. We might never reach the kind of world he envisions, but our everyday imaginations could help bring us closer to that state of affairs. Often the unintended effects of communication are most prominent and, historically speaking, most troubling.

In *The Idea of Progress since the Renaissance* Warren W. Wagar concludes that the "idea of progress has inspired most of the great political and intellectual movements of the last two hundred years."[165] It has inspired some of the most influential ideas about media technologies as well, for behind the mythos of the electronic church is the simple but attractive belief that communication technologies are potent forces that will enable people to transform evil into good. The history of the telegraph, the wireless, and even the latest digital technologies should dispel the myth, but especially in North America the enchanting arias of the Franciscans and the pansophists still play to rapt audiences. Now the mythos has new religious visionaries whose livelihood depends on the hopes created instead of on the actual progress achieved. Americans effortlessly substitute the apparent promises of technological progress for the hard work of communicating with each other, identifying the technological vices as well as the virtues and eventually negotiating public spaces for community life. The rhetorics of technological praise and global communion seem to ameliorate the rhetoric of exile as the world becomes a stage for enacting ritualistic paeans to the power of mass communication. Popular theology sounds like science fiction, while science fiction often reads like apocalyptic tragedy or spiritual quest. As Morse said in that first telegraphic transmission across the Eastern seaboard, "What Hath God Wrought?" What would Americans perceive in those telegraphic symbols if they were broadcast live today on CNN?

3

Leading the Tribes Out of Exile:
The Religious Press Discerns Broadcasting

◩ ◩ ◩

In 1936 General Francisco Franco and other military leaders revolted against the Popular Front government of the Second Spanish Republic, plunging the country into a devastating civil war that would last until 1939. American Roman Catholics faced divided loyalties in trying to stake out positions in the public discourse about the war. Hoping that the Republic would become more democratic, and fearful of Franco's "crusade," some Catholics argued for supporting the new Republican government even in the face of its violence against clerics of the state church. Other Catholics believed that Franco's campaign enjoyed clerical support and might, in spite of its fascist followers, be the better of two imperfect sides in a messy revolt. American Catholics faced a potentially divisive quandary about a war that could threaten all of Europe.

Many Catholic periodicals in America hoped to shed some light on the war and thereby serve the church more fully than could the mainstream media. The Catholic press generally sided with Franco and against the Republic, believing that the government was not truly democratic but rather a front for anarchism, socialism, and Communism. One writer portrayed Franco's efforts as "a nearly faultless crusade to preserve Iberia's ancient liberties and traditions, including the special place of the Church within Catholic circles." Only a few Catholic voices spoke publicly against Franco. One of them was a weekly lay periodical, *Commonweal*, whose managing editor, George N. Schuster, called Franco's efforts a "military cabal" and a "nightmarish incident." Schuster challenged the Jesuit journal *America*, which "stood solidly behind the rebel legions." A "Right" victory, said *America*, could not result in anything worse than what was already perpetrated by the "Red" government of the "United Communist Front." Many of *Commonweal's* 15,000 subscribers angrily wrote letters to the editor, while some irate clergy cancelled subscriptions.[1]

In the months ahead, Catholic magazines and papers vied with each other over the issue of how Catholics should think about the Spanish Civil War. The *Catholic Worker*, led by former Communist Dorothy Day, condemned every aspect of Franco's revolt. Regional and national Catholic periodicals in the United States opened their pages to voices from Spain and from American Catholic activists and intellectuals. Father Henry Palmer, a diocesan priest from Long Island, wrote that "the sword [of Franco] does not convert. It kills the good with the bad. It wages against truth as well as error." "Do you suppose," he added, "that St. Thomas would justify slaughtering these deluded fools, no matter what their sin? Would he countenance shooting them to death with curses on their lips against God and the Church, when these deluded people might have been so easily brought back to the faith by a more sympathetic appreciation of their grievances and a more intensive manifestation of Christian charity?" Citing Catholic periodicals' attacks on Day, Schuster, and others, Palmer wrote that a "Catholic paper which makes such frequent charges against the unfairness of the Secular Press, might well examine its own conscience, if it treats so badly an honorable adversary within the Church itself." Father Charles E. Coughlin, the legendary radio preacher from Detroit, criticized *Commonweal* for its "silk-stocking class" and its "pussyfooting" on Spain.[2]

The Catholic press during the Spanish Civil War documents some of the major conversations that American Catholics were having about the war— conversations within parishes, between vocational orders, among clerical and lay leaders on both sides of the Atlantic, within the pages of particular periodicals, between periodicals, and even among Catholic periodicals and mainstream news media. Religious organizations in America have always included in their ranks the kinds of publications that engage clergy and lay members of churches in vigorous conversations about important events, ideas, and artistic expressions that are shaping culture far beyond the boundaries of the ecclesiastical channels. Christian periodicals sometimes focus narrowly on official, institutional information and events, but often they vigorously engage the surrounding culture, pushing the range of their conversations to new geographic areas and social strata that might otherwise not be able to participate directly in the religious discussions of the day. By engaging religious communities in such conversations, religious periodicals become part of the public mind as it is recorded in their pages and remembered by their participants.

Media history, suggests James W. Carey, should not be limited to the official version of social progress, technological improvements, or professional development—what he calls, based on the work of historian Herbert Butterfield, a "Whig" interpretation of the past.[3] Religious history, too, is more than ecclesiastical pronouncements and official church histories. It should include the voices of the people who communicate through religious media, including what they say, hear, and see about themselves and the cultures in which they live. Religious media are not only social institutions worthy of intellectual and institutional histories; they are also arenas of symbolic action in and through which cultural groups form their self-identities and create interpretations of other social groups' motives and actions. As a form of cultural history, religious media history is concerned not just with events but also with people's thoughts, sentiments, and imaginations. When the Spanish Civil War broke out, the Catholic press in America quickly became a complex series of overlapping and interacting conversations through which various Catholic groups in America and abroad tried to make sense of the competing claims about the politics, economics, and culture of Spain. The Catholic press thereby entered the very history that it was discussing.

As forums for public conversations, religious periodicals are also ways of collectively knowing about the world.[4] Religious groups use these media partly to gain shared understandings of what it means to think and act in accord with their faith. Moreover, just as the history of communication is a major part of the "history of civilization"—culture is expressed and passed along through communication—the history of religious communication is central to the history of religion.[5] The "natural history" of the religious press in America is a doorway to some of the conversations that comprise the history of Christianity in the United States.[6]

The purpose of this chapter is two-fold. The first section provides a social context and a language for interpreting the role of the religious press in the life and thought of Christian groups in the United States during the twentieth century. It addresses the important social functions of the religious press in the formation of religious groups' self-identities and in the shaping of religious tribes' understandings of the wider culture. The remainder of the chapter interprets the tribal rhetoric of five Christian periodicals in the period from 1920 to 1970, focusing on the different ways that each of them conversed about the development of radio and then television. Included are three Roman Catholic journals—*Commonweal*, *America*, and *Catholic World*—and two Protestant periodicals—*Christian Century* and *Christianity Today*.[7] Of particular importance is how each of these periodicals imagined the role of broadcasting in furthering the "public interest, convenience and necessity," to use the phrase created by the U.S. Congress to guide the regulatory activities of the Federal Radio Commission (FRC) in the late 1920s and its predecessor, the Federal Communications Commission (FCC) beginning in 1934. The journals' conversations about broadcast regulation helped each tribe to develop its own perspective on the interaction of religious tribes and the government in the wider society. In addition, the periodicals often became the public venue in and through which a tribe addressed how the broadcast media could best serve the wider public interest, not merely its own tribal interest.

When *Commonweal* opened it pages to a conversation about the Spanish Civil War, it knew that the issue would be controversial and perhaps even divisive. As a facilitator of tribal conversation, however, the journal thought that it had a responsibility to address the topic directly and openly, speaking for the interests of Spain and humanity rather than merely for Roman Catholics or intratribal interests. Hoping to convert readers to its anti-Franco stance, *Commonweal* took a public stand, defended its position, and offered public room for other points of view. Along the way it responded directly to related conversations taking place within the Roman Catholic Church as well as to those occurring in mainstream media. In short, *Commonweal*'s voices became part of the national and even international conversation about what the United States and the church should do about a civil war that was taking place in a largely Roman Catholic country but had worldwide implications. The editors, writers, and readers of *Commonweal* conversed about ways of relating their tribal loyalties to the public interest. As this chapter documents, religious journals can foster rhetorics of communion and discernment that help the tribe to locate itself at the intersection of tribal tradition and the public interest. In so doing they serve society, not just the tribe.

Pressing for Tribal Loyalties in a Strange Land

In her survey of the religious press in America, Sister Mary Patrice Thaman discovered a "tapestry of opinion of life in the 1920s." Religious periodicals, she said, were a "panorama, a cross section, of life" in America. "In viewing this gamut of life, from the literature going into the American home to the sundering of the home itself by divorce," she found that "manners and morals were no longer being channeled in traditional streams." Religious editors and spokespersons, she discovered, were "keenly alerted to the shiftings in the contemporary scene, and in their journals have reconstructed for future generations a picture of their day. . . . Combined with other sources at the command of the historian, it is a definite aid in the task of rebuilding the buried past." In addition, Catholic groups had "moved from the center to enter their protest with the others who decry immodest styles." Like the other periodicals, the Catholic press "presented a period of liberation of the human spirit, but for the majority of them that spirit seemed to be liberated in a maelstrom of worshipers of the body, of champions of speed, of adventurers in the ephemeral, of creators of the imaginative movie-world."[8] She found that the religious press was not just an organ for religion news but also a forum for religiously engaging the wider culture.

Thaman discovers in the religious press of the 1920s imaginative conversations about religion and culture that address both tribal and mainstream American culture. She sees the religious press as a window through which people of a later period will be able to view American life in the 1920s. Thaman recognizes that religious periodicals record both tribal structures of feeling and the broader cultural shifts in American life. In fact, the religious press became ongoing conversations occurring at the intersection of tribal culture and mainstream American society. It mediated discerningly between the broader society and the subculture of the tribe—especially between what I call the tribe's transcendent metanarrative and the wider culture's subnarratives of immanent meaning and significance.[9] Media technologies can be "especially powerful mechanisms for reconstructing an inauthentic humanness," but they can also be a powerful means for a tribe to create, maintain, and change its collective identity in tune with its own traditions.[10]

Stewart M. Hoover suggests that in the modern world religious "institutions are in the position of having to surrender control over their own symbols, in exchange for access to the public sphere and are unlikely to be entirely comfortable with this exchange."[11] Looking especially at the news media, Hoover recognizes that religious tribes cannot simply re-create in mainstream media their own interpretation of public issues. If a subculture wishes to participate directly in the mainstream media, it is more or less at the mercy of professional media gatekeepers who select stories and shape them publicly for their own economic or professional interests. Unlike the ways that some nations around the world allocate broadcast media time to particular religious groups, American commercial media maintain their own tight control over the messages that they create and distribute. "As journalists construct their narratives," writes Hoover, "they are writing for a different audience than the object group or individual. They are attempting to make that group 'make sense' to a more general audience."[12] Tribes depend upon nontribal media to present their own concerns, ideas, and perspectives to the wider public.

Historically speaking, however, Hoover may not be entirely correct, because of the major role that specialized religious media have played in American society. The public world has included more than merely high-profile, mass-audience media. Religious tribes have always had many alternative opportunities to enter public conversations in the United States. Indeed America might actually be moving toward a national culture that is riddled with every imaginable kind of special-interest group and its corresponding print, digital, and electronic media. Looked at through the lens of the last 200 years, the current media scene seems to be much more like the nineteenth and early twentieth centuries than the period since the rise of the national radio networks in the 1930s. The crucial turning point for religious media in the United States probably was the shift from the late nineteenth to the early twentieth century, when the daily newspaper became the major means for the average American to orient himself or herself to the growing national culture and to the increasingly heterogeneous local community. Before that time the religious press was phenomenally popular and influential in America, acting as a countervailing cultural force to the news media in the inchoate nation; many religious periodicals even viewed themselves as competing news media. As the century turned, however, mainstream news won tremendous social significance as the primary vehicle for professional versions of community conversations. Mark Silk suggests that these new, professional daily papers transformed religion news into a "journalistic commodity like book and car news, with editorial content designed to accompany the advertisements on the adjacent page . . . [and] coverage of religion became increasingly bland and promotional."[13]

The remaining specialized religious media, on the other hand, were free to converse theologically about the news, especially to employ their idiosyncratic rhetorics of tribal discernment.

The rise of powerful, general-interest mass media in America seems to elicit the development of the more specialized, countervailing media aimed at particular speech communities, including religious groups. In the 1830s the penny press offered readers an additional source of fairly inexpensive news and human-interest stories in some large American cities. During the same era religious groups created many alternative media. By 1850 there were 181 religious periodicals in the United States, at least half of which were newspapers.[14] Although the mainstream media tend to assimilate marginal groups in society, countervailing subcultures are always emerging to form their own communities of interpretation. Assimilation creates new social groups on the margins of society, whether they are the "Jesus freaks" of the 1970s or home schoolers of the 1990s. Moreover, long-standing religious tribes sometimes reconnect with their traditions through the printed word, thereby gaining a renewed sense of appreciation for and commitment to the stories that carried their forebears through earlier times and places. In modern, literate societies, religious tribes often have access to the sacred documents, recorded rituals, and cultural practices that once gave the group its particular self-identity. Oral cultures are hard to reclaim but also hard to transform; literate subcultures, on the other hand, come and go as they alternatively reach out to their pasts, assimilate into the broader society, and then try once again to reclaim their distinctive self-identity in a new forum.

In the United States the religious press has always been a crucial vehicle for tribes to differentiate themselves from other subcultures as well as to participate critically in the conversations occurring in the larger society. The printed word enables religious groups to form across geographic space; periodicals can foster regional or national identities in the midst of other social changes taking place in the country. Both parachurch movements and denominations have used journals, magazines, and books to establish national and in some cases even international speech communities with shared theological perspectives and common religious sensibilities. Printed media even help such groups to establish their own symbolic leaders and to engender in-group pride that transcends the local settlements. By 1850 the Congregationalists alone published at least twenty-five periodicals in the United States.[15] Many of these nineteenth-century religious periodicals were more than denominational news organs; they addressed the relationship of the tribe to American society, including tribal and public interests.

Print media in nineteenth- and especially twentieth-century America provided a means for religious tribes to spread their public conversations
across geographic space. As Park argues, technology "profoundly modified"
human geography, dissolving some distances of space while creating new
ones between generations even within the same races and peoples.[16] Religious journals did not simply receive local parish conversation; they also
created discourse as a means for religious movements and traditions to organize their conversations and to reimagine what it meant to be faithful in
a national and international world.

In the twentieth century, however, many mainline religious periodicals
struggled to find their niches in the expanding media marketplace. The
powerful mainstream media, especially radio and later television, increasingly eclipsed the religious press. As daily newspapers began seriously covering religion news after 1900, many Christians in America apparently felt
little or no need for a distinctively tribal press with its own rhetorics of discernment and communion. Mainstream media used capital and expertise
to create attractive products for mass markets—so attractive, in many
cases, that busy Americans dropped their religious press subscriptions in
favor of special-interest magazines and popular radio and television programming. Dennis N. Voskuil documents how mainline Protestant periodicals lost readers to mainstream media during the twentieth century.
Mainline readers fled in droves to other media, leaving behind hard-
pressed religious magazines that often were able to stay afloat financially
only through denominational subsidies. As late as 1931 there were 542
Protestant denominational journals and magazines, many of which were
state and diocesan publications and a few of which were foreign-language
monthlies, Sunday school weeklies, and missionary reviews. But by 1961
there were only about seventy-five mainline journals still publishing, and
over a third of them were United Methodist journals. In addition, some of
the writers and editors of these religious publications began working instead for nonreligious magazines such as *North American Review, Harpers,
Scribner's,* and the *Atlantic Monthly.* The staggering decline in the number of
mainline religious periodicals during that thirty-year period is even more
incredible given the fact that the membership in mainline churches grew
from about sixteen million to more than twenty-four million.[17] One of the
editors of *Christian Century,* Martin E. Marty, summarized the difficulty
faced by all religious periodicals: "Choosing the course of staying religious
in a secular day, staying complexly Christian in a simplistic spiritual

market, will involve the board, editors, staff and 'Christian Century family' in remaining delicate and endangered."[18]

The transformations among Catholic periodicals throughout the nineteenth and twentieth centuries illuminate other institutional dynamics at work in the decline of religious media in America. Michael R. Real divides the period into six eras that reflect changes in the structure and policy of the Catholic press. From the early years of the nineteenth century to about 1889, the Catholic media were independent publications that offered immigrant Catholics a vehicle for maintaining and defending their ethnic and religious self-identities in the largely Protestant nation. The number of Catholic publications continued growing through the first two decades of the twentieth century, often cooperating with each other through the new Catholic Press Association (CPA), formed in 1911, but maintaining their independence from the church. Then Catholic periodicals, particularly the newspapers, consolidated between the World Wars, forming national news media with diocesan editions under the control of local prelates. From 1946 to 1961, says Real, the Catholic press expanded from less than fifteen million to a total circulation of about twenty-six million, partly as a result of "diocesan saturation subscription plans" that called for dioceses to purchase copies of papers for every member and to mail them directly to the homes. Also during this period the lay leadership of Catholic periodicals lost considerable control over news content to a central news service in Washington, and the first priest was elected president of the CPA. Between 1962 and 1966, according to Real, the Catholic periodicals gained additional freedom under the impact of the Second Vatican Council, attracting strong lay leadership and creating a "boom period" for critical and controversial news coverage as well as for church-related muckraking. Finally, after 1968 the Catholic press stabilized or, as Real argues the case, suffered repression, retrenchment, and de-sensationalizing.[19] The periodicals' rhetoric of discernment was now controlled largely by ecclesiastical officials.

Regardless of whether Real's analysis of the Catholic press accurately interprets its history, his account suggests at least an interaction between a tribe's own ways of imagining and those of the broader society. Real contends that changes in the structure and policy of the American Catholic newspaper "reflect trends in the economy in general, those of consolidation and monopolization of industry, concentration of decision-making information and power in relatively few hands, and conflicts between corporate interests, and the public interest."[20] In other words, the professionalization of news gathering and distribution along with the industrialization of the news business essentially put the Catholic press on an economic and cultural ground the mainstream news business. In addition, if Real's analysis of the changing content of the Catholic press is any indication, these periodicals' definition of "news" followed that of the mainstream papers toward objectivity and detached reporting. After 1968, Catholic journalists were less likely to be advocates for particular perspectives or to use news to reform the church. Perhaps the one major difference between the mainstream news media and the Catholic press during the latter period was the Catholic media's increasing reliance on "hierarchical economic institutions with authoritarian roots," compared with the daily news media's emphasis on "free speech with libertarian roots."[21] Catholic news periodicals essentially combined liberal news-gathering philosophy with a commitment to the church's official beliefs and its own news-distributing agencies.

Real's assessment of the rise of the Catholic newspaper after 1968 seems to contradict Voskuil's staggering review of the decline of Protestant denominational periodicals beginning already in the 1930s. While the Catholic Church standardized and professionalized the news-gathering and publishing processes, most Protestant media had neither the denominational loyalty nor the national economies of scale to launch and sustain such media endeavors. Few large cities had enough residents from a single Protestant denomination to sustain newsworthy content, let alone to fund the contributions or subscriptions necessary to pay for it. By contrast, heavily Catholic cities such as St. Louis and Chicago provided a readership base for local Catholic media as well as contributing to the audience needed for national news media. American Protestantism was still deeply fragmented not just among mainline groups but also among evangelicals. Finally, the mainline churches continued through the 1980s and 1990s to lose members by attrition to independent and evangelical churches. Mainline groups had neither the necessary membership numbers nor the strong denominational identifications among members to support the kind of news-periodical growth experienced by the Roman Catholic Church.

In any case, the most significant religious media in the United States during the twentieth century were not the local, regional, and national newspapers but rather the monthly or biweekly journals of comment and opinion. These periodicals are a variation on what Mary Biggs calls "small publishing"—the more or less low-circulation journals aimed at people who want to participate in public life through the work of literary artists and the thoughts of public intellectuals.[22] Such media extend back to the early newspapers of the American colonies that tried to develop a concept of news in the context of divine providence. They are perspectival periodicals that frame public conversation through the lens of faith commitments, including assumptions about human nature, democratic life, religious liberties, and the like. Instead of simply reporting news in the Enlightenment tradition of telegraphic, objective journalism, these journals open up public reasoning, dialogue, and debate about the intersection of tribal beliefs and current public issues.

Religious journals of comment and opinion provide both priestly and prophetic ways of imagining for the religious tribe. As priestly media they help the tribe recognize what it believes as well as confirm those foundational beliefs in the midst of a wider culture that might dismiss such beliefs or even attack them. The journal as priest says to the speech community: "This is who we are and what we believe. This is our self-identity. Thanks be to God!" As prophetic media, however, these journals apply their own faith traditions to an ongoing critique of the life of the church and the wider society; they provide a forum for faithful members of the tribe to discuss the implications of the tribe's faith commitments for its understanding of human culture, including the media and popular culture, but also politics, economics, and the sciences. Such prophetic conversations are moral discourses, not telegraphic reports. And the conversations extend beyond the journals to parishes, E-mail messages, telephone discussions, coffeehouse dialogues, and other venues. Real's analysis of the history of Catholic newspapers in the twentieth century suggests that such periodicals moved from the prophetic to the priestly role, becoming priestly spokespersons for uncritical ecclesiastical authorities rather than prophetic conversations for critical discourse. Nevertheless, most religious periodicals continued to be both prophetic and priestly voices for religious tribes in the United States.

The prophetic and priestly functions of religious media are not necessarily independent of one another or even contradictory. In fact, the prophetic role of religious media depends on the existence and maintenance of a priestly community of believers. Without a shared religious language and common core beliefs, tribal media cannot sustain significant prophetic conversation. The religious prophet is not a loner in the wilderness but rather a wise communicator of the implications of faithfulness. Prophets assess and critique the present in light of the wisdom of the ages. They assess the possible future from the perspective of history, not from the perspective of a historical prognostications expressed in the mythos of the electronic church. Religious journals can provide a vehicle for cultivating such memory as part of a critique of the current conversation. The contemporary world wrongly tends to imagine prophets as socially isolated persons, disconnected from community and uninterested in history and tradition. As theologian Walter Brueggemann puts it, the biblical prophet is not a foreteller or social protester but rather one who uses the human imagination and the community's symbols to *bring to public expression those very hopes and yearnings* that have been denied for so long and suppressed so deeply that we no longer know they are there." Such public expressions of hope, he continues, are not merely optimistic statements about social development or evolutionary advances. "Speech about hope cannot be explanatory and scientifically argumentative; rather it must be lyrical in the sense that it touches the hopeless person at many different points," says Brueggemann. In addition, such prophetic speech of hope must be "primarily theological, which is to say that it must be in the language of covenant between a personal God and a community. Promise belongs to the world of trusting speech and faithful listening."[23] Hopeful religious periodicals are necessarily both priestly reminders of tradition and prophetic critics of the gap between traditional tribal hopes and present social reality. Developing this kind of prophetic voice requires a respect for both the tribal rhetoric of communion and the expression of a tribal rhetoric of discernment.

Religious journals of comment and opinion, then, can be a means for a community of faith to locate itself in the wider world as well as within the particular community of faith. Such media are not a substitute for worship or for local assemblies of believers, of course, since faith, according to Christian tradition, is embodied in fellowship, liturgy, and sacrament. These media depend on the existence of such local communities to provide most of the priestly affirmation that anchors individuals to communities of shared interpretation and belief. The journals extend the sphere of that local faith to the broader culture, creating public space in and through which believers can converse discerningly about how their faith should illuminate their actions beyond the bounds of worship. In the United States the religious press has been one of the most important vehicles for bringing people of faith into a shared public space to converse about the broader society. Without such journals, believers are much more likely to assume that their religious faith has no bearing on how they think and act in public life; they might even be less inclined to participate in the common life of their communities and nations. Certainly without shared public space in which members of a community of faith are invited to participate, humankind will tend to find public action either absurd or

trivial, and will be much more inclined either to give up on collective action or simply to act according to perceived self-interest. "Only the existence of a public realm and the world's subsequent transformation into a
community of things which gathers men together and relates them to each
other depends entirely on permanence," writes Hannah Arendt. "If the
world is to contain a public space, it cannot be erected for one generation
and planned for the living only; it must transcend the life-span of mortal
men."[24]

Religious journals of comment and opinion can engage people in such
time-binding public arenas by facilitating and recording the conversations
of communities of faith across geographic space and through generational
time. As centrifugally organized media, these organs sustain the particular
conversations of specific religious communities, dividing up the realm of
religion into tribes that share a language of belief and a way of interpreting
the role of faith in life. Usually these media emerge from the existing
speech communities organized locally at particular churches or religious
institutions such as universities and colleges, or sometimes even nationally
from the interactions of members of specific denominations or parachurch
associations. Tribal journals extend the specialized conversations across geographic space, organize collective sentiment, focus the discussion, and
somewhat centralize the ways that the participants imagine their faith in
the world. During the century between 1880 and 1980, for instance, religious journals such as *Christian Century, Commentary*, and *Commonweal* sustained discussions about immigration trends and policies in the United
States. Partly as a result of their conversations about the issue, religious
groups in America played a role in shaping the country's immigration policies.[25] As this chapter documents, religious periodicals also addressed the
role and impact of the media in America. J. Daniel Hess says that each religious periodical tends to offer a distinct view of the mainstream media,
sustaining a particular community of interpretation and critique.[26]

The religious press in America has always been a significant part of the
public square where communities of religious interpretation can establish
common agendas for discussion and coordinate their thinking for collective
social action. The religious press in America extends the influence of the
congregation and the denomination into the public realm, offering priestly
confirmation of the community's faith and prophetic imaginations that
apply the tradition's beliefs critically to the church and to the wider social
world. These media thereby affect both church and society, as participants
in the mass-mediated conversations shuttle back and forth between the

tribal discussions and their daily lives in the world. But such impact can occur only in the context of a society that encourages a freedom of the press. The clash of perspectives in the religious press is a cynosure of democratic life in the United States—a land in which Alexis de Tocqueville found already in the 1830s a bewildering array of local journals, each with its own perspective and idiosyncratic slant on life.[27] From the outside, the range of such journals might resemble chaotic speech at the Tower of Babel. But from the inside they each carry their own logic and passions for imagining a more faithful church and more just society. These media can help to decelerate the secularization that marks public life in large, highly differentiated and disintegrated societies such as the United States. As Louis Wirth puts it, secularism blends new cultural "syncretisms" by mingling the "symbol and slogans" of one group with "those of others in order to woo more effectively the greatest number of adherents. Ideas and ideals that formerly stood for one set of objectives come to be perverted and diluted."[28] By enabling and focusing religiously grounded discussion, religious journals at their best enable a tribe to discern such dilution and then to reintegrate the tribes' thoughts and actions. They also can foster tribal public opinion that transcends mere provinciality as the tribe assesses its location in geographical space and generational time. Such public opinion, argues Wirth, is "formed in the course of living, acting, and making decisions on issues."[29] In short, religious periodicals can press for forms of rhetorical discernment that engage the tribe in the broader conversations about the nature of the good life in contemporary society. As the remainder of this chapter illustrates, some religious periodicals seriously engaged America's conversations about the role of broadcasting in American life.

Commonweal: The Primacy of Community

The establishment of *Commonweal* in 1924 roughly parallels the beginning of broadcasting in the United States. Launched by Michael Williams with funding from Calvert Associates, the journal aimed to interpret American social problems through broadly Catholic principles in a public conversation that was free from ecclesiastical control. The periodical was particularly interested in its early days in improving the image of Catholicism in America, partly through encouraging strong interfaith understanding. It became a forum for thoughtful lay Catholics to discuss problems such as relatively low working-class wages, national and regional employment, concentrations of wealth, agricultural depression, and the routinization and mechanization of work. The magazine argued strongly against totalitarianism, engaged European-Catholic thought, often promoted liturgical reforms within the Catholic Church, combated secular and radical movements that had existed in the Catholic Church since the Reformation, and consistently proclaimed a cooperative Christian social ideal.[30] *Commonweal* also became one of the few periodicals to advocate strongly for a change in immigration and rescue policies in the light of persecution of European Jews.[31] Without question, *Commonweal* is one of the most important Catholic journals in twentieth-century America.

Commonweal's content from 1924 to 1970 ranged over an incredibly broad spectrum of public concerns, nearly always with intellectually rigorous standards.[32] The founders of the journal explained the periodical's rhetoric of discernment, "The idea, broadly stated, was this: How can Catholic thought, the Catholic outlook on life and the Catholic philosophy of living, as distinct from what might be called the Catholic inlook and individual religious experience, be conveyed to the mind of the whole American people?"[33] *Commonweal* published much on the arts and literature and from the beginning critically eyed electronic media as institutions and cultural forms. But as a "nonmovement movement in American Catholicism," the journal was a "detached intellectual force rather than a popular movement."[34] It engendered discussion and debate far more than it tried to mobilize people to act in a given way on a particular issue. After the Second Vatican Council many of the seemingly liberal ideas advocated in *Commonweal* entered the Catholic mainstream and became institutionally respectable, according to the Jesuit journal *America*.[35] Nevertheless, some of the conservatives in the Roman Catholic Church continued into the 1990s to criticize *Commonweal* for "replacing the tradition with the stifling truncated tradition of modernity."[36] *Commonweal's* rhetoric of discernment elicited such criticisms from some of those in the church who looked only to traditionalism as their guide. Jaroslav Pelikan distinguishes between tradition—the living faith of the dead—and traditionalism—the dead faith of the living.[37] A prophetic religious periodical can embrace tradition without succumbing to traditionalism.

During the 1930s and 1940s, *Commonweal* repeatedly addressed one major question associated with broadcasting in America: Should the federal government regulate radio stations? While it is not accurate to say that the journal became a single-issue periodical in regards to radio, it is fair to suggest that *Commonweal* viewed the question as the most significant public issue with respect to broadcasting. It felt obligated to speak in favor of regulation because "some things promulgated in the name of art must be hidden or destroyed if the community is to prosper. In other words, there is an antisocial test which creative individualism must pass if it wishes to live. Thereby, and immediately, the problem of censorship is created."[38] "Sensible government regulation" is not "censorship," wrote Michael Williams in a column about the radio dramatization of H. G. Wells's *War of the Worlds*. He called for regulation of the "many other programs that daily and weekly are corrupting children's minds and souls; and demoralizing horror and gangster stories; and vicious, moronizing adult programs of an even more debasing sort; and programs which are merely a flood of silliness; a tidal wave of stupid jungle music, and jungle morality."[39] Feeling like members of a tribe under exile, *Commonweal*'s writers discerned the nefarious effects of unbridled individualism on media content and on society. They consequently saw regulation as an important means of avoiding a commercial radio system that would become indifferent to social needs.

Commonweal's stand in support of media regulation was cogently defended by Edward J. Heffron, executive secretary of the National Council of Catholic Men, in an essay apparently directed at *America* and other publications, whose editors "have a greater love of freedom of speech than they have knowledge of the nature of radio." In support of regulatory powers, Heffron maintained that "radio is free to be fitted into the category of public utilities subject to federal regulation or of those businesses that are said by the Courts to be 'impressed with a public interest.'" He compared radio with street railways, which, while privately owned, were publicly regulated. Heffron argued that without such regulation the streetcar companies and radio stations would likely pursue only self-interest. He concluded that it was clearly in the public interest for the government to censor the anti-Catholic broadcasts of Rev. Robert "Fighting Bob" Shuler and other anti-Catholic preachers.[40] Heffron warned that unless the government required stations to provide equal opportunity for the broadcasting of alternative viewpoints on controversial issues, "anti-Catholic stations, anti-Semitic stations, anti-Labor stations, White Supremacy stations, will inevitably spring up."[41] The government had a public responsibility to regulate extremist programming on behalf of society.

Commonweal similarly endorsed different forms of broadcasters' self-regulation as a means of ensuring that programming met community standards. "If radio is to serve the interests of its true owners, the public, it can't be free in the sense that newspapers are free," wrote Joseph A. Roney. He supported the National Association of Broadcasters' (NAB, which later became the National Association of Radio and Television Broadcasters) code that apparently led to the removal of Coughlin from the airways. The NAB was guided by "principle rather than by opportunism," he argued; he commended the organization for taking the popular priest off the air.[42] Roney took issue with rival *America*, which argued that radio stations are merely private businesses and should therefore be as free as newspapers were to determine editorial stands. *Commonweal* also defended the three major networks' self-imposed code for the coverage of war, which was designed to protect the radio audience from "misinformation, propaganda and sensationalism."[43] The editors of *Commonweal* believed that public cries for "uncensored" radio broadcasting were fabricated by those members of society who were unsympathetic to the central role of moral sensibility in community life. The journal's view of the necessity of censorship was similar to the stand that the Roman Catholic Church had taken in the public debate over governmental regulation of the motion picture industry; in fact, one writer called for the formation of a radio group similar to the Catholic-supported Legion of Decency that rated shows based on moral criteria.[44] The periodical looked for ways of integrating the media's self-regulation with broad moral standards that Catholics and non-Catholics alike could affirm.

During the late 1940s and 1950s, *Commonweal* continued expressing its concerns about broadcasting's influence on community life, warning of the dangers of unregulated television programming. One writer described the new medium's "arresting" effects on human senses, cautioning Americans that television posed the threat of functional illiteracy and encouraging parents to implant their children early with enough "intellectual curiosity and desire for reading."[45] Regarding television's role in national and community politics, *Commonweal* editorialized, "To hold major political office, it will be increasingly necessary to have an effective radio voice, a face that can be made presentable and an ever bigger bankroll. . . . The attributes of intellect, training and a certain public spiritedness fall still further down on the list."[46] "If ever a single domestic gadget came along to change the habits of a nation it is television," warned the periodical.[47]

The social impact of television, emphasized *Commonweal*, was tied to the medium's political economy. While the technology itself affects the nation's habits, television industry executives determine in the end the medium's role in American cultural life. Since "advertising pays the piper," wrote *Commonweal* in 1951, "it is easy to discern the direction of the motivating force. It is an axiom of American advertising to give the public what it wants."[48] Because of industry economics, few programs are permitted to "make some positive contributions to the life of the community."[49] The Catholic periodical saw similar flaws in England's British Broadcasting System (BBC), which operated through an annual tax levied against owners of radio and television receivers. "In America," observed *Commonweal*, ". . . immediate competition directs the bulk of the funds toward supplying more of the same—the stuff marketing surveys have shown to be surefire. Producers here could use more imagination; the BBC could do with bigger funds. There are mountainous handicaps either way."[50] The periodical saw no perfect method for funding television, no way of ensuring that programs would meet the moral and aesthetic standards and collective needs of the community. It worried that the market system rather than social values per se was shaping broadcast content and affecting the nation negatively.

Commonweal's response to the development of television clarified its seemingly incompatible support of the collective interests of the community and of the individual rights of particular religious organizations and broadcasters. The journal sought to uphold the primacy of community in a nation lacking any common cultural heritage. To make this argument, the journal viewed "community" as the common values that existed across the various groups in the nation. Its views were similar to those of early twentieth-century Progressive reformers such as John Dewey, whose book *The Public and Its Problems* called for the restoration of collective interests and the formation of a public consciousness.[51] *Commonweal* reasoned that only fringe political or religious groups, who rejected society's common values, should be excluded from the airways. The journal sharply criticized Chicago Catholics for their "deplorable" role in pressuring a television station in that city not to broadcast the film *Martin Luther.* "No matter how good their intentions, they have damaged the fabric of our democratic society; they have damaged relationships between Catholic and Protestant in this country."[52] *Commonweal*'s stand in the debate among Catholics about the airing of the film drew predictably harsh responses, but the journal maintained that minority rights would be squelched and the broader interests of the community would be undermined if broadcasting stations succumbed to pressure from any particular groups in society.[53] John Cogley summarized *Commonweal*'s philosophy of broadcasting in a 1957 article satirically bemoaning the lack of controversy on television: "We hear no Socialists on television. Atheists and even Agnostics . . . are practically non-existent in the United States. There are no 'soft-headed liberals' and soon there will be no 'hard-headed conservatives.' The [television] industry seems intent on walking down the straight and narrow path between truth and falsehood."[54] According to the periodical, avoiding controversy in the media could be just as socially unwise as supporting a wide-open, unregulated media marketplace.

Commonweal served from 1924 to 1970 partly as a public space for lay Catholics to discuss seriously the impact of broadcasting on American culture. The journal sought to balance the freedom of the press and broadcasting with the common values that Americans held—or should have held—as a democracy and a national community. Moreover, *Commonweal* defined those shared values not as purely Catholic but instead as public ones. By upholding the rights of other religious traditions to use radio and television to express their tribal beliefs publicly, *Commonweal* maintained a strong belief in the overarching communal values of freedom of speech for the entire nation. In summary, *Commonweal*'s conversation about broadcast regulation highlighted a remarkably subtle but rhetorically powerful integration of individual freedom, on the one hand, and public values, on the other. Certainly religious tribes benefited from such freedoms, but so did the nation. According to *Commonweal*, the best means of ensuring the greater good was self-regulation, not government intervention. The government should enter the fray only when the conflicting tribes cannot solve the issues themselves. *Commonweal* combined a rhetoric of Catholic communion, a strong rhetoric of public discernment, and a rhetoric of praise for freedom of speech in America.

America: Freedom of the Airways

The Society of Jesus (Jesuits) of the United States and Canada began publishing *America* in 1909, when "daily newspapers and weeklies were the primary shapers and distorters of public opinion" and when many WASPs were "either indifferent or hostile to Catholicism." The Jesuits established *America* in order "to supply in one central publication a record of Catholic achievement and a defense of Catholic doctrine built up by skillful hands in every region of the globe." Editors believed that "there is a way of looking at the issues and events of each week that is distinctively Catholic, even if it does not always and necessarily yield 'the one Catholic answer.'" The journal's founder, Father John J. Wynne, said that the new periodical would "be a weekly review of events and questions of the day affecting religion and morality," "contain short articles of timely interest," and "treat the broadest range of subjects that might be of interest to contemporary readers." Wynne preferred to call the magazine the *Freeman* as a symbol of both the Jesuits' historical legacy of St. Ignatius's spiritual exercises and the American experience of liberty from 1776, but Jesuit provincials rejected the name because of its "potential association in people's minds with a racist, intemperate publication called the *Freeman's Journal*."[55] *America* was committed to Jesuit ideals but also flexible about how to express those ideals effectively in the broader national culture.

During the period from the late 1940s to the early 1960s *Commonweal* and *America* were the only two Catholic journals of opinion published weekly in the United States. Not surprisingly, the two sparred over a wide range of issues, sometimes even addressing each other in the journals' ongoing conversations about Catholic life in the nation and the world.[56] The two periodicals mediated the transformations taking place in the United States in the years leading up to the Second Vatican Council, providing public forums for lay and clerical Catholics to discuss seriously the meaning and implications of the changes taking place in the Church.[57] While both journals published serious Catholic commentary on contemporary culture, *America* was more of a tribal forum for those who taught at Jesuit colleges and universities. In its early years *America* was conservative theologically but liberal in its economic views. Later in the century it moved closer in editorial stand to its more liberal but less widely read counterpart, *Commonweal*. Both weeklies displayed lively interests in the arts, in general, and the media, in particular, and sought Catholic interpretations of human actions in historical and contemporary events. But *America* was a bit more earnestly committed to the ideal of totally unfettered media representing an open marketplace of ideas. *America*'s rhetoric of free speech was both idealistic support for the Constitution and a very pragmatic endorsement of its own cause, namely, to keep the media open to Catholic as well as to other forms of religious expression.

If *America* accurately reflected the order's collective opinion during the early days of broadcasting, Jesuits were preoccupied in their assessments of radio with the problem of maintaining a free marketplace of ideas on the airways. Unlike *Commonweal*, *America* sometimes considered individual freedom to be significantly more important than the shared values of the community. *America*'s views appealed more strongly to the individualistic spirit of the Enlightenment, while *Commonweal* sided with the collectivist thought of early-twentieth-century reformers. *America*'s support of the free market for media was also a way for the Jesuits to participate in the

American experiment, a means of affirming publicly the rights expressed in the Constitution and of sharing in the rhetoric of free speech shaped so directly by early American Protestant culture. The Catholic Tocqueville had argued already in the 1830s that American Catholics were among the greatest supporters of freedom of the press and that Catholicism seemed to be even more democratic in spirit than was Protestantism.[58] Moreover, it was likely that if broadcast regulation were to be culturally biased it would support the WASPs who largely controlled broadcasting across the country. As cultural outsiders, Catholics had more to lose if the government began adjudicating religious content on the airways. If Catholics were not strong supporters of an unregulated broadcasting system in the United States, all religious tribes could find themselves in cultural exile.

Already in the earliest days of broadcasting *America* strongly opposed any form of radio censorship. The journal appealed directly to the Constitution, arguing that prior restraint of any broadcasts should be forbidden and even challenging the federal government's role in regulating broadcasting. While not in principle opposed to government "supervision" of radio—meaning basic licensing and technical standards—it called into question the constitutionality of the FRC's authority to rule on matters of radio station programming. *America* feared that such supervision would "mean control of property rights and the destruction of the First Amendment."[59] The periodical editorialized that regulation might lead to "a radio censored by the party in power, and wholly devoted to that party's interests."[60] Editors warned, "Whoever can control . . . radio . . . can control public opinion."[61] These Jesuits were especially concerned about a popular proposal that would grant free radio time only to public officials, thereby excluding political challengers from the offer of free time. "It is impossible to think of a licensed press in this country. It should be equally impossible to think of a licensed radio," wrote the weekly.[62] In spite of the fact that broadcasting was more expensive to operate than a printing press and that broadcasting relied on the limited electromagnetic spectrum that technically made it impossible for everyone to operate their own transmitter without interference from others, *America* feared government regulation of content more than it worried about the chaotic results of wide-open airways.

By the early 1930s *America* was publishing insightful and cogent discussions of the problem of broadcasting censorship, usually addressing the necessity for freedom of speech in the context of constitutional guarantees. *America* believed that penalties for "every alleged abuse of a Constitutional right" of free speech should be imposed only after the abuse had been broadcast.[63] Prior restraint of speech should never be imposed, but "broadcasting injurious to the public welfare and community of feeling" should be penalized.[64] The freedom from restraint of the broadcaster should supersede the a priori moral claims of the community. The result of censorship, feared John LaFarge, might be the use of propaganda techniques being employed in Germany and Soviet Russia: "The disquieting picture arises to my mind of a world censorship under which it will be impossible to obtain any more news that can be recognized as news." He saw a critical role for the media in democracies and warned readers of the possible authoritarian consequences of censorship.[65] As World War II approached, *America* maintained its strongly anticensorship position. The journal praised freedom of broadcasting in the United States and contrasted it with political propaganda on European stations.

America's unequivocal defense of freedom was particularly significant because it took place amid the rise of anti-Catholic radio programs. In 1933 the journal editorialized against the FRC's revocation of Shuler's station license even though the minister used the airways to become one of the most outspoken critics of Roman Catholicism. "To Mr. Shuler, for years an unmitigated nuisance, we offer no sympathy, for we feel none," wrote the periodical. "But that is not the whole case. The issue here is whether or not the Constitutional guarantee of free speech is a reality or only a pretense."[66] *America* believed it was more important to support freedom of speech in broadcasting than to worry about the Catholic image construed by propagandists such as Shuler. In a seemingly inconsistent case, *America* editorialized six months later that Joseph F. Rutherford, an early leader of the Jehovah's Witnesses, should be "denied the privilege of broadcasting his attacks on the clergy."[67] Apparently Rutherford's malicious and fallacious attacks on the Catholic priesthood so angered the editors that they turned their attention toward the nefarious effects of radio's commercial system. Rutherford had been allowed to broadcast, reasoned the journal, not because of government intervention in the affairs of the radio industry, which the periodical would have opposed, but because of the strictly commercial motives of broadcasters who sold air time to Rutherford. In other words, the greed of broadcasters, not the market system, was the real villain.

Beginning in about 1935, a year after the establishment of the FCC, *America* began criticizing the venal mentality of the monopolistic broadcast industry while simultaneously supporting a nonregulated broadcast system. *America* first criticized the two major radio networks—CBS and NBC—which had grown "to a degree of power which enables them to look upon these wave lengths as their exclusive property." It editorialized that a license granted by the FCC to a radio station was not a property right but a privilege. "The relations of this new monopoly to the generally discredited power trust in this country are close. . . . New Federal legislation which will destroy once for all the idea that all the best wave lengths must be assigned to a few highly capitalized companies is an imperative necessity."[68] *America* argued that without some governmental regulation the large, for-profit broadcasters might prohibit others' access to the airways.

Along with its strong support of freedom of the airways, *America* perceived a crucial role for critical, interpretive analysis of programming. The journal offered readers an ongoing critique of the spiritual and aesthetic dimensions of radio programming. George Henry Payne, for example, wrote about radio "officials" and the more "sophisticated" listeners who, he believed, were unsympathetic toward the spiritual aspects of life and culture. Radio "sophists" have little respect for programs that teach "truth and inculcate justice and a respect for the spiritual aspects of life and culture," wrote Payne; "materialists and sophisticates" control the airways.[69] Theophilus Lewis similarly argued that "aesthetics and commercialism will not mix at all." While complimenting NBC for its Saturday night symphony broadcasts and CBS for its Sunday afternoon philharmonic concerts, he decried network radio's penchant for mass entertainment and recommended that a foundation be established to provide "radio entertainment exclusively for adult listeners either by operating its own broadcasting chain or by purchasing time on an existing system."[70] Defining itself as a critic of broadcasting, *America* increasingly developed a rhetoric of discernment that probed the cultural biases of commercial broadcasting.

The commercial broadcasting system was, in the eyes of *America*, anathema to the development of a healthy religious experience in the community and the home. "Religion cannot be put into the home by radio," proclaimed the periodical as early as 1923, during the same period that journals such as *Catholic World* were predicting tremendous evangelistic potential in the new medium of mass communication. "Sermons and church music can supplant the popular song, but they do not constitute religion. As far as individual and family are concerned, religion is a conviction. . . . Family and homes find their focal point in the heart. So does religion."[71] In this regard the Catholic view of early radio espoused by both *America* and *Commonweal* was quite different from that articulated by the Protestants.

While Protestant journals typically examined radio's impact on the church, Catholics usually emphasized its effect on the family and the local community. "Religion and radio . . . need not be enemies," *America* wrote in 1923, but radio religion should not be allowed to supplant "Christian homes."[72] It applauded CBS in 1932 for providing a special Holy Week message from Rome, saying it is "indeed a relief to listen to programs of this type . . . to be freed from the insistent cordiality, the commercialized comradeship, of the announcer with his 'hello, everybody!' which nothing can excuse by the necessity under which the poor man rests of making a living."[73] The journal also commended the National Council of Catholic Men for its production of *The Catholic Hour:* "The schedule of subjects was well devised, the successive speakers were men of ability and distinction, and the musical programs reached high excellence."[74] During the formative years of radio broadcasting, however, *America* only once expressed unbridled optimism about the medium's potential as a means of evangelism. The writer was an Australian priest who used radio "to speak in the homes of people who would not set foot inside a Catholic Church." Based on the limited success he had while using radio to gain Catholic converts, the priest nonetheless concluded that "radio is an apostolate of immense significance and power."[75] Broadly speaking, *America*'s rhetoric of praise extended to the constitutional guarantees of free speech but not to the resulting radio programming.

America's anticensorship principles were strongly tested during the late 1930s and early 1940s by the political broadcasts of Coughlin, who spoke via radio networks to the nation from the Shrine of the Little Flower in Royal Oak, Michigan. The liberal economic views of *America*'s editors and writers contrasted sharply with the increasingly reactionary and anti-Roosevelt tenor of Coughlin's speeches. When the three major networks—NBC, CBS, and Mutual—refused to sell time to Coughlin, allegedly because of the priest's controversial political sermons, *America* nevertheless angrily protested: "We bitterly resent interference by any public official to keep us from hearing Father Coughlin."[76] The Jesuit publication criticized the "radio chains" for yielding "to a pressure group, simply because the members of this group disagree with Father Coughlin's opinions," and it implicated the FCC in the move by the networks to remove Coughlin from the airways.[77] *America* saw no problem with the Catholic Church's own censorship of Coughlin's sermons when Archbishop Rev. Edward Mooney of Detroit required the radio minister to submit for approval all radio sermon texts. "The Catholic priest is not at liberty to preach sermons or to deliver addresses wherever he wishes, under whatever circumstances he may prefer, and in any sort of manner. . . . He is bound to follow the directions of his Ordinary."[78] In *America*'s view the church's own self-regulation of Coughlin's radio propaganda was totally reconcilable with the journal's support of freedom of the airways.

But *America* worried about even broadcasters' self-regulation of speech, including the industry's efforts to silence Coughlin. In a two-part essay on the self-regulatory code of ethics published by the NAB in July 1939, John P. Delaney charged that one sentence of the code was written specifically to remove Coughlin from the airways. That sentence, located in the code's "Controversial Issues" section, stated, "Time for the presentation of controversial issues shall not be sold except for political broadcasts." Delaney revealed that although NAB officials denied the charge, one of the NAB's own pamphlets on the likely impact of the new code concluded that it would have the effect of "silencing" Coughlin and "other spokesmen for controversial issues."[79] He warned readers of *America* that the overall effect of the code would be to place "absolute control of both speakers and material in the hands of station owners, who are empowered to grant or refuse permission of American citizens to use the airways. . . . The Code establishes just such a monopoly, control and domination that it pretends to fear."[80] If the industry could silence Coughlin, it could potentially remove any other religious broadcaster from the airways, including any or all Catholics.

The move by the NAB to silence Coughlin through the adoption of a self-regulatory code soured *America* for a time on the possibilities of improving the quality of radio programming without government interference. When CBS wrote its own code in 1935 to limit the "vulgarity and coarseness" of radio programming, *America* cautiously expressed its support but also charged that CBS "has apparently become fearful that the same kind of uprising might come against radio as rose against its older sister, motion pictures."[81] The removal of Coughlin from his radio pulpit in 1939 appeared to confirm the Jesuits' worst fears about the self-interested nature of broadcast codes. Not until 1948 did *America* again speak in favor of formal radio self-regulation. The NAB then adopted a code prohibiting programs "which induced the radio audience to 'listen in hope of reward rather than for the quality of entertainment.'" These "give-away" shows built large, profitable audiences by promising listeners a chance of winning free prizes.[82] By late 1949 the game-show situation had become so competitive among the networks that *America* editorialized in favor of a temporary FCC ban on shows such as *Stop the Music* and *Break the Bank*.[83] When the FCC ban was challenged in the courts, however, *America* reversed its stand in favor of industry self-regulation: "This is a situation for the industry to face and solve within itself. It would be a shame if the FCC . . . should ever feel it necessary to step in and curtail such programs."[84] No matter how much *America* distrusted the broadcast industry's own regulation, it feared even more any government involvement in dictating program content for stations and networks.

America optimistically turned its attention from radio to the novel medium of television during the late 1940s. Wynne wrote that television could be used as an "instrument of inestimable value in the promulgation of world brotherhood, permanent peace and the fuller life promised so blithely by our statesmen." He predicted that "the addition of televised education will make the schoolroom a more attractive and exciting spot for the average youngster. It will also play an important part in the eventual elimination of juvenile delinquency as a major national problem."[85] The journal was particularly hopeful about the role that the new medium might play in public and parochial education. Given the Jesuit publication's close ties to colleges and universities, it predictably favored regulatory allocation of television channels specifically for educational stations and encouraged instructors to "develop a large audience which will appreciate the good educational (including religious) programs that are already provided on both radio and TV."[86] *America* also supported a bill introduced in the U.S. Senate giving the FCC the authority to require television stations to devote a portion of their "best hours" to educational programs.[87] And it suggested that all educational institutions in a given geographical area "pool their funds and resources" to establish their own educational television stations.[88] During the early years of television the journal established a surprisingly upbeat rhetoric of praise for the potential of educational television broadcasting in the nation.

America's hopeful vision for educational television programming disappeared in the early 1950s, however, as the nation's nascent "ETV" system, which later became public broadcasting, struggled with inadequate funding and unclear objectives. Supporting the concept of broadcast freedom but convinced that television's commercialization would probably be as nefarious as radio's journey into almost purely commercial fare, the journal quickly concluded that the new industry should be permitted to regulate itself without government interference. It criticized the FCC in 1952 for requiring NBC to air the acceptance speeches of Progressive Party candidates for president and vice president, calling members of the party "commie stooges."[89] The editors cautioned the networks not to "yield to undiscriminating and McCarthyesque pressure groups" that were calling for the elimination of Communist sympathizers from the talent pools of broadcasting.[90] *America* once again favored self-regulation over government regulation, in spite of the broadcasting industry's self-serving motives. Commenting on the fact that the National Association of Radio and Television Broadcasters code of ethics did not spring "purely from the Galahad heart of the industry," but was instead prompted by a bill before Congress calling for a "national watchdog committee to keep TV on the reservation," *America* called the code "good and wise."[91] The Jesuits continued to espouse freedom of the airways, but they repeatedly relented to the need for industry-imposed restrictions on those freedoms. The reality of commercial broadcasting increasingly tarnished the periodical's hopes for culturally worthwhile programming.

The conversations occurring publicly in the pages of *America* between 1920 and 1970 frequently were vigorous defenses of freedom of the airways. Of course protecting freedom of the airways also meant that Catholics would not be blocked from radio and television channels. But there were so few examples of such Catholic broadcasting even in the open media market that it would be unfair to interpret *America*'s position as essentially self-interested. The journal's support of freedom of the airways was grounded philosophically in the idea that only a free market could protect all voices and ultimately lead to reason on the airways. In the spirit of social justice, the Jesuits wanted for themselves no more than what others in society would have a right to as well. *America* cared along with *Commonweal* about community values, but it placed freedom above such community standards; freedom guaranteed open admission to the public square, whereas community always required a community of interpretation, which could easily exclude some people from participating in public conversations. Voskuil suggests that during the early years of radio broadcasting *America* championed a kind of neo-orthodoxy that valued realism, insisted on the transcendence of God, and offered a sober analysis of human nature.[92] If so, this kind of theological stance would help explain the journal's fear of any attempts to socially engineer a better society through governmental regulation of radio and television.

Christian Century: The Ecumenical Spirit

Although it never achieved large circulation, the *Christian Century* garnered a loyal audience of thoughtful mainline Protestant pastors, denominational leaders, theologians, and reporters from the mainstream media. James M. Wall, one of the publication's editors in the 1980s and 1990s, recalls first seeing a copy of the journal when he was a graduate student at the Candler School of Theology at Emory University. "Having spent the previous six years in various forms of journalism, my first impression was that the *Christian Century* could use a design artist. But my second impression was the one that stuck: Here was a world Christianity presented with sophistication that challenged the parochialism of my southern Methodism."[93] Wall argued the significance of the journal by recalling one of editor Marty's insightful summaries of the place of Protestantism in American life. Marty suggested to readers that John F. Kennedy's inauguration as the first Catholic president symbolically marked the end of Protestantism as the national American faith and reflected the "distinctive faith of a creative minority."[94] *Christian Century* provided this kind of important discussion of the place and role of mainline Protestantism in the United States and increasingly the world. Without question it was the most frequently quoted and discussed mainline Protestant journal during the century.

Originally called the *Christian Oracle*, the journal was founded in 1884 by the Disciples of Christ denomination. Linda-Marie Delloff describes the structure of feeling among mainline Protestants during the turn of the century as "positive, optimistic and liberal" and suggests that *Christian Century*'s readers "welcomed the modernism heralded by the new age: the spirit of rationality and scientific inquiry, the growth of social awareness, and the sense of an expanding world." These Protestant liberals "were bent on proving that genuine Christian faith could live in mutual harmony with the modern developments in science, technology, immigration, communication and culture that were already under way."[95] The editors of the journal celebrated that liberal optimism in 1900 by changing the name of the publication to *Christian Century*. "No name could have better symbolized the optimistic outlook of that period," wrote the journal. The periodical never gained a substantial circulation even within its sponsoring denomination in spite of a series of denominational editors in the early years. Editor Charles Clayton Morrison in 1916 labeled the journal "undenominational" and paved the way for *Christian Century* to become a "broad-based nondenominational magazine."[96] By the end of the second decade of the century, thanks partly to an advertising campaign in other publications, the periodical had acquired about as many Congregational, Presbyterian, and Baptist subscribers as Disciples—and twice as many Methodists—and it began vigorously covering news across the American denominational spectrum.[97] From then on the journal combined religious news and commentary with feature articles, book reviews, and even film and eventually television criticism.

After the 1920s, however, with the Great Depression, problems of immigration, conflicts in state and church relations, the Second World War, and eventually the civil rights movement, the journal became increasingly realistic and far more pragmatic about taking specific action in the world.[98] It adopted a rhetoric of mainline Christian discernment, opening its pages to everything that might be discussed in mainstream journals of comment and opinion, including foreign and domestic political affairs and social justice. The magazine's group of editors-at-large, which represented numerous denominations, contributed provocative articles and editorials from around the world and from a variety of viewpoints. At the hundredth anniversary of the publication in 1984, the journal editorialized that "the tune" the periodical had been "banging for 100 years" comes "from Scripture, tradition and experience. It also arises from the society we seek to serve, for this magazine has insisted that its task is to stand poised at the intersection of religion and society, with pencil (and now word processor) in hand, ready to report, analyze and propose solutions for the events occurring at that intersection."[99] *Christian Century* took an explicitly critical, prophetic role in the church and society, at one point even losing its tax-exempt status for endorsing John F. Kennedy for U.S. president.[100] The publication was deeply determined to provide American Protestantism with an ecumenical rhetoric of discernment.

Of all the periodicals included in this study, *Christian Century* was the most preoccupied with the role that broadcasting would play in the spiritual life of the local church and the nation. The periodical addressed other issues related to the electronic media, such as censorship and federal regulation, but its assessments of radio and television repeatedly returned to one fundamental question: Does broadcasting—tribal and mainstream—create harmony or discord among Christians? More specifically, *Christian Century* viewed broadcasting in the context of the media's apparent role in fragmenting the American church landscape. The journal embraced ecumenism, and it evaluated broadcasting according to whether particular types of programs, means of financial support, and degrees of governmental regulation were contributing to cooperation and understanding among the various strains of American Christianity. According to its rhetoric of ecumenical discernment, radio and television industries and religious broadcasters should pursue nonsectarian rather than religiously divisive programming. The periodical believed that this would be good for society, not just for the church.

Christian Century praised ecumenical radio preachers and initially held great hope for nondenominational broadcasting. "No one could 'tune in' on Dr. Fosdick or Dr. Hugh Black on recent Sunday evenings and not be impressed and inspired," wrote the periodical in 1923 about two early radio preachers. The magazine editorialized optimistically about the

> new device which contributes appreciably to the realization of the fellow-
> ship of the church universal, for there is now no limit to the size of congre-
> gations. What sectarianism has always forbidden has now come to pass. Vast
> congregations, without thought of name or creed, repeat the Lord's Prayer
> after the minister and hear his sermon, critically but intelligently. Mean-
> while, the ministers feel the competition of preaching by the side of the na-
> tion's greatest pulpiteers. Village pulpits must turn out a better product. City
> congregations will soon know what real preaching is. The new invention for
> spreading the gospel is likely to work many a change in preaching style, in
> religious attitudes and in the coming of a more catholic consciousness to the
> church of Christ.[101]

Christian Century never wavered from its support of nonsectarian, ecumenical broadcasting, embracing the new media as potentially powerful technologies for reuniting a deeply divided American church.

Christian Century at first was reservedly enthusiastic about the possibility that the developing radio ministries in the United States could supple-
ment rather than substitute for the local congregational preacher. When
in 1928 Dr. S. Parkes Cadman began broadcasting nationally on NBC
under the auspices of the Federal Council of Churches, a national coalition of mainline Protestant churches, *Christian Century* expressed "satisfaction" in learning that he was not to give up the pulpit of his Brooklyn
church. "The radio ministry is a tremendous power for good," wrote the
journal. "But there is that about preaching which seems to require that
the preacher, if he is to be genuinely effective, must do most of his
preaching in the presence of living men and women. . . . Contact with an
actual congregation is the best means of guarding against the encroach-
ments of this insidious artificiality."[102] Calling radio "an inconvenience to
religious narrowness," *Christian Century* sanguinely editorialized that
"thousands of Catholics are now hearing occasional sermons by gifted
Protestant preachers. . . . Meanwhile the stations in their broadcasting of
these sermons are enlarging the straitened concepts of many a Catholic
mind."[103] Radio might help the ecumenical spirit by overcoming some of

the local as well as the national stereotypes and biases among congregations and denominations.

The editors of *Christian Century* also expressed misgivings about broadcasting church services because "so many churches are now using this method . . . that the result may become a non-ecumenical nuisance, a cacophony of different traditions and theologies. Some radio enthusiasts assert that there is hardly an hour on any Sunday when there are not as many as a dozen church services on the air. What the effect may be on church attendance has been debated . . . without clear conclusion." The journal reported that some critics believed there should not be radio broadcasting of religious services on Sunday morning, and it called for "some method of cooperation" among all the churches. "Wisely used, the possibilities of the radio are beyond imagination, but abused they may lead quickly to a popular reaction that will drastically curtail the outreach of this form of service."[104] The growing religious cacophony on local stations might undermine the medium's potential to foster ecumenical dialogue and understanding.

Recognizing that sermonic forms of religious radio broadcasting would almost invariably be denominational, the journal sought alternative modes of religious communication on the airways. Looking for ecumenical alternatives to church broadcasts, *Christian Century* suggested that "a religious broadcast without a sermon might offer attractive and edifying possibilities."[105] The journal frequently asked why traditional religious broadcasting, with its sermons, evangelistic appeals, and exposition of scriptural texts, "was apparently so ineffective." It concluded that such methods served only "particular doctrinal viewpoints." "The content of the message also will have wider appeal if it deals with the great things of religion than if it is devoted to the exploitation of sectarian specialties," the periodical speculated.[106] In the 1940s *Christian Century* began its own campaign for "nonsectarian" religious broadcasting.[107] It often criticized the trend toward denominational radio programs, challenging readers to consider the effects of such broadcasting on the American public's image of Christianity. By accentuating and highlighting religious differences, sectarian broadcasting was merely making Americans "as conscious as possible of the divisions which disgrace Protestantism. . . . If the denominations are not careful they may find that all they will get for their separate outlays will be a new set of denominational secretaries, complete with offices and stenographers and well oiled and ceaselessly turning mimeograph machines." Only a "united" approach to religious broadcasting would "make a real dent on the mind of the nation."[108]

When the FCC opened up noncommercial FM radio channels in the mid-1940s, *Christian Century* wrote that "religious radio" would have "its chance of the century. . . . If the churches try to meet this opportunity on the basis of separate denominational programs . . . they will surely muff it. . . . The sole question is whether, in this matter where the church has a chance to repent of past mistakes and make a new start, they show a primary loyalty to denominational interests or to the kingdom of God."[109] Part of the problem, from *Christian Century*'s point of view, was the plethora of fundamentalist broadcasts. As one writer put it, many of those shows "are cheap and tawdry and tend to bring Protestant radio into disrepute."[110] Mainline and evangelical groups sparred over who would have access to broadcast outlets; the mainline groups generally favored free, or "sustaining," time, while evangelicals increasingly learned to market their programs to stations and the networks on a paid basis. By starting over with the new FM band, the government might be able to work with mainline Christian broadcasters to create a less sectarian and more ecumenical way of allocating radio resources for religion.

Christian Century strongly advocated the broadcasting activities and policies of the Federal Council. In 1926 the Federal Council had created the National Religious Radio Committee "for the purpose of maintaining cooperative relationships" with the major networks.[111] The Radio Committee worked with the networks to produce religious programs that satisfied both parties: noncontroversial, ecumenical programs that were well produced. By 1943 such successful "cooperation" led to the Mutual network's elimination of paid religious programs; instead of accepting payment for such programs, the network agreed to provide "free" time only to the three major religious "groups"—Protestants, Catholics, and Jews, with Protestants represented by the mainline Federal Council. To the delight of *Christian Century*, other networks later followed suit, forcing some independent religious broadcasters off of the national airways. Evangelicals and fundamentalists responded by forming the National Religious Broadcasters (NRB), which eventually reestablished the right to purchase time on most stations and networks. Battles between the networks, the NRB, and the Federal Council continued for decades, escalating again in the mid-1950s when the availability of television broadcast time became the major issue.

While the ecumenical-minded *Christian Century* championed the efforts of the Federal Council, its readers disagreed over what were the roadblocks to truly nonsectarian religious broadcasting in the United States. Charles M. Crowe, chair of the Department of Radio and Television, Federation of Churches of Chicago, believed that the broadcast industry was to blame. "The crux of the problem . . . lies in the difficulty of convincing top station management and the radio interests of the responsibility of the industry for the presentation of religious telecasts as part of their normal expense. Such presentations should be a recognized part of the station budget for both time and production costs. They should be controlled by the station or the sponsor with the expert advice of qualified religious leaders."[112] J. Edward Carothers, taking the position supported by the broadcast industry, criticized the churches for producing poor-quality religious shows. He believed that churches should have pooled their "talent" and financial resources to produce a few excellent, nonsectarian shows that broadcast industry officials would air enthusiastically.[113]

In spite of its support for the work of the Federal Council, *Christian Century* objected to any organized self-regulation of religious broadcasting by particular religious groups. While it favored cooperation among denominations involved in radio, it rejected any attempts by churches to limit the broadcasting activities of others. When Methodists outlined a proposal for "Protestant" radio stations that would be used by cooperating denominations, *Christian Century*'s editors applauded, but the periodical criticized the section of the Methodists' plan prohibiting any discussion on the air of "disputed" questions (such as millennialism) and forbidding any on-air appeals for funds. "There is a danger . . . that its shortcomings lie in its apparently wise restrictions. A censor takes the life out of any matter, and religion most quickly of all."[114]

Christian Century's preoccupation with ecumenical broadcasting that could present a united image of Christianity to the nation also influenced its views of radio regulation. During the first few years of commercial radio the journal saw no need for governmental restrictions of radio broadcasts. It even upheld the rights of Shuler and Coughlin to address the nation with their inflammatory rhetoric. "There is but one workable rule," wrote *Christian Century*, "to apply to radio broadcasting the same restrictions that apply to public discussion in any other form, whether spoken or written. . . . Once time has been secured, then let the minister have absolute freedom of speech, subject only to those legal safeguards which exist in the form of laws against libel and slander." The editors admitted that "the available supply of radio facilities will . . . always exercise a form of censorship on clerical broadcasting," but they did not view such technical limitations as a form of censorship.[115] The periodical's rhetoric of ecumenical communion supported wide-open airways even though some of the sectarian broadcasts would challenge the magazine's stand for ecumenicity.

In the case of Shuler's anti-Catholic broadcasts, *Christian Century* worried about the potential for governmental control of the content of religious shows. Conceding that Shuler's attacks on the Catholic Church were not "marked by . . . canons of good taste which [should] obtain throughout radio," the journal nevertheless criticized the FRC for revoking the minister's radio station license. "The precedent has now been established that the commission can, for unexplained reasons and in response to unrecorded and unspecified charges," remove some broadcasters from the airways, the periodical warned. "A more vicious and danger-fraught basis for censorship could not be set up." The editors' strong stand on this issue was precipitated in part by Shuler's charges that prominent and influential Catholics—Henry J. Robinson, a Los Angeles banker and close friend of President Hoover, and Louis B. Mayer, a motion picture magnate and intimate of William Randolph Hearst—put "behind the scenes" pressure on the FCC to deny Shuler's license renewal.[116] The journal feared that the politicization of federal regulation of radio might have a religious dimension.

By 1930, however, *Christian Century* was seriously questioning its "freedom of the air" stand toward all types of programming, including religious broadcasts. The growing number of ministers, particularly anti-Catholic preachers, who began using the airwaves as a forum for disseminating religious bigotry greatly concerned the publication. Writing in an ecumenical spirit, it editorialized that anti-Catholic broadcasters should "be put off the air by the federal authorities, together with attacks on all other forms of religion." Hoping to protect the growing religious tolerance between liberal Protestants and Catholics, editors of the journal joined the Catholic press in its condemnation of hypersectarian, fundamentalist diatribes against the pope and Catholic beliefs. The editors argued that broadcasting had become a "nuisance" that would be "infinitely aggravated if the highways of the sky are going to be crowded with the traffic of jangling voices for and against all the varieties of religion whose adherents consider them the ultimate truth." For the first time, the periodical told readers that the public's interest is to censor religious bigots rather than to allow them "free rein."[117] In 1939 *Christian Century* went so far as to applaud the NAB for its new self-regulatory code designed to "clip the wings" of Father Coughlin.[118] Clearly the journal's rhetoric of discernment finally excluded some broadcasts.

Like the other religious journals included in this study, *Christian Century* increasingly deplored the overly commercial motives of the broadcasting industry. Radio's profit-oriented system of attracting eager audiences for lucrative advertising agencies produced deep cynicism among the editorial staff. When CBS composed new guidelines for self-regulation in 1935, *Christian Century*'s jaundiced view of the industry was clearly evident: "Undoubtedly there are fertile minds already at work in advertising agencies and in the radio departments of the firms which buy time over the air devising tricks by which [the] new regulations may be circumvented."[119] "Is radio to be nothing but an adjunct of big business?" asked the journal rhetorically.[120] It criticized the radio "chains" for being merely "profit-seeking corporations" whose "share in the nation's cultural future will always be conditioned by balance-sheet considerations." *Christian Century* saw hope for cultural enrichment via radio only in a completely different system of program production and distribution that would be financed "by hearer's fees rather than by advertising income."[121] The periodical hoped that John D. Rockefeller and other philanthropists would "soon come to see that the value of 'cultural' broadcasting is largely conditioned by the fact as to whether or not it is under commercial control or must meet the expediencies of commercial operation."[122]

During the development of television in the late 1940s and early 1950s, *Christian Century* reconsidered its criticisms of broadcasting's commercial and sectarian nature, but in general the conclusions reached were the same as in the earlier years of radio's popularity. Mildly optimistic at first, the journal called for "a revolution in the moral sense of those who create the public's entertainment" and asked whether "TV brought the longed for equivalent of town-meeting democracy."[123] It also predicted, "As the novelty of television sets wears off, the lure of the sexy and the macabre also wears thin. . . . If the television producers cannot provide better programs than they have so far, we predict that they—and their advertising sponsors—will soon be frantic for viewers."[124] A. Gordon Nasby wrote of the new medium's "miraculous opportunity for witnessing" and challenged the church to develop effective ways of using television. He suggested that Roman Catholic "pageantry and color" were particularly well suited to the medium's visual appeal. Nasby also hinted at television's negative potential to "cut largely into our church life in certain areas."[125]

From the mid-1950s to 1970 *Christian Century* again focused on what it believed to be the negative effects of sectarian approaches to religious broadcasting on the church in America. Its criticism of fundamentalist radio programs grew sardonic, prefiguring the tone of analyses that it would publish about the electronic church in the 1970s. Michael Daves's essay on Bible Belt stations chastised radio managers for not having the courage to cancel commercial religious programs that promote "free" booklets and other gifts, engage in on-air healing practices, call for Communist witch-hunts, and repeatedly solicit funds. He told readers that part of the blame for Bible Belt broadcasting should be directed at the liberal churches that are "usually not disturbed enough to take any action either in protesting the programs or in offering the stations any constructive alternatives."[126] In spite of *Christian Century*'s repeated pleas for an ecumenical approach to religious television, individual denominations, not the National Council of Churches, pioneered novel approaches to religious programming. The journal enthusiastically endorsed the successful *This Is the Life* show produced by the Lutheran Church—Missouri Synod; when the show was made available to all churches in the National Council, the periodical asked its readers, "What denomination is ready to follow its lead?"[127] *Christian Century* also continued its campaign against broadcast stations' "censorship" of religious programs, in spite of its own disdain for the growing tide of fundamentalist shows. Citing evidence that a Chicago television station canceled the film *Martin Luther* in 1957 under pressure from Roman Catholics, the journal editorialized, "A television station which permits de facto censorship by yielding to anti-Protestant pressure should not be permitted to continue to use airways to which access is controlled by the FCC."[128] It concluded that "sectarian censorship is based on fear of the truth and fear of the uses people will make of their democratic freedom."[129]

The *Christian Century*'s rhetoric of communion during the half-century period from 1920 to 1970 was remarkably consistent and focused. The journal repeatedly argued that broadcasting could harm the Christian faith in America by giving every religious zealot, each denominational group, and all of the parachurch organizations their own public voice. This would create a confusing cacophony of disparate religious ideas and practices in America, ultimately serving only the most ostentatious and flamboyant Christian broadcasters who could use the medium to build their sectarian movements and expand their intolerant forms of religion. If *America* pushed rhetorically for freedom of speech on the airways, *Christian Century* pressed just as forcefully for fairness, for balance, and especially for mainline Christian dominance as a means of protecting the public and the church from bogus religious ideas on radio and television. *Christian Century* fostered a lively conversation about the proper and legitimate role of mainline Protestantism in the nation. The periodical wanted mainline Protestantism to be the most influential and tolerant version of the Christian faith in America—the type of Christianity that reflected the mood and optimism of early-twentieth-century liberal thought, with its emphasis on tolerance and hope rather than on dogma and conflict. The journal praised the networks and stations when they adopted policies favoring ecumenical broadcasting and apparently feared the possibility that evangelical broadcasters would garner larger audiences and squeeze mainline Christian programs out of the marketplace. Defining its voice cross-denominationally, *Christian Century* hoped to leverage its ecumenical rhetoric of discernment into a new plea for a cross-tribal rhetoric of communion. The journal praised a wide range of regulatory and broadcasting efforts that seemed to support such rhetorics.

Christianity Today: Marketing the Gospel

Christianity Today is probably the most influential and certainly the most publicly visible of the broadly evangelical periodicals in America. Established in 1956 by evangelist Reverend Billy Graham and colleagues, the fortnightly periodical tried to gain some of the public profile of *Christian Century* by similarly appealing to pastors and educated lay leaders. But it also hoped to create a new, broadly evangelical rhetoric by avoiding the fundamentalism that, largely because of the modernist-fundamentalist debates, often carried a negative connotation in the public square. Graham recalls, "We were convinced that the magazine would be useless if it had the old, extreme fundamentalist stamp on it. . . . It needed to avoid extremes of both right and left."[130] Editors initially described evangelical Christianity's position in America as "neglected, slighted, misrepresented" and in need of a "clear voice." They sought to "apply the biblical revelation to the contemporary social crisis, by presenting the implications of the total Gospel message for every area of life."[131] In a priestly sense the publication hoped to speak for evangelicalism, while in a prophetic sense it sought to evaluate and critique the wider culture and society from a biblical perspective. Although initially the magazine had difficulty building a decent circulation apart from sending out free copies to pastors, it eventually became a commercial success, achieving nearly 200,000 subscribers under the leadership of Harold Myra, a businessman with a mandate from the journal's board to make the magazine profitable.[132] *Christianity Today*'s circulation was greater than the combined circulation of all of the other periodicals discussed in this chapter. It was also the most commercial of the publications, filled with advertising and aggressively soliciting new subscribers.

Christianity Today was partly a journal of comment and opinion during these years and partly an "evangelical consumer" publication. Like the other journals analyzed in this chapter, *Christianity Today* sought to generate serious discussions about the intersection of evangelical Christianity with American culture. The periodical gained support from some of the most influential pastors and leading university seminary faculty in the evangelical movement. In addition to addressing the pragmatic needs of the pastoral ministry, the magazine displayed a concern for political and economic issues as well as directly theological ones. Mark G. Toulouse describes the magazine's editorial stand as partly priestly because of its "emphasis on American values and cultural ethos," its tendency to "define the 'normative' in American life and society," and its raising of "certain aspects of the status quo to an ultimacy." The publication was concerned about Roman Catholic influence in American politics and favored strong American support for the nation of Israel. Moreover, argues Toulouse, *Christianity Today* increasingly narrowed the "ideological gap" between itself and *Christian Century* on "most every social issue."[133] These editorial positions were not just commercial moves designed to broaden the subscriber base but also rhetorical moves to establish American evangelicalism as a more respected voice in the public square. *Christianity Today* originally was designed to provide both a rhetoric of evangelical discernment and a rhetoric of evangelical communion that would be taken seriously in American society. Along the way, however, *Christianity Today* instead increasingly tended to establish a more tribal rhetoric of conversion that championed the potential power of the new media to save souls and populate evangelical churches.

Unfortunately, the magazine's relatively recent birth excludes it from early comparisons with the other journals included in this study.[134] *Christianity Today* was established roughly ten years after the first television broadcasts in the major American cities. By the time the premiere issue of the magazine appeared, members of the evangelical community had ample opportunity to reflect on the role of television in American culture and to consider ways that the church might appropriately use the medium to accomplish its work. Instead of refined thought, however, one finds in the first years of publication a sense of inferiority and tardiness; *Christianity Today* immediately proclaimed that evangelicals lacked the technical expertise and marketing know-how to use television for effective evangelism and that it was high time to seize the medium for the evangelical cause. "Evangelicals have not spent time in workshops and on basic research as they ought, in order to use this new channel most effectively to the glory of God," editorialized the journal.[135] Evangelicals might be late adopters of television for ministry, but they were determined to catch up quickly. A rhetoric of conversion quickly dominated the journal's interpretations of broadcasting in the United States.

Beyond evangelism, *Christianity Today*'s most pressing concern regarding religious broadcasting was the alleged monopolization of program time by the ecumenical National Council. It alleged that "the Council itself has secured more and more of a monopoly of free [sustaining] religious radio time on the networks for its own agencies, so that noncommunicant groups are increasingly discriminated against in the assignment of sustaining time." The publication called on the networks to provide equal amounts of free time to evangelicals who, the magazine claimed, were entitled to 63 percent of available radio time based on a national constituency of 36,719,000. The journal supported the formation of the NRB, which lobbied the networks on behalf of evangelicals and offered broadcasting "clinics" for technical instruction in 1958. It also encouraged churches to work with the broadcasting industry to create the "best techniques" for bringing "invisible spiritual and moral forces to the network."[136]

Encouraged by *Christianity Today*, evangelicals entered broadcasting with a provincial optimism about media technology that was expressed in only one other journal examined in this study—*Catholic World*. *Christianity Today* envisioned in 1966 the emergence of "space-age Christian pioneers" who, in the midst of America's successful space exploration, would "strip away any vestige of suspicion about technology or intelligence employed in God's service."[137] The magazine became an uncritical supporter of the rhetoric of the so-called communications revolution. Disregarding any historical or theoretical evidence to the contrary, writers such as George Patterson claimed that the "communications revolution" presents "an exciting and wholly satisfying way of communicating the Christian Gospel in all its fullness to all peoples and all classes in our own generation. . . . *This is the challenge to the Christian Church: to reach everyone in the country within ten years with everything from education to salvation for $100,000.*"[138] Such exaggerated claims became incantations for the faithful to recite frequently, presumably until people began to believe them and act upon them. Campus Crusade for Christ's "I Found It" campaign, which teased citizens during the 1980s with broadcast advertising and billboards, is one later example of this faith in technology.[139] The recurring emphasis on a rhetoric of conversion often led *Christianity Today* to a very instrumental and pragmatic view of broadcasting—fundamentally the same kind of conversionary optimism that guided the commercial broadcasting industry. Yet it arrived at that perspective via its rhetoric of discernment, which concluded that tens of millions of Americans needed to be saved from their sins by the blood of Jesus Christ.

Ron Spargus, in a *Christianity Today* article labeled by the editors as a "well-thought-out proposal," asked television networks and evangelicals to work together to put "religion" on in prime time.[140] A public relations consultant, Spargus addressed "the economic possibilities" that might tantalize businesspeople and advertising executives, especially those "whose products or budgets have not previously seemed conducive to TV sales. Sponsorship of religious-bloc programs can, for example, come from major church-related business and industries. There are large insurance companies that direct sales programs primarily at church members and ministers, and there are book publishers and record manufacturers who do the same."[141] Hoping to transform the economic market into a mechanism for religious conversion, he envisioned such a financial partnership between broadcast ministries and for-profit corporations. Although his article was not typical of those in *Christianity Today*, it represented an important articulation of later evangelical aspirations to baptize the free market positively as a potential force for good in society.

Between 1957 and 1970 *Christianity Today* published few articles critical of television programming or the political and economic aspects of the television industry. It devoted most editorial space to fairly simple and straightforward theories and techniques for evangelizing the nation. Although the situation began to change dramatically in the late 1960s, prior to then there is little evidence in the journal's pages that evangelicals desired the kind of insightful media criticism that had been articulated for decades in the other journals surveyed in this chapter. The periodical seemed to be enamored with the conversionary rhetoric of the mythos of the electronic church. Prior to the tumultuous Vietnam War protest years, *Christianity Today*'s response to broadcasting was primarily an uncritical attempt to integrate the practices and theories of modern marketing with the goal of worldwide evangelization.

Christianity Today sometimes distinguished between evangelical discernment and both fundamentalist and mainline Protestant discernment.

Fundamentalists and the mainline groups tended to be much more critical of technology and American consumerism. But when Graham concluded in 1981 that *Christianity Today* had "helped bring about an evangelical revolution in America" and given "intellectual respectability" to the movement, he might have overstated the historical case with respect to the journal's assessment of American broadcasting.[142] Certainly the journal established a major forum for evangelical conversations about the faith and its relationship to American culture, but its understanding of broadcasting was so tightly wedded to a rhetoric of conversion that it struggled to establish an independent voice of discernment. *Christianity Today* addressed the subject of broadcasting with priestly propaganda designed to confirm what the tribe wanted to believe about the alleged power of the media to convert people to Jesus Christ, not with a prophetic witness to the reality of mass communication as a business in the United States. Toulouse concludes that the periodical generally lacked a sense of "social sin"—a cognizance of the wider reality of evil in the world as both a social and institutional force rather than just a personal evil.[143] The rhetoric of conversion, without a countervailing rhetoric of technological discernment, put too much hope in the ability of evangelicals to overcome institutional as well as cultural and technical difficulties in mass-media evangelism. Moreover, *Christianity Today* demonstrated little interest in a rhetoric of communion that would connect mass evangelism to local community. Up to 1970 *Christianity Today*'s assessment of broadcasting was largely an expression of the mythos of the electronic church in America.

Catholic World: An Apostolic Tool

Catholic World (since 1972 called *New Catholic World*) is the oldest Catholic magazine in the United States, founded in 1865 by the Society of Missionary Priests of St. Paul the Apostle (Paulists), an order dedicated originally to proselytizing in America. The periodical's evangelistic role in the nascent industrial nation eventually waned, however, and the magazine broadened its focus and began exploring various aspects of American life from a Catholic perspective. Although typically more theologically conservative than *Commonweal* and *America*, it addressed some of the same problems and themes. In many respects it was more similar to the style and rhetoric of *Christianity Today* than to those of *America* and *Commonweal*, suggesting that the rhetoric of conversion was not limited to evangelicals and that not all Catholic groups were fundamentally concerned with any dangers of broadcast religion.

Catholic World published only a few articles on radio and television broadcasting, but they are significant statements from the Paulist Order of the Catholic Church. The journal saw both the sacred and the profane in the new medium. Broadcasting was simultaneously a special gift from God for mass evangelization and a wicked instrument of Satan for cultural destruction. The journal never worked out the implications of its views, but its Janus-headed commentary insightfully portrays another form of Catholic thought about the media—a paradigm that integrated a rhetoric of communion with a rhetoric of discernment. *Catholic World*'s discussion of broadcasting shows that some Catholics adopted the mythos of the electronic church.

Catholic World began proclaiming the benefits of domestic and international radio as early as 1926, when the medium was still a cacophony of largely unregulated broadcasters, including many Protestant stations. William H. Scheifley wrote, "From the first application of wireless telephony in 1915 it was evident that the discovery was destined to become one of the most marvelous of science." In glowing terms and with almost mystical adulation, Scheifley rhapsodized about how "broadcasting has more than fulfilled" people's sanguine expectations. "Notable is its cooperation in the great work of social solidarity. For not only does it disseminate knowledge; in 'wet' countries it combats alcoholism by entertaining workers at home during the hours that they formerly spent in the cabarets. Similarly, in transmitting to the farm the best artistic treats, broadcasting tends to check desertion of the countryside for the cities. It even diverts the aged and the sick, who otherwise would have many long, cheerless days." His article doxologically described "the beneficent ethereal waves, which function instantaneously for man's instruction and entertainment."[144] Like *Christianity Today*, *Catholic World* saw tremendous religious potential in the power of the medium to convert people to faith.

By the 1930s, however, *Catholic World* was analyzing radio programming. It wrote that "radio is a miracle but also a menace." The journal asked readers to "take a glimpse at the daily or weekly menu of radio fare. . . . The impression is that of a madhouse. . . . The air seems to be given over to astrologists and 'psychologists,' hillbillies and gypsies; to cheap comedy, stupid, pointless, dramatic sketches; dialect sketches, mostly inane; detective stories, sales talks; patent medicine ads, orchestras, orchestras, orchestras, orchestras, most of them fifth rate interpreters of tenth rate music." The writer complained that radio was in the hands of the "*vulgas humanum*, the vulgar horde, who lack good taste and intelligence and ambition for culture, the moronic mob, the kind that patronizes shameless musical comedies and crude vaudeville, the kind that laughs loudest at smutty jokes in plays brazenly advertised as 'bawdy'; the kind that prefers the more lascivious type of motion picture, seeking from the screen sexual titillation or a substitute for it; the kind that devours salacious fiction and buys the obscene periodicals exhibited brazenly at the corner newsstands; the kind that demands jazz and more jazz and nothing but jazz on the radio." This "'hotcha' element," continued the writer, "knows no modesty; it is a total stranger to reserve of manner; it knows what it wants and gets it; but meanwhile the quieter people, the unobtrusive who still cherish the old-fashioned virtues of modesty and decency and retirement, are crowded out, ignored, laughed at. They, too, know what they want but the mob won't let them have it. It is held a weakness in them that they don't push and pull and scramble, don't get into the common mêlée and fight for what they want."[145] It seemed that this scathing indictment of the inferior culture transmitted by radio might signal the end of the Paulists' love affair with the new medium.

But *Catholic World* found a villain responsible for radio's quick decline into Bohemian culture: government regulators. The villain was not the "hotcha" culture itself but the federal government, which *Catholic World* believed, through the FRC "knowingly or unknowingly . . . played into the hands of the mob."[146] The periodical cited as an example the case of radio station WLWL operated by Paulists in New York City. The order's attempts to keep the cultural and educational programs of its station on the air were repeatedly frustrated by the FRC under strong pressure from commercial station interests. WLWL was eventually limited to two hours of operation daily. "We are . . . trying to repel the suspicion that the Federal Government put a premium upon commercialism and an embargo or near-embargo upon education, culture and religion," concluded an editorial.[147] Not only was *Catholic World* concerned about mainstream radio programming; it further worried about the federal regulators who favored commercial broadcasters over educational and other "cultural" broadcasters.

The Paulists' disdain for federal control of broadcasting apparently had no effect on their optimistic views of radio evangelism. "We can bring the Gospel of Christ to such a great number of people that it seems like folly to neglect this vehicle," wrote John J. McMahon. "There was a time when we used to wonder how we could get Christ's World beyond the pews and out through the door to those who never came to church. Radio has solved this." McMahon concluded, "When radio reaches [the] point of universal use in the work of the apostolate, the words of the ancient Psalmist will be fulfilled: 'Their sound hath gone forth into all the earth: and their words unto the ends of the world.'"[148] Such rhetoric of technological praise sounded amazingly like that of evangelicals. *Catholic World* strongly endorsed *The Catholic Hour*, which began on NBC in 1929 under the sponsorship of the National Council of Catholic Men. "It is the Church really being herself—the Church as she lives, thinks, feels, worships. . . . The non-Catholic listener is made a part of a family group."[149] In 1940 the journal estimated that about fifty conversions to Catholicism yearly could be credited to the show."[150] *Catholic World* proudly endorsed the first major national Catholic radio broadcast in America.

According to *Catholic World*, however, radio was not being used to its religious potential partly because of the refusal of station management to permit the broadcasting of controversial subjects. "Any radio speaker who tries to be strictly non-controversial condemns himself to sheer banality," stated one editorial. "One may preach exclusively sweetness and light, but it will not be the gospel." Lamenting the fact that there was so much "wishy-washy religion" on the air, *Catholic World* chastised "radio companies and other soft-peddlers (who) demand that we should preach an inoffensive gospel. . . . The moral is obvious. No Catholic, or for that matter no Christian, can open his mouth two nights in succession and speak the faith that is in him without stirring up opposition. The avoidance of 'controversy' on the radio resolves itself, therefore, into a prohibition against the preaching of the authentic, undiluted Gospel of Jesus Christ."[151] Unlike *Commonweal* and *America*, which situated this dilemma in the contexts of community standards and free speech, *Catholic World* offered a much more pragmatic analysis tied to the journal's rhetoric of conversion. Without the freedom to be controversial, Catholic radio broadcasters would simply not be able to transmit the church's gospel through the public medium.

Of the Catholic journals analyzed in this chapter, *Catholic World* was the most sanguine and the least critical of television during the medium's formative years. An editorial entitled "I Believe in Television," for instance, assumed that in spite of television's nearly identical commercial system it would not follow in radio's footsteps. "Television will be more successful than was the radio in presenting so-called 'high-brow' programs," predicted the magazine. It further divined that television would, if "properly controlled," "exert a tremendous and beneficial influence on our way of life," positively "revolutionize politics," and further the proselytizing activities of the "telegenic" Catholic Church.[152] The journal never defined "proper control." Fearful of broadcasting falling into the hands of "some bureaucrat in Washington," however, *Catholic World* strongly preferred industry self-regulation, in spite of the ineffective and largely symbolic attempts at self-regulation that existed in radio. The journal also declared that television "would become whatever public opinion makes it and in this early formative stage of the industry, thoughtful people by writing letters to TV stations and by leading discussions can mold television into a lever capable of raising the level of popular taste and intelligence."[153] *Catholic World* had far more faith in the market to dictate quality radio programming than did either *Commonweal* or *America*.

Catholic World focused primarily on the likely role of radio and television in apostolic work. The periodical tended to see the media neutrally as "tools" and expressed little interest in the ideological and even the theological consequences of adopting particular evangelistic methods most suited to the new technology. At times *Catholic World* seemed most interested in developing religious programs that imitated the commercially successful techniques of mainstream broadcasters. In a 1948 article that endorsed the use of commercial radio techniques in religious broadcasting, Brooke Byrne explained that many religious shows "fail" because the producers and writers blindly overlook the successful methods employed by commercial radio to build and hold audiences. "The basic rules of a good broadcast are few and simple. 'Catch 'em—hold 'em,' about sums it up," wrote Byrne. Effective religious shows "can't be done by ignoring all that commercial radio has painfully learned in the process of selling patent medicines any more than the missionary preacher ignores the tricks of rhetoric or the religious writer ignores the rules of grammar."[154] Such uncritical acceptance of marketing techniques is remarkably similar to the trend found in *Christianity Today*, showing that it was not merely evangelicals, let alone Protestants, who were lured by the enchanting rhetoric of the communication revolution and the successful techniques of Madison Avenue. Although *Catholic World* found much at fault with secular programs, it was willingly co-opted by the ways of thinking that dominated the commercial broadcasting system in the United States.

A column conducted by William H. Shriver for *Catholic World* during 1950 and 1951 cogently illustrates how the Paulists' rhetoric of discernment sometimes wavered. Shriver began a monthly column, "Radio and Television," in July 1950 with the promise that the "aim of this department [will be] to try to keep you posted on 'Whither radio and TV' always with four very important phases of these two lively arts in mind": children's programs, top-rated shows, commercialism, and religious programs.[155] He encouraged readers to act as "spotters" by sending him information about programs that they viewed and heard. In the months that followed Shriver wrote about everything from the *Howdy Doody* show to Catholic programs and the Peabody awards. He even attempted to organize a "Bedside Brigade" made up of people "sick abed who would look and listen and send in from time to time their appraisals of various programs."[156] Oddly enough, Shriver's critical reviews apparently had no effect on the journal's overall perspective on the media. The column, which stopped after just over a year, dealt with religious broadcasting only infrequently and super- ficially, in spite of Shriver's often-deep barbs at the commercial broadcast- ing industries. *Catholic World* saw much at fault with the media, but it also clung confidently to radio and television as means for evangelizing the world. The journal seemed unable to reconcile its rhetorics of discernment and conversion.

Catholic World's rhetorics of technological praise and conversion were re- markably close to the rhetoric of some of the articles and editorials in *Chris- tianity Today*. But the rhetorical continuities between these two journals might say less about their theological and religious commitments than they do about their common cultural commitments. Both periodicals expressed a kind of American sentiment reflected in technological optimism and evangelistic hope. *Christianity Today* and *Catholic World* offered their readers not primarily a critical conversation about the role of the media in society, but rather an optimistic discussion of the possible future for the new medium as a transmitter of religious faith and values. Of course if the medium offers such evangelistic potential to every religious group, then the power of the media is a mixed blessing; the gain of one religious group is at the expense of a different one. This might be why both of these mag- azines tended to lament the relatively late use by their respective tribes of television and radio for evangelism. Whoever first seizes the power of the technology has a leg up on the religious competitors in society—or so the periodicals' rhetoric suggested. Time was more important than criticism, and technique more crucial than perspective.

Conclusion

During the twentieth century Protestant and Catholic groups used religious publications to converse about faith and its relationship to the wider world of American culture, economics, and politics. The religious press struggled to compete against the mainstream media, trying to maintain serious religious discourse in the face of tremendous competition for attention from entertainment media that flaunted comparatively enormous budgets and extensive publicity programs. In terms of their national visibility or their power to shape overall public opinion, the religious journals were probably a failure. Judged more in terms of their rhetorical role as conversational arenas, however, some religious periodicals continued to play an important role in American society. They nurtured religious conversations within cross-geographic communities that existed primarily in and through the pages of the journals. As centrifugally organized media, these journals helped to establish and maintain distinct religious tribes with their own language, leadership, and perspectives on the American experiment. Sometimes the magazines spoke about each other and to each other, extending the conversations across their respective communities of discourse. Moreover, some of the periodicals vigorously discussed broader public issues and sought to discern public as well as tribal interests.

In the half century included in this study, the religious press published many remarkably insightful analyses of broadcasting—often more insightful than those found typically in daily newspapers and in mass-circulation magazines, let alone in radio and television broadcasts. *America*, *Commonweal*, and *Christian Century* are particularly noteworthy as journals that cogently critiqued media programming, financing, and regulation. Like the other magazines discussed in this chapter, these three displayed interests and concerns idiosyncratic to their particular traditions. But they also had the courage to challenge repeatedly some of the most widely held myths about commercial broadcasting: that radio and television were necessarily good methods for winning souls to Christ; that federal regulation of broadcasting might help ensure that stations operate in the public interest; that advertiser-supported media were preferable to public-funded broadcasts; that public interests were just as important as—sometimes even more important than—tribal interests. Robert S. Fortner concludes in his study of the role of churches in public debates about radio that churches made two fundamental errors: they let the broadcast industry define the terms of the debate, and they focused too exclusively on the goal of protecting the Christian "orthodoxy" of the airwaves.[157] Although there is some evidence in these journals to support that conclusion, *Commonweal*, *America*, and *Christian Century* were major exceptions. These publications provided Americans with some perceptive examinations of the electronic media.

Did the religious press actually influence the development of broadcasting? Here Fortner might be correct. Perhaps religious press editorials and articles did not themselves directly influence the industry's operation or the government's policies, although the articles sometimes implied that the periodicals were part of the larger public conversations. Religious journals may have been little more than impotent voices exiled in the wilderness of a society narcotized by the same mass culture that the religious press often sought to expose and chastise. If the general public listened to religious opinion about the electronic media, it heard disparate voices. As the periodicals examined in this study reveal, the religious press was clearly at odds over what should be *the* Christian response to radio and television broadcasting, to the point where *Commonweal* and *America* sparred openly over the necessity of strong federal regulation of the airways. The five journals demonstrate that there was no single Christian perspective on the media at even the most basic level of whether each church should use electronic means to spread the Gospel. Most of the journals took seriously the rise of radio and television, but they relied often on conflicting rhetorics of conversion, discernment, communion, exile, and praise. Taken as a whole, the religious journals sensitively addressed most of the significant issues related to the role of broadcasting in the United States. But they also lacked a unified rhetorical voice, especially contrasted with the broadcast industry's univocal drive for audience share, profits, and regulatory freedom. American Christianity's lack of common voice is also probably a major reason for its own internal dynamism and democratic spirit in the marketplace of belief.

Each of the journals analyzed here assessed radio and later television in terms of a particular crisis that seemed paramount. *Commonweal* saw in the early twentieth century the eclipse of community, and it evaluated the media in terms of whether radio and television contributed to or mitigated that loss. *America* decried what it saw as the decline of individual freedoms and the rise of corporate power, and it looked to radio and television as means of helping to guarantee the longevity of a classical liberal marketplace of ideas in the democratic nation. These two Catholic weeklies represented opposing views of how American society should have responded to what Edward A. Purcell Jr. has called "the crisis of democratic theory."[158] *America* sought to reform the media and society by the maintenance of individual freedoms, thus harking back to an Enlightenment view of society. *Commonweal*, on the other hand, looked to community for the values that it believed should be reflected in the media and protected by federal regulation. This search for community in early-twentieth-century American life might have been particularly attractive to urban Catholics whose strong ethnic ties were sustained through neighborhood and family relations as well as through church life. It also showed that a significant segment of lay Catholic intellectuals more or less adopted the social Progressivism of the WASP establishment.

The similarities between *Catholic World* and *Christianity Today* are fascinating. Their sanguine, typically uncritical editorials about the opportunities for "electronic evangelism" prove that such thinking was not limited historically to evangelicals or even to Protestants. When coupled with the optimism found sporadically in the other tribal periodicals, this technological optimism suggests that the mythos of the electronic church is a significant feature of Christian-American experience.[159] Certainly evangelicals have been the most steadfast believers in the spiritual efficacy of religious broadcasting, but they have not been alone in espousing a Pollyannaish faith in technology. Belief that the media would usher in a more harmonious City upon a Hill had its political and economic as well as its religious versions.[160] The adapting of marketing principles to the proclamation of the Gospel makes for a Horatio Alger story of evangelistic success.[161] As reflected in these two journals, the rhetoric of conversion was a symbolic solution for the crisis of religious unbelief and the breakdown of community in the nation.

Christian Century's preoccupation with ecumenical broadcasting at least partly reflects the journal's early relationship with the Disciples of Christ, which was itself concerned about the sectarian tide in American Protestantism and which tried to restore American Christianity to its early forms of belief and practice, without humanly devised doctrines and dogma. The fact that this preoccupation continued through the rise of television, however, is difficult to explain. Perhaps the sectarian issue gradually became a loosely defined rationale for the journal's growing criticism of fundamentalists and other evangelicals. Maybe *Christian Century*'s reasonable assertion that sectarian broadcasting presents a sorely divided image of Christianity to the nation became a basis for the arguable claim that evangelicals were the worst offenders of ecumenism. One need only cite the numerous Catholic programs that drew little or no comment from the journal. In any case *Christian Century* saw in religious broadcasting the same trends and threats that it was witnessing in American religious life as a whole, and it responded with pleas for cooperation and tolerance. For *Christian Century*, the crisis at hand in America was primarily a lack of religious tolerance and a failure of Protestants to present a unified view of the faith to the wider society. The hope that this reunification of Christianity might ever be possible reflects deeply American sentiments about the ability of disparate groups and individuals to talk through their differences and work toward a shared rhetoric of communion.

These religious publications established important agendas for Americans to use to examine the nation's broadcast media. In fact, the concerns of these periodicals are still the issues that face the American public and that are being addressed once again with the funding, operation, and regulation of the new communication technologies. Clearly Americans have not solved institutionally the major concerns of these journals: how to create a system of broadcasting that will enhance community life, enliven nonbigoted public discussion, maintain cultural diversity, unify disparate but closely aligned groups, and nurture a respect for religion as a crucial part of what makes American society deeply democratic.

4

Converting to Consumerism:
Evangelical Radio Embraces the Market

◩ ◩ ◩

When Everett C. Parker conducted the first major study of religious radio broadcasting in America, he had no idea what he would discover.[1] It was 1941, and World War II was drawing the nation's attention to Europe as the commercial radio networks already garnered large national audiences. Parker sent questionnaires to the management of all commercial radio stations in Chicago, hoping to gain a snapshot of their religious programming, including how much of it they aired, which types of religious programming seemed to hold listeners' interests, and how station management funded such broadcasts. Parker also sent questionnaires to the sponsors of each religious broadcast.

The results of Parker's research showed conclusively that Chicagoans liked religious radio broadcasts. Commercial stations aired seventy-seven different religious programs, from the *National Catholic Hour* to *Religion in the News*, the *Old-Fashioned Revival Hour* (Rev. Charles E. Fuller), *Call to Youth*, and the *Hebrew Christian Hour*. Approximately 3 percent of all commercial radio time in the city was dedicated to religious broadcasts, primarily on Sundays. The two most frequently aired types of broadcasts were sermon or talk shows (fifty-seven programs) and church services (thirteen

programs). Most were Protestant broadcasts, especially what Parker
dubbed "fundamentalist" programs. Moreover, only two of the seventy-
seven programs were aired with the endorsements of a denomination. Un-
aware of the eventual commercialization of religious radio in America,
Parker began his report with a paragraph that in retrospect was prophetic,
"Within the last ten years radio has become a powerful force in the life of
the people of America. It has affected every phase of that life, and religion
is no exception. Religious programs have emerged upon the air without
any concerted plan on the part of the great Christian bodies of the nation
and today are competing with soap, cigarettes, cosmetics, gasoline, food
products, symphony concerts, world-views—and even with churches—for
the attention of and, in many instances, for money contributions from the
listening public."[2]

Broadcasting offered religious tribes a means of building their own local
and national speech communities in the expanding industrial nation. But
religious broadcasting also challenged the government to clarify whether
any of the nation's limited electromagnetic spectrum, presumably a public
resource, should be dedicated to tribal interests. In the United States regulatory agencies tried to articulate broadcast policies that would protect the
"public interest, convenience and necessity," as both the Federal Radio Act
of 1927 and the Communications Act of 1934 put it.[3] Along the way, however, the regulatory agencies both hindered and facilitated the broadcasting
of different Christian tribes. Emphasizing the importance of the free market even for a regulated medium, American broadcasters and regulators in-
advertently tipped the scale in favor of those religious groups that could
function most effectively in a market system—the evangelicals. The history
of American radio is a fascinating case study in both the rhetoric of governmental regulation of religious broadcasting and the rhetoric of the various religious tribes that used radio to gain a public voice in the expanding
industrial nation. Although evangelicals legitimized tribal use of radio with
a rhetoric of conversion that emphasized preaching the Good News, over
time evangelical radio began converting its tribes to consumerism.

The first section of this chapter reviews the explosive growth of early religious radio as a local, grassroots phenomenon across the country. Evangelicals and various fringe religious groups championed the new medium,
first as an evangelistic tool for converting the nation to their own beliefs
and second as a means of elevating their social status in a national culture
that favored mainline Protestantism. Feeling increasingly exiled in secular
society, evangelicals looked to radio as a means of legitimizing their beliefs

and creating a powerful public voice. Before the government seriously began to regulate the new medium, evangelicals had already established a significant presence in local radio markets across the nation. Radio helped these tribes to forge unified identities across geographic space in the midst of rapid urbanization and industrialization that otherwise challenged and attenuated the role of traditional religious institutions in society.

The second section describes how evangelicals tried to develop program formats in a market system. Since there was not yet any public consensus about regulation of the new medium, the U.S. Congress granted the authority to regulators to determine the public interest; these regulators defined the "public interest" in order to give the American people a representative voice in regulation. The resulting licensing requirements, which favored commercial over religious "propaganda," were a blessing in disguise for evangelical broadcasters. Forced to vacate their broadcast frequencies and to negotiate time on commercial stations, evangelicals learned how to create competitive programs in a market system dominated by commercial licensees. Evangelicals' rhetorics of conversion and community led them to work vigorously to secure airtime and build sizeable audiences in the growing system of commercial broadcasting.

The next part of the chapter considers the impact of the ensuing commercial broadcasting policies on religious programming. Once commercial broadcasters had secured the new medium as an advertising-supported system, mainline Protestant and Roman Catholic groups collaborated to ensure that they would receive from networks and stations some free, or sustaining, broadcast time. Mainline religious groups promised to use their airtime to represent only "broad truths," not to express the beliefs of Christian sects or other fringe religious tribes. Mainline groups' attempts to restrict evangelicals' access to free airtime, like the earlier federal regulations that prohibited religious groups' ownership of radio stations, created barriers to entry that forced evangelicals to learn how to create and fund broadcasts in a commercial market system. By equating "public interest" with commercial broadcasting, federal regulations unintentionally favored evangelical broadcasters, whose strong rhetoric of conversion was most compatible with the conversionary motif in commercialism. Regulation backfired.

The fourth section looks at the struggle between mainline and evangelical broadcasters over control of the time available for religious programs on radio networks. Since networks were not licensed and therefore, unlike stations, were not directly accountable to broadcast regulators, networks were free to establish broadcast policies that favored particular programming. Radio networks generally sided with the government position that sectarian broadcasts were not as fully in the public interest as more ecumenical ones. Nevertheless, the networks increasingly realized along with radio stations that evangelicals represented the best religious source of program time revenues. The more sectarian programs seemed to have a knack for building audiences and raising funds to pay their broadcast time bills.

Finally, the chapter explores the incredible growth of evangelical radio in the television era. In sheer numbers the growth of evangelical radio has been impressive. Over 1,000 evangelical stations and a few networks helped these tribes to create a small, powerful subculture. Relying on a rhetoric of conversion, religious tribes built an amazing system of local and national broadcasting. But the system served only a small percentage of even evangelicals. In spite of its rhetoric of conversion, Christian radio served primarily the interests of a subgroup within the evangelical tribe. As a "place" for gaining a shared sense of evangelical identity, these radio programs implicitly embraced a rhetoric of tribal communion. Striving for popularity within the evangelical ranks and funded increasingly by commercial interests, however, religious radio both isolated the tribe from mainstream media and increasingly converted the tribe to American consumerism. Evangelicals' broadcasting in the long run may have actually ushered the tribe into religiously oriented consumer lifestyles. As Parker discovered already in 1941, religious radio was competing not with other religious tribes as much as with "soaps, cigarettes [and] cosmetics."[4] In short, evangelical radio won a somewhat Pyrrhic victory in the commercial broadcast marketplace, effectively ushering its own tribe into exile under the dominant power of consumerism.[5]

The Rise of Religious Radio

The rise of religious radio is an important but largely unexamined chapter in the history of American broadcasting. In the early 1920s Christian organizations began using radio to preach the Gospel to the nation. Even some Roman Catholics relied upon a rhetoric of conversion to justify their broadcast endeavors. "Behold," wrote *Catholic World* in 1922, "now is the acceptable time for the Catholic Church to rise to this great and unique occasion, before the privilege is entirely preempted by those outside the Faith, and not allow the wireless telephone, like the classics of the English language, to be used as the medium of heresy." The magazine called upon the church to *"erect a powerful central wireless telephone transmitting station . . .* [to] reach untold millions at the very poles of the world." This transmitter, the journal continued, would put the world "in touch with Christ's truth instantaneously and simultaneously since the wireless telephone leaps over all barriers of time and space."[6] Since the AM radio spectrum was largely unregulated, religious groups could easily launch their own broadcast ministries.

Evangelicals, in particular, saw radio as a golden opportunity to recruit members to the faith. Like later televangelism, early radio preaching circumvented local churches, delivering a group's message directly to the people. As R. Laurence Moore puts it, radio was these Protestants' "dream medium." Radio represented "the perfect blend of the public and the private. The notion of a public church service carried into the home was wonderfully compatible with ideals of domesticity they had championed."[7] Religious radio was a kind of public populism, a means of mass-mediating the presentation of religion with commonsense rhetoric and easy-to-apply examples and illustrations. Radio could potentially circumvent liberal church pastors and denominational structures by delivering the evangelical gospel to every living human being.[8] Radio's "marriage of science and religion," predicted a church-growth consultant, would likely lead to "a new quickening of the spiritual life of America."[9] A Rhode Island radio preacher criticized the church for being "content with her oxcart methods" and proclaimed that it was time to "step on the gas."[10] Evangelical communication in early America, says Nathan O. Hatch, reflected the belief that "the principal mediator of God's voice has not been state, church, council, confession, ethnic group, university, college, or seminary [but] . . . the people."[11] Radio preachers eventually became some of the most popular broadcast personalities in the country, building strong constituencies largely independent of established churches and denominations. Evangelicals took the lead, using the new medium to publicize their movement and raise financial support for new parachurch organizations, including Bible institutes and colleges, summer Bible conferences, domestic and foreign missions, and publishing houses.[12]

Particularly important for the development of evangelical radio were three related cultural developments. First, the nation's relatively weak Protestant traditions left "revivalism an almost open field for determining the distinctive characteristics of American religious life."[13] Radio appeared to be a great conversionary medium that, like the sawdust trail and the camp meeting revival, could take religion directly to the people. Second, feeling increasingly like "outcasts from respectable religious life," some evangelicals turned to radio not only to spread their religious truths but also to battle media stereotypes of their faith and elevate their social status.[14] Third, evangelical tribes often resented the immorality and seemingly antireligious tenor of mainstream popular culture. Radio gave them a soapbox to discern publicly the apostate spirits behind American culture.

Evangelicals' concerns about secular popular culture were particularly important. As movies, vaudeville, comic books, and radio gained steam in the emerging industrial nation, many conservative Protestants felt both outraged and beleaguered. Contrasted with the popular commercial media, religion "became of marginal value, cultivated by marginal people on marginal time."[15] In 1937, for instance, the nationally broadcast *Edgar Bergen-Charlie McCarthy Show* aired a skit that essentially reinterpreted the biblical account of the Fall from grace. Eve, played by sex-symbol Mae West, used "love groans and promiscuity" to cajole Adam to take her "outta this dismal dump and give me a chance to develop my personality." Eve tricked Adam into eating the forbidden fruit and then declared that she is "the first woman to have her own way, and the snake'll take the rap for it." Eve finally seduced Adam with what Eve called "the original kiss."[16] Another media event that angered evangelicals was news coverage of the Scopes trial. The newsworthy drama pitted creationists against evolutionists, symbolizing a new social world in which conservative Protestants would have to take a provocative, perhaps even militaristic public stance against heresy and satirical criticism of their faith.[17] Many Protestants also criticized newer forms of public entertainment, from vaudeville to film.[18] In short, conservative Protestants wanted a say in the national conversations about faith and morality, and radio seemed to give them such a public voice.

Compared with mainline religious rhetoric, evangelical rhetoric was remarkably optimistic about the power of radio. By contrast, the liberal rector of Calvary Church, which sponsored the legendary first religious broadcast on KDKA in Pittsburgh during January 1921, later expressed publicly his misgivings about religious radio.[19] He compared the temptation to air religious programs with King Jeroboam's desire to lord it over the early nation of Israel by making sacred calves for the people to worship.[20] Mainline Protestants, perhaps more closely aligned with the professional and managerial class rising to power in urban America, decried the undignified and unprofessional character of many religious broadcasts.[21] Many programs were "cheap and tawdry and tend to bring Protestant radio into disrepute," wrote one mainline observer.[22] As religious insiders in American life, mainline Protestants preferred using free broadcast time instead of soliciting viewer contributions to pay for programs. Evangelicals were critical of mainstream radio programming, but as outsiders to mainstream religious culture they wanted a chance to use radio, even if they had to pay for the opportunity.[23] Their rhetoric of conversion, bolstered by premillennial theology, led evangelicals to endorse radio as a God-given means of evangelizing the unsaved souls.[24]

From its beginning local religious broadcasting was dominated by various religious minorities, especially evangelicals, who hoped that radio would amplify their religious presence and increase their cultural power in the expanding industrial society. Among evangelical broadcasters in the mid-1920s were the Echo Park Evangelistic Association, the Bible Institute of Los Angeles, and the Moody Bible Institute of Chicago—all supported by the contributions of listeners and patrons.[25] Baptists operated the largest number of stations, including church-run stations in Shreveport, Worcester, Rochester, New Orleans, Columbus, and New York City. Probably typical of the early evangelicals on the air was the Calvary Baptist Church, one of the oldest Baptist congregations in New York City. In 1922 the church appropriated $1,000 for installing a transmitter to broadcast sermons and music. Within five months listeners heard WQAQ's 250-watt signal under good conditions from Maine to Georgia. Pastor John Roach Straton explained the station's purpose: "I shall try to continue to do my part . . . tearing down the strongholds of Satan, and I hope that our radio system will prove so efficient that when I twist the Devil's tail in New York, his squawk will be heard across the continent."[26]

The "Bazaar" Rhetoric of Public Interest

As evangelicals chased the devil on the airways, the broadcast radio spectrum in the United States began sounding increasingly like an electronic Babel. As with CB radio in the 1970s[27] and the World Wide Web in the 1990s, radio in the 1920s was a free-for-all of conflicting ideas as well as competing electromagnetic signals. If this was electronic democracy, it sounded more like anarchy. Grassroots religious programming was only one part of the racket; practically anyone who wanted to get on the air could do so. Commercial broadcasters, dependent upon advertising revenue, were having trouble being heard above the cacophony of interfering signals. For radio hobbyists, the whole mess was exciting and promising— they never knew what signals they could receive on a given day. For the inchoate broadcasting industry, however, the chaos was intolerable. The federal government, they believed, should bring industrial order to the electronic Babel. Commercial broadcasters got what they wanted, much to the anger and disillusionment of most of the nation's many religious broadcasters.

The growth of religious stations was quickly curtailed in the late 1920s by new federal regulations designed to minimize signal interference and to establish public standards for issuing and renewing licenses. The rapid entry of evangelicals into station ownership was stalled in 1927 by the newly formed Federal Radio Commission (FRC). In one year the number of stations operated by churches and other religious organizations decreased from about seventy to fifty.[28] Only eleven noncommercial religious stations remained on the air fifteen years later.[29] Developing a new policy of "public interest," which defined religious broadcasts as "propaganda," the FRC was able to remove most religious stations from the airways.

Prior to the FRC's crackdown on religious ownership of stations, the Department of Commerce treated broadcast licenses of commercial and noncommercial stations equally under the Radio Act of 1912, which had made no distinction on the basis of public interest between the two types of broadcasting. Also, the case in 1926 of *United States v. Zenith Radio Corporation* ruled that the Department of Commerce had no power to require stations to broadcast on assigned frequencies or to limit their hours of operation.[30] The Department of Commerce was little more than a powerless license registration bureau that merely granted licenses without any authority to determine which applicants should be awarded licenses and which ones should not.[31] The agency could not make any distinctions among licensees—religious or secular.

Congress responded to this growing broadcast anarchy with the Federal Radio Act of 1927, which first gave the FRC the authority to assign frequencies, establish hours of operation, and classify radio stations according to the "public interest, convenience and necessity."[32] That phrase—the "public interest, convenience and necessity"—became the rhetorical core of American broadcast regulation for the next seventy years. As a rhetorical construct, it captured both unity and diversity; it suggested that there was such a thing as a public, yet it also opened the way for stations and regulators to define this public interest in terms of a host of categories or subjects that broadcasters would be required to address in their programming. The concept seemed to harmonize the conflicting interests of various tribes in the American cultural landscape while simultaneously giving the regulating agency the authority to determine which types of broadcasting met the public interest. In effect, the FRC got to act *for* the public, even *as* the public, by dictating the criteria by which vendors would be allowed to display their wares on the airways, at the broadcast bazaar.

By the fall of 1928 the FRC had reassigned almost all religious and educational stations to frequencies that these broadcasters would have to share with other stations.[33] While the explicitly commercial broadcasters gained large tables at the broadcast bazaar, other broadcasters found themselves sharing tiny tables with other small-market vendors. The FRC "took the stand that *special interests* had no proper claim to *general* broadcast facilities" (emphasis added).[34] The FRC would try to serve all listeners rather than a few broadcasters. As much as possible, stations should serve the "entire listening public within the listening area of the station."[35] Although "public interest" was yet to be defined, clearly it was not the same as a "special interest." Within a few years most noncommercial stations were squeezed off the air along with dozens of other broadcasters that lacked the equipment and funding necessary to become major commercial broadcasters.[36] Meanwhile some key members of the FRC left government service for more lucrative and secure opportunities in the growing commercial radio industry.[37] The business of broadcasting was about to take off as a grand, national bazaar of corporate sellers who more or less owned their own booths even though the bazaar used public space, the limited electromagnetic spectrum. For all practical purposes, the FRC had created a vibrant market for for-profit broadcasting, eliminating most religious and educational radio in the process.

In 1929 the FRC justified its treatment of religious broadcasters by officially classifying them as "propaganda stations." According to a principle of "nondiscrimination," the FRC argued that stations would be favored in the allocation of limited broadcast frequencies if they offered a "well-rounded program [in order] to best serve the public. In such a scheme there is no room for the operation of broadcasting stations exclusively by or in the private interests of individuals or groups. . . . As a general rule particular doctrines, creeds and beliefs must find their way into the market of ideas by the existing public-service stations."[38] The burden of deciding which religious groups were granted access to the airways was the province of commercial stations, not the government. These commercial operators could rent space at the public bazaars that they, in effect, owned. After all, the FRC argued, there is only so much space at the market. The FRC promoted "well-rounded" programming because "there is no room in the broadcast band for every school of thought, religious, political, social, and economic, each to have its separate broadcasting station, its mouthpiece in the other."[39] By placing "religion" first in its list of "private interests," the FRC signaled its intention to devalue all forms of "sectarian" broadcasting in the regulatory process.

Clearly the FRC had reasons to believe that broadcasting would never be able to serve all special interests equally and that some interests should be treated unequally. The FRC's attitude toward religious stations likely was influenced by the controversial broadcasts of "Judge" Joseph F. Rutherford and Rev. Robert "Bob" Shuler. Rutherford, leader of the Jehovah's Witnesses, openly preached anti-Catholic and antigovernment sermons.[40] Beginning in 1924 he used the church's Brooklyn station to broadcast his views to the public.[41] "The Lord has, just at the right time brought radio into action, which permits the people to remain in their homes and listen to a proclamation of the truth, regardless of the opposition of the clergy," wrote Rutherford.[42] Meanwhile fundamentalist Shuler was denied a license renewal in 1931 after he had repeatedly attacked public officials and other religions.[43] In both of these highly visible cases the FRC faced the difficult issue of how to deal with a contentious religious broadcaster who was using the public airways to attack other faiths. The "sectarian" nature of much religious broadcasting, as many observers called it, was a troubling issue, but public attacks on other religions no doubt bothered the FRC even more. The FRC had to figure out a means of solving at least the latter issue in a way that seemed to be equally heavy-handed with respect to all faith groups in America. The regulators concluded that there would be no tribal religious broadcasting in America unless commercial broadcasters themselves were willing to take the grief and potentially lose their audiences by airing sectarian programs. The market, rather than the regulators, would have to decide the fate of propaganda broadcasting.

According to FRC policies, no new licenses were to be issued to religious groups, and existing "propaganda" licensees were to be reassigned to "part time or inferior channels."[44] Few religious stations had the legal or technical assistance necessary to challenge the FRC.[45] Evangelical broadcasters, in particular, discovered that their tribal broadcasts were little more than propaganda in the eyes of the FRC; these broadcasters had little recourse other than to accept the FRC's decision to revoke their licenses or to reallocate them to a frequency that they would have to share with other broadcasters. In effect, the FRC deemed that religious broadcasts in themselves were not diverse enough to meet the "public interest, convenience and necessity"—unless commercial broadcasters aired religious programs and counted them as credit toward the FRC's "public interest" requirement. As Stewart M. Hoover and Douglas K. Wagner conclude, broadcasters "had an important incentive to give account of religion as part of [their] overall service obligations, and a further incentive . . . to ensure that what religion was aired was of a variety that involved broad truths and was non-controversial."[46] Commercial broadcasters were now poised to exploit the new medium with considerable capital and expertise, but they still had to show the FRC that they broadcast a wide enough range of programming to meet the public interest. Noncontroversial religious broadcasts could help them do so.

One of the few evangelical broadcasters with the resources, expertise, and tenacity to challenge the FRC was the Moody Bible Institute in Chicago. Moody's WMBI remained on the air only because of the remarkable efforts of Henry Coleman Crowell, who served as assistant to the president of the institute. In addition to making ten trips by rail to Washington, D.C. to plead the case of WMBI, Crowell kept Moody's administration apprised of the legal status of the license in his forty-page reports to the organization's board of trustees.[47] Crowell's advice repeatedly paid off as Moody administrators fought the FRC's plan to "consolidate" WMBI on the frequency of Chicago's WBBM—a plan that would have reduced WMBI to limited broadcast time on the other station. Eventually WMBI retained its license because of the well-argued cases it made in hearings before the FRC. The station held that it did not broadcast to a small, sectarian audience but rather that it served many different Christian churches and citywide organizations. By 1930 the station was receiving over 20,000 letters annually from listeners.[48] Some of the programming was evangelistic, but most of it was more broadly educational and inspirational. WMBI produced the *Young People's Hour*, a children's gospel variety program, piano and orchestra broadcasts, and many foreign-language shows for Chicago's immigrant communities. Reflecting the increasingly transdenominational character of American evangelicalism, WMBI also broadcast services from different conservative churches in the Chicago area.[49] By 1942 WMBI was syndicating programs to 187 different stations.[50] WMBI's fairly broad-based religious fare, plus its instructional goals as a radio voice of a Bible institute, provided one of the best cases for challenging the FRC's view of religious broadcasting as "private interest" radio.

Another one of the handful of religious survivors of the FRC's move to eliminate propaganda programming was KFUO in St. Louis. The evangelical Lutheran Church—Missouri Synod started the station on the campus of Concordia Theological Seminary in late 1924.[51] Using a rhetoric of tribal communion, Pastor Walter Maier appealed to the conservative denomination to establish the station on the grounds that it would "assist preventing our people from hearing other sermons and addresses which might injure their spiritual growth."[52] Like many other evangelicals, Maier wished to broadcast the "pure gospel" to the nation, but he also recognized that intratribal broadcasting was a potentially powerful means of building tribal loyalty, denominational identity, and theological cohesiveness. Aided by the city's relatively large Lutheran population, as well as by generous newspaper coverage of the station's activities, KFUO created within six months a mailing list of 4,500 supporters.[53] In January 1926 alone more than 3,000 listeners wrote to the station. One pastor said, "KFUO has put our Church on the map. To me it is the greatest and most effective missionary and publicity movement ever set on foot in the history of American Lutheranism."[54]

Like WMBI, KFUO successfully cultivated a fairly broad audience of evangelical listeners with a menu of evangelistic, prophetic, and entertaining programming. The station's programming extended well beyond Lutheran church services to an evening program called *Views on the News* in which Maier offered Christian critiques of world movements and national events.[55] Maier's preaching style was highly evangelical, stressing the inerrancy of Scripture and attacking the follies and sins of "modern man," including evolution and divorce.[56] But his style was also irenic and cultured—not the bombastic approach taken by some evangelical radio preachers. During the first few years of broadcasting KFUO publicized the station's program schedule in the *Lutheran Witness* magazine, reflecting the station's denominational ties. But by 1926 the station's success, as well as its broadening evangelical constituency, warranted its own magazine, *Gospel Voice*. "On radio one could not speak only to one's congregation of fellow Lutherans," says historian Alan Graebner.[57] KFUO's case echoed that of WMBI: it positioned itself not as a "propaganda" station for "private interests" but rather as a public expression of many people's religious convictions.

In the American West the controversial and charismatic Aimee Semple McPherson challenged the FRC with her own station, KFSG.[58] The station's unstable signal elicited complaints from some listeners and even resulted in a threatening telegram from Secretary of Commerce Herbert Hoover.[59] But in spite of the technical problems, the station's programming was enormously popular in southern California. One entertainment magazine claimed that the station had the second-largest listening audience in Los Angeles and that McPherson was "pastor" of the largest "radio church" in the world. Hinting at the growing commercialization of market-driven Christian radio, McPherson boasted that KFSG was the "first missionary station, completely owned, maintained, and operated by its audience."[60] Hyperbole aside, her creative programming likely appealed to many radio listeners. Among the shows were dramatic series such as *Jim Trask—Lone Evangelist* and *Half-way House*, various live and recorded music programs, and an amateur talent show.[61] Thompson Eade, a former vaudeville performer, created many of the programs.[62] McPherson knew how to entertain a wide, cross-denominational audience.

The popularity of stations such as WMBI, KFUO, and KFSG, as well as their success at challenging the FRC's rhetoric, attested to the diversity within American evangelicalism as well as to the impact of American popular culture on conservative Protestantism. Their efforts to maintain their licenses illuminate the tension between private and public interests, between commercial and noncommercial views of media regulation, between religion and government, and between the centrifugal growth of specialized media and the centripetal expansion of national media in a market economy. Defining "the public" and especially "public interest" in America has been a difficult process frequently born out of pragmatic solutions to larger social issues. Robert E. Park argued during the early years of radio that communication makes possible "consensus and understanding among the individual components of a social group which eventually give it and then them the character not merely of society but of a cultural unit."[63] FRC regulations were not only maps of the public interest but also maps for creating a particular kind of public in society. The regulators sought to create regulatory rhetoric that would presumably protect the broader interests of national unity over the specialized interests of tribal cohesiveness.

Marketing Religion on the Radio

The FRC's stricter policies about religious stations encouraged evangelicals to create programs that could compete for audiences in a largely commercial broadcasting system. Most religious stations could not survive license challenges, but religious broadcasters could get on the air anyway either by purchasing airtime from commercial stations or in some cases securing free airtime from stations that would use the religious broadcasts to demonstrate to regulators a diversity of fare. Both the FRC and the Federal Communications Commission (FCC), which replaced the FRC in 1934, included religious programming as an option in the lists of public-service requirements that commercial broadcasters had to fulfill.[64] Although the federal agencies frowned upon distinctly religious stations, they required commercial radio stations to demonstrate that they served the public with some religious programming. Radio stations could meet this requirement in many different ways, by paid and nonpaid (sustaining) religious programming and by broadcasting anything from church services to religious discussions. Although some stations met these requirements by providing sustaining time for religious programming, most commercial stations simply sold airtime to evangelicals.[65] As a result, evangelicals began learning how to produce programming that would attract audiences and garner financial support. The FRC had unwittingly done religious propagandists an enormous favor by forcing them to master the market system.

Many stations sold time to religious groups, opening up a new kind of religious broadcasting market that required religious tribes to produce audience-generating programs. The tribes had to garner enough listeners and solicit adequate contributions to pay for the program time. Prior to the formation of the FRC, about 4 percent of the programming on nine major-market stations was church services and sacred music, although such meager data were not necessarily representative of radio across the country.[66] Nearly all the largest stations scheduled "precious time for religious messages or music."[67] Already in 1927, half of the stations on the air included religious programming in their schedules.[68] AT&T's commercial station, WEAF, received more requests from religious groups for airtime than it could honor.[69] Although commercial broadcasters were not willing to turn their stations into purely religious media, they did provide some religious broadcasters with airtime partly as a means of meeting the regulatory requirements for diverse fare and partly as an additional revenue stream.

In spite of, or perhaps because of, FRC regulations, by 1932 more than 8 percent of all radio programming in the nation was religious.[70] By restricting religious station ownership, the FRC had closed some markets for religious programming. But by requiring commercial stations to broadcast religious fare, the FRC's policies were now opening up new local and regional markets for paid as well as sustaining religious broadcasting. Nearly all of the new paid programming was evangelical. The fundamentalist

Sunday School Times, with a circulation in 1931 of about 100,000, regularly listed in its reader-contributed "Radio Directory" over 400 evangelical programs across the nation.[71] At least some of this evangelical fare was very popular with radio listeners. A poll conducted by the *Kansas City Star* the same year determined that a local evangelical broadcast was the city's most popular radio program, more popular even than the national *Amos 'n' Andy* situation comedy.[72] Evangelical propaganda apparently appealed to many listeners in the competitive marketplace.

Among the most active radio evangelists of the 1930s was Chicago's Paul Rader. Rader began his broadcasting career with free time provided by the mayor on the municipal station. Within five years Rader was on all of the major Chicago stations, and he briefly secured a one-hour morning broadcast on the CBS network called the *Breakfast Brigade*. Meanwhile the indefatigable Rader persuaded another station to permit him to use its idle transmitters for fourteen hours every Sunday to broadcast *The March of Ages*, a combination of hymns, songs, and Bible-story narration improvised around a weekly theme.[73] Like other savvy evangelical broadcasters, Rader had learned to work the commercial broadcasting system to his ministry's advantage. For him, the commercial radio market was an opportunity to reach a broad audience, thereby expanding his prominence as a national religious celebrity. He discovered how to produce an attractive show that would garner a fairly heterogeneous audience from across the more conservative churches and denominations.

As the U.S. economy improved after the Great Depression, religious groups found it increasingly difficult to secure free airtime. In 1932 three-fourths of all religious programs were broadcast free.[74] Five years later only three-fifths of them were aired on a sustaining basis.[75] Clear-channel stations generally carried more religious broadcasts than other stations, but this may have been because of their longer broadcast hours or greater commercial profitability.[76] Swamped by requests for sustaining airtime from numerous religious groups, some stations took the easiest and most profitable route of limiting religious broadcasts to paid programming.[77] Network affiliate stations sometimes replaced network programs with paid evangelical broadcasts, but they probably evaluated such religious broadcasters carefully before giving them access.[78] CBS discontinued selling airtime in the years after the Depression because of its fear that paid religious broadcasting "would develop into a racket, because it was perfectly clear that if you did them effectively you took in a lot of money."[79] By the late 1940s radio stations derived "a good proportion of their income from the sale of airtime to religious groups."[80] Nine percent of all paid broadcast time on "low-power" stations was for religious programs, more than for any other type of sponsor except "groceries."[81] Paid evangelical radio was becoming a significant part of the commercial broadcasting business.

Evangelicals, who had long been developing successful paid programming, were in the best position to take advantage of openings for paid programs. Fundamentalists accounted for 246 of the 290 weekly "quarter hours" of religious programming aired in Chicago already in 1932.[82] Nationally, Baptists (presumably the more conservative ones) were by far the largest religious broadcasters in 1937, accounting for about a fourth of the total time devoted to religious programs in the county. The Gospel Tabernacle churches, which included a variety of independent fundamentalist congregations, were the next largest category of religious broadcasters. Even the Holiness and Pentecostal churches had more broadcast time than mainline Presbyterians and Lutherans.[83] Of the seventy-seven different religious broadcasts aired in Chicago every week on commercial stations during 1946, twenty-five were sponsored by fundamentalist churches and only three by liberal Protestants. The rest were Roman Catholic, Jewish, Christian Science, and unclassified Protestant.[84] *Christian Life*'s incomplete "Radio Log of Evangelical Broadcasts" in 1948 included over 1,600 programs in the United States.[85] Evangelicals apparently had the motivation and could raise the contributions necessary to support paid religious radio broadcasts.

The growth of local evangelical radio broadcasting suggests considerable financial support from the cross-denominational evangelical community in America. Baptist and Gospel Tabernacle broadcasters, for example, purchased about two-thirds of all of their airtime, while Lutherans and Presbyterians were charged for only about one-third of their program time.[86] In fact, the more removed a religious group was from mainline Protestantism, with the exception of the Roman Catholics, the more likely that it had to purchase airtime for religious broadcasts. Jehovah's Witnesses purchased nearly all of their programming.[87] When the FRC designated religious stations as propaganda broadcasters, the regulatory agency probably had no idea that evangelicals, in particular, would eventually garner respectable audiences on commercial stations. Evangelicals' strong rhetoric of conversion motivated them to master the business of commercial broadcasting.

Even into the early 1940s, when the radio networks and the Federal Council of Churches were strongly opposed to selling time for religious broadcasts, about a fourth of the broadcasts were commercial because of the "demand of militant ministers for time on the air."[88] In Los Angeles alone there were over forty religious programs broadcast daily, and one station had a waiting list of 200 evangelists desiring to purchase program time. Some of the stations in that city derived more than half of their revenues from paid religious broadcasts.[89] The smaller the station, the more likely it charged for religious broadcast time.[90] Religious broadcasting had become a significant source of revenue for many commercial stations, reflecting the existence of viable markets for radio religion. In 1945 men preferred religious broadcasts to all types of daytime programming except news; two years later women indicated that they preferred religious broadcasts to all daytime fare except news and homemaking programs.[91] World War II news reports and the scarcity of musical programming during this period partly explain these preferences. Nevertheless, 34 percent of U.S. adults liked to listen to daytime religious broadcasts, more than liked to listen to quiz shows, dance and popular music shows, talk shows, semiclassical and classical music, homemaking programs, hillbilly and western music, and farm shows.[92] Rural Americans wanted religious broadcasts more than any other programming.[93] A survey of thirty-eight counties in Kentucky and southern Indiana found that residents preferred religious programs to everything except hillbilly music.[94] The more sectarian religious broadcasters seemed to have garnered the largest audiences. By the 1940s religious broadcasting had become one of the more commercially viable and certainly one of the most public expressions of religion in American life. If not officially in the public interest, evangelical broadcasting was certainly part of the commercial interests of the stations that aired the broadcasts. It had found its place at the radio bazaar.

The Struggle over Network Broadcasting

One manual for early religious radio wisely explained how religious broadcasters could stay on the good side of stations and networks: "Don't alarm listeners with long lists of what is wrong with the world. Don't speak dogmatically. Remember it's normality we're striving for."[95] The idea of seeking "normality" captures the spirit of the broadcast regulators, stations, and networks during the 1930s and 1940s. But normality, of course, is somewhat in the eyes of the beholder. Like the concept of public opinion, the idea of normality begged for self-interested definitions—for statistical averages or popularity contests. In station and network policies normality connoted the "broad truths" shared by all of the major Protestant groups and

the Roman Catholic Church. In spite of the large market for popular evangelical broadcasts, the FCC could not officially sanction the sentiments of
tribal evangelicalism. Nor could the tribes get too involved in the bitter passions of governmental regulation. As Alexis de Tocqueville said in the
1830s, "As long as a religion is supported only by sentiments that are the
consolation of all miseries, it can attract the hearts of the human race to it.
Mixed with the bitter passions of this world, it is sometimes constrained to
defend allies given it by interest rather than love."[96]

The growing prominence of religious radio in America in the 1930s and
1940s tested the spirit as well as the letter of federal broadcast regulations.
How could broadcasters operate in the general public interest by programming particular religious interests? Perhaps America faced two irreconcilable goals—to allow the stations to broadcast religious programs while
expecting such programming to reflect the "normal" beliefs of mainstream
faith. Maybe the radio market itself would tend to favor particular traditions while disenfranchising others. Perhaps only those tribes strongly motivated by rhetorics of conversion would likely succeed in a market system.
When Tocqueville investigated the enormous popularity of newspapers in
early America, he discovered a built-in check to the power of any particular paper. The only way "to neutralize the effect of public journals," he
wrote, "is to multiply them indefinitely."[97] But radio was not like the press.
A journal could be launched rather inexpensively by nearly anyone,
whereas radio stations used the limited electromagnetic spectrum and were
increasingly costly to maintain and manage. Recognizing this fundamental
distinction between the abundance of paper and the relative scarcity of the
electromagnetic spectrum, the regulators tried to develop a rhetoric of public interest that distinguished between private and public interests, on the
one hand, and between particular and general interests, on the other. In
theory, general-interest radio programming would serve the greatest number of individuals while minimizing any offense that might be caused by
private, sectarian perspectives. But the realities of everyday life rarely
match theoretical definitions, especially when public-policy rhetoric conflicts with the realities of the market.

This tension between public and private interests in the case of religious
radio grew even more pronounced as evangelicals became national broadcasters. As long as religious radio remained only a local or regional phenomenon, it could not meet the growing needs of the evangelical
movement and some denominations for national leadership and cohesion.
The evangelical press and national revival circuits had already established

authors and evangelists as influential leaders and convinced the tribes of the importance of national media. Moreover, mainline Protestant and Roman Catholic periodicals had helped to build national cohesiveness and symbolic leaders. But a personal voice on the radio was a new means of establishing a national symbol of authority.

Radio seemed to offer American religious groups a more powerful means of creating strong national identities and charismatic leadership. As *Radio Stars* magazine wrote, "Whatever your beliefs or your creed may be you can hear the greatest of its leaders. Men whose greatness have [*sic*] made them world names in the realm of religion now come to your home, as John the Baptist once came to the doors of people who lived in that earlier age."[98] Both mainline and evangelical groups desired that kind of public presence and symbolic authority in the developing national medium of radio. Both wanted a means of delivering their creed to the nation, not just to communities. Mainline groups generally had the advantages of close relationships with management in radio stations and networks and a seemingly more generic and less sectarian message. But evangelicals already had experience in the commercial marketplace; for them, national syndication or network broadcasts were simply opportunities for expanding proven fund-raising and audience-generating techniques. The ensuing struggle between these two groups pitted the market-proven evangelicals against the less sectarian but better-connected mainline groups.

At first it appeared that evangelicals had little chance of successfully taking the network stage. Many mainline Protestant leaders, the networks, and the FCC perceived evangelicals as intolerant and sectarian. Harry Emerson Fosdick, one of the best-known mainline Protestant broadcast preachers, declared, "What one says on the air must be universal, catholic, inclusive, profoundly human."[99] He predicted that mainline Protestant broadcasters might "outflank, overpass, and undercut sectarianism in religion."[100] Critics repeatedly associated evangelicals with radio hucksters who espoused self-serving beliefs in order to profit financially from unwary listeners.[101] Fundamentalist programs "have long been distasteful to liberal church leaders," declared the influential and ecumenical *Christian Century*.[102] To make matters even worse for them, evangelicals were implicated in other groups' attempts to politicize Christianity, especially the broadcasts of the anti-Semitic Father Coughlin.[103] Mainline Protestants repeatedly criticized evangelicals publicly for their sectarian rhetoric and worked with broadcasters to exclude proponents of such rhetoric from the airways. These critics preferred broadcasts by the "major established faiths," the "outstanding denominations of the Protestant Church" whose broadcasts were "evangelical in quality, but nonsectarian."[104] Mainline leaders in America sought what Moore calls "radio ecumenism."[105] They believed that the public presentation of Christianity on the airways should be as general and cross-denominational as possible—regardless of how divided the Christian community was privately in its own tribal denominations and parachurch groups.

Hoping to preclude government regulation, the National Association of Broadcasters (NAB) formalized in 1939 its concerns about sectarian programs in its revised Standards of Practice Code.[106] Although not entirely designed to restrict evangelicals from purchasing radio time on member stations, the code required all religious programs to be "nonsectarian" and prohibited the sale of time for "controversial issues."[107] The "purpose of the religious broadcast," it stated, was to "promote the spiritual harmony and understanding of mankind and to administer broadly to the varied religious needs of the community."[108] Some stations did not support the new code, but other NAB members used it to rid the airways of Rutherford, Coughlin, and others.[109] The NAB code apparently had no long-term impact on evangelical broadcasting, although at the time evangelicals feared that they would be excluded categorically from the airways. Relevant sections of the code remained essentially the same through the 1950s, but evangelicals continued to purchase time on NAB and non-NAB stations around the country.[110] In other words, the code gave member stations the rhetoric that they needed to justify excluding particular religious broadcasters—evangelicals or others. They could apply the code as a means of justifying their authority to censor the more uncivil and antagonistic religious broadcasters who disrespected other faiths. The code's ecumenical rhetoric of communion became a basis for maintaining religious civility on stations without excluding profitable evangelical program revenues.

Only the more independent Mutual Broadcasting System, a network established in the 1930s, unequivocally sided with evangelicals by refusing to adopt the NAB code. Mutual decided to offer broadcast time to any religious group that would pay for it, thereby endorsing a market-based approach to religious broadcasting that would eventually favor evangelicals. Fuller's *Old-Fashioned Revival Hour* became Mutual's largest broadcast customer during the early 1940s. In fact, about a quarter of the network's revenue came from religious program time sales.[111] Mutual demonstrated what local stations had already proven, namely, that evangelicals could generate loyal listeners who would contribute funds to keep the broadcasts on the air.

Lacking the cushion of free program time, evangelicals were learning how to leverage national markets successfully. They were, in effect, developing a new form of "commercial broadcasting" that relied on listener donations instead of on spot-advertising sales or program sponsorship.

In spite of the popularity of evangelical broadcasts, the radio networks generally supported policies that largely restricted evangelicals from gaining access to such national distribution. NBC specified that it would accept only "nonsectarian and nondenominational [programs] . . . of the widest appeal; presenting the broad claims of religion." CBS prohibited the sale of airtime to religious groups or individual clergy, preferring instead the cautious approach of offering free program time to "representatives of the major faiths of the religious community."[112] Of course there was no single "religious community" in the United States, although there were ecumenical associations such as the Federal Council and its successor, the National Council of Churches. Rader and Donald Grey Barnhouse were probably the only evangelicals to gain regular access to CBS; Rader secured time before the network's policies were tightened, while Barnhouse's style of Presbyterian evangelicalism was theologically and stylistically palatable to many mainline Protestants.[113] Even Mutual limited such programming in 1943 to Sunday mornings and refused to accept any new religious broadcasts.[114] Mutual also prohibited preachers from soliciting funds and from addressing controversial topics or criticizing other faiths; these restrictions probably kept most fundamentalists, if not most evangelicals, off the network.[115] Of course religious broadcasters could still solicit funds through direct-mail appeals aimed at listeners who had sent cards or letters to the program. Evangelicals formed the National Religious Broadcasters (NRB) in 1944 largely to combat these restrictive network policies, believing that the mainline groups were conspiring with the broadcasting industry to keep evangelicals off the air.[116]

Although both federal regulatory policies and trade-association restrictions were designed to strengthen mainline religion's control of religious broadcasting, they probably weakened it in the long run. The FRC and FCC requirement that stations serve the public interest partly with religious broadcasts would eventually lead the stations and networks to seek the most profitable or at least the most audience-generating means of meeting the requirement—and evangelicals were increasingly savvy about garnering audiences and eliciting the contributions necessary to pay station and network airtime costs. Mainline religious groups were not particularly interested in paying for airtime and were principally opposed to asking listeners for contributions to support the costs of production and broadcast time; in their view, fund-raising appeals were inappropriate and would lead religious preachers to pander to audiences. During the late 1930s and early 1940s, CBS and NBC reduced the amount of sustaining network religious programming, almost all of which had been provided to mainline Protestant and Roman Catholic broadcasters.[117] In return for the network promise of free time, these broadcasters consigned themselves unwittingly to an ever-smaller role in the nation's religious broadcasting. In spite of the costs involved, evangelicals stood to gain; forced to learn how to create programming that would attract audiences and raise funds, they were ready to enter radio markets when later federal regulations opened up station ownership to religious groups. While evangelicals learned how to market religion on the radio, mainline Protestants became increasingly complacent about, and uncreative with, their programming.[118] Radio listeners apparently wanted engaging styles of programming and easily understood messages, not highbrow sermons or theological lectures.

Evangelicals' greatest difficulty in achieving national syndication without the networks was operating capital. It often took several years for a new program to establish an audience of loyal contributors. Maier originally purchased time on CBS for *The Lutheran Hour* in 1930, before the network eliminated paid broadcasts. CBS permitted him to buy one half-hour program period weekly on affiliates in only thirty-six cities at the full commercial rate of $4,500.[119] The Lutheran Laymen's League raised half of the annual $200,000 budget in advance of the first broadcast, but the program had to be taken off the air for financial reasons within a year.[120] In spite of excellent ratings there was not yet adequate listener support.[121] It took four years for the league to raise enough money to get the program back on a network, this time Mutual. By 1939 *The Lutheran Hour* was carried on all of the network's 178 stations.[122] *Time* magazine called the show "radio's most popular religious broadcast"; the program may have been more popular nationally than even prime-time sitcoms.[123] During the mid-1940s the program elicited 30,000 letters weekly from listeners, more than three times the mail received for all of the programs sponsored by the mainline Federal Council.[124] In 1948 the show received 450,000 letters and was aired on 684 stations, a third of all of the stations in the country.[125] *Time* called Maier the "Chrysostom of American Lutheranism."[126] His replacement on *The Lutheran Hour*, Oswald Hoffman, suggested that Maier "helped stimulate the . . . evangelical resurgence."[127]

The most popular national radio preacher of the first two decades of U.S. broadcasting was Fuller, whose *Old-Fashioned Revival Hour* became a symbol of the growing public popularity and respectability of evangelicalism in America. More than any of the other radio preachers, Fuller learned how to package the old-fashioned Gospel for mass appeal in the new medium. He started inauspiciously with two Bible lessons weekly on KJS, operated by the Bible Institute of Los Angeles. In 1934 he contracted with 50,000-watt KNX, the "Voice of Hollywood," for a half-hour *Heart to Heart Talk* program on Sunday evenings.[128] Within a few years the syndicated program was so popular, and the financial support from listeners so encouraging, that Fuller purchased time for a radio revival hour on Mutual while continuing to bear the costs of syndicating it to independent radio stations across the country. By 1939 Fuller's broadcast had the largest prime-time distribution of any radio program in the country. In 1940 it aired on 456 stations, 60 percent of all stations in the United States.[129] Fuller paid $1.6 million for time on Mutual in 1944 in order to reach a weekly audience estimated at twenty million persons.[130] At its peak during the war, the program also aired internationally on 1,154 stations, and Fuller's popularity inspired many later broadcast evangelists, including Billy Graham and Jerry Falwell, who named his *Old-Time Gospel Hour* after Fuller's broadcast.[131] "Between the death of Billy Sunday in 1935 and the rise of Billy Graham fourteen years later," wrote *Newsweek*, "Americans who sought that same kind of old-time religion turned to an evangelist named Charles Edward Fuller."[132] No mainline Protestant or Roman Catholic radio preacher ever attained Fuller's popularity—even with sustaining broadcasts provided by networks and supported by the NAB.

In spite of the FCC regulations and broadcasters' self-regulatory policies, by the late 1940s audience-funded evangelical radio broadcasting was an established institution in American radio. Faced with the loss of advertising to television, radio networks and stations loosened even further their restrictions on paid religious broadcasts.[133] The National Association of Evangelical's periodical, *United Evangelical Action*, concluded in 1950 that gospel broadcasting had grown because of the decreased demand for commercial radio advertising resulting from the advent of television.[134] ABC sold thirty minutes weekly to Fuller beginning in June 1949, followed several months later by the network's commitment to air *The Lutheran Hour*.[135] Although mainline Protestants still fought for sustaining time under the auspices of the Broadcasting and Film Commission of the National Council of Churches, evangelicals had already won the real battle for religious broadcast supremacy. Evangelicals' propaganda, to use the FRC's term, had met with popular appeal, if not the public interest. By the advent of television, evangelicals had already learned how to make creative and entertaining programming that would successfully "sell" the old-fashioned Gospel to a new-fashioned society. Evangelicals might not have converted millions of Americans to their faith, but they were able to use the medium centrifugally as a means of creating a national evangelical identity, promoting their own symbolic leaders, publicly legitimizing particular values and attitudes, and raising funds to build other evangelical institutions, including Fuller Theological Seminary and the Moody Bible Institute.

The conflicts between mainline and evangelical broadcasters over regulatory and network policies toward religion involved different rhetorics. Tribal rhetoric of conversion usually focused on the sectarian goal of conforming the nation to a tribal unity. Regulatory rhetoric of communion focused instead on the public interest as a form of consensus. Robert White argues that as the public sphere in America "began to be identical with the state, the discourse of the press and other forms of mediated communication were also considered a volatile threat to orderly public consensus and, like religion, were either consigned to the sphere of private opinion or were allowed into the public sphere as a form of circulating the information necessary for industrial progress." He further believes that this social process "provided a framework for including a kind of nondenominational religion" in radio programming. Mainline religious leaders, he says, "joined hands with broadcasters and political leaders to ensure that their message was recast into the nondenominational language of public progress, instrumental rationality, and nation building." As a result, White concludes, "competing sectarian groups were excluded from broadcasting."[136] While White's assessment may be accurate, it is also true that evangelicals' conversionary rhetoric was just as deeply anchored in instrumental logic and a mythos of technological progress. Both mainline and evangelical religious broadcasters justified their use of radio on the basis of deeply seated American views of progress and efficiency. In this regard they shared with regulators a rhetoric of technological praise. All of these parties were tuned to the deep cultural imaginations of optimistic Americans who believed that radio itself represented progress. The real distinction between evangelical and mainline rhetoric was how they related public and private interests to religion, or how they discerned the role of religion in the public square—as conversion or communion.

In any case during the heyday of the radio networks, stations and regulators were more interested in protecting and even advancing the immediate market opportunities for the new medium than they were in secularizing the public square as part of the "Enlightenment political-economic project."[137] The public debates over the place of religion in American radio broadcasting were fundamentally struggles between public and private ways of imagining broadcasting, undergirded by the conflicting rhetorics of conversion and communion.

The increasingly diverse character of American society simply made it more and more problematic for any subculture or tribe to legitimize a moral order for the entire society. If, as Park and John Dewey suggest, one of the functions of communication is to "maintain the unity and integrity of the social group in its two dimensions—space and time," then regulators and networks faced the task of defining "unity and integrity" in a heterogeneous society.[138] If society lacks a common tradition or a shared moral order, one or more cultural groups will simply posit a conversionary rhetoric intended to achieve a social order more or less in their own interest. In the end, regulators, stations, and even many religious broadcasters implicitly judged that the market should frame the moral order for society. As Park suggests, "Commerce invariably expands more widely and rapidly than linguistic or cultural understanding."[139] In this historical case, the market became the mechanism for facilitating competition without explicit moral order. Unable to find any reasonable definition of religion that would respect the diversity of American religious life, the regulatory agencies and others turned the problem of moral order over to the marketplace.

Perhaps the most salient issue in this historical case study is how to understand the relationship between the market and public interest. The radio broadcast market is a competitive arena that pits different cultural imaginations against each other. Such a market mechanism looks to the future both rhetorically and financially; religious broadcasters become pecuniary prophets who believe that they can tune their messages to always-emerging audiences. Evangelicals apparently were better at this market prediction because they could imagine a wider range of futures without the unifying influence of tradition. Mainline groups, on the other hand, tried to forge nonsectarian messages out of the past as represented in their theology and tradition. By and large the market, as a largely impersonal process of competition, is uninterested in tradition. Moore rightly argues that mainline groups' desire to "remain non-controversial was sincere enough," but that desire hardly represented a marketable religious message.[140] The mainline rhetoric of communion was essentially a moral claim that lacked market appeal. As Moore puts it, mainline Protestants "had to wonder whether their broad messages were worth anyone's attention."[141] The concept of "worth" is a moral claim, a rhetoric of discernment for articulating value. Evangelicals had a dynamic, market-sensitive message but little moral vision about the impact of the market on that message. They assumed that the market could make the moral claim, that popularity would ultimately adjudicate moral value. Mainline religious broadcasters had a grand moral vision about the civil relationships among religious faiths in public life, but they lacked a message that would "work" pragmatically in the marketplace.

The FRC and FCC essentially let the market decide the fate of religious broadcasting in America. "We have already witnessed in the United States," stated Louis Wirth in his presidential address before the American Sociological Association in 1947, "the rise of what might be called 'government by Western Union,' which reminds one of the story of the lady who went to the telegraphy office and said, 'I should like to send a telegram to my Congressman to use his own judgment.'"[142] It is not altogether clear who was sending the FRC and the FCC telegrams, but history suggests that it was not the public. There was no public—only cultural competitors dancing tribally around their own rhetorics of conversion and communion and perhaps celebrating together a rhetoric of technological praise that ultimately contributed to their divisions.

Marketing Religious Consumerism

In the 1920s statistician Roger W. Babson urged large Christian congregations with access to radio transmitters to organize smaller congregations within signal reach, a concept he patterned after chain stores. Hoping to find a way for mainline churches to monopolize religious time on local radio stations, he looked forward to the day when large mainline congregations could "combine and purchase the time for all day Sunday from our great broadcasting chains, and thus outbid secular competitors with their jazz contests."[143] Babson's wild hopes were in retrospect rather prescient. Mainline churches never were able to control the airways as he envisioned, but they nevertheless achieved the spirit of his plan. After television exploded in American society to become the major national medium, evangelicals began transforming the face of religious radio into a kind of chain-store model, leading both nonprofit and commercial religious radio into American consumerism.

Between the early 1950s and the early 1970s, religious radio chugged along on the momentum that it was gaining in the broadcast marketplace. Then evangelicals roared ahead of other tribes by taking advantage of the new FM radio band as well as the loosening regulatory standards for broadcast licensees. The FCC opened up many less-desirable FM radio frequencies to nonprofit organizations, including religious and educational groups. At the time, commercial broadcasters saw no great market for FM radio and felt little concern about competition from the new band. In fact, FM was becoming a new arena for broadcasters to experiment with novel formats and to program alternative musical styles for subcultural taste groups. The FCC also permitted religious ownership of stations, including commercial stations, truly a strange development given all of the FRC's fuss in the 1920s over special (propaganda) versus general interests. Many evangelicals saw the FM band as an opportunity to get into broadcasting without having to purchase an expensive AM license from an established broadcaster.[144] Now religious groups could license and operate even for-profit stations, competing directly with all of the other broadcasters. At the time the FM band was not commercially viable, so it seemed as though religious groups had no great advantage in the broadcast marketplace. But before long FM became the cutting edge of commercial radio, and evangelicals found themselves with many valuable FM frequencies, both commercial and noncommercial.[145] Evangelical "propaganda stations" achieved precisely what the FRC had denied them fifty years earlier—a means of dedicating a station's entire program schedule to special interests.

In sheer numbers evangelical radio was a success story from the 1970s through the 1990s. In 1973 there were 111 radio stations in the United States that devoted at least twenty hours weekly to religious programming, including inspirational music, spiritual talk shows, and Bible instruction. Three years later there were 341 such stations. By 1979 there were 449 religious stations representing nearly every state in the country.[146] One decade later there were 1,052 special-interest religious stations in America, and the number continued to climb.[147] The average top-100 market in 1988 had three or more noncommercial religious stations.[148] By 1993 one in ten American radio stations classified its content as "religious," making religious programming the third most common format in the country.[149] What the FRC had deemed "propaganda" in 1927 had become an institutionalized part of the radio market by the 1990s. The turning point occurred in the 1970s, a period that Carey identifies as the decline of general-interest, national media and the rise of a plethora of special-interest media segmented by lifestyle, demographics, and political interest.[150]

Although statistically evangelical radio seemed to be a booming industry, behind the scenes things were not nearly so encouraging. Trumpeted within the tribe as a medium for evangelization, religious radio nevertheless settled into tribal patterns that virtually guaranteed it would reach few nonevangelicals. By the early 1980s evangelical radio served primarily a small religious subculture. Very few nonevangelicals listened regularly to religious radio programs. The most optimistic surveys concluded in 1980 that about seventeen million adults regularly tuned in religious radio programs—about a tenth of the population.[151] Many of these listeners, however, did not hear religious broadcasts on religious stations. One survey found in 1982 that only about 2.5 million Americans listened specifically to gospel music programs.[152] In the mid-1980s the typical religious station generally attracted the smallest audiences of any local stations; most religious stations were not even included in local audience measurements by the major research companies.[153] From 1977 to 1984 the national audience share for religious stations (the percentage of radio listeners who tune in to religious stations) increased from .89 percent to 1.76 percent, but much of that growth could be explained purely by the increase in the number of stations, not as an overall increase in the audience for each evangelical station.[154] Evangelical radio audiences were growing, but they were still remarkably small, older-aged, and static.

This tribalization was furthered when the fledgling gospel music business became an independent industry largely disconnected from the mainstream music industry. Gospel music had always had its fans who bought records and tapes from performers after church concerts. In the early 1970s, however, evangelical artists and businesspersons saw potential profits in new forms of religious music. The evangelical Gospel Music Industry grew partly out of the established evangelical book-publishing business, using Christian bookstores as retail outlets and imitating secular styles of popular music. As William D. Romanowski documents, gospel music soon included religious versions of practically every style of nonreligious music, differentiated only by the spiritual lyrics.[155] Among the most successful genres were Southern Gospel, Jesus Rock, religious MOR (middle-of-the-road music), and eventually a wide array of even more specialized styles of religious music. Suddenly the expanding evangelical radio business had plenty of recordings to play, but the lyrics were largely tribal, emanating from evangelical speech communities and aimed at tribal markets. Within the churches there also was little agreement over what styles of music were appropriate for evangelical parents and children to listen to at home and in the car. If radio stations played one type of "Jesus music," as it was sometimes called, they could easily offend some devout believers who preferred other styles. If Christian FM stations played too many different types of gospel music, they might drive away every evangelical listener. Evangelicals were copying the styles that characterized mainstream commercial radio, but typically they had only one or two stations in each market.

In addition, religious stations turned away people from outside the tribe by depending heavily on prerecorded programs from preachers and teachers of virtually every evangelical stripe. These broadcast "pastors" realized that religious stations best reached their target market—evangelicals. They also figured out that airtime on religious stations was much cheaper and more cost-effective than equivalent time, if they could purchase it, on nonreligious stations.[156] Syndicated broadcasters preferred religious stations because the audiences were more responsive and the program costs were significantly lower than those of mainstream stations.[157] From the 1970s on most religious stations became public pulpits for syndicated Bible teachers and pastors who bought fifteen- and thirty-minute program periods to reach their radio flocks. By the late 1980s about 37 percent of all programming on religious stations was preaching or teaching programs.[158] Some of these ministers were local pastors, but far more of them were national or international broadcasters who independently syndicated their programs to religious stations or syndicated them through one of the growing numbers of agencies that served the increasingly specialized religious market. But not all evangelicals liked these preaching programs; younger listeners, in particular, disliked pedantic or fiery radio teachers, preferring to listen instead to secular rock music stations.

Evangelical stations liked more than just the revenues they received from daily and weekly program time sales. Taped preaching programs gave them an excuse not to play divisive gospel music. Whereas musical formats sometimes generated complaints from offended listeners, taped preaching and teaching shows elicited few objections; unhappy listeners simply tuned to other stations. Contemporary Christian music especially elicited objections from conservative listeners who believed that such music was more secular than religious. Older listeners, in particular, complained vigorously about the music's beat; to them, the overall sound of contemporary Christian recordings was too similar to secular equivalents.[159] These older listeners preferred traditional hymns to the more "worldly" popular tunes that sounded like the music on secular rock music stations. Even in the late 1990s many evangelical stations refused to broadcast popular religious musical recordings, fearing that they would lose the small but loyal audience for Bible programs. Too much music, they realized, could kill the cash cow of paid teaching programs by driving away the older listeners who financially supported syndicated broadcasts.

These three factors—FM radio, religious musical recordings, and program time sales—combined to transform evangelical radio into a tribal medium that could hardly fulfill its own rhetoric of conversion. Like secular radio, religious stations were increasingly aimed at an identifiable American subculture. Evangelical radio joined the heavy-metal rock music stations, jazz stations, classical music stations, and all of the other formats. Instead of reaching out to the general public for listeners or even expanding significantly their evangelical audiences, most religious stations in the 1970s through the 1990s settled for rather small but comfortable niches in the broad mosaic of American broadcasting. They offered listeners edification and education instead of evangelism. They told the more conservative wing of evangelicalism what it wanted to hear about the world and about its own faith. They offered largely nonoffensive and noncontroversial musical recordings—except perhaps late in the weekday evening or on Saturdays, when some stations bravely aired Christian rock music programs. Evangelical radio became a vernacular form of broadcasting less interested in extratribal conversion than in intratribal communion. As one observer put it after listening to one of these stations, "This was a clear display of in-group language on an in-group medium going to an in-group audience. It probably reached none of those it was intended for. It never left the ghetto."[160] Evangelical radio's rhetoric of conversion became a patina that pleasantly disguised the underlying tribal rhetoric of communion.

Compared with some of the nationally syndicated evangelical radio broadcasts of the 1940s and 1950s, programs in the new religious ghetto were largely invisible to the public. Fuller's *Old-Fashioned Revival Hour*, for example, had established an enormous national audience in the 1940s by purchasing time on major nonreligious stations as well as on religious ones across the country. One estimate put Fuller's audience at twenty million—certainly more than the total national audience for all religious radio stations in the late 1980s and even larger than the audiences for syndicated religious television programs during the same period.[161] By contrast, the new evangelical radio served essentially its own subculture. Unlike nationally syndicated television programs, few of these newer evangelical radio shows were familiar to the general public. Most American radio listeners were too loyal to their own mainstream radio stations to switch to a religious station. More than that, few syndicated religious programs attracted many listeners—evangelicals or nonevangelicals. After all, such syndicated programs required only a small but loyal following that would regularly send financial contributions to keep the program on the air. As long as these programs pleased their supporters, they were successful in the eyes of both local religious stations and the preachers themselves. As one critic put it, syndicated evangelical broadcasters did not have to "understand the medium well enough to really use it wisely."[162]

During the 1980s and 1990s, then, evangelical radio's conversionary power was limited increasingly by the medium's own allegiance to the tribal marketplace. The successful preaching and teaching programs deepened the roots of the evangelical radio in the tribe but also cut it off from the broader American culture. By pleasing the very small audience for these kinds of broadcasts, stations virtually guaranteed that they would never attract a wider group of listeners. Relatively few evangelicals listened for long to continuous blocs of syndicated programming. By 1980 merely 20 percent of the religious radio audience tuned in for three or more hours weekly.[163] As an educational and inspirational medium, evangelical radio was rather solidly entrenched in the small evangelical subculture. The raison d'être of evangelical communication, religious conversion, was little more than triumphalistic rhetoric even for the larger syndicated broadcasters. Preaching and teaching programs normally created small audiences for particular programs rather than larger audiences for the station overall.[164] The easy route to financial liquidity for evangelical stations, namely program time sales, further fragmented such stations' audiences. Although evangelical programs raised contributions largely on the basis of the rhetoric of conversion, they functioned more as a tribal means of self-identification. Radio symbolized technological power and social status while delivering tribal propaganda.

Of course local evangelical radio successfully raised financial support for some national broadcast ministries. But even evangelical donors were not necessarily listeners; a donation was a means of voting symbolically for evangelicalism amid the broad and confusing array of religious tribes in America.[165] Supporters likely perceived evangelical radio as an important presence in American society that lent legitimacy to the evangelical cause even if it did not attract many unconverted souls. And those few who listened regularly were often remarkably responsive to stations' pleas for help in fighting secularization in America. When rumors circulated among evangelicals in the 1970s and 1980s that well-known atheist Madalyn Murray O'Hair had petitioned the FCC to eliminate religious radio stations, the federal agency received millions of letters of protest from evangelicals.[166] The FCC eventually hired a public relations agency to try to quell the outlandish rumors. One of the FCC's strategies was to encourage evangelical stations to correct the errors on the air—which many of them did. To some evangelicals, religious radio was a rather sacred symbol of their faith, a sign that evangelicalism had a voice in the wider culture.

A growing number of evangelical broadcasters believed in the 1980s and 1990s that musical formats were one answer to relatively poor audience ratings. Popular Christian music, they thought, might pull evangelical radio out of the religious ghetto by attracting a broader spectrum of younger listeners. In a nation where about a third of all adults identified themselves as "born again" Christians, audience ratings suggested that no more than three or four million adults regularly listened to evangelical radio.[167] Virtually everyone in evangelical radio agreed that part of the meager audience problem was the dull programming offered by most stations, especially the predictable preaching and teaching programs. Since the advent of network television, musical recordings increasingly dominated American radio. Americans turned largely to television for talk and to radio for music. Music-oriented evangelical stations certainly attracted larger audiences than those that emphasized preaching and teaching programs. On average, the audiences of religious music stations were 70 percent larger than their preaching-teaching counterparts. In addition, music audiences generally listened longer without tuning to different stations.[168] But the younger listeners to the music stations were not the contributors to the syndicated teaching and preaching programs. If a musical station alienated older listeners, it could cut off its major source of revenue, namely, revenues from selling program time.

As if rubbing salt into radio stations' wounds, some gospel music industry executives told evangelical stations that they were rather unprofessional compared with their secular counterparts. Artist manager Ed Harrell, whose clients included evangelical pop-star Amy Grant, expressed this openly to a group of religious radio station managers and employees at the Gospel Music Association convention in Nashville in 1989. Christian radio had yet to prove whether it was a trend or merely a fad, he said. Lamenting the lack of vision and creativity among stations, he said that stations' desire to "please God" had become a "crutch and an excuse for mediocrity."[169] Frustrated with religious stations' minuscule young audiences, he and others criticized the religious broadcasting industry. Only 2 to 6 percent of the average religious station's audience was under eighteen years of age.[170] Young evangelicals simply were not listening to Christian radio stations. In 1988 only a fifth of the subscribers to *Campus Life* magazine, the major publication for evangelical young people, had become aware of new Christian music the previous year through Christian radio. These young evangelicals listened to twice as much mainstream as Christian radio each day. In fact, half of them did not listen to any Christian music.[171] Perhaps Harrell was correct that the style of evangelical radio was too nonprofessional by mainstream radio standards. Even into the 1990s, however, evangelical radio was still largely invisible to all but a small group of dedicated listeners; less than 2 percent of radio listeners in America tuned in religious stations.[172]

While evangelical radio programmers and listeners muttered about their future, they faced the greatest challenge of all—outright assimilation into the prevailing consumer culture. History shows that larger social entities tend slowly to assimilate the "secondary groups" into larger public rituals.[173] Evangelicals are far more assimilated into mainstream American life than they often are willing to admit, and the fact is that religious radio stations will likely have to imitate their mainstream radio competitors in order to gain younger evangelical listeners. Real growth might require willing cultural co-optation. To put it starkly, evangelical radio could become so commercial that it would lose all of its religious distinctiveness, including the countercultural aspects of its evangelical message. Herein lies the greatest hope and the deepest despair of the industry. Like the man in the biblical parable who got everything on earth and nothing in heaven, evangelical stations faced their greatest challenge in defining the terms of their own success.[174] At issue in evangelical radio from its earliest days has been whether it will be able to remain evangelical or whether it will invariably be transformed along with its constituency into solid-gold commerce.

If the industry desires to achieve greater "success," it will likely model itself even more fully after nonreligious broadcasting. This is already evident in the rise of various companies that provide religious stations with audience ratings, demographic audience profiles, and spot advertising. None of these developments will likely drive all of the evangelical ethos out of religious radio, but each of them could be a sign that the consumer marketplace is beginning to set the agenda and determine the course of tribal radio. Research shows that religious radio audiences are more highly educated, more affluent, and more likely to be employed as professionals—more "upscale."[175] To put it crassly, religious radio listeners are an increasingly lucrative market. They are even more likely to own a car than is the reader of *Car and Driver* or *Road and Track* magazine. They buy more entertainment devices than viewers of MTV. If that were not enough to attract advertisers, these audiences enjoy spending their way through leisure time—even more than viewers of ESPN—and they buy more groceries, household products, appliances, term life insurance, and personal-care products than listeners of other radio formats.[176] Evangelical audiences tend to be loyal female listeners who will support advertisers by buying advertised goods and services.[177] The religious audience is increasingly composed of "Guppies"—God-fearing Urban Professionals.[178] The rhetoric of conversion is shifting from "ministry" to "marketing" and from "evangclism" to "segmentation." Although the noncommercial religious stations are somewhat immune from these trends, they nevertheless have to compete for audiences against increasingly commercial religious stations and networks.

It was a long road from the evangelical teachers of the 1930s to Guppies of the 1990s. The story of evangelical radio in America is the tale of a religious subculture that nevertheless draws much of its sustenance from mainstream American society. Evangelical radio has become what Wirth calls a "trade area" of bustling economic activity that expresses its own area customs and depends on outsiders to bring in tradable culture and adequate revenues to maintain the regional ways of life. "The listening areas of radio stations," says Wirth, may indicate how far a regional culture extends and "where it comes into collision with a competing center."[179] In the case of evangelical radio, the surrounding consumer culture permeates the social and economic landscape, right up to the doors of the studio and the residences of listeners—if not through the doors of the area churches.

Conclusion

In an ethnographic study of a Christian radio station, Jay D. Green examined the case of WCRF in Cleveland between 1958 and 1972.[180] After securing an FM radio license the local nonprofit corporation contacted the Moody Bible Institute in Chicago in hopes of securing funding to build the station. Believing that FM radio was a "gamble," Moody turned them down.[181] But Moody and the Cleveland nonprofit group eventually agreed that if the former raised the funding to get the station operating the latter would then take over operations and ongoing expenses. Alas, there were no listeners on FM, so once again the Cleveland group looked for a way to make its dream a reality. In an amazing demonstration of their commitment to the idea of Christian radio, the original nonprofit group recruited a "small army of volunteers" to travel throughout northeast Ohio extolling the virtues of FM radio and selling FM receivers that they had purchased directly from manufacturers at wholesale prices.[182] Green's case study suggests that the tale of evangelical radio in America consists of the many stories of grassroots energy and collective actions of people who were not professional broadcasters as much as hopeful believers in the power of electronic media.

As Green documents in the case of WCRF, the station's major impact in the Cleveland area was to revive and coalesce the region's sleepy evangelicalism. Area evangelicals wanted to climb out of the "graveyard of evangelism" by organizing themselves publicly under a shared, cross-church label.[183] But instead WCRF enabled Cleveland evangelicals to cocreate a new public self-identity. In short, radio gave the group a common cause, established symbolic leaders from the local community, and connected the local tribes to the wider evangelical movement. The station provided a decentralized, segmented network loosely conjoined by various personal, structural, and ideological ties. Radio for this community was a missionary activity, but even more important it was a means of building symbolic community among various local congregations and even across churches from different denominations. Connected to the broader evangelical movement in America though the network programming, Cleveland's evangelicals could transcend their geographic community by imagining themselves as part of the larger symbolic world of American evangelicalism. This station, says Green, "served to amplify the previously muted voice of conservative Protestantism within Cleveland's diverse religious matrix, and also built a transdenominational 'big tent' under which an ecumenical evangelical community joined together."[184]

The ironies and paradoxes of evangelical radio in America reflect the synergies and tensions between tribal faith and mainstream culture. Up to the 1970s evangelical radio had grown as a grassroots movement without much market research or careful market planning. Ironically, the eventual success of evangelical radio might come as a result of the industry's cooptation by American consumer culture. From the 1920s forward evangelical radio fought to be a viable public medium for conversion, and perhaps its dream was finally becoming reality. After all, evangelical radio could finally become as commercial as it was religious, thereby joining the throngs of mainstream broadcasters hoping to convert listeners to their formats, personalities, and advertisers. This time the rhetoric of conversion probably was in the "public interest" as defined in the 1920s by the FRC.

5

Searching for Communion:
The Christian Metanarrative
Meets Popular Mythology

◪ ◪ ◪

In a short story entitled "The Lost Civilization of Deli," raconteur Jean Shepherd projects a future world where archaeologists excavate the ruins of the great North American culture of "Fun City," known previously as New York. Deep in the remains of a skyscraper the archaeologists exhume the dusty contents of a gray metal vault, perhaps a sacred burial site. The interior of the vault reveals row upon row of reels wound with celluloid and labeled in small script, "TV 60 Second Commercials." Months later the scientists determine in a laboratory that the films were strangely imprinted with images of special people—perhaps idols? Passing light through the rapidly moving celluloid, the scholars watch the icons magically come alive: uniformed dancers singing "We do it all for yoo hoo hoo!"; a group of sun worshipers dressed in outlandish pagan costumes of staggering immodesty chanting, "Join the Pepsi Generation, come alive, come alive!"; three women in a repository confronting a uniformed guard who is trying to stop them from ecstatically fondling small white scrolls with the admonition: "Don't squeeze the Charmin!" Soon the archaeologists realize that their find was far "more revealing than any of the poor fables and tepid myths that these people had left behind, what they called Arts and Literature." Watching the drama about Charmin toilet tissue unfolding before their eyes, one of them exclaims, "Those tightly rolled white scrolls . . . they were worshiping! Are you ready for a cosmic theory? . . . If we can find out what was on those Charmins, or what they were used for, I believe we would know what their civilization was all about, what they believed in. Do you follow?"[1]

Shepherd's story may be a bit far-fetched, but his thesis, if not a "cosmic theory," merits serious consideration. Advertising, for example, might serve a mythopoetic function in society, affirming the communal beliefs and shared values of a consumer culture. Perhaps popular culture plays a "priestly" role in contemporary America, confirming mainstream beliefs, expressing the nation's collective dreams, and molding "the soul's geography."[2] In Robert E. Park's language, maybe such expressive public communication manifests shared sentiments and attitudes.[3] If television is a major storyteller of our time, perhaps American churches need to exegete TV, like a theologian interprets the themes and myths of sacred literature. "Freedom in community," writes Ronald C. Arnett, "can only be found when what we take for granted is critiqued against a narrated vision of how things 'should' be."[4] Lacking their own perceptive critics, Christian tribes might never discover that secular mythology has challenged implicitly the veracity of their tribal metanarratives.

This chapter addresses the relationship between the Christian metanarrative and the subnarratives of the mass media, especially television. In small tribal societies, religious narratives and the folk culture are tightly interwoven. But in large, industrial societies, particularly pluralistic democracies, the life-world of individual religious tribes will invariably conflict at least partly with the popular stories distributed by mainstream media institutions through a market system. Of course the various religious tribes usually have their own media as well. But the mainstream national media aim their narratives at broad markets that transcend religious differences among citizens. These media are not in business so much to serve tribal subcultures as they are to deliver definable markets to advertisers. In short, the forces of the capitalist market and Christian ministry sometimes overlap, but just as often they reveal conflicting allegiances and irreconcilable notions of reality. By its very nature as a function of metanarrative, religious rhetoric often claims a more or less hegemonic view of reality that eschews the market system as the ultimate arbiter of truth.

The first part of this chapter discusses the importance of both narrative and cultural theory in understanding the interaction of religion and mainstream mass media within an industrial society. The mythopoetic foundations of human culture-making give nearly all cultural expressions a quasi-religious quality. As Louis Wirth suggests, mass communication in society requires a "consensual basis" for shared meaning to occur.[5] This consensus is a kind of social "faith" in shared values and beliefs. Even popular art breathes some form of spiritual reality into a society's narratives. Stories come alive, acquiring meaning within the wider community, thereby enabling people to imagine a different social world from the taken-for-granted one that they inhabit. Both secular popular culture and religious narratives can help people to think and act collectively, to share a faith. Such faith in turn facilitates how religious tribes and the wider society see the world, including how each perceives the other. Everyday popular culture thereby often imitates the transcendent character of religious myth. As Northrop Frye goes so far as to argue that nearly all narrative forms derive from the Bible's mythological forms of explanation.[6]

The second part examines how popular narratives communicate "liturgically" in mass-mediated societies as quasi-religious rituals. James W. Carey contends that mass communication is a ritual that portrays and confirms a particular view of the world, or a drama that relies on familiar genres to satisfy a culture's desire for form, order, and tone.[7] The centripetal force of mainstream media creates formulaic genres that affirm the broadly conceived values and beliefs of consumer society. Comedic stories, in particular, perform like priestly jesters—confirming mainstream beliefs while "sacramentally" entertaining their audiences. Comedic television programming is in some ways analogous to the Christian metanarrative. Popular American comedy, however, generally rejects the vertical dimension of the Gospel metanarrative, which represents God as the ultimate agent in human affairs. Mass-mediated comedy instead offers America a horizontal view of "salvation" that focuses on human agency as the means to a better world.

The subsequent part of the chapter considers the crucial role of the religious critic in mediating the wider social world for the religious tribe. A tribal critic should maintain a healthy skepticism for the tribe about the wider cultural world. He or she employs a rhetoric of discernment to counter what Wirth calls the "disenchantment of absolute faith which expresses itself in the secular outlook of modern man."[8] The religious critic is an observer and interpreter of the mass media, a rhetorical exegete of the popular narratives that fill everyday media, and a steward of the prophetic imagination of the tribe. The tribal critic discerns the value of popular culture and enacts a rhetoric of praise for cultural forms that favorably pass his or her scrutiny. The critic ultimately engages in a form of religio-exegesis that uses the tribe's own metanarrative, as interpreted by the community of faith, to evaluate nontribal culture. In doing so the tribal critic often illuminates aspects of popular mythologies that should concern the general public as much as the tribe.

The final section examines four Christian critics' approaches to and understandings of the relationship between the biblical metanarrative and the broader culture's many subnarratives: Edward J. Carnell, William F. Fore, John Wiley Nelson, and Andrew M. Greeley. Each has developed a theology of culture that is also a theory of narrative communication. In addition, each approaches criticism from within the intellectual and cultural contours of a tribal tradition. They offer different ways of exegeting popular culture even though they rely upon essentially the same Christian metanarrative. In the process, they can both affirm distinctive tribal beliefs and provide the broader public with insightful critiques of popular culture. Wirth argues that mass communication invariably produces "skepticism toward all dogmas and ideologies."[9] Perhaps it also elicits renewed tribal convictions in response to exterior threats to the tribe's collective identity.

Religious Uses of Narrative Communication

For centuries scholars have addressed humankind's abilities to reason and symbolize. Now narrative theory is moving to the center of some academic disciplines as scholars recognize that human culture is usually expressed and maintained through shared stories. Narratives often establish paradigms for human understanding in scientific, aesthetic, and religious pursuits. Narrational interpretation is one of the most characteristic aspects of humanness. People are not merely storytellers, story listeners, and story watchers, but they are also story interpreters and, most important, story doers. We all imagine who we are and express our communal lives through shared storytelling. Narrative is not merely part of our leisure time or an isolated form of artistic expression; it is a crucial means of human self-awareness and part of the very drama of human existence. Our lives are partly participation in stories—the tales spun for us, those that we spin for others, and those that we spin collectively with others in work, play, and worship. Biography and autobiography are stories. So is community life—the tale of our lives together. Each of our lives could be transformed into a novel, an opera, or even a sitcom. By our very nature we interpret and understand our lives as narratives played out in the real world and recorded selectively in our own memories and in those of our friends and associates.

Narrative, then, is a natural way for human beings to structure experience and express sentiments. We do not think of our lives so much as scientific formulas, mathematical equations, or computer programs, but rather as stories. Narrative is the dominant metaphor that humankind uses to make sense out of its past actions (retrospection), to guide its future actions (anticipation), and to analyze its current actions (introspection). Our friends say "Tell us what happened!" when they seek to get to know us. Story becomes both a style of expression and a mode of interpretation. As theologian Stanley Hauerwas observes, "Stories are thus a necessary form of our knowledge inasmuch as it is only through narrative that we can catch the connections between actions and responses of man that are inherently particular and contingent."[10] Stories bind events and agents together in intelligible patterns, articulating the richness of humans' intentional action. They help us to see that our own actions are purposeful but not always necessary; we make choices that could change the story of our own lives and those of our communities, nations, and world. Like the daily news reporter, we wonder why people do what they do—what motivates and engages them to act wisely and foolishly. Even fictional stories enable us to imagine the consequences of our and others' actions. By identifying with a character in a story, we consider not just what the character should do but also what we might do in similar circumstances. Without the human ability to "story," our lives would be much more chaotic and fragmented than they already are.

Human beings often express and maintain religious faith and spiritual traditions through sacred narratives. Unlike a mere listing of religious truths or an enumeration of moral commandments, religious stories can be rich, dynamic, and reflexive. Spiritual verities frequently survive best as stories precisely because they can often embrace both literal and metaphorical meaning. The narratives of the Hebrew Torah and the Christian Bible, for instance, are regularly reinterpreted for new situations and applied to novel human actions and situations that could not have been fully elucidated by the original writers of the narratives. Moreover, sacred stories equip religions to account for human origins, responsibilities, and destinations. Religious faith is necessarily communicated as a story because "the beginning and the end can only be discussed in narrative form."[11]

Religious narratives have an inherently sacramental quality, suggesting the existence of a reality beyond the stories themselves. Hasidic philosopher Martin Buber says that a "story is itself an event and has the quality of a sacred action. . . . It is more than a reflection—the sacred essence to which it bears witness continues to live in it."[12] Yet at the same time religious stories often address the yearnings and experiences of everyday people, not just the actions of the gods in some distant realm. The biblical writers focused on the interaction of God's will with the "everyday doings of random persons."[13]

The importance of story for religious faith extends well beyond canonical writings. Through the ages much of the influential Christian testimony (devotional, theological, and philosophical) was cast in the form of narrative (for example, St. Augustine's *Confessions*, which set the form for autobiography in the West, and Bunyan's *The Pilgrim's Progress*, one of the most influential allegories of the Christian journey). The Christian community lives in and through tribal stories, often finding in them a spiritual path and expressing through them the great mysteries of life as well as the majesty of God. Humankind's consciousness is "entwined in stories," says Johann Baptist Metz, and it "always has to rely on narrative identification."[14]

Long before rationalizations and orthodoxies expressed religious faith, human cultures organized religious life around ritualistic reenactments of narratives. These stories served as "paradigms for understanding" by expressing each tribe's primordial myths about good and bad, origins and endings.[15] Without myth and symbol, human language is "too feeble to convey all the thoughts aroused by the alternation of life and death."[16] The Christian Gospel, for instance, expresses the story of the human Fall from grace, the redemption of humankind in Jesus Christ, and the promise of eternal life in heaven; the Bible fills out, amplifies, and interprets the meaning of this story of Good News. Moreover, many of the Christian doctrines derived from this Christian metanarrative "can be grammatically expressed only in the form of metaphor. Thus: Christ is God and human, in the Trinity three persons *are* one, in the Real Presence of the body and the blood *are* the bread and wine."[17] The Christian Gospel is a dynamic story filled with history, metaphor, and symbol. It is not reducible to prepositional claims or scientific verification. As Galileo once suggested in a letter to the Grand Duchess Christina, the Bible teaches "how one goes to heaven, not how heaven goes."[18] Sacred narratives grant faith a kind of dynamic power to shape generations of culture in new, revelatory ways.

The Christian Gospel frames all human activity within the context of God's story. It points to the ways that even the future of God's work in the world is related to the present. The Gospel is a narrative lens through which the Christian views the world—a way of seeing God's truth in the mundane as well as the sublime. Christian community in turn becomes the cultural vessel in and through which Christians interpret this godly way of seeing the world. In this sense, the Christian metanarrative is both hermeneutical and hegemonic. It claims to be the one great story for interpreting all other stories. It is meant to be read both as particular (that is, as a story about specific people and the one God) and as universal (that is, about the human condition and about all people). The Roman Catholic Church, for example, believes that to interpret the Bible "we must first seek out what the inspired author intended to communicate through the particular language, culture, historical situation, and type of writing (historical writing, poetic texts, etc.) in which the teaching was presented and from which it emerged."[19] From such revealed particulars the church derives its universal truths.

Christian communities of interpretation generally see the Gospel as the supreme story that gives meaning, significance, and shape to the stories of individuals and communities. Christians look to the Gospel, as interpreted through the traditions of Christian tribes, to make sense of their everyday lives as well as their ultimate destiny. Theologian Joseph Sittler writes, "All things are more bearable if we make a story of them. And the ultimate desolations are made both more bearable and significant when the story is the Ultimate story."[20] This ultimate metanarrative frames the Christian view of truth, centers worship, directs the preaching of the Word of God, and interprets the sacraments of the faith. The Gospel story provides the narrative context in and through which the church understands its identity and makes sense of the particulars within the Old and New Testaments. The Gospel reminds the community of believers, over and over again, that God created the world, that humankind fell into sin, and that God is restoring the world to its rightness through Jesus Christ. The various Christian denominations have their own ways of interpreting scripture and allocating the importance of traditions, but they agree on the central importance of this Gospel story.[21] For Christian tribes the Gospel is *the* metanarrative.

In modern societies religious metanarratives like the Gospel often compete with "secular" narratives in the indispensable task of locating people in broader patterns of meaning, identity, and intimacy. Such secular narratives can express widely held sentiments and beliefs but usually do not

claim universal or ultimate truthfulness. These subnarratives admit more
or less to their conditionality within the larger social and cultural world.
Metanarratives and subnarratives compete within a society for influence
and popularity.

Nevertheless, metanarratives and subnarratives are important vehicles
both of and for cultural expression. By gaining an understanding of and
appreciation for these stories, we can achieve some knowledge of or acquaintance with a culture—just as our relationships with individuals depend on our capacity for sharing their life stories. Hannah Arendt says that
the only way we really come to know a person is through sharing that person's story; a person's biography gives us more of a sense of the true person
than any mere description or list of qualities, which almost always loses
the uniqueness of a person in a type or character.[22] At the same time,
however, a story can link the uniqueness of its characters and actions to
broader significance, experience, and themes. Most of our narratives are
"about" something; they speak meaningfully to us in the chaos of busy
lives and in a changing world that otherwise might seem to defy logic and
to reflect meaninglessness. Sacred stories, in particular, can help us, in Lud-
wig Wittgenstein's words, "to know how to go on" in the face of fate, anxiety, and tragedy.[23] Situated within the Gospel, every human life becomes
a parable.[24] Our life stories point to deeper spiritual truths about ourselves,
others, and God. The "once upon a time" of our everyday lives finds meaning in the "beginning" and "end" of religious myth. But each religion's
metanarrative might claim to make different sense out of the particularity
of human lives, just as different movies can interpret reality in contradict-
ing ways. The heterogeneity of modern society reflects a wide range of
competing metanarratives and subnarratives.

Apart from its practical value in organizing human experience, shaping
community life, and affirming the uniqueness of individuals, narrative capacity reflects the human ability to imagine other worlds, including better
ones. Storytelling itself says that life could be different than it is now. As
Michael Edwards puts it, the human capacity for storytelling assumes that
something is wrong with the current state of affairs. "According to the old
adage," he writes, "a happy people has no history; it also has no story."[25]
Stories both enable humans to see what is wrong with the world and equip
them to imagine a better, redeemed world. Stories thus enable people to
talk of beginnings and endings, to connect those delimiting events to the
present, and to relate the stories to their own lives. We teach our children
with stories, build religious communities around narratives, create business

legacies and political campaigns anchored in tales, and spend some of our later years reflecting on our own lives as nearly finished autobiographies. As Edwards suggests, stories recount their own recounting; they are naturally reflexive, providing us with a means of imagining and thinking about the state of affairs that they recount. Stories are the "fiction of a fallen world remade."[26]

The interaction of Christianity and the media, then, occurs in a world filled with all kinds of parallel and contradictory stories. One type of story is the religious metanarrative, which claims a kind of universal truthfulness for its community of believers. At the same time, however, a modern nation witnesses many mythlike tales displayed through the mainstream mass media. These mass-mediated subnarratives are less reflexive about their cosmic implications; unlike religious metanarratives, they do not wear their cosmic assumptions or theological prejudices on their sleeves. Contemporary cultures have their own escapist fictions that may "confirm a 'reality' we continue to encounter even if we no longer have a way of accommodating it."[27] Sometimes a particular film or novel will generate obvious public discourse about the nature of human existence, the beginnings of the cosmos, or the end of the world, but most popular culture is not so deeply reflexive about human origins and the human condition. Nevertheless, some of these stories help people "aspire to new hopes and beliefs," if only by imagining a better state of affairs.[28]

Both metanarratives and the subnarratives are expressed through signifying systems—or cultures—that organize the creating and sharing of narratives in society.[29] Each of the Christian denominations, for example, maintains its own signifying systems through publishing houses, worship, and other communal practices. Although the denominations share some of the values and beliefs of the broader American culture, they also try to maintain some distinctive practices and beliefs. The mainstream media are not so closely connected to particular subcultures such as ethnic or religious groups. Instead their signifying systems are linked on one side to the audiences that they supposedly serve and on the other side to the businesses that profit from their operation. While religious media closely serve particular religious tribes, the larger and presumably more influential mainstream media are more diffuse and generic—less tied to the particularities of any subculture. Compared with media in much of the rest of the world, which are more directly linked to the government, political parties, or religious groups, American media stand apart as fairly independent businesses operating in a market system. In addition, the mainstream media rely upon professional communicators who "broker" symbols for their businesses rather than express their own points of view or those of the tribe to which the broker claims allegiance.[30] Their storytelling is shaped more by the abstract concept of the marketplace than by the distinct beliefs of particular subcultures.

American religious groups exist simultaneously in both types of culture— mainstream media signifying systems and religions. Religious individuals, so long as they are part of a community of faith, will usually feel a tension between the subnarratives of the mainstream media and the metanarrative of their own religious signifying systems. Using the terminology of Raymond Williams, Michael Warren suggests that "a particular religion represents a distancing zone of signification, a culture that exists within a wider culture." A religion, he says, "is more specific and intentional in its meanings than the wider culture, but its claims about its meanings are broader and more explicit."[31] While the broader and the more explicitly religious types of storytelling sometimes match, just as often they conflict, causing tension between religious tribes and the more general mass-mediated culture. As St. Augustine once put it, a Christian always lives simultaneously in two realms, the "City of God" and the "City of Man."[32] In many respects the interplay of media and religion in America is the give and take between these two, often competing, systems of signification, one anchored in the tribe's view of reality and the other one forged out of market-driven mass media.

Whenever a society opens up its signifying systems to the market, new forms of religious language and experience emerge from the chaos. Moscow professor Anri Vartanov tells how the Russian media market under perestroika suddenly created a new myth in Soviet society. During a morning news and information program, *120 Minut*, Alan Chumak's five-to-seven-minute séances offered viewers healing from all kinds of medical problems and diseases. The short segments became daily spectacles, generating tremendous viewer interest. Chumak asked viewers to put water and cream in front of their TV sets, "persuading them that this would 'charge' them with a special healing energy."[33] Soon Chumak gained nationwide fame, and the government honored him publicly with an international press conference at the Ministry of Foreign Affairs. Eventually one of his colleagues in the art of mass-mediated healing was granted a TV show of six half-hour séances broadcast on national television during the highest-rated time periods. People who claimed to have been cured offered testimonies on the show, and the program host read letters and telegrams from people across the nation who said that they, too, were healed by the séances.[34] Although Chumak's séances hardly constitute a religion, they illustrate the power of the media market to generate storytelling that competes with more traditional religious cultures, such as Eastern Orthodoxy. American media similarly produce popular syncretisms that, as Wirth describes, "seek to combine a variety of hitherto incongruous elements in such a way as to attract the greatest number of followers."[35]

The reason why some stories capture national markets and others do not is largely a mystery. If the major media companies knew the answer they would be far more profitable, and advertisers would be inclined to spend even more money on commercials. Carey believes that most popular culture creates moods and motives that normally do not reach beyond the media to the street corners and churches "where other dramas are being enacted and other melodies played."[36] Anyone who can read the tea leaves of popular markets accurately might temporarily become a guru. In the 1970s, for instance, Fred Silverman of NBC television somehow managed to predict one hit show after another. He seemed to "know precisely what the American people [would] resonate to."[37] Market research firms, pollsters, newspaper pundits, and even some academicians sometimes act as gurus who are able supposedly to identify and predict changes in the markets for popular stories.

The interactions between the secular subnarratives of the mainstream media and the metanarrative of religious tribes in America are complex and paradoxical. Popular culture sometimes knocks at the gates of the church, offering its own ways of worshiping attractive icons, sanctifying saintly performers, and sermonizing about moral life. "All cultures are dependant on cultic forms, even our technological culture," says M. Daniel Bryant. He adds that cinema is one "place where we can learn the myths of the culture, meet its heroes, and be instructed in the characteristic habits."[38] As national media intentionally identify and coalesce a nation's beliefs, they sometimes resonate with a hopeful audience. More often by accident, popular culture breaks loose from its position in society and temporarily resonates with people's vague mythological yearnings. In short, popular culture can serve a mythopoetic function in Americans' lives, creatively reflecting and directing audiences' sentimental desires through the expression of quasi-religious stories. The market sometimes turns the secular signifying system on its head, transforming banality into perceived beauty and mass taste into seemingly mythic tales. Audiences become fans—fanatics—of television characters, film stars and sports celebrities.

Market-driven subnarratives and religious metanarratives both usually confirm existing cultural beliefs more than they challenge them. Market-driven mass communication tends to use narrative implicitly as a rhetoric of communion, a means of recalling the audience's shared beliefs. Of course the immediate purpose of a mass-mediated story is probably to maximize audience ratings, to sell a product, or to increase box office receipts. This is the primary difference between folk and popular art; popular art nearly always has a patron waiting at the bank or collecting at the cash register, whereas folk art usually serves more organically to affirm collectively the historical story of a tribe. But the market does not automatically obviate the mythopoetic function of popular art. Popular art often offers the audience the means to unquestioned ends—beauty, happiness, and success.[39] Popular culture can help people wish collectively for the state of affairs that they desire, coalescing audiences' desires and moods through particular story formulas. Just as religious myths retell the sacred narratives for expectant believers, popular stories try to affirm what the more generic marketplace desires to be true.

Television commercials, for example, are quasi-religious rituals for people who wish to be better than they already are or to improve their lot in life. A handsome young man overcomes unpopularity by using a new toothpaste or mouthwash; a wife restores her husband's love for her by serving him "home-style" spaghetti; a homemaker squelches her feelings of inferiority after discovering the secret of her neighbor's "whiter-than-white" wash. These kinds of tales do not encourage audiences to question a telos—popularity, love, and self-esteem—even if the advertised claims about particular products appear to be outrageous. A spaghetti sauce will not lead to a harmonious marriage, but who doubts that serving the right meals will not help build a happy marriage? And who dares question the goal of a happy marriage? Even TV commercials invite our participation in the making and remaking of largely confirming myths. They do not try to subvert consumers' faith any more than religious narratives dislodge the faith of true believers. Commercials are part of what Williams calls a "magic system" that simultaneously helps create the very needs that the products will supposedly meet.[40]

All types of popular narrative can function mythopoetically in the wider society as well as in the tribal community. Both religious and market-driven stories are able to project a human world that ritualistically affirms already-held beliefs. In the market the stories tend to affirm by accepting us as we are and then making us more that way. They "teach" us interpretations of ourselves by using us as examples. All true stories, says Walter Benjamin, "have an overt or hidden use—a moral, a practical instruction, a rule of life."[41] Stories often display this didactic quality even when they are not intended to educate. The narrative of a "religious community retains and rehearses its characteristic words and acts to maintain its identity against those alternatives of vacancy, chaos, or evil power which seem ready to preempt their place."[42] Public performances of popular narratives, like the rituals of worshiping God, instruct the community of believers and enable them to share their stories and their own meanings of those stories. Religious stories aim primarily at the tribe, whereas popular culture points less precisely to markets defined by demographics and life styles.

The rituals of both popular culture and of religious tribes invite people to share the meanings of narratives. Over the centuries Jews gathered around the Passover table and Protestants met in homes and churches to celebrate Communion. Today television audiences meet in front of the tube for a ritualistic enactment of a community's shared hopes and fears. Like religious rituals, mass media rituals can dramatize communal belief. The daily news, says Carey, "is not information but drama; it does not describe the world but portrays an arena of dramatic forces and action; it exists solely in historical time; and it invites our participation on the basis of our assuming, often vicariously, social roles within it."[43] The media, like religious rituals, do not merely transmit information; they portray symbolic actions among real and imagined people and invite audiences to join in the expressions of these stories by thinking wishfully with others. In the process, religious and popular narratives frame for their audiences many of the everyday rituals of life.

Mass-mediated stories, then, can function like religious myths as they ritualize the values, beliefs, and even the sensibilities of people in a market system. Some stories do this specifically for the metanarratives of particular religious tribes, while others do so more generically through the market and for the cross-tribal society. Even in modern industrial societies narratives can serve as cultural paradigms, organizing a community's experiences around a common repertoire of widely known personae and dramas. Stanley Hauerwas observes that "stories suggest how we should see and describe the world—that is how we should 'look-on' ourselves, others, and the world—in ways that rules taken in themselves do not." As a result, our "character is constituted by the . . . stories that are combined to give a design or unity to the variety of things we must and must not do in our lives."[44] Our culture and our characters are more or less made in the image of our stories.

In spite of the mythopoetic similarities between metanarratives and subnarratives in society, there is also one fundamental difference: Religious metanarratives not only confirm the particular tribe's existing belief system, but they also tend to subvert the mainstream values and beliefs of market societies. The Christian metanarrative, for instance, is significantly at odds with the basic values and beliefs expressed through many mass-mediated subnarratives in market economies. Market-driven media serve a priestly role that largely confirms the existing mainstream culture. Professional communicators thereby become expert mythmakers who tell stories supposedly on behalf of the market. Although the Christian metanarrative plays a similar priestly role within the Christian community—and relies upon prelates and other "experts"—it also serves a prophetic role by challenging various aspects of mainstream culture. Especially when the Christian metanarrative is embraced only by a minority of people in society, it challenges the validity of competing subnarratives as well as other metanarratives. Novelist Walker Percy argues, for instance, that "the Christian notion of man as a wayfarer in search of his salvation no longer informs Western culture." In such a transformed milieu the Christian metanarrative calls for a new consciousness that explores epistemological options that now exist outside of the assumptions of the age.[45] The Gospel metanarrative refuses to pay obeisance fully to the established kingdoms of this world, challenging the "principalities and powers" of each age.[46] Tribal media critics, in particular, use tribal metanarratives and related ideas to critique the established media institutions.

The Christian metanarrative, as interpreted by various tribes, invariably confronts the priestly mainstream media with its own prophetic voices. In the process, the secular media and the religious tribe jockey for rhetorical ground by imagining very different stories of and for society. Religious metanarratives can, to use Percy's words, expose humankind's "nakedness," explore a "new world," or rediscover forgotten language and meanings.[47] Religious metanarratives thereby re-create and reintegrate the disheveled array of human culture that has been fragmented and restructured by the tyranny of ideologies, the logic of mass markets, or simply the inattentiveness of tribes to their own histories. "Except in the rare instances of assassination," says Carey, "news no longer functions aesthetically, for it does not bring back into an integrated whole the fragmented pieces of modern experience."[48] Yet that is precisely what tribal rhetoric under the banner of its own historic metanarrative, claims to do—using the Good News to exegete critically the mediated tales of the day.

The Liturgical Character of Mass-Mediated Narratives

In 1996 public television aired the five-part series *The Wisdom of Faith*. Produced by Bill Moyers, the series was scheduled to run through Passover and the Christian Holy Week as a salute to religion. *Newsweek* called Moyers's guest for the series, Houston Smith, a pioneer in the study of world religions, "the original New Age spiritual surfer." Smith spent much of the previous fifty years in India, Iran, and other regions, "experiencing first-hand the mystical highs of Hindu holy men, Buddhist monks and Sufi saints." He called his own membership in the Methodist Church "a kind of ancestor worship." "The enduring religions at their best," said Smith, "contain the distilled wisdom of the human race."[49]

The mainstream mass media, like Smith, often look for a distilled religion, an archetypal faith without the particularities of time and space, a generic and homogenous religion that captures the imaginations of as many Americans as possible without offending existing religious traditions. In developed societies this homogenized faith can be found in an endless array of mass media subnarratives that collectively constitute a secular "liturgy." Mass-mediated liturgies are analogous to tribal liturgies with respect to two characteristics: the priestly relationship between media and audiences in a market economy, and the formulaic character of storytelling. The priestly role of the media leads media producers to create mythopoetic stories that largely confirm what audiences either believe or want to believe, while the formulaic nature of industrialized storytelling results in predictable and easy-to-produce story forms that coalesce the priestly message. Although there are probably millions of distinct stories in American media, they fall largely into a few established narrative genres that are reworked repeatedly with minor variations. Like traditional religious practices, the mediated rituals invite participants to imagine and to believe in a shared reality.

The centripetal role of the mass media is evident in the large, national media with fairly heterogeneous audiences of religious and nonreligious people. These include the radio and television networks, the national magazines, and a few national newspapers. As Carey suggests, these national media "allowed individuals to be linked, for the first time, directly to a national community without the mediating influence of regional and other affiliations."[50] Novak says that television, in particular, is an instrument of the national, mobile culture and "does not reinforce the concrete ways of life of individual neighborhoods, towns, or subcultures." National television, he concludes, "shows the way things are done (or fantasized as being done) in the 'big world.' It is an organ of Hollywood and New York, not of Macon, Peoria, Salinas, or Buffalo."[51] During the twentieth century national media centralized much of the production of mythological story-telling in American society, amassing large audiences of consumers whose attention could be delivered to hopeful advertisers. Centripetally organized media simultaneously serve the needs of business for profit and the needs of society for solidarity and integration among the many specialized cultures and divergent speech communities. Television, probably more than any other medium, provides a common body of narratives that help define, for good or for bad, America's shared beliefs.

The many subnarratives of popular culture collectively carry tremendous mythological weight. Popular stories come to represent the archetypes of mainstream American culture, the mythological glue that binds together the many disparate subcultures. "Though it may well be true that our present-day archetypal heroes cut pale figures when set side by side with those of earlier cultures," writes drama critic Martin Esslin, "the genesis of today's archetypes is by no means as different as it might appear at first glance." He suggests that the "archetypal characters in ever-recurring situations on present-day American television . . . accurately reflect the collective psyche, the collective fears and aspirations, neuroses and nightmares of the average American, as distinct from the factual reality of the state of the nation." Esslin asks rhetorically, "Does not the prominence of hospitals and disease in story lines indicate a national preoccupation with health, even a certain hypochondria? Do not the sex kittens of the evening series actually represent current ideals of beauty? Are not the mix-ups and grotesqueries of family situation comedies an accurate, if exaggerated, scenario of the embarrassments and triumphs of family life, real or fantasized?" Television dramas, he concludes, are the "collective daydreams of American culture."[52]

Popular stories can be at least superficially mythopoetic as well as entertaining. They provide cultural formulas that help individuals to locate the meaning of their personal lives within the broader society. These ritualized stories function like acolytes in the liturgies of news, drama, sports, and advertising, wielding significant cultural power as they ritualistically project fictional worlds with real-life consequences. Yet their authority, like that of a priest, must always be granted by the faithful followers. If their narratives are totally at odds with what the mediated "parishioners" wish to believe, the mass-mediated rituals run the risk of losing their congregational audiences. This is partly why tragedy has never been particularly popular in American popular culture; the congregation of viewers hopes that life will end happily for all "good" characters. Faithful audiences want to be able to think wishfully about even the everyday narratives that they consume through the media. Americans desire predictable liturgies of hope.

Throughout the history of American television the networks have avoided distinct expressions of particular religious tribes in favor of a more generic faith that is palatable to large, heterogeneous audiences. Distinct religious expression has always been a scarce commodity in prime time television.[53] Father Ellwood Kieser, whose program *Insight* largely pioneered distinctly religious TV in the 1960s, says, "Since the beginning of television, God has been a taboo word. . . . The industry was convinced that entertainment and religion were incompatible."[54] As Joel Stein argues that mainstream television seemed during the 1990s to reverse its stand, largely because of the phenomenally popular CBS series *Touched by an Angel.* Launched in 1993, the commercially successful drama "got the reformation rolling." As Stein tells the story, the network "went hunting for something fluffy to cash in on the New Age angel craze." Instead executive producer Martha Williamson delivered to CBS "some heavy religious programming" about three angels who "come to earth to counsel souls in crisis. Basically, they tell them to shut up and trust God, and then the angel of death takes someone away." As Stein suggests, however, even a New Age craze might not be enough to sustain a new wave of spiritual television fare. The problem, he concludes, is that "the young and reckless still rule. Sinners, after all, have killer demographics."

But the mythopoetic lure of sin in the media is nearly always related to comedic outcomes that affirm the triumph of good over evil in the world. The market system, oriented primarily to mass taste rather than tribal sensibilities, encourages the producers of popular liturgies to emphasize hopeful stories with happy endings. As David Marc argues, American television has always emphasized predictable, formulaic comedies. This most popular of all of the storytelling media, says Marc, acts like America's jester.[55] Americans turn to the tube to be entertained or amused, to have a few laughs and to enjoy a happy ending that at least temporarily seems to solve the confusion of everyday life. Of all of the television genres, sitcoms have been the most consistently popular and profitable. Begun in radio, which took aspects of the genre from vaudeville, the sitcom is both the most formulaic of all network television genres and also arguably the most priestly. In order to please American audiences night after night the broadcast industry repeatedly returns to comedic ritual.

The comedic shape of American popular culture is not just a means of amusement, a thoughtless form of entertainment. Critics like Neil Postman assume that simple, comedic stories represent an intellectual and mythological "descent into a vast triviality."[56] This kind of criticism is akin to evaluating the parables in the New Testament according to their ability to engage deep intellectual responses. In fact, the parables were aimed at average citizens, common believers in God, not at the legalistic Pharisees or the scholarly Sadducees. Like the stories of Jesus Christ, contemporary popular culture is meant to be immediately relevant and meaningful to the childlike people of faith. Both types of story—parable and popular narrative—intentionally ask the hearers and listeners to suspend worldly belief and purely rational discourse in order to let the tales speak to them. To the faithful listener who is already living out the spirit of a biblical parable, the story is an affirming comedy, an assurance that he or she is on the right religious path. Comedy, more than any other liturgical form, culturally confirms without pretense. Sitcoms, in particular, are a populist expression of faith that all things will work together for good.

As a narrative formula, comedy might owe its meaning analogously to religion. In both the Hebrew and Christian traditions, for instance, the work of God in the world is always filled with surprises and impossibilities. The events that should not normally occur somehow do happen. God reverses the tide of normalcy and ultimately redeems otherwise hopeless situations. God gives Abraham a son, Isaac, in spite of the elder's age and personal pessimism. Abraham laughingly asked when God told him that he would have a son, "Will a son be born to man a hundred years old?"[57] Similarly, the Gospel of the New Testament defies all of the odds and saves humankind by sacrificing the Son of God, Jesus Christ. The Hebrew and Christian traditions contain comedic narratives that cast all other stories within the framework of God's often unpredictable mercy and compassion. Viewed within the Christian tribe, the Gospel can be seen as the ultimate comedy, the essential happy ending that results in eternal life for people who do not deserve it.[58]

Comedy, then, is the liturgical inverse of tragedy. Comedy is not composed merely of funny or humorous tales but also of a mythopoetic

rhetoric that creates hopeful meaning out of the chaos of everyday existence and the awful events of actual human life. Comedic narrative is an
interpretive grid, a popular hermeneutic of everyday life, that embraces the
serendipitous good and unpredictable joys of human existence. Both religious metanarrative and secular subnarratives address the discrepancy between how things are in the world and how they should be. A comedic
story "represents a desirable otherness."[59] Comedy is probably the most
popular and humane way of organizing human experience in an imperfect
but improvable world; it is a quasi-liturgical expression of both the value of
human life and the need for grace in human affairs. We laugh not just because a happy ending is funny or humorous, but also because every happy
ending points to hope in the future. When it captures grace—good things
that happen in spite of human foolishness—comedy can transcend the limits of purely human agency. Programs such as *Touched by an Angel* leverage
the power of comedy within a dramatic formula, confirming audiences' expectations that good things can happen even unexpectedly to imperfect
people. Such programs cross the line between tribal metanarratives and
secular subnarratives. Every time comedies touch on reconciliation, they
seize some of the mythopoetic power of liturgy. As Nelvin Vos says, "For
God's sake, laugh!"[60]

Nevertheless, the liturgies of mainstream media are not synonymous
with those of any particular religious tribe. This comedic analogy of the
biblical tradition is easily transformed into hope in mere human agency.
The subnarratives of popular culture replace the God-centric metanarrative of the Gospel with popular religious thought, such as a generic belief
in angels or a trust in the goodness of heroes. The source of hope, the very
cause of salvation, distinguishes traditional Christian doctrine from mass-
mediated narratives of hope. Roman Catholic novelist Flannery O'Connor, for instance, authored seemingly tragic tales in order to point to the
utter futility of human beings who hope to save themselves. "The religion
of the South," she wrote, "is a do-it-yourself religion, something which I,
as a Catholic, find painful and touching and grimly comic. It's full of un-
conscious pride that lands them in all sorts of ridiculous predicaments."[61]
Indeed mainstream popular culture is filled with such pride because it almost invariably diminishes the authority of God and exaggerates the
power of human beings to extirpate evil from the world. From the perspective of the Christian metanarrative, human agency is insufficient for
the deepest form of comedy, which no longer depends on God's agency.

Under the pressure of a market system, most popular comedy is stripped of tribal referents. Mass-mediated narratives often use the liturgical structure of divine comedy without the theological and biblical particularities. As suggested earlier, they typically shift comedy from the vertical realm of God-human relationships to the purely horizontal setting of person-to-person relationships. Many sitcom characters, for instance, overcome complications and confusions in order to resituate themselves in the equilibrium of normalcy. Similarly, film companies test different movie endings to find the one that most satisfies the audience. When popular tales are seemingly tragic stories instead of affirming comedies, the media typically re-contextualize the tragedies in order to cast them in a more hopeful light. Television news, for instance, often concludes each day's litany of tragic events with a hopeful story of human triumph, a secular "doxology" that reminds viewers that things work out for good even in the world of American news. Popular novels, comic books, broadcast commercials, sports reporting, and other forms of narrative capture this comedic liturgy in a market system.

The tug of consumer markets de-traditionalizes mass-mediated expression of comedic liturgies. For instance, popular sitcoms, soap operas, cop shows, and the like are so generic and formulaic that they appear to be produced by no one in particular for everyone in general.[62] But generic appeal is often not enough to hook massive audiences. Hoping to express religious sentiments without expressing tribal convictions that might divide audiences, makers of popular culture often replace belief in a particular God with more "eccentric notions" from "the margins of spiritual life." In the waning years of the twentieth century, writes James Bowman, people were writing of new religions that mixed elements of Western and Eastern faith, including "'Christian-style eschatology with a space-alien obsession.'"[63] Even journalists, he said, were syncretizing the "journalistic impulse" with "the religious and the merely kooky."[64] "Television promises its mortal viewers a magic transformation—youth, love, joy—by imbibing the nectar of the gods," writes Harold M. Foster.[65] Centrifugal pressure of mass marketing leads the storytellers to satisfy the mythopoetic yearnings of millions of consumers with quasi-liturgical tales that promise unusual, bizarre, and incoherent experiences—the formulas of supermarket tabloids and, increasingly, mainstream media. As national media chase broad audience demographics, they generally turn to generically comedic fare that either ignores traditional religion or adopts paranormal spiritual themes, from flying nuns to magical genies and alien creatures. The producers care little about actual religious tribes; they seek cross-tribal allegiances in the marketplace of comedic liturgies.

In a market system, then, centripetal narratives tend to replace indigenous folk tales, family storytelling, and community performances of cultural history.[66] Barry Levinson shows in his fine film *Avalon* how three generations of the Jewish community of Baltimore increasingly lost their own religious, ethnic, and family roots. Striving to become Americans, seduced by the dream of wealth and upward mobility, the family in the movie increasingly replaces cross-generational, domestic rituals with the new, solitary habit of watching television. The medium grafts these individuals' identities to an amorphous national media culture at the expense of their own generational ties and cultural traditions. Having bought houses in the suburbs, earned financial success, and even changed their last name to sound less Jewish, the grandchildren eventually lose ethnic and familial cohesiveness. Although they came to America for liberty and prosperity, they seem to earn little more than the freedom to watch television. Their comedic hope for a happy ending—the American Dream—precipitated a tragic tale of their own religio-cultural demise.

Of all of the media, television most reinforces centripetal liturgies of a common public belief that transcends ethnic and religious variations among the American populace. Through easily apprehended settings, stereotypical characters, and predictable plots, televised stories project meaningful, widely experienced fictional worlds that become part of Americans' shared symbolic universe. The television gathers together a wide spectrum of viewers and then addresses each one individually. In the process, this mass-mediated liturgy comes to speak to and for the individual viewer. By organizing, standardizing, and ritualizing the many subnarratives into a few comedic genres, network television creates a quasi-sacramental viewing experience that effortlessly ushers viewers into a reality that seems to transcend everyday banalities and boredom. As the mythological subnarratives reflect and reinforce each other liturgically within common narrative structures, they communicate collectively even if amorphously. Sitcoms and other largely comedic genres tend to speak from within their popular formula as a unified voice with a coherent mythological meaning. Thanks to the marketplace, the many subnarratives together carry a quasi-religious, univocal cultural weight. John J. Navone writes, "The attitudes and images, the symbols and metaphors of the myth, disclose the character of the individual's hopes, the quality of his dreams."[67] Other media, such as newspapers, radio, and magazines, reinforce the role of televised narratives by discussing and describing them, relating them to other areas of life, and expanding the contexts in which Americans share and learn about televised stories.

These quasi-liturgical subnarratives, then, are more or less a univocal sacred text. The pressures of the marketplace produce less variety of content than repetition and redundancy, a fairly uniform mythological world predicated on social conformity and social control. The mass media function like God, promoting their own processes of "self-thematisation, self-observation and self-description." The media, argues Guenther Thomas, attempt to "bridge the gaps between, and link the differential parts by a general and vague knowledge resulting in an encompassing version of the 'world.'" He believes that television, in particular, acts like a secular liturgy for society, stipulating and accepting established social conventions and "conventional states of affairs." He calls this ritualistic self-defining that takes place through television "metaperformative" and "metafactitive."[68] Like religion, the mass media provide individuals and even entire societies with "normative expectations to which other events may be correlated."[69] This quasi-liturgical function of the media mirrors the way that religion historically has provided self-referential rhetoric tied not just penultimately to itself as a social institution but ultimately to God.

Popular subnarratives locate individuals in a quasi-liturgical world of comedic sentiments. As Sallie TeSelle writes, "We learn who we are through the stories we embrace as our own—the story of my life is structured by the larger stories (social, political, mythic) in which I understand my personal story to take place."[70] *New York Times* religion writer Peter Steinfels admits that for the news media "popular fiction provides a reference point that was once provided to an earlier public by Shakespeare or the Bible."[71] James M. Wall adds, "People who no longer resonate to stories about prodigal sons or unfaithful servants are familiar with lines from popular movies."[72] Popular films allow people to see "religious themes, theologies, morals, myths, and archetypes represented in a visually compelling medium their ancestors never experienced."[73] Americans live amid a "spirited interplay among faiths and between the sacred and secular in the broader culture."[74] The result might be a nation whose religions often seem to look like its mainstream culture and whose mainstream media function mythologically like liturgical religion for millions of consumers in a market system.

The many people who produce mass-mediated stories are acolytes serving these mythopoetic liturgies to the American people. Popular narratives require the work of many people, not the handiwork or even the vision of just one person.[75] On the production side, for example, television requires writers, directors, performers, technicians, and especially producers.[76] These creators work from "available imaginative materials: stories, models, symbols, images-in-action"—a "storehouse of imaginative materials" that Novak calls a "repertoire."[77] Each person influences the resulting dramatic production; however, there is no way to explain or even interpret the content of popular stories merely as a reflection of the values of the people who make it, as some conservative critics have tried.[78] As Warren puts it, "The specific imaginations are planned, produced, and communicated, but the precise way they come together to create an overall sense of reality may not have been planned by any single person or group."[79] Media companies produce popular narratives within an organizational paradigm that indicates the rules of conduct, a kind of professional folklore that is established over years as various types of tales succeed or fail in the marketplace. Popular culture's producers are not gods but priestly acolytes who conserve the liturgical events through the imaginary re-creation of an existing genre.

These popular liturgical myths and practices often conflict with traditional religious metanarratives. The market and tradition never fully mesh. Williams says that the word "tradition" generally implies age-old, ceremony, duty, and respect.[80] Whereas tradition is primarily active and oral—a purposeful "handing down"—mass-media consumption is far more passive and unstable over time. The acolytes of popular culture may not even believe in the stories that they produce—particularly if they hold personally to a religious tradition. Audiences generally do not expect entertainment to affirm their religious traditions. Traditional religious tribes still sometimes reject the rhetoric of communion proffered by market-driven media. As the next section of this chapter clarifies, the media and Christianity in America interact through continuities and divergences in their hermeneutical modes of expression. Often a Christian tribe nurtures its own media critics who use the tribe's interpretation of the Gospel metanarrative as a means of critically interpreting popular culture. At the same time, tribal media can become countercultural modes of prophetic discourse by emphasizing a particular rhetoric of discernment over the mainstream media's comedies of communion.

Media Criticism As Tribal Exegesis
and Prophetic Imagination

In 1993 journalist and filmmaker John Pilger delivered the Raymond
Williams lecture at the Hay-on-Wye festival of literature. His wide-ranging
address examined the nature of "thought control" in capitalist democracies. He recalled writer Simon Louvish's story about a group of Russians
visiting the United States before glasnost. The Russians were amazed to discover that so many reports about the vital issues of the day were simply re-
statements of the same opinions. "In our country," the Russians admitted,
"to get that result we have a dictatorship. We imprison people. We tear out
their fingernails. Here, you have none of that. So what's the secret? How
do you do it?" Pilger also recalled an interview he conducted with Zdener
Urbanak, one of the writers banned by the government in Czechoslovakia
for seeking political reforms under Communism. "You in the West have a
problem," said Urbanak. "You are not sure when you are being lied to,
when you are being tricked. We do not suffer from this; and unlike you,
we have been forced to acquire the skill of reading between the lines."
Truth, concludes Pilger, "is almost always subversive. Otherwise, why
would elites and their hierarchies fear it so much and go to such lengths to
suppress it."[81]

The interaction between tribal metanarratives and mainstream subnarratives in America is both a rivalry and an accommodation between contrasting views of the truth and of the subversion of truth. In a democracy,
tribal cultures both compete via the market and seek a rhetorical common
denominator, depending on the situation. Through the process of tribal
media criticism, however, religious tribes sometimes subvert popular notions of truth while asserting their own, contrary notions of reality. Moreover, tribal critics occasionally use mainstream narratives to critique the
tribe's own misplaced grasp of truth. Tribes' critiques, often publicized in
the tribe's own centrifugal media, help locate tribes as distinct groups
within American society. Tribes thereby maintain tribal faith as an option
within society. P. van Dijk argues that faith "is not hereditary and is not
culturally transferable."[82] Religious tribes must constantly renew their
own identities within society, or they will lose them to mainstream market
assimilation or possibly to co-optation by other tribes. Tribes can easily
transfer religious information from generation to generation, but faith is
much more dynamic and often even unpredictably elusive. As a constella-
tion of internalized beliefs, sentiments and values, traditional faith is not

easily communicated through the mass media. Just as the mass media cannot readily engineer a particular society, a tribe cannot fully mandate its vision of truth even for those within its subculture. As van Dijk puts it, the tribe "can present evidence," but it "cannot forcibly convince. In other words, the essential information transfer must be left to God. That is the most profound reason why we cannot build a Christian culture or society."[83]

Tribal critics often provide a countervailing force to secular culture, a subversive mode of thinking anchored in tribal assumptions. To borrow a phrase from Michael Walzer, we could say that tribal critics in a democratic society are "connected critics" who serve a tradition as well as society.[84] Informed by tribal perspectives, they consider "what is" and the "what if" in ways that often are incompatible with mainstream subnarratives. Tribal criticism frequently subverts the mass media's largely humanistic notions of secular faith. In the Christian tradition such criticism posits a "view of life as contingent upon a source of being which lies ultimately beyond it."[85] Tribal media critics frequently use that ultimate human contingency to exegete the penultimacy of popular culture's vision of truth and reality. In the process, they reveal to the tribe and to society what the surrounding culture "worships" in lieu of God.

Christian media critics usually begin hermeneutically with a concept of what their faith is and what its implications are for biblical or theological interpretation. Philosopher Nicholas Wolterstorff calls these root assumptions the "control beliefs" of faith.[86] The religious critic likely acquires control beliefs from his or her community of faith as the tribe interprets and then applies its understanding of its metanarrative to the wider culture and society. Using a tribe's metanarrative and its modes of interpretation, a critic applies the resulting beliefs and methods to rhetorical situations that confront the exiled tribe. Of course the religious critic might also acquire critical ideas from the wider culture, including from mainstream media critics and news reports about the media. Sometimes the member of one tribe gains meaningful insights from critics of other tribes, as when a Protestant critic considers Catholic discourse or when an evangelical Protestant borrows insights from mainline or Hebrew criticism. Cross-tribal conversations are often enormously influential, especially when the critics in one tribe learn a rhetoric of discernment from another tribe.

In addition to using control beliefs the Christian critic implicitly or explicitly forms a theory about how popular narratives function in the world—how they communicate, how such stories shape their own narrative into meaningful messages or ritualized understandings of culture. Of course the tribal critic might apply to the mediated narratives the same hermeneutical process that he or she uses to make sense of his or her own tribe's sacred stories. In this case the critic assumes that popular stories function for mainstream culture essentially the same way that religious metanarratives function within the tribe. Or the critic might offer a different mode of interpretation of popular stories on the assumption that they are not of a kind with sacred stories. In either case the religious critic assumes both particular control beliefs and a theory of mythopoetical communication.

The tribal critic in America works with one interpretive foot in mainstream popular culture and the other one in his or her own community of metanarrative interpretation. As literary critic David Thorburn puts it, the interpreter of popular culture has to "achieve something of the outsider's objectivity or partial neutrality" while remaining "something of a native informant."[87] The tribal critic is positioned like an Old Testament prophet between the culture of Baal and the tribe's sacred traditions. Working with the tribal control beliefs, the critic invariably discovers points of dissonance between that tribe's overarching story and the media liturgies. Frank D. McConnell even claims that "all art is religious" and that art demands outrage by challenging conventional thinking.[88] This kind of aesthetically contrived control belief invariably elevates the cultural value of secular art and diminishes the significance of religious art. Popular culture, for instance, often imagines particular situations and characters, but it is not necessarily driven by distinctly religious convictions. Much popular art is pastiche that refers only to other popular art.[89] For some people, popular art can function like a religion, but that does not transform the art into a religion. Tribal criticism is not primarily the criticism of learned academicians, professional intellectuals, or elite critics, but rather a form of communal exegesis undertaken by discerning members of a particular religious tradition. I call this *lower criticism with a higher purpose*, namely, using a religious metanarrative and its accompanying hermeneutic to exegete the patterns and meanings of mass media's mythological formulas.

Most Christian criticism of mainstream media is patterned after one or another mode of biblically informed exegesis. The tribal critic gains an understanding of popular culture by appealing to his or her community's sacred narratives, identifying the significant cultural context for those stories, and finally illuminating the popular narratives in the light of the metanarrative. This kind of metanarrative-based criticism first assumes the veracity of its presuppositions as tribally discovered within the metanarrative. Then it defines what the popular cultural text is, such as a TV series. Next it elucidates contexts of the popular text, such as the cultural and historical setting of the people for whom the text is meaningful as well as the material conditions of its creation and financing. Finally, the tribal critic "applies" the religious metanarrative to the derived meaning of the popular text, looking for points of tension, synergy, allegory, irony, and the like. At this point the Christian critic relies deeply on his or her own tribe's notions of morality, aesthetics, biblical significance, and evangelistic mission. In Leszek Kolakowski's terms, the Christian metanarrative functions as a guiding or interpretive narrative that precedes empirical reality and empirical time.[90] American evangelicals tend to be less reflexive about the contingent nature of their understandings of the metanarrative, whereas mainline Protestants tend to be less reflexive about the contingent nature of their interpretations of mediated subnarratives.[91] Both groups generally understate the crucial importance of the market in shaping priestly media content.

In the United States, however, tribal criticism of popular narrative is often moralistic rather than hermeneutical criticism. Some moralistic critics believe that they have the ethical right to moralize in the name of their ultimate cause—to twist the interpretation of popular texts in order to make them conform to preconceived hobbyhorses or tribal fears. They do not believe that the critical interpretation of a public narrative must first be grounded in an honest review of that narrative's text, context, and apparent meaning for a given audience. Religious critics face the same temptations that preachers face within the religious tribe. "If pastors only carry moral sayings in their pockets," warns theologian Eugene H. Peterson, "and go through the parish sticking them like gummed labels on the victims of the week, there will be no pastoral work; they must learn how to be gospel storytellers."[92] Similarly, the tribal critic needs to be able to tell the story of the interaction of the Gospel with popular narratives without succumbing to knee-jerk moralism.

As moralistic provocateurs, some religious critics essentially skip the process of contextualizing the popular text that they are critiquing in order to engage immediately in evaluative rhetoric. Having seen the televisual text and reacted without reflection to one part of it, they are ready to condemn the text's producers and in some cases to attack its sponsors as well. In fact, some tribal critics even skip any analysis of the original text and launch their attacks based merely on hearsay or news media reports about the text. In the case of the public outcry over the film *The Last Temptation of Christ*, for instance, the resulting moralistic campaign used hearsay, media reports about the hearsay, and a smuggled copy of an earlier version of the script.[93] Moralistic criticism becomes a parody of real tribal relationships— a parody that often says more about the critics' penchants than it does about their tribe's metanarrative or the text that is under attack. The most incisive religious critics are primarily exegetes, not moralists; they frame the popular story in terms of tribal control beliefs instead of couching criticism in separate moralistic language. Moralism actually secularizes the religious critic's distinct role in society, turning the community's metanarrative into simplistic delineations of good and evil. Much tribal criticism in America is little more than moralistic hectoring of the media, not metanarrative-based interpretation and evaluation. If religious critics lose their distinct perspectives, the "mantle of the prophets" might descend upon "secular shoulders."[94] Their criticism slips from cultural insight into moralistic labeling.

The other major temptation for tribal critics is condescension. Given many educated people's existing veneration of fine art and their disdain for popular culture, condescending attitudes among critics are often the leading motivation. When tribal critics forget that they, too, are creating a work of human imagination, they are less likely to listen intently to the narrative conversations of the text under review. Tribal critics are not above culture but rather work from the insights of a particular religious culture. They are essentially tribal storytellers who help the tribe fashion its own interpretations of texts that exist outside of its own community of interpretation. A good storyteller is "unwilling to reduce anyone to the formula of a case history, or depersonalize anyone into a statistic."[95] When tribal critics fail to empathize with the people who enjoy popular culture, they will be far more inclined to look down on them as unrefined, uncouth, or even unworthy of intelligent criticism. Andrew M. Greeley and Richard J. Mouw have both admonished their respective Christian tribes for engaging in this kind of condescending rhetoric.[96]

From the early years of the twentieth century numerous American religious tribes have both feared and condemned Hollywood as a worldly and immoral culture. Sometimes they have criticized virtually all popular culture and tried to restrict their members' access to movies, recorded music, and the like.[97] This fear, regardless of how justifiable in a given situation, sometimes leads religious critics to begin their exegesis of a popular text condescendingly—to assume that the media texts are thoroughly evil and worthy of only negative evaluation. This type of initial bias against popular culture encourages some tribes to look arrogantly upon an entire genre, industry, or medium and to blindly dismiss exceptions to their own stereotypical condescension.[98] As Mouw points out, some theologians' views of popular culture are far too elitist and too insensitive to the ways that average believers desire valuable religious truths from nonacademic culture.[99] After all, religious truth itself is often expressed through popular culture, not just through academic theology or fine art.

So the Christian critic uses a vertically oriented rhetoric, which includes God's revelation, to exegete the horizontally oriented myths of mainstream media. If the American church relies on a purely horizontal paradigm, it is merely using the contemporary culture to exegete other contemporary cultures. The vertical twist in tribal criticism brings together the "meta" and "sub," the ultimate and the penultimate. As the next section shows, Christian criticism is often dynamic, multifaceted, and robustly multifarious. Although such criticism is informed by tradition, it is also frequently aimed at capturing a "true" interpretation that can serve the wider society as well as the tribe with valuable insights.

Four Examples of Tribal Criticism

In a revealing assessment of mainstream television's coverage of the Los Angeles riots in 1992, Patrick O'Heffernan says that the medium had become the "nerve system of national societies and of the World society." He argues that television "constructs our reality, it tells us what is going on out there, past the places we can see, illuminating the nuances of our planet that we cannot see, but which affect our hometowns." He adds, however, that a "Television Heisenberg Principle" is emerging from the medium's ambiguity. The media do not just reflect reality; they also question widely accepted American values such as individualism, consumerism, and the legitimacy of violence. Everyday television "tells us that violence is a routine part of life and that individuals use it to get the things that they want to consume."[100]

O'Heffernan's interpretation of how television shapes American culture points to the crucial role of the tribal critic in making sense of the mass-media's view of society. Using his or her own imagination, the critic can cast alternative stories that question the real value and impact of mass-mediated narratives. The critic can imagine a different, presumably better world and consider whether the media are moving us toward or away from his or her tribal concept of the good life. In some cases the critic illuminates existing roadblocks and articulates the communication-related means that the tribe should use to achieve that better world. O'Heffernan, for instance, not only evaluates the media coverage of the Los Angeles riots; he also asks his readers to consider what kind of world they wish to inhabit. The tribal critic can help the community of believers imagine an alternative vision of social reality that is in tune with its tribal beliefs and sentiments. In this sense, tribal criticism does not aim merely to deconstruct mainstream mythologies; it also aims to reconstruct tribal liturgies of shared understanding and to reassert tribal expressions of hope.

This section examines how four tribal critics make sense of the interaction of the Christian metanarrative ·and the mainstream media's liturgical subnarratives. Each of these four Christian exegetes of American popular culture—Carnell, Fore, Nelson, and Greeley—represents a particular method of interpretation, although they all rely upon the same Christian metanarrative for their control beliefs.

Edward J. Carnell, a leading evangelical theologian in the 1950s, explicitly uses the Christian metanarrative and accompanying theological commitments to evaluate the new medium. His book, *Television: Servant or Master?*, is a remarkable achievement given the fact that it was published when television was just starting to eclipse radio as the primary national storyteller in America. Many evangelicals at the time simply rejected the new medium as Hollywood's decadent intrusion into the home.[101] Filmmaker Paul Schrader, who was raised in a conservative Protestant family, says that "when TV *did* come in, it undermined the church position. . . . The value system of the outside world shot straight into the homes. After TV there was no way to keep the outside out."[102] In Carnell's view, television had the potential, however unlikely, to become a moral, theological, cultural, and aesthetic force for good. Quoting Charles Dickens's *A Christmas Carol*, Carnell writes in his preface, "'Men's courses will foreshadow certain ends, to which, if perused in, they must lead. But if the courses be departed from, the ends will change.'"[103] Hoping to redirect television toward the proper ends, Carnell suggests four ways that the new medium "threatens" church and society.

Carnell begins with the tube's preeminent threat: the "secularization of our culture." Television might make the "things of the flesh" so alluring that a "chronic televiewer, deluded into thinking that man may live by bread alone, will sell out his divine sonship in favor of the baseness of animality."[104] The problem is television's power to mirror the outside world in the formerly protected enclave of the home. Television's subtle appeal is "stunning." It does not ask "man to kill or steal; it only commands that stones be made bread"—Carnell's reference to the devil's temptation of Jesus Christ.[105] The main problem is not the obvious portrayal of drunkenness, erotic nudity, gambling, and other sins. Television is far too subtle for such easy corruption. Carnell suggests that television might pass the letter of moral law—especially moralistic Westerns like Hopalong Cassidy films aimed at children. Television's subtle corruption is much more "covert"; it expresses a "philosophy" that "makes no room for Jesus Christ. All problems are happily solved without any serious reference to His cross. Life can successfully be met without the slightest petition for grace."[106] In other words, television's subnarratives are fundamentally secular.

Carnell calls television's humanistic view of life, devoid of serious reference to God, the "greatest hoax in history." He compares it to the scientist's pretension that "through the control and prediction of natural forces one can carve out a utopian civilization." Only a "serious reference to God," says Carnell, "can elevate man to that position of dignity which he senses by intuition ought to be his." Even scientists recognize the need for "narrative ethics," he adds, whereas television moguls glut the airwaves with "ball games, puppet shows, water carnivals, circuses, ancient films, comedians with a hundred gimmicks, jugglers, wrestling burlesquers, acrobatic dancers, card players, and a dump truck full of other balms to soothe man into believing that he is able to know life's fullness by bread alone." The evangelical tribe ought to worry about the medium's self-referential view of reality, its spiritually impoverished rhetoric of pretense, and its assumption that human beings have no allegiances or responsibilities beyond this world and their own life. Carnell's other three critiques of television—the desecration of personal initiative, the exploitation of fleshly lust, and the warping of children's minds—fall within his overarching assessment of the medium's secular worldview. [107]

Carnell acknowledges at the end of his book that he is acting as a gadfly of the church, just as Socrates was an Athenian gadfly. Carnell penned the book in order to "nettle people into critical thought, not to make them peaceful." He hoped to bother the "pessimists and perfectionists who see nothing but evil in video and who feel justified washing their hands of the entire matter," as well as the "chronic optimists" who perceive the medium through "rose-colored glasses." History without the eternal archetypes is "chaos," he writes, "but the eternal archetypes without history are an irrelevance."[108] His nuanced critique was relatively rare in American evangelicalism, which settled into largely moralistic attacks and de-contextualized interpretations of how subnarratives shape culture. In fact, Carnell's book may yet be the single most perceptive and sobering critique of television from an evangelical perspective. Like Paddy Chayefsky's blisteringly sardonic film about the American television network industry, *Network*, Carnell's book is a stinging critique of a medium that is portrayed as lacking any cosmic compass.

Without question the most influential tribal critic using the Christian metanarrative to critique the mass media is mainline Protestant theologian and church leader William F. Fore. In a number of influential books, through speaking engagements around the country, and via his participation in the World Association for Christian Communication and the Communication Commission of the National Council of Churches, Fore became the leading spokesperson for the mainline Protestant assessment of popular culture.[109] In addition, Fore did as much as any Protestant theologian to illuminate the mythological character of American popular culture. In his 1970 book, *Image and Impact: How Man Comes Through in the Mass Media*, Fore presents a mythological critique of mass communication that has significantly shaped mainline Protestant theory and theology about the media. "Technology and the media constantly tell us about ourselves, who and what we are," begins Fore. "The media add perspective to our flat ego-centered worlds" and "transmit culture," including a kind of religion. Television is not primarily entertainment but rather a form of "education" that helps Americans to "apprehend" their world.[110] In more recent writing, Fore defines myths as "stories that unfold the worldview of a people." Fore says that in the ancient world "the most powerful people were the mythmakers. It is the same today and today our most powerful mythmakers are the mass media." Fore suggests *"how Christians can relate their understanding of the Gospel to this culture, especially as communicated by the mass media."*[111] His rhetoric of discernment assumes a major conflict between the Christian metanarrative and the subnarratives expressed in popular media.

As he exegetes the media world, Fore explains the "myths about society in general," the "total cultural worldview" of the mainstream media. First, the media promote the myth that *"efficiency is the highest good."* According to Fore, this myth reflects the "spirit of capitalism" and places "getting things done" above all other human values and goals. Second, the media express the myth that *"technology defines society"*—that technological "progress" is necessarily good and inevitable. Third, the media tell Americans that *"the fittest survive."* Fore associates this myth with Social Darwinism and suggests that the media reflect a worldview in which the fittest in society are *"not* poor and nonwhite Americans." Fourth, Fore argues that media mythology expresses the idea that *"power and decision making start at the center and move out."* Political communication emanates from Washington, whereas financial communication comes from New York and entertainment from Hollywood. He contrasts this centralization of power with the American Declaration of Independence, which says that government derives its power from the consent of the governed. "Center-out clearly is essential to the maintenance of both centralized governmental bureaucracies and capitalist economies," concludes Fore. Fifth, Fore rounds out his view of the major media mythologies with this myth: *"Happiness consists of limitless material acquisition,"* including the corollaries that *"consumption is inherently good* and that *property, wealth, and power are more important than people."* Reflecting on the impact of these five myths, Fore concludes that the media place more value on property than on life.[112] In his tribal view, the mainstream media reflect a deeply materialistic and capitalistic view of reality.

Fore eventually summarizes his view of how American mass-media mythology integrates the individual myths into a coherent media worldview. The media value power, wealth, property, consumerism, narcissism, immediate gratification, and creature comforts. The mass-media worldview tells Americans that they "are basically good, that happiness is the chief end in life, and that happiness consists in obtaining material goods." Perhaps worst of all, concludes Fore, Americans "become less and less able to make the fine value judgments that living in such a world requires." Focusing on the institutional aspects of the media, he contends that mainstream media are the "obedient servants of the economic system" because "capitalism tends to turn everything into a commodity."[113] As a result of how the media are institutionalized in modern market economies, they transform human culture into a mere commodity.

Contrasted with Carnell's critique, Fore's is much less personalistic, far more ideological, and not nearly so tied to specific biblical texts. In fact, in his chapter "How to Read Television," Fore first offers a pragmatic theory of signs and symbols and then analyzes television from the perspectives of economics and psychology—with no overarching theological or biblical perspective. He describes the "fragmentary puzzle" that the Scriptures paint about Jesus Christ—the ambiguity of the metanarrative—and the value of scholarly and even scientific modes of inquiry. He argues that "the task for theologians must be to remain true to the church-community of which they are members, while at the same time being committed to the methods and insights of current scholarly inquiry." The biblical Gospels about Christ, he says, are "parables," not "mystical abstractions" or "complicated theological systems." Fore concludes his theological excursion into human communication with a claim that most evangelicals probably would reject: *"there are no meanings except as people give meaning to things and relationships."*[114] Fore accepts the control beliefs of the sociology of knowledge.

Fore's implicit theory of communication is not in tune with his expressed theory of communication, but he nevertheless ends up in nearly the same symbolic arena as the other critics. Although he claims to embrace a postmodern theory of symbolic subjectivity, he affirms particular truths that are historically associated with cross-tribal interpretations of the Christian metanarrative. Fore certainly calls the church to achieve and maintain "distance" from the media by cultivating its own tribal perspective informed by faith.[115] But unlike Carnell, Fore defines the Christian metanarrative in terms of broadly theological motifs rather than more personalistic and pietistic claims about the meaning of Christ and message of the Bible. In order to distinguish between the media mythology and these basic Christian motifs, Fore summarizes five of the church's control beliefs: (1) the goodness of creation, (2) the human "fall," the "recognition that evil can come into the world through the self-centeredness of individuals," (3) the "covenant story" in which God reconciles people if they worship only God, (4) the "reign of God" that occurs "within us" through the work of the Holy Spirit, and (5) "the servant and Savior" Jesus Christ, who by "his death and resurrection became the Lord of history, providing both reconciliation and hope for us all."[116] For Fore, these are the nonnegotiables of the faith that the tribal critic should use as rhetorical equipment for discerning media. Although he accepts the more relativistic theory of the sociology of knowledge, he also adheres to particular Bible-centric control beliefs widely accepted among Christian tribes.

Reflecting his belief in the parabolic nature of the Gospels, Fore concludes his critique with the claim that the Christian metanarrative and mainstream media myths are largely incompatible. The media affirm wealth and possessions, he decides, whereas Christ tells the rich young ruler to sell all that he owns. Similarly, says Fore, Jesus questions the idea that money can buy anything and affirms the idea that "anyone who wants to be a follower must leave self-centeredness behind and follow him, which involves taking up the cross." Fore adds that the Christian worldview urges believers to love their enemies, give power to the poor and other powerless people, create and maintain inclusive community, and live in harmony with all of creation.[117] Although Fore's theology is different from Carnell's, both critics conclude that the Christian metanarrative and the mass-mediated subnarratives are worlds apart. They define the "City of God" somewhat differently, but they agree that it is not the same as the "City of Man." Moreover, they both hold open the possibility that if the church does not develop and apply a meaningful rhetoric of discernment to society, it may be forced entirely into cultural exile. To some extent, they agree, the Christian tribes already live in exile.

Finally, much of Fore's critique of the media would likely be shared by non-Christians who would affirm Fore's critique of unbridled capitalism, the poorly regulated market economy, and the resulting consumer culture. Fore's rhetoric, far more than Carnell's, assumes some commonality of belief with nonreligious groups in society. His exegetical model shares cultural assumptions about democracy and industry that many liberal and some conservative critics alike could affirm. Fore speaks not just to the tribe but also to scholars and educated citizens who share his concerns about venal media in contemporary society. At its core, Fore's critique addresses the media's institutional love for mammon and the resulting American principalities and powers in the world of mass communication. But in the end Fore, like Carnell, is deeply American. He thinks optimistically about a better future: "The media can be reformed. Its myths can be changed."[118] His rhetoric of discernment leads to a rhetoric of conversion that holds out hope for a better media world and hence for a better society.

Presbyterian John Wiley Nelson offers an unusual variation on tribal criticism. If Carnell moves from Scripture to culture and if Fore travels from sociology and theology to mythology, Nelson works from mythology to theology. Nelson presumes that media myths are a secular theology or worldview. He applies to the mass media five essentially theological questions that, he believes, are answered by all "belief systems": (1) the nature of evil, (2) the source of evil, (3) the source of good (that is, who will deliver us from evil), (4) to what are we delivered, and (5) the way to that deliverance.[119] In other words, he exegetes the mass-media liturgies by interpreting their implicitly theology-like form and substance. Like Jean Shepherd in the opening story of this chapter, Nelson plays the role of a theologically oriented anthropologist, hoping to discover the "cosmic ideas" within American media mythology. In Nelson's eyes the American media together represent a belief system that is "a systematically arranged set of answers to basic life-problem questions. All such answers are directed toward the resolution of unsatisfactory present experience in the direction of optimum fulfillment."[120] Nelson's functionalistic approach to the tribal exegesis of secular texts assumes that the life-and-death questions answered by the Christian metanarrative are also answered implicitly by the media mythologies. The media are transmitters of the "American cultural 'religion.'"[121]

Assuming that mainstream media express a kind of civil religion, Nelson discovers a popular theology presumably embedded in American media and perhaps even in American culture. The media's answers about the nature and source of evil are: Families and other social institutions are threatened by external forces, by evil people or organizations, not by internal factors such as weaknesses among the members of the social groups threatened. Mass-mediated salvation, says Nelson, comes from a specially gifted individual who often has "uncanny coolness and imperturbable self-control in the face of evil incarnate." The hero delivers people back to "family and the family-community, stabilized and promoted by schools and churches, by law and order, by peace, tranquility, and domesticity." Finally, argues Nelson, there is no room in popular stories for a way toward ultimate salvation because the tales do not imagine a world that requires a final, eschatological battle. In popular mythology the goal is merely for people to overcome day-to-day problems. Media salvation is practical and immanent, not final and transcendent.[122] The media emphasize the horizontal relationships among people while largely ignoring the vertical relationships between human beings and their creator or savior.

Nelson comes to these conclusions about popular culture's quasi-theological worldview after an extended analysis of films, country music, popular magazines, and detective fiction. He finds the American Western story, in particular, to be the best expression of the "dominant belief system in American life." Westerns and the other forms of American popular culture help sustain the "secular" beliefs of most people in the United States. "Popular culture," contends Nelson, "is to what most Americans believe as worship services are to what the members of institutional religions believe."[123] The mass media thereby function as a default religion, the lowest common denominator of American mythological belief for those who do not acquire their worldview from a real religion.

Only after his extended cultural exegesis does Nelson connect the Christian metanarrative to American mythology. In popular culture, writes Nelson, the community must be worth the hero's sacrifice, whereas the Christian "Gospel says exactly the opposite." "Far from being essentially immanent, humanity not only was not worth the sacrifice, and didn't want it anyway, but was also responsible for Jesus' death—and would be any-time if he came!" Nelson also argues that the tendency of the American be-lief system to identify the source of evil as external to the community conflicts with the Christian assumption that evil by original sin exists in all people. He claims that the American mythology about external evil might shape Americans' views of criminality and their inability to feel empathy for the "criminal element." Nelson even wonders if mass-mediated mythol-ogy accounts for the popularity of capital punishment. American Chris-tians, he says, "have the opportunity to raise critical questions about the necessary connection of justice and violence, and the simplistic distinction between good (community) and bad (sources of evil), with which we have all grown."[124]

Nelson's religio-anthropological exegesis of the main themes of popular culture is considerably removed from the interpretive methods of both Carnell and Fore. Nelson looks for the system of meaning that he assumes is embedded in popular media narratives. Starting with this kind of bibli-cal-theological control belief, Nelson examines how in each genre the var-ious quasi-liturgical characters and plots mesh to form coherent meaning. But in striving for such discursive symmetry, he overlooks the fact that much of popular culture is meant to be experienced, not to be read like a well-integrated argument. Nelson is likely more correct than misguided about the quasi-theological nature of mass-mediated stories, but he should not conclude that his hermeneutics are accurate without also communicat-ing with the people who enjoy such popular culture. He needs to deter-mine if the audiences of detective stories, for instance, read the genre the same way that he does. Do they seek restored social balance, retribution, physical health, and well-being—to summarize Nelson's conclusions about the genre? Or do they appreciate primarily the sense of aesthetic satisfac-tion in a cleanly finished tale? Nelson assumes that such meaning exists in the cultural artifacts, where anyone would discover it. Fore's sociology of knowledge, more in tune with postmodern theory, assumes instead that various individuals and tribes might read the same television text differ-ently, while Nelson's Platonic Theory of Mass Communication assumes that all human culture codifies particular answers to some of the most fun-damental issues of life.

Nelson also is uninterested in the political economy behind mainstream media production and distribution. He assumes that mass-media genres automatically take on the particular quasi-liturgical structures and mean-ings in tune with the surrounding culture. Presumably the economics of

production and the ideologies of media companies at least partly account
for the resulting story lines. Nelson virtually ignores the ideological issues
that Fore emphasizes. If Fore sees media content as shaped primarily by
economic structures and interests, Nelson assumes that such content results almost purely through the workings of the market. Nelson's Platonic
exegesis is a quest for the undiluted truths inherent within particular cultural forms. Fore, on the other hand, believes that there are no meanings
inherent in message forms; the meanings emerge from real cultural practices, especially economic activities. Nevertheless, Nelson and Fore come to
some of the same critical conclusions about American popular culture.

True to American optimism, Nelson concludes his critique of the nation's popular culture with a practical agenda. His hermeneutic, he argues,
"will not only renew interest in Christian theology, but will also enable
clergy and lay people to determine their logical priorities." The most relevant theological issues will "leap out at us," and pastors will better understand their parishioners' "particular frustrations and anxieties." Above all,
the church will be able to do a far better job preaching the Gospel meaningfully to congregants and discipling new believers in the church. In
short, by exegeting popular texts as if they were systematic expressions of
secular theology, the church will be far more effective at evangelization.[125]
As a tribal critic, Nelson relies partly on a rhetoric of conversion to uphold
the value of critical discernment for the benefit of the tribe and the nation.
Nelson argues that his mode of media exegesis is especially valuable for
what it can contribute to the goal of evangelism.

In *God in Popular Culture* Roman Catholic priest, sociologist, and novelist
Andrew M. Greeley sets out on a personal journey to develop a "theology
of popular culture." He argues that popular culture is a *locus theologicus*, a
theological "locale in which one may encounter God." Popular storytelling
provides an opportunity, he says, for people to "experience God and to tell
stories of God, or, to put the matter more abstractly, to learn about God
and to teach about God."[126] In short, God and theology can be expressed in
and through even the most popular mass-mediated narratives, because religion is an imaginative activity before it is a cognitive one.[127] If Nelson
strains critically to reveal popular culture's substitute for true religion,
Greeley looks hopefully for signs of God's grace within the media. Greeley
assumes that all human culture will reflect sacramentally some of the
goodness of God.

In a virtual reversal of Nelson's highly systematic and deeply cognitive
hermeneutic of popular story, Greeley offers a sacramental hermeneutic of

ordinary culture—the ability of God to work through everyday people, to speak through "the objects, events, and persons of life." Culture, suggests Greeley, occurs when the creative imagination of a writer or artist "leaps" to the creative imagination of a reader or viewer. In other words, both the initial creator and the user (or "re-creator") of popular culture engage in creative works of their imaginations. "Creativity," says Greeley, is "that experience when something inside the self takes over and tells you, often quite imperiously, what comes next." Communication occurs when the artist and the "creative consumer" of the artist's work share their experiences, when the two people's mutual experiences tell them that they have experienced the same thing. In addition, because in Catholic theology the "world is seen as a metaphor for God," it is possible for artists and their creative consumers to experience God by way of the analogies for God that are embedded in even "secular" popular culture. In fact, there really is no such thing as thoroughly secular popular culture. Any reality, says Greeley, "may trigger a 'grace' experience (and hence everything is sacramental in the sense that everything has the potentiality of revealing the source of our hopefulness)."[128]

In order to make his case for a sacramental control belief, Greeley exegetes many varieties of popular stories, looking for the ways that people's experiences "in the secular" are then "correlated and re-presented through liturgy." After viewing *The Cosby Show* and other sitcoms, for instance, Greeley says that he is "prepared to propose that anyone who can certify that they have viewed two of these programs during the preceding week can be dispensed, if not from Sunday church attendance, then at least from listening to the Sunday homily/sermon. They do it a lot better than we do it." Greeley calls Bruce Springsteen a "blue-collar prophet" and a "Catholic troubadour" who defends the American Dream, rages against how the country mistreated Vietnam War veterans, and expresses the meaning of the nation's flag. He celebrates fantasy literature for continuing the fairy tale and the legend, castigates the Roman Catholic Church for "giving up" storytelling, criticizes theologians for fleeing from stories on the false assumption that myths are unhistorical and unsophisticated, and laments the fact that his own Catholic tribe has lost its "storytelling tradition." He calls Stephen King the "most popular storyteller in America" and suggests that King's novels remind readers of the fact that life is filled with potential horrors—with far more potential disasters than actually occur. Writes Greeley, "I'm not sure whether Stephen King really sighs with relief at the end of the day and announces to his wife, 'Well, they didn't get me again today.' But it's not a bad prayer of gratitude to utter every night."[129]

Greeley saves his most trenchant exegesis for his analysis of the ways that God and theology surface in American films. "Film in the hands of a skilled sacrament-maker is uniquely able to make 'epiphanies' happen," he proclaims. Examining films such as *Places in the Heart*, *Purple Rose of Cairo*, *A Day in the Country*, *Ladyhawk*, *The Breakfast Club*, and *The Gods Must Be Crazy*, Greeley finds "homily material" and "hints that are obvious and even easy to comprehend of the Being who lurks in beings." Woody Allen is the best contemporary filmmaker, Greeley argues, and even an artist "preoccupied by God," a "God-haunted person." Greeley wonders "who else makes films that honestly and unambiguously ask about the existence of God and the purpose of life and suggest tentative answers that . . . are acceptably Catholic?" There might be more Catholic films, he argues, except for the fact that the motion picture industry was "shaped by Eastern European Jewish immigrants who were mostly agnostic and very ill at ease with religion in any manifestation." Meanwhile, the Catholic Church in America was "caught up" in its urban immigrant experience and "deeply committed to protecting a presumed fragile faith of the immigrants and their children." Instead of engaging the movie-making process, he says, the church responded defensively through the Legion of Decency and Hays Office. Nevertheless, religion continued to appear in American cinema and beyond. Greeley finds, for instance, that Clint Eastwood's character in the spaghetti Westerns is a "proto-Christ figure" that reveals the human hunger for a "paladin," even a "savior figure in our culture of Jesus of Nazareth." By the time of Eastwood's role in *High Plains Drifter*, the "man with no name has become a predestined savior and avenger."[130]

Greeley anchors his sacramental view of imaginative storytelling in a love for the tribe and a desire for the community of believers to reclaim their narrative sensibility and their storytelling skill. He denounces the "heretical notion" that the human imagination is not to be trusted, the elitist idea that only academic critics know the best way to approach cinematic culture, and the tribal assumption that the most effective way to indoctrinate young people is the "agonistic approach" rather than an empathetic approach. Greeley is convinced that popular culture could lead many more people to God if the church were open to popular storytelling and less committed to approaching culture with an "adversarial intellect." "The agonist is almost necessarily mean spirited" and "always on the attack," settling "only for the perfect." Under such a hermeneutic of suspicion, says

Greeley, "[t]he critic may never be entertained," but he or she will "have a hell of a lot of fun attacking." Regardless of what the church thinks about popular culture, Greeley concludes that even some of the most popular stories have "theological, homiletic, and catechetical implications. We must listen to the rumors of angels."[131]

Greeley argues that the church's own moral blinders prevent it from seeing how much popular culture, from sitcoms to romantic novels, reveals moral issues and ethical dilemmas. He finds God at work in the biblical ideas and sacramental analogies to Christ and to the Gospel expressed in much popular art. Greeley observes that popular culture is loaded with biblical and theological insight that common folks can grasp, even if the theological scholars wrongly look down upon such narratives. He attacks cultural elites who hold up the aesthetic superiority of "fine art" and categorically assume that popular culture is inferior. Using a quasi-liturgical argument, Greeley argues that it makes little sense to evaluate the aesthetic merits of human culture across different genres; he argues that such judgments should occur largely within genres. Finally, Greeley contends that tribes are losing an opportunity to spread the faith through powerful, narrative-based, largely nondiscursive modes of electronic communication. Poor media criticism leads to ineffective evangelism.

Greeley's optimism about popular art, his relentless pursuit of signs of grace in everyday cultural artifacts, is at first unnerving. He initially seems not to see any significant tension between the Christian metanarrative and the mass-mediated subnarratives. But here and there Greeley lucidly critiques particular expressions of popular culture, sometimes even severely. For example, he wonders if novelist John le Carré's fictional portraits of the "shadow-world" always teeter on "the brink of nihilism and despair." Greeley asks if humans are no better than those in le Carré's world—and if not, "What difference is there between good and evil?"[132] Greeley repeatedly identifies the tension between the quasi-liturgies of popular story genres and the real sacraments of the church, but he always begins on the side of grace rather than on the side of the fall into sin. This deeply Catholic rhetorical move is anchored in two assumptions: the idea of the goodness of all people created in the image and likeness of God, and the sacramental qualities within all human culture that more or less reflect something of the goodness of God to all persons. Greeley's Catholic control beliefs are also culturally liberating for Christians who might otherwise sense only the antagonistic tension that his paradigm intentionally tries to overcome on behalf of both the church and the media. Finally, Greeley's sanguine posture might be the most characteristically American sentiment among all four critics. His rhetoric of communion sacramentally extends God's grace to all people, saints, and sinners. Such grace is the biblical-theological center of his criticism.

These four critics of American popular culture document how vibrant, interesting, and provocative religio-tribal criticism can be when it avoids moralism and condescension in favor of metanarrative-based interpretation. They also reveal some of the disparate strains of interpretation that result from various Christian traditions as well as from alternative methods of using the Gospel to exegete contemporary culture. Oddly enough, Greeley's critique might focus most ardently on a rhetoric of conversion even though American Roman Catholics are often among the least evangelistically inclined Christian tribes. Mainline Protestant Fore's biting attack on American consumerism carries the kind of moral language that Americans might associate with evangelicalism or even fundamentalism. Fore's critique shows that mainline Protestants care deeply about morality but that, contrasted with an evangelical critic such as Carnell, they may focus on institutional rather than personal moral issues, and on collective as much as personal sin. Nelson's well-integrated critique of American media's self-contained worldview suggests that the field of popular culture studies has at least somewhat influenced religious criticism. His formalistic hermeneutic is a telling illustration of how a community of interpretation can systematically use genre criticism to illuminate contrasting control beliefs.

One more point is worth noting about tribal criticism. Each tribe's understanding of other religious tribes is mediated largely through the mass media. Americans may learn more about Roman Catholics, evangelicals, and mainline Protestants from the media than they do from serious dialogue with each other. If this is the case, the role of religious critics is even more important. Presumably they can help each tribe know what it believes, how those beliefs differ from media mythology, and how such beliefs are at odds with or in harmony with the beliefs and practices of other tribes. William Donahue of the Catholic League for Religion and Civil Rights says, "The more dissenting the Catholics, the more reasonable they're portrayed [in the media]. The more Orthodox, the more Neanderthal."[133] If he is correct, Catholics and the other tribes stand to lose in many mass-mediated portrayals. Tribes face not only mythological competition from mainstream subnarratives, but also a distortion of their tribe's and other tribes' beliefs and practices.

Tribal media criticism is one way for religious groups to participate in conversations about their faith and about the wider society. Using a rhetoric of discernment, tribal criticism focuses primarily on the interaction of the religious community's metanarrative and accompanying traditions with the wider media culture. Such criticism can also express a rhetoric of exile to warn the tribe about its minority stake in the mainstream culture. Tribal criticism even establishes criteria that enable the tribe to express a rhetoric of praise about those aspects of mainstream culture that are more or less in tune with the tribe's metanarrative. These four examples of tribal criticism in the United States suggest that tribes find value in criticism both because it helps them to affirm their distinctive self-identity and because it gives them hope that discernment can lead to conversion and eventually greater community. Thus the rhetorics of conversion and communion become two sides of the same meta-exegetical acts of tribal criticism.

Conclusion

When the archaeologists in Shepherd's tale uncover the tins of television commercials in a long-abandoned skyscraper basement along Madison Avenue, they quickly assume that the short vignettes are religious icons from the history of the United States. Their far-fetched assumptions might be more accurate than illusionary. Under the pressures of mass marketing and the overall quest to commercialize American culture, the mass media developed during the twentieth century an amazingly extensive system of liturgical propaganda. Yet the centripetal forces that try to leverage the national media into one enormous, hegemonic force invariably meet with resistance from various groups, including religious tribes. American society remains at the beginning of the twenty-first century a remarkably vibrant and dynamic arena in which competing subcultures and shared interests interact. As Alexis de Tocqueville observed, the United States has "no capital: enlightenment like power is disseminated in all parts of this vast region; the rays of human intelligence, instead of starting from a common center, therefore cross each other going in all directions."[134] America is a nation of crisscrossing narratives that inform, inspire, confuse, and confound.

In the case of Christianity in America, clearly tribal critics are frequently at odds with the national media's mythopoetical formulations of the American experience. As Park suggested already in the earlier years of the twentieth century, the "art of the moving picture" might be among "the most profound and subversive cultural influences in the world today."[135] The tribes should foster and listen to their own critics who help direct the tribe through the confusing combinations and permutations of mass mythology. Optimistic Americans certainly love their media comedies, but tribal critics are not so quick to accept the media's smooth tales of happy endings. In addition, the evangelistic impulse still shapes much tribal theologizing and dreaming. Nevertheless, when Americans adopt tribal systems of significa- tion, they likely become more critical of the priestly liturgies promulgated by the mainstream media. Tribal media criticism is nearly a cottage indus- try in America, partly because of religious persons' desire to live faithfully in a confusing world of narrative excess and spiritual deflation. But it is still an important part of democratic life. We all would be worse off without tribal critics, because as Jean Bethke Elshtain argues, the churches should play a critical role as interpreters of the culture to the culture. "In recog- nizing and holding ever before our eyes the dignity of the human person created in God's image, one is called to articulate and to work to achieve a common good, not as enforced homogeneity but as a type of community that turns on and recognizes the particular gifts each brings to the banquet table of life."[136]

"Meta" and "sub" narratives often seem to find synergies of both coop- eration and competition. At times Americans appear to be nonreflective media spectators "clamoring for new and more exotic entertainment out of heaven."[137] Mass-media storytellers are happy to fill the need through the market. But at the same time the tribes often realize that they have been taken advantage of, and so they rebel against the media, using their own rhetoric of discernment to strengthen tribal cultures of resistance. The media pundits may talk about a "Judeo-Christian tradition," but the tribes generally know better; they find their critical language in the particularities of their own denominations, church communities, and traditions. The mass media try to bridge the mythological gaps among tribes, to create a unified "version of the world," but such generic narratives are "never com- plex enough for those people who have to act within their respective sub- systems."[138] In the United States some of the mainstream commercial media probably still press toward a market-driven hegemony that continu- ally redefines reality in tune with the nation's dreams. But the tribal critics, among others, sometimes reveal the media's covert orchestration of homo- geneity. "No dominant culture," says Williams, "in reality exhausts the full range of human practice, human energy, human intention."[139] Americans are not just generically religious, as the public opinion polls suggest year after year; Americans tend to yoke themselves to particular religious tribes whose own metanarratives both compete with and energize mass-mediated mythologies. The media are probably less pastiche and more narratively rich because they can call upon the rich metanarrative traditions to give their stories more life.

To the extent that tribal critics can help religious traditions decode the language of everyday media, they can play a vital role in maintaining cultural pluralism and facilitating wise communities of religious resistance to centripetal media. Without them the world would be less wise about market-driven propaganda. But how will tribal critics simultaneously represent the interests of the nation and their own tribes? Strong religious subcultures can seek theocracy as much as democracy; they might push to make their metanarrative the only story of America. The rhetoric of the City upon a Hill sometimes leans in that direction. Who will criticize the critics? As Arnett argues, communities find freedom only when they critique the taken-for-granted aspects of their culture, when they maintain a narrated version of how things should be.[140] As the final chapter of this book suggests, however, a good and just America requires not just a collection of competing tribal mythologies but also a unifying political narrative that simultaneously privileges all people and groups in the public square and provides its own democratic narrative of peace and justice. The clash of tribal and cross-tribal criticism is probably one of the most important features of public life in democratic societies, for each can learn from the other how dependent they both are on common stories of goodness and grace as well as on particularistic tales of humans falling into evil and being rescued by grace.

6

Communing with Civil Sin:
Mainstream Media Purge Evil

◩ ◩ ◩

In his classic book *Public Opinion* Walter Lippmann distinguished between the "world outside" and the "pictures in our heads." Writing in the early 1920s, he observed the growing role of the mass media in modern society. He cogently argued that the media were a "pseudo-environment"—a human creation that people insert between themselves and their external world. This media environment, said Lippmann, is made up of "fictions." "By fictions I do not mean lies," he wrote. "I mean a representation of the environment which is in lesser or greater degree made by man himself. The range of fiction extends all the way from complete hallucination to the scientists' perfectly self-conscious use of a schematic model. . . . For the real environment is altogether too big, too complex, and too fleeting for direct acquaintance." In order for people to "traverse the world," he concluded, they "must have maps of the world. Their persistent difficulty is to secure maps on which their own need, or someone else's need, has not sketched in the coast of Bohemia."[1]

Lippmann's "fictions" are mass-mediated representations of reality. Long before the rise of television, Lippmann recognized that the media were taking on mythological significance as epistemological "maps" of and for the social world. Like religion, the mass media implicitly offer answers to a wide range of human questions about life. News, entertainment, advertising, and the like are rhetorical interpretations of reality. Lippmann called for an elite class of public interpreters who could construct pseudo-environments that presumably would better match the underlying reality of society. Without this new group of intellectuals, he suggested, human ignorance and self-indulgence might so taint symbolic reality that Americans would lose touch with the world that they inhabit. The classical liberal marketplace of ideas was not enough. Neither was a self-informed public. Americans needed experts, veritable priests, to explain reality and to lead people in the right direction. James W. Carey writes of the journalist's prescription for social progress, "Lippmann turned the political world over to private and specialized interests, albeit interests regulated by his new samurai class."[2]

Nearly half a century later, Jacques Ellul addressed a similar theme but with far more pessimism. In his view, the public is not just lost but self-propagandized—intellectuals and journalists included. Mass propaganda does not have to be forced upon people in order to shape effectively the public's views of reality. Nor would any media intelligentsia be able to solve the problem; in fact, they are part of the problem. Ellul alleged that human beings want distorted pseudo-environments, to use Lippmann's term. Propaganda is actually a result of mass society's insatiable but misguided quest for certainty, security, and power. People willingly seek simplistic slogans and join moralistic causes that embrace delusions and distortions of truth. In the modern world, argues Ellul, propaganda simplifies and panders by telling people what they want to believe.[3] Even religion becomes a victim of mass propaganda that feeds symbolically thirsty yet self-delusional audiences what they desire. "Everyone takes it for granted," writes Ellul, "that fact and truth are one; and if God is no longer regarded as true in our day it is because He does not seem to be a fact. Now it is this kind of intimate conviction which constitutes the religion of the masses. To have a 'religion' there is no need of creeds and dogmas, ceremonies and rites: all that is necessary is that men in the mass should adhere to it in their hearts."[4] As traditional religion loses its anchors in tradition, mass-mediated "religion" emerges in the courts of mass opinion. To put the issue most critically, the media eclipse traditional religious faith and practice, substituting the winds of mass opinion for the stability of age-old truth as expressed in tribal sentiments. No social class of priestly intellectuals or journalists can reverse the tide of self-delusional propaganda. Intellectuals are just as self-delusional as every-one else, says Ellul—maybe even more so.

Lippmann, Ellul, and other media critics have contributed to a quasi-religious understanding of both the media and culture.[5] Perhaps the most important aspect of this paradigm is the way that media generate popular culture—culture that is not an expression of particular traditions, but rather is formed out of mass-mediated opinion through the mechanisms of the market and the means of industrial production.[6] Popular culture, as part of the contemporary pseudo-environment, continually challenges ex-tant religions, ideologies, ethnicities, and nationalities. Lacking respect for any particular cultures, markets generate audience-oriented popular cul-ture that is neither historical nor traditional. Popular culture thereby mas-querades as mere entertainment or news when in fact it is a major cultural force that often competes with traditional religious and nonreligious cul-tures. Using the markets as their guides, media moguls create endless loops of predictable messages, formulaic news, entertainment, and advertising. Professional communicators act like religious priests by adjudicating sym-bols, legitimizing genres and rituals, and opening and closing the gates to public participation. American media, in particular, control much of the public storytelling around the world. One critic concludes that "the media are American."[7]

But who should regulate the media market? Do we need Lippmann's priestlike disseminators of wisdom, or are tribal critics and public opinion adequate as means of assessing the meaning of messages in the pseudo-environment? How can a democratic society establish a rhetoric of discern-ment in the context of a market system? Karl Menninger wrote in *Whatever Became of Sin?*, "Fluctuations in the authority and popularity of the church have tended to let the brightest torch of moral leadership pass to the press and television."[8] Should the tribes pass the torch to the media?

Building on the previous one, this chapter argues that the popular the-ology espoused by the media can threaten as well as energize Christian tribes in America. Popular theology—the quasi-religious myths perpetu-ated by the media—needs the restraints of religious traditions and guid-ance from communities of critical religious discourse. Without these influences, popular theology will tend to be the product merely of the market for popular culture and will over time subvert historic faiths. Chris-tian tribes, for instance, maintain rhetorics of discernment and communion that enable the tribes to maintain their fidelity to tradition—the living be-liefs and practices of a historic religion. As communities of moral discourse,

Christian tribes can morally leaven the broader society, including the popular theology of the media. Without strong tribal theology, the market, rather than tradition, will tend to guide religious thought and practice.

The chapter first addresses a small but critical part of the interaction of tribal and popular theology—the mainstream media's view of evil. In order to be commercially viable in a market system, mainstream media gravitate away from the unpleasant tribal concepts of sin and toward the more acceptable notion of evil. The mass media understandably have little regard for one of the most essential elements of the Christian metanarrative—the Fall from grace. In fact, sin is virtually nonexistent within the media's rhetorical construct of evil. The biblical idea of sin, an alienation from and a rebellion against God, influenced Western culture for centuries and shaped the worldviews of gifted artists in music, painting, sculpture, and architecture. Today, however, sin has virtually disappeared from public, mass-mediated discourse except in specialized tribal media.

Second, the chapter examines the newer, mass-mediated version of evil—what I call *civil sin*. American mass media foster a tradition-free, cross-tribal motion of evil that is morally palatable to the broad markets for their media products. Apart from what our tribes might tell us, we generally do not want to believe that we are sinners. As Robert Wood Lynn suggests, the media tend to accept our assumption and then proceed to conform us even more closely to that image.[9] Obviously there are dissenting voices and various minority opinions, especially in journals of comment and opinion, newspaper columns, explicitly religious periodicals and broadcasts, late-night radio, books, non-Hollywood cinema, and specialized cable-TV fare. But the weight of public opinion and the scope of national communication technologies tend to overcome the particularities of tribal differences, geographic regions, historical traditions, and catechetical doctrines. Mediated narratives assume a common and amazingly consistent view of evil that is "civilized" rather than tribalized. Communication researchers and media critics often contribute to this concept of civil sin by assuming their own moralistic perspectives on the effects of media on culture and society. Civil sin is a crucial part of America's quasi-religious rhetoric of communion.

Third, the chapter addresses the way that popular media turn civil sinners into victims. Lacking a transcendent worldview, the mass media explain evil largely in terms of immanent causality. If God cannot enter history and change the course of human events, the actions of human beings are essentially the result only of immediate factors. Moreover, if evil is unrelated to any primal cause, it does not directly affect human nature and can presumably be eliminated or at least greatly attenuated by purely human effort. Humankind can then self-engineer a better, less evil, more civil society. The American infatuation with mass-mediated morality campaigns is a product of this kind of popular theology of self-salvation from civil sin. Public-service advertising campaigns, didactic sitcoms, media boycotts, and media-reform movements often try to use moralistic rhetoric to rid society of evil persons. Moralistic language becomes part of America's quasi-religious rhetoric of progress—a secular notion of conversion.

Fourth, the chapter suggests that this popular theology of civil sin leads the media to demonize particularly evil people whose symbolic sacrifice will supposedly assuage the guilt of society. Addressing the relationship between victimage and sacrifice, Kenneth Burke notes, "The Bible with its profound and beautiful exemplifying of the sacrificial principle, teaches us that tragedy is ever in the offering."[10] In the media, too, "good" depends on "evil." Someone or something must be sacrificed, at least in an earthly sense, for a greater good. "Let us be on guard ever," says Burke, "as regards the subtleties of sacrifice, in their fundamental relationship to governance."[11] The Christian metanarrative emphasizes the sacrifice of God's only son, Jesus Christ, for the salvation of fallen human beings. Mass-media theology, on the other hand, "governs" the world by equipping human beings with symbolic victims who are sacrificed day in and day out in the media. The media offer a priestly means for media experts to rebuild social relationships and reengineer society for the good of humankind. In addition, the media make this sacrifice rhetorically without any necessary reference to God. The media affirm a rhetoric of discernment that distinguishes between good and evil people and offers an earthly means of salvation.

As the media and Christianity interact in America, the Christian metanarrative both facilitates and challenges the popular theology of immanent causality. In an odd case of mutual dependence, the media need Christianity's sense of hope and progress, while mass-mediated portrayals of evil can remind Christian tribes that the human race is indeed fallen. Like literature, the mass media rely implicitly on both the doctrine of the Fall and on the hope of redemption.[12] Driven by the market rather than by tradition, however, the popular theology of the mainstream media interprets these doctrines very differently than do the Christian tribes. Lippmann's optimism about a new class of information experts is merely one example of the foolish optimism that results from the rhetorical suspension of sin.

From Sin to Evil

One of the most memorable American television programs about sin in the 1980s was not a news report, drama, comedy, or commercial. It was televangelist Jimmy Swaggart's own confessional sermon. When he returned to the TV pulpit in 1988 after a sex scandal forced him off the air, Swaggart made no bones about his predicament: "I call it sin." The news media and audiences loved the dirty little drama about a big-time televangelist caught with a low-priced prostitute. Television stations repeatedly flashed sound bites of Swaggart's confession, showing the world his teary-eyed face and quivering lips. The most popular weekly American televangelist was apparently a hypocrite. Now *that* was sin—or so the TV stations and networks suggested rather self-righteously. After all, Swaggart himself had called his actions sin. In a rare reversal of roles, the mainstream media became the heralds of a preacher's sin, borrowing Swaggart's rhetoric of evil to reveal the televangelist's own hypocrisy.[13] Apparently the media loved the role reversal, and so did Americans; the scandal boosted the market for newspapers and television news programs. Comeuppance sells.

Theologian Cornelius Plantinga Jr. says that sin is "not only the breaking of law, but also the breaking of covenant with one's savior. Sin is a smearing of a relationship, the grieving of one's divine parent and benefactor, a betrayal of the partner to whom one is joined by a holy bond."[14] In short, sin is not merely wrongdoing but also alienation from God and other people. Historically speaking, Hebrew and Christian tribes have accounted for and defined evil in such explicitly theological terms.

In spite of the existence of religious broadcasting, this biblical and theological concept of sin rarely appears in mainstream media. And when it does, it is hardly distinguishable as sin. In 1993, for instance, MTV aired an hour-long prime-time broadcast called "The Seven Deadly Sins." At least one television critic called the program "illuminating," echoing what MTV itself described as a "new and more meaningful way to talk about these things." This reviewer concluded that the show was a "TV rarity: a program to make us think."[15] In fact, the program was little more than an amazingly superficial, promotion-laden peek at how some celebrities and "average" teens feel about words that were once connected to sin: lust, greed, sloth, pride, anger, gluttony, and envy. Instead of asking theologians or even religious laypersons to define the deadly sins, MTV turned to a remarkably uninformed group. One Hollywood star, Kirstie Alley, said, "I don't think pride is a sin, and I think some idiot made that up." Music celebrity Ice-T added this theological insight: "Lust isn't a sin. Just from that being the first sin, I'm willing to believe that these are all dumb." Steven Tyler of the rock music group Aerosmith admitted, "I live for lust." And Evan Dando of the group Lemonheads offered this wisdom: "Lust seems like a really, really bad joke on humanity."[16] According to the press release for the program, this quasi-documentary "digs down deep into the soul of the MTV generation." If the program claims such a lofty goal, writes John Leo of *U.S. News and World Report*, "the whole generation can sue for libel."[17]

In his biting criticism of the MTV program, Leo illuminates how this kind of mass-mediated rhetoric about sin lacks any theological or even moral significance. One of the people on the program, for instance, said that sloth was a good thing because "sometimes it's good to sit back and give yourself personal time." Ice-T similarly revealed a dearth of theological insight by suggesting that pride is "mainly a problem of the inner cities. The kids don't have pride." Leo concludes that instead of talking knowledgeably about virtue, moderation, and self-control, participants on the program spoke the "therapized language of feelings and self-esteem."[18] Nearly the entire program lacked any reference to God, let alone to relationships between God and humankind. In this show's worldview, the church's traditional understanding of sin evaporated into a hodgepodge of individual feelings, at worst, and superficial moralism, at best. Horizontal relationships among people eclipsed vertical relationships with a deity. With God out of the picture the concept of sin was ripe for any and all personal definitions. Producers reduced sin to a vacuous theme that could generate viewers and please advertisers.

The MTV broadcast on the seven deadly sins captures the way that market-driven mass media tend to transform sin into something far less troubling and far more superficial. If traditional theology is "God talk," mainstream popular culture is "people talk." Public rhetoric in America has increasingly steered away from using any language explicitly owned by a particular religious tribe or tradition. Sin, for instance, is simply too tribal a term to use in the media unless one is talking about religious people. Since Swaggart used the term in his own TV sermons, it was fair game to describe him as a sinner. On MTV, however, there was no reason to refer even to the seven deadly sins as "sins." They might be problems, issues, or concerns, but not sins. "We don't have sin anymore," quips Jean Bethke Elshtain. "We have syndromes."[19] The word "sin," when used in the media, seems to many people to legitimize a particular religious worldview;

it lacks respect for nonreligious perspectives and other religious traditions; the language challenges the feelings of those who do not agree with Judaism or Christianity and simply appears to be intolerant of nonreligious people. In this sense, the argot of the tribe and the commercial demands of the mass market seem to be largely incompatible.

Popular media therefore replace sin with a very generalized notion of evil tied to the horizontal relationships among people but separated from any transcendent relationship to God. Morality, for example, is either what people feel is right or wrong in their relationships with other people or sometimes what is the norm according to public opinion polls. MTV decided to air the program on the seven deadly sins because, as the show's producer put it, "It seemed that a lot of young people were anxious to talk about moral matters."[20] In other words, the concept of talking about the seven deadly sins offered the potential for building an audience. The producer admitted that a set of "rules," such as the Ten Commandments, was not as good a vehicle for this kind of market-driven program.[21] As secular ideas, however, each of the seven deadly sins offered enough theological ambiguity and tickled adequate prurient interest to attract a curious audience.

Rather than relying on the biblical notion of sin, the media express little more than personalized notions of bad behavior. *People Weekly* used this personalistic idea of wrong-doing to construct a questionnaire. The magazine first asked readers to rank the Ten Commandments by the degree of difficulty in keeping them (editors called this the "Top 10"). Then the periodical created the "Sindex," ranking fifty-one activities—such as spouse swapping and bigotry—according to how guilty readers would feel if they committed them. Finally, the editors selected "TV's Top 10 Sinners," the nastiest television characters who were most likely to "kill, cheat, lie, covet, embezzle, kidnap" and the like.[22] The magazine essentially redefined sin according to the results of public-opinion surveys and vagaries of editorial license, all with an eye toward attracting rather than offending readers.

The concept of sin, as a distinctly religious contextualization of evil, has virtually disappeared from the mainstream media.[23] It took the fall of a hellfire-and-brimstone preacher from Louisiana to get the word "sin" on the nightly news. Day in and day out the mass media instead offer a more palatable and secular rhetoric of evil that permits moral claims without assuming any theological basis. On the evening after the terrorist attacks on the World Trade Center in 2001, President George W. Bush even used the word "evil" four times in his public address. "Today our nation saw evil—the very worst of human nature," he told the country. Newspaper editorials and other political figures similarly used the word "evil" to describe both the attacks and the terrorists themselves.[24] These strong uses of the word "evil" to describe actual people are atypical for media rhetoric. The mainstream media understandably are not open to the idea of sin as a state of existence, a perversity of human nature, or a condition of human alienation from God. Certainly the biblical marks of sin exist in the media (for example, jealousy, pride, sensuality, greed, and self-pity), but they are rarely put into a distinctly biblical or theological context.[25] Clearly the classical formulations of sin found in Judaism and Christianity are largely at odds with the softer notions of evil found in the popular media. This is probably less true in forms of public expression that are not so market driven, such as world cinema and literature.[26] As part of a distinctly religious worldview, sin is still largely an "improper opinion," to use Martin E. Marty's apt phrase.[27]

One explanation for this shift from vertical (God-to-person) to horizontal (person-to-person) rhetoric in the media assumes that modern worldviews premised on reason and objectivity—especially Enlightenment, scientism, and the resulting naturalism—have finally worked their way from intellectuals to common citizens. In this perspective, religious belief, or at least belief in God, is passé in the contemporary culture of empirical data, objective information, and scientific knowledge. Alvin W. Gouldner distinguishes between religion, which is based on an epistemology "that makes knowledge a phenomenon that is *bestowed* on man and vouchsafed by higher powers and authorities," and ideology, which emphasizes the "self-groundedness of men's knowledge, involving his reason and his experience: cogito ergo sum."[28] If he is correct, perhaps the secular ideologies of scientism and naturalism dominate media gatekeeping.

But how would we reconcile this kind of ideological rationalism with the individualistic morality of MTV's program on the seven deadly sins? Why, too, would television programs like *X-Files* and *Touched by an Angel* be so popular in the late 1990s? For that matter, what would account for supermarket tabloids' exposés of space abduction and reports of miraculous healings? Even apparent agnostics such as Wendy Kaminer, author of *Sleeping with Extra-Terrestrials*, argue that the American public craves seemingly irrational and highly subjective views of reality.[29] If God died in the media, some other types of gods have appeared in other bodies, movements, or inexplicable events. The market system, which leads media to maximize audience size for the sake of advertisers and revenues, drives American media toward alternative forms of spirituality that leave little or no space for sin. Maybe the vertical rhetoric of God-human relationships just takes different, less traditional forms in contemporary media. In any case scientific understandings of reality hardly dictate the content of popular culture's view of evil. Much popular fare, from *X-Files* to the late-night clairvoyants on cable channels, looks far more like "irrational" religion than rational science or naturalistic ideology.

A second explanation for the lack of a rhetoric of sin in the media is nearly the opposite of the Enlightenment thesis. In this argument contemporary postmodern sensibilities have rendered all public discourse subjective and individualistic. Even if people have never heard the word "postmodern," they have been swept up by popular versions of the philosophy. Both individualistic and group relativism, the latter represented in endlessly competing "communities of interpretation," have tended to put traditional religious belief on a par with all other religious and nonreligious systems, philosophies, and methods of belief. Indeed many of the comments by guests on the MTV special about sin sound like pop-postmodernism. According to this perspective, the market for media products is highly dynamic and deeply fragmented, creating all kinds of contradictory values, beliefs, and practices with little or no coherence. If references to evil as sin appear in the media, they will likely be relegated to tribal programs or publications. The media express merely the postmodern smorgasbord of subcultures extant in society—but without exclusivism.

If postmodern sensibilities shape people's everyday understanding of life, people might indeed assume that no human being can know God with certainty and that the market-driven media should express a wide array of subjective religious options. The vagueness of language alone might make people feel increasingly comfortable with the idea that even if God exists, we cannot know God and should be skeptical about the veracity of those who claim that God transcends human symbolizing. All human rhetoric about God is deeply imprecise; it might say more about the speaker's assumptions than about the reality of an alleged God. So all language, all metaphor, is merely conjecture. As one theologian puts it, "no human being can have a literal 'fix' on God. . . . God transcends human language and human comprehension." Sacred texts such as the Bible are mere midrash, at best.[30] In this type of postmodern perspective, MTV and even the supermarket tabloids are on to something, namely, the amazing ways that human intersubjectivity coalesces at times around particular quasi-religious interpretations of the "transcendent other." MTV, *X-Files*, and Jimmy Swaggart all reflect the same symbolic imprecision with respect to knowing God and discerning God's language for understanding the world. The media markets are simply doing their job by serving up cultural fads and fashions, some of which are spiritual. Martin Kaplan, director of the Norman Lear Center at the University of Southern California, argues that the contemporary postmodern condition "deprives us of grand narratives." Living happily requires telling ourselves "a story that makes sense, a narrative that satisfies, an autobiography—both individual and collective—worth handing down." But the days of such metanarratives, Kaplan suggests, are long gone in the vapor of postmodernity.[31]

Whether struck down by scientism or postmodernism or the needs of marketers in a heterogeneous society, sin is almost always unacceptable in public rhetoric, whereas evil is more compatible with popular culture, rhetorical tolerance, and civility. So the mainstream media use the freedom of the marketplace to avoid expressions of ultimate and knowable reality. "Where sin still pops into our vocabulary," writes Os Guinness, "it is trivialized beyond recognition." The Puritan rhetoric of "sinners in the hands of an angry God," he adds, "has evaporated into a misty concern for low self-esteem."[32] As a biblical-theological construct, sin makes sense only in the context of a religious metanarrative that is too controversial for the news reports, sitcoms, and teen flicks of the day. Of course Christian and Hebrew worldviews, like those of other religions, implicitly challenge the media by claiming an "ultimacy" for their meanings.[33] The concept of sin assumes a totalizing rhetoric at odds with the totalizing tendency of scientism and the relativism of postmodernism. As Raymond Williams offers, the rise of the language of "isms" in the Western world shifted from disputes within theology to political controversy.[34] The movement from talking about "sin" to conversing about "evil" in public life, including the media, partly reflects a growing uneasiness in accepting Christian, Hebrew or any other religious metanarratives—and their traditional and tribal interpretations—as ultimately true. The shift also probably reflects tolerance for those religious worldviews that are not dominant in the industrialized Western world.

The doctrine of sin could be assessed publicly in terms of how well it comports with reality—even with reality as recorded by the media. The historian Herbert Butterfield, for instance, claimed that "the doctrine of original sin is the only empirically verifiable doctrine that Christians have."[35] Another historian, John Lukacs, comes to the same conclusion after a lifetime of study of the actions of real people in different cultures.[36]

Theologian Reinhold Niebuhr also agreed, defining the Christian concept of sin as "pride and arrogance of individuals—a definition of evil that is hardly limited to the Christian tradition."[37] According to the worldview articulated by theologians like Niebuhr, the concept of sin accurately describes what humans do when they engage in wrongful thoughts and actions. Using the biblical metanarrative, but also grounding the metanarrative's veracity in empirical reality, they see real evil in theological terms. Moreover, they apply their definition of evil as sin not just to themselves but more broadly to all people. In their view, because of the tragedy of the Fall from grace, humans are naturally sinful; human beings "reoriginate sin," passing it down from generation to generation from its origin in the first human sinners. Theologian Walter Rauschenbush states that the "kingdom of evil" is as real as the kingdom of God: "The sin of all is in each of us, and every one of us has scattered seeds of evil, the final harvest of which no man knows."[38] But of course one can accept the grotesque evil within history without also accommodating the corresponding theological assumptions about the Fall. From a biblical frame of reference, the media might ignore the existence of sin because the tribal language does not comport well with mass marketing; the media, too, are fallen.

These three ways of understanding the eclipse of sin-talk from the media—Enlightenment scientism, contemporary postmodernism, and historic Christianity—hardly exhaust all of the epistemological options, but they do suggest at least three widely different approaches to interpreting the secular language of the mainstream media. They are grounded, respectively, in objectivism, subjectivism, and divine revelation. Each one also tends to produce its own metanarrative that isolates problems and provides methodological as well as theoretical solutions to those problems. Each interpretation also addresses at least implicitly the problem of evil and suggests a means of dealing with evil actions and evil people. In addition, each of them can be expressed in popular terms through the mass media, although they are then likely to be shaped by the market.

The most practical and immediate explanation for the lack of references to sin in the popular media is economic. Mass markets can survive only by implicitly adjudicating among tribal differences. The easiest and most charitable way for media gatekeepers to do this is to look for the common ground among different worldviews, theological orientations, and cosmologies—to affirm what most people can embrace even if it no longer carries explicit tribal language. It does not amount to a new consensus as much as a language of exchange that enables tribes to talk with each other about issues over which they might otherwise be deeply divided.

As Christianity and the mainstream media interact in America, then, the media have to find their own rhetoric of evil that is at least somewhat consonant with the dominant beliefs of members of society and thus marketable. Sin is too particularistic and too deeply tribal for this popular rhetoric; sin assumes a tribal metanarrative, even a biblical theology. Evil, on the other hand, is not only more acceptable but crucial for many forms of popular storytelling. There can be no strong heroes without deep expressions of evil. Evil is a crucial dramatic device for films, television, comic books, and the like. There is nothing "improper" about evil, to use Marty's word once again. The power of the mainstream media to build audiences rests on professional communicators' ability to capture markets with persuasive narratives that resonate with audiences' moods and sentiments. Upon his own conversion, St. Augustine, previously a successful teacher of rhetoric, cried out, "What is wrong with us? Uneducated people are rising up and capturing heaven, and we, with our high culture without any heart—see where we roll in the mud of flesh and blood."[39] Augustine realized, long before the rise of mass markets and mass communication, that sentiments can be as persuasive as the intellect. Today's mass media sometimes use evil as part of the language of exchange necessary to evoke emotion and garner audiences. Charles Krauthammer even suggests that mainstream journalism has "taken up the slack" caused by philosophy's uninterest in the problem of evil.[40] When religion is weak, secular popular culture seems to fill the theological and especially the spiritual voids.

Many contemporary Americans grow up with competing masters, tradition and the media. Jeffrey H. Mahan recalls that when he was a child his Sunday mornings "may have belonged to the Sunday School Jesus, but Saturdays were happily spent with Roy Rogers, Wild Bill Hickock, and the Lone Ranger." Mahan remembers being "fascinated by the Westerner's stylish assertion of a moral self." Thinking back on those days, he concludes that the popular media communicate a "rich body of lore which modern Americans use to interpret their collective and individual experiences." He asks Christian tribes to "wrestle seriously" with the "inevitable interaction" between the church's own religious texts and those of the popular media. He cites the character Ethan in the film *The Searchers*, a tough man who repeatedly presses Captain/Reverend Clayton to "clarify whether he speaks and acts as a preacher or a captain of the Texas Rangers."[41] Clayton's predicament echoes that of the tribal believer who now resides in a mass-mediated world.

Civil Sin

Literary critic Frederic Jameson suggests that contemporary art is more pastiche than parody. Whereas parody requires a perspective outside of the work of art—a critical stance—pastiche is little more than a self-referential caricature of itself, with no larger perspective for reference. Jameson speaks as a Marxist presumably with commitments to a materialistic view of the world. One could make essentially the same argument about pastiche from a religious perspective. Sin makes sense only when it is connected to a metanarrative that frames evil actions in a larger religious context. The story of the biblical Fall from grace places evil in the context of a biblical world where all evil actions are repeat performances of the original misdeeds of Adam and Eve. In this perspective, human beings' evil actions today are serious parodies of the greater cosmic struggle between good and evil. Tied to the biblical metanarrative, evil as sin reflects the corrupted relationships between God and God's people.

If the concept of sin is disconnected from this traditional metanarrative, it becomes more pastiche than parody. So the trick of contemporary media is to hang on to the pretence of sin without accepting the accompanying cosmology. The media in a market system need to rely on the expression of unfettered evil for dramatic effect, without vacuous pastiche. Somehow they have to create the sense of moral certainty—perhaps even Natural Law—without using anything more than the language of exchange afforded within expressions of evil without expressions of God. As a result, mass-mediated narratives hint at the tribal worldview, thereby working off of existing tribal beliefs within audiences while rarely making those beliefs explicit.

Examining contemporary film, for instance, Reinhold Zwick concludes that media "attempt . . . to question evil as to its very roots, to offer interpretations, and moreover at times to suggest a path for coping with and overcoming it." He even suggests that "there is a religious dimension to the discussion of evil when it is carried out with a view toward hope or the prospect of an end to evil." What would film be like, he wonders, if the medium did not rely upon the "eternal, archetypal-mythical fight between good and evil?"[42] By rejecting explicit expressions of sin, the mainstream media do not necessarily reject all tribal motifs, such as the battle between good and evil that marks Christianity, Judaism, and Islam. In short, the media avoid total pastiche by borrowing some of the structure, if not some of the meaning, of tribal religion. Tribal believers thereby can find some accommodation to their beliefs as they consume mass-mediated story-telling. In this way the media's popular theology still owes much to religious worldviews even though the mass-media's implicit theology is not tribal.

As it both borrows and rejects aspects of tribal narratives, popular culture replaces religious sin with civil sin. In a market system the media frame evil horizontally as a problem among people rather than vertically as a corruption of the divine relationship with God. Civil sin does not replace the idea of religious evil in American society, but it does recontextualize it as a purely human problem with presumably human solutions. Civil sin gives the nation a language of evil that is not fully commensurate with any particular faith but which nevertheless shares the general moral outlook of most Americans.[43] In fact, when the nation is under severe distress, as in the case of the 2001 terrorist attacks in New York and Washington, D.C., the public language of exchange about evil comes remarkably close to tribalism. News reporters and politicians talked not just about "evil" but also about the need for "prayer," thereby presuming the existence of a personal God.[44]

Even civil sin does not usually include the everyday moral improprieties found in the media—things such as white lies, rudeness, and anger. Most people would argue that such behaviors are not good, but neither would they call them evil. Nor does civil sin necessarily include actions about which society lacks moral consensus, such as homosexual practices, abortion, fornication, gluttony, and drunkenness. These kinds of contested actions are largely outside of the scope of civil sin and are not necessarily morally right or wrong by mainstream media standards, even though particular citizens or tribes might define them as evil. In the media such actions are less matters of parody than pastiche.

Civil sin does include the human practices that are evil by both wide-spread public sentiment and ongoing media consensus. Like civil religion, civil sin calls upon vaguely religious rhetoric, without reference to any distinctly religious values or beliefs. In the media it takes the place of tradition, sacred text, or religious community as the popular paradigm for identifying real evil. Civil sin functions within society as a type of invisible moral measure of collective opinion or shared public will, both reflecting and directing public opinion within existing public rhetoric about evil. Public opinion, as a mediated consensus, provides the external basis for moving mediated expressions of evil from pastiche to parody. Public opinion thereby substitutes for a more obviously transcendent view of evil tied to tribal metanarrative. In the process, the media nearly sacralize civil sin. Instead of fully consigning the biblical frame of reference to the past, the media continually re-create and rejuvenate it in a more civil form.[45]

Civil sin retains a generic moral outlook, namely, the plausibility of clear good and devilish evil. Such an outlook facilitates not only dramatic storytelling and news reporting but also popular media criticism, especially the kinds of moralistic criticism practiced by media watchdog groups concerned about mass-mediated violence and profanity. Civil sin enables us to identify evil in public life and provides the social space for a shared hope that evil can be transformed into good. Without at least civil sin, there would not be evil that is bad enough to merit criticism and necessitate amelioration. Rhetorically speaking, we need some kind of collective notion of evil in order to share any routes toward a common good. Mass-mediated civil sin, propped up by the tribal beliefs held by audiences, provides the popular diagnosis of the human problem that the media then must solve.

The media doctrine of civil sin addresses at a popular level the same theodicy that confronts theologians. Paul Ricoeur argues that the "worlds of myth" contain a "primordial dramatic structure" that addresses mythological evil in one of four ways: (1) evil is coextensive with creation, (2) evil comes about as a result of a fall of humans, (3) evil results from the tragedy of a god who "tempts, blinds, leads astray," or (4) evil emerges from the exiled soul, the division between human soul and body. The "sacred," says Ricoeur, "takes contingent forms" because humans can experience it only through the "indefinite diversity of mythologies and rituals."[46] In a democratic nation these explanations of the origin of evil are open to tribal claims and popular opinion. No particular religion can dictate one or the other interpretation to the rest of society. Nevertheless, the broader religious attitudes or sensibilities of the culture cannot help but shape the popular theology that defines evil in everyday life. The mass media both articulate and affirm society's shared sense of a contingent version of evil.

In a mass-mediated society significantly influenced by the biblical metanarrative, particular forms of a "myth of evil" are more likely to be more popular than others. The first of Ricoeur's types of evil seems to offer little hope; all that humans can do in this scenario is reenact the tension between good and evil, with no clear and final resolution. Why enjoy happy endings in comedy, for example, if they are simply lies? The second kind of myth pins all human beings to evil. It requires people to acknowledge their own tendency toward evil. Who would naturally find this kind of self-indicting perspective to be entertaining or enjoyable in popular stories? It would probably destroy broadcast ratings and print-media circulation. Under such a myth, popular media might even sound like Jonathan Edwards's famous sermon, "Sinners in the Hands of an Angry God." Ricoeur's third myth of evil may be the most troubling of all to mass audiences, especially those shaped by biblical ideas of God's sacredness and holiness. If God is the problem, how can mere mortals improve their lot in life? How could the media possibly deal with this myth in a market system? Finally, the fourth myth seems far too confusing to make popular sense. Although biblical theology posits a distinction between body and soul, the soul itself is not easily identifiable in popular storytelling. How can the media portray the soul? The body, on the other hand, is ideally suited to television, film, and the Internet.

Civil sin modifies the second of Ricoeur's types, equating evil only with the actions of distinctly evil people. In one sense, this Hollywood mythology accepts the Christian notion of the human fall into sin, although the media hardly go as far as Jonathan Edwards. Civil sin symbolically "solves" the problem of evil by assuming that creation overall is good but that some people are not. Most people will tend to be good and righteous members of society, but a small number of people will cause the real trouble. *They* are the fallen ones, the real sinners, and the sources of conflict in the world. The next section of this chapter examines the nature of these evil people. For now, suffice it so say that the media tend to delimit "fallenness" in order to shift guilt and blame from the audience's "self" to "others."

As part of the Hollywood mythology, civil sin also is a "peep hole" into American society that reveals both how we define evil and how we think we can deal with it.[47] Striving to create narratives that will attract mass audiences, the media rely upon secular narratives that resonate with broadly American sentiments. American movies, for example, often reflect an Edenic "yearning to go back, to return to a simpler form of life where values were clear-cut; good and evil distinguishable."[48] Nostalgia affirms our view that there used to be less evil in the world and gives us a good past worth recovering.

Sin requires a savior, whereas evil requires only heroes. So we can now create rugged do-gooders who will supposedly overcome evil. After the Los Angeles riots of 1992, Patrick O'Heffernan concluded that American television reflects the "national ethos of rugged individualism" and legitimizes personal, heroic violence as a means of solving conflicts. He viewed the riots, in which poor citizens looted area businesses, as a living out of the

Hollywood idea that "violence is a routine part of life and that individuals use it to get the things they want to consume."[49] The media also look to science, the market, and love to eliminate evil. Neil P. Hurley concludes that some films even try to "write another Genesis with the machine as made in God's image." Popular science fiction proposes "through imaginative works that scientific, technical, and organizational advances can alter, radically and irreversibly, human nature made in God's image and likeness." The most popular films, he suggests, "postulate a pervasive benevolent and guiding force assisting humans of good will and courage to use technical and scientific knowledge" to integrate the universe, despite "undeniable evil forces and the frailties of the human condition."[50] The media accept the second of Ricoeur's myths of evil but reformulate it more palatably for cross-tribal audiences.

As the previous chapter suggested, tribal critics often point out the conflict between generic media concepts such as civil sin and the particularity of tribal metanarratives. In a stinging indictment of the very popular TV series *Touched by an Angel*, television writer and producer Coleman Luck addresses the most crucial point of theological tension between the program's implicit theology and what Luck sees as historic Christian theology. Calling the show "Touched by a Fallen Angel," Luck contends that it "represents everything that is transcendentally powerful about Western Civilization." He satirically compares watching the series to "eating 7000 spiritual Twinkies" that make "everyone's emotional taste buds Tingle." The program's "inclusiveness," Luck writes, makes it "transcendentally powerful." "For over five thousand years of recorded history," he says, "religious people have been battling each other in the name of God, imagining that their religions were mutually exclusive. Now, thanks to Martha [Williamson] and her team, that's all over. Everyone from Tantric Buddhists to Santerians to evangelical Christians to ritual axe murderers can know that there is only One, True, Faith and we're all part of it. Hardened atheists and New Age mystics can join hands. For one hour on Sunday night, we can all Tingle together. And if the Tingle gets big enough . . . if it girdles the globe . . . my friends, there will be PEACE." Luck even suggests that the program might represent the birth of "a new media religion."[51] In his view, this popular American program is a threat to the Christian metanarrative because it both limits the biblical notion of the Fall and consequently terminates the human need for a transcendent savior who is capable of taking away the sins of the world.

Of course a show that presents theologically ambiguous angels will be interpreted differently by various audiences, perhaps each viewer according to his or her own tribal theology. The polysemic nature of quasi-religious messages might avoid offending particular faiths while letting viewers interpret the symbols in light of their own tradition. Possibly tribal viewers of *Touched by an Angel* are able to interpret the television stories in the context of the biblical portrayal of angels and the need for human beings to seek salvation from their transgressions against God, even though the program itself does not offer this kind of tribal expression.

Luck's stinging criticism suggests that the nonparticularity of the program *is* the message. In his view as a tribal critic, the program might be less polysemic than it is distinctly general; the program's own particularity is its nontraditional message, which does not comport with the metanarrative of any historic tribe. Luck calls the series' producer a "genius" for discerning what "all good religious people in Western Civilization want," a "Redemption that costs nothing. Stories that warm the heart, but do not convict the soul. And most of all, a happy, tear-filled ending to every damnable week."[52] From Luck's perspective, *Touched by an Angel* is not polysemous but ultimately anti-Christian. He thus calls the program a new "media religion." Luck's tribal criticism of *Touched by an Angel* suggests that media markets create their own "theologies" based on mass taste and cross-religion sensibilities. So Luck uses his evangelical tradition to parody the series—to argue that the program is essentially pseudo-theological pastiche with no tribal anchor.

Luck's critique points out that dramatic generalities can also be expressions of cultural particularities. He recognizes that Hollywood's concept of evil is inextricably linked with its view of salvation. If organized religion offers salvation, it must always offer salvation from something in particular. In his biblical tradition, that particularity is sin. So Luck includes himself rhetorically in the list of fallen human beings who need salvation from their sin. "Worst of all," says Luck, "I've smelled the sickly-sweet odor of my own ambition. I am not a 'nice' person. Left to myself I'd be one of the worst people in Hollywood. When someone gets in my way, I feel an overwhelming urge to rip out his/her heart. In short, I am immensely qualified to write about somebody else's TV series."[53] Like a theological ethnographer of the television industry, Luck turns his critique of the series on himself and on the entire entertainment business. He parodies the program because he believes that producer Williamson is untrue to her own tribal metanarrative in the Southern Baptist tradition. She has, from his frame of reference, sold out to an industry that equates success with popularity and that cares little for the veracity of the Christian metanarrative. He ironically concludes that the series, which ends every week with a tearful happy turnaround of hurting people, is a tragedy. When he first met Williamson, the show's producer, opines Luck, "she believed in something other than her own empire. Back then, she was struggling for success, now she's desperately afraid of losing it."[54] According to Luck, Williamson has become a willing victim of the evil social institution of commercial network television. She has forsaken the particular tenets of the Christian metanarrative in favor of a mass-mediated, feel-good faith. As a tribal critic, he takes no stock in civil sin.

The media need evil for dramatic purposes, but in a market system they want to be more civil than the concept of biblical sin will allow them to be. So the media must formulate the idea of evil in a way that only loosely comports with distinctively tribal notions of sin. One way of doing this is to confine evil largely to sociological and especially psychological language. Guinness argues that the media are not merely opposed to Christian theology; they embrace therapeutic concepts of evil that de-mythologize the particularity of any religion's beliefs.[55] The media transform theological issues and biblical perspectives into moralistic rhetoric. By cutting off humans' relationship to God, the media recontextualize evil as a matter of social mores or personal conscience. "Talk shows," he says, "have their topic du jour," the daily moral outrage that draws angry listeners.[56] Everybody gets "mad as hell," to quote the rather mindless but charged-up TV audience in Paddy Chayefsky's movie *Network*.[57] But what are they really so angry about? And why? Without an illuminating metanarrative, fashionable moralism slips into quasi-religious pastiche.

Although mainstream media express civil sin daily in the taken-forgranted displays of evil, they present civil sin most strongly when public opinion turns from loose sentiments to moral outrage. Suddenly there is a strong, collective impulse among audiences in response to seemingly wicked and especially uncommon actions. This occurred in media responses to extremists' takeover of the American embassy in Iran during 1979, Iraq's invasion of Kuwait in 1990, reports during 1991 about Jeffrey Dahmer's mass murders in Milwaukee, and the video coverage of terrorists flying jet planes into the World Trade Center and the Pentagon in 2001.[58] Although television drama and films can create scenarios where evil seems unambiguous, such real-world expressions of evil are always the most powerful and the longest lasting. They frame civil sin as a nonambiguous rhetoric of moral outrage that is seemingly in harmony with the particular metanarratives of any religious tradition. Rhetorically speaking, civil sin is a kind of prereligious expression of moral certainty that fulfills the human desire to identify evil and discuss it with others.

The news is a particularly fertile field for identifying the expressions of civil sin that emerge out of the public's moral outrage. During the Christmas holidays of 1992, one of Chicago's major news stories concerned the arrest of a married couple at O'Hare Airport for child abandonment.[59] Police and news media discovered that the couple apparently had gone to Acapulco for a week's winter vacation, leaving at home alone their two children, the oldest of whom was only nine. If the news stories were accurate, clearly the couple acted irresponsibly. Public sentiment quickly coalesced around the growing moral outrage, leading prosecuting attorneys and the judge to act rapidly and decisively on behalf of the interests of the state; the couple was arrested at the airport, booked on child abandonment charges, and saddled with a large bond. Within a day the story attracted national attention. Here was a tale about evil that people could find compelling for what it said about the immoral actions of others. News media dubbed it the "home alone" case, after the popular Christmas movie.

The fact that the story broke during the Christmas holidays certainly gave it special moral weight—like house fires and stories of indigence, which are more heartrending when most people are thinking about their families. News media effectively contrasted the outrageousness of the parents' actions with the pitiful situation of the kids, who had been found alone, barefoot, crying in their yard after a smoke detector went off in their house. The news stories coalesced ongoing public frustration about child neglect. Readers and viewers wondered how the couple could relax on Mexican beaches while their children had to cope with the anxiety of being home alone. News reports both created and reinforced a sense of public outrage. The public was indeed mad as hell. As public anger grew around media reports of the case, civil sin emerged from the everyday moral ambiguity of the news. Everyone seemed to agree that the parents' actions were evil and deserved punishment.

Although this example of civil sin came as close as the news media ever do to the recognition of distinctly religious sin, it was still a tale of only civil sin. The story was not defined specifically in terms of sin—as transgression against God or God's moral law. Even the obvious selfishness and self-centeredness of the parents did not elicit any tribal contextualizations of their actions. Second, there were few attempts (National Public Radio was one) to put the story in a broader moral context regarding the overall responsibilities of parents to their children. The episode was generally treated as a freak tale, not as a revealing example of latent evil that resides in the hearts of all parents. News reports focused again and again on the outrageousness of the particular parental actions, thereby eclipsing the likelihood that the story might reflect universal lessons about humankind. In other words, the news reports and analyses typically were oblivious to the story's possible parabolic significance. Third—and this is crucial—the news reports expressed the idea that the parents' actions were so outrageous as to be inexplicable—beyond words and even beyond human understanding. News stories analyzed the event in purely human terms as an aberration in human nature, as an example of "normal" human nature inexplicably run amok. Public sentiment, as reflected in news reports and letters to the editor, did include the possibility that there was something far more wrong with the parents than merely their idiosyncratic mistreatment of children. But even all of the media groping for psychological explanations ended with more unanswerable questions. Journalists simply lacked a language for making sense of the senseless. They faced the epistemological as well as the moral limits of civil sin.

If nothing else, mass-mediated expressions of civil sin could direct people to an understanding of evil as part of the human condition. The media's own preoccupation with stories about evil reflects the widespread existence of evil in all societies. Anson Shupe suggests that evil survives in industrial societies just as it has in preindustrial ones.[60] He argues that all societies define some things as sacred and others as evil, or profane. According to Robert N. Bellah, both good and evil play crucial roles in maintaining social order.[61] Although people's definition of evil may change over time, their belief in the existence of evil remains, explicitly or implicitly, an important part of their understanding of the world. Experience teaches us all that evil is a tenacious part of life. "In essence," says Shupe, "technology and science do not eliminate the theodicies and injustices of life. Evil, explicitly conceived theologically or implicitly realized, certainly does not lack for new forms to assume."[62] In a sense, evil is socially normal, even if religious tribes and other subcultures disagree about what to include in the category of evil. The concept of sin in the biblical tradition focuses on the normalcy and pervasiveness of evil as one aspect of the human heart and the resulting human condition.

If Bellah is correct, the mass media do not create the concept of evil as much as they codify it and express it in tune with civil sin. The media may overemphasize some types of evil or fail to address others or even misrepresent evil motivations of real people. But the media express evil ultimately because evil is simply a part of the human condition, a crucial element in the drama of life. As Bellah suggests, however, evil has to be expressed in specific social mores; the concept of evil, like the overall concept of sin, requires some type of symbolic content, some specific meaning for a particular people in a specific time and place. The generic idea of evil is itself too vague and amorphous, if not too abstract and impersonal. Every society defines evil, just as parents normally teach their children what is right and wrong. When the media address evil, they typically codify it as the particular rhetorical construct of civil sin in tune with the market.

When British literary critic C. S. Lewis wrote the BBC radio addresses that were later printed as *Mere Christianity*, he anchored his belief in God partly in the tendency of all cultures to establish moral contours for public and private actions. "It seems," writes Lewis, "that if we are to think about morality, we must think of . . . relations between man and man: things inside each man: and relations between man and the power that made him." Moreover, posits Lewis, we "can all co-operate in the first one. Disagreements begin with the second and become serious with the third."[63] The media avoid differences of opinion about the latter two relationships; they seek cultural conformity for the sake of building a consensus as reflected in audience ratings, print-media circulation, and especially morally charged public opinion. "A mass medium must concern itself with the common denominator of mass interest," remarked CBS president Frank Stanton in the early years of television. "It can only keep its great audience . . . *by giving people what they want*."[64] So the media satisfy this "want" by creating moralistic narratives without necessarily accepting any of the explicitly tribal rhetoric of sin that would divide or offend audiences. In this sense, American media may be among the most secular media in the world, avoiding ideological or religious parody when pastiche will make the market.

Civil Sinners As Victims of Immanent Causality

In an essay on the state of television docudramas, Elayne Rapping describes how producers are increasingly representing the views of abusers over those of the victims. Citing docudramas about well-known events—O. J. Simpson's trial for allegedly murdering his wife, the Menendez brothers' murder of their parents, and Amy Fisher's attempted murder of her lover's wife—she argues that these "high-profile cases involving sexual abuse of young people and violence within families are presented not from the victim's point of view but from the abuser's." She suggests that the women and children who have probably suffered abuse by males are "blamed, condemned and demonized in ways which have audiences screaming for blood." Rapping cites five TV-movie versions of these stories that never even mentioned the possible sexual and physical violence against the defendants.[65]

The popular media often define evildoers as victims. This is a very subtle but enormously powerful rhetoric that affirms civil sin. The implicit theology is something like this: individuals would not do evil except for the circumstances that cause them to do it. Behind evil actions are previous evil actions. If someone did something evil, even terribly evil, he or she must have been provoked by other evildoers. Thus Simpson, the Menendez brothers, and all other possible evildoers must have been motivated externally by the evil actions of others. In short, evil is the product of previous evil committed by other people. Evildoers are also victims.

This "victimage" approach to the popular portrayal of evil implicitly rejects the possibility that evil is intrinsic to the human condition and seeks instead to explain evil phenomena purely on the basis of immanent causality. In the news story about the abandoned children, for example, news reports shifted in several days to the question of what went wrong in the parents' background to cause them to leave their children home alone. Mainstream media often seek to answer the question of causality by looking to immanent understandings, such as psychological and sociological explanations, rather than to distinctly philosophical or theological ones. Under normal circumstances parents would not do such a horrible thing to their children. Therefore something must have caused these particular parents' actions to leave the equilibrium of normalcy. Whatever the answer, these parents were idiosyncratic, not typical. Immanent causality thus includes its own quasi-theological assumptions that evil is a product of society, not the result of individual hard-heartedness and certainly not the result of some species-wide flaw. Immanent causality is the basis for the secular rhetoric of discernment expressed in mainstream media explanations of evil.

James R. Keller addresses immanent causality in a study of films that portray humans with physical disabilities. For centuries, says Keller, people regarded physical disability "as a sign of spiritual corruption."[66] In literature physical disability represented "chaos," the "distortion of natural law" or of the "moral order."[67] Just as the lack of moral law in society led to social chaos, the lack of "natural" form in the body supposedly foreshadowed moral anarchy. Keller suggests that literature, reflecting the broader religious values of society, linked physical disability and depravity.[68] American writers believed that sin or at least some terrible moral deeds led people to physical manifestations of their unnatural, evil ways. Turning to recent films, however, Keller finds that directors are de-spiritualizing physical disability. Films such as *The Elephant Man* (1980), *Mask* (1985), *Johnny Handsome* (1989), *Darkman* (1990), and *The Man without a Face* (1993), he concludes, attribute much of the "culpability for criminal activities to the social forces responsible for alienating and abusing the physically handicapped."[69] In popular media psychological and sociological explanations overshadow any distinctly theological interpretations of evil, regardless of the veracity of either account. This shift from theological to psychological language might reflect the larger movement from a worldview that includes human nature and evil to one that looks instead at immanent causality.

Immanent causality contextualized a CBS docudrama, *Overkill: The Aileen Wuornos Story*. Based on the life of the first convicted female serial killer, the story depicted Wuornos as a victim of male child abuse who turned to prostitution and eventually murdered male clients. It portrayed Wuornos not only as a murderer but also as a victim. In fact, the cable channel Court TV, which covered the trial of *Florida v. Wuornos*, later presented a two-hour condensation of the trial titled *Aileen Wuornos: Serial Killer or Victim?* Even though no one contested that she committed the crimes, the media presented the possibility that her own background caused her to commit the heinous murders. Perhaps she was a tragic victim of earlier abuse.[70] The television programs suggested that her background is the best way to explain her motive for the killings.

Certainly Wuornos's childhood probably did influence her adult view of men. Even a cursory examination of her life suggests an important psychological connection between her childhood victimization and her adult actions against the men that she killed in Florida. Nevertheless, the media's tendency to transform evildoers into mere victims is an implicitly philosophical as well as a psychological assumption. As the media try to interpret the news and as writers compose compelling fictional drama, they assume a cause for evil in the world. They take a rhetorical position, implicitly or explicitly, that frames the meaning of evil by attributing a reason or cause to its existence in particular situations. By assuming immanent causality these stories largely reject a biblical concept of sin and civilize the evil in human terms. When this type of victimization establishes the moral context for action, transcendent considerations are largely irrelevant. Evil is then only a matter of human cause and effect, never a more troubling matter of human choice or the human condition. To borrow language from Elshtain, we forget "how far we have fallen."[71] The secular "doctrine" of immanent causality even shifts responsibility from the latest evildoer to earlier evildoers who presumably caused the resulting evil. In a biblical framework evil is passed along from person to person and spread through social institutions from generation to generation; the mechanism for passing along evil is not merely psychological or sociological but a more primary defect in the heart of people. Whereas the victimization motif focuses on the sequential strings of human causes, the biblical tradition emphasizes an ultimate cause as well, namely, hard hearts caused by alienation from God and neighbor. This alienation is part of the human condition, original sin, not merely the product of society.

Many of the pop culture wars between the media and media watchdog groups illuminate the cultural as well as the economic significance of immanent causality.[72] When critics assail the media for causing particular social ills, they usually assume that little or no fault rests with the audience. In fact, social-scientific studies of the effects of mass communication historically assumed that the "sender" was more or less responsible for the effects of messages on audiences, which by definition were passive and malleable.[73] Television critics and media researchers together still often assume a posture of immanent causality even though later studies virtually reversed the early ones and defined the audiences as "obstinate."[74]

A study of "slasher" films, for instance, begins with a reference to TV critics Gene Siskel and Roger Ebert, who on their own television program dubbed a new genre of movies—"woman in danger" films. Concurring with Siskel and Ebert, the researchers suggest that these films feature "grotesque and sadistic victimization of women" and frequently mix sex and violence. Then, after analyzing the content of thirty such movies, they nevertheless agree with earlier studies suggesting that "females are not the predominant victims" of these types of films and that these movies "apparently dwell on the woman's terror, prolonging her suffering and the viewer's uncertainty about her plight."[75] How can researchers determine from an analysis of movie content how the movies affect women? Males, the researchers contend, "have had to endure a greater share of the brutality as producers have toned down attacks on females."[76] Do male audiences "endure" these kinds of movies? Or do they "enjoy" them? Again, the study assumes a rhetorical and a moral position of immanent causality with respect to the impact of such movies on their audiences. This assumption, which lies at the core of much mass-media research, tends to shape both the questions that researchers ask and how they answer them. In this sense, the media critics and the media researchers share a similar paradigm that defines audiences as the victims of media content and locates the "cause" of evil primarily in the media, not in audiences.

A tribal perspective, anchored in the Hebrew and Christian traditions, might assume instead that audiences and the media "cocreate" evil that is always latent in the human heart. Evil runs deep within the human condition, not merely in the people who work in the entertainment industry. As Lynn puts it in his theological excursion into the effects of the media in the early days of television, "radio along with the movies, television, and the press intensify the distress of unseen audiences." Lynn contends that there is some truth to a broadcaster's claim that the "faults of the radio are the faults of the America people." The media, Lynn claims, simply make people more dependent upon "alien identities" and "distorted reflections" of themselves. He compares modern media audiences to Willy Loman in the play *Death of a Salesman*, a tragic figure who "looks upon himself as an object to be manipulated."[77] The assumption of original sin resists limiting all culpability for evil to the media or to the audience. This perspective assumes, based on both a reading of the biblical text and the wisdom of tradition, that media producers and consumers are both "fallen creatures." The biblical metanarrative, as interpreted by many Christian and Jewish tribes, suggests that audiences might desire and even enjoy reading about evil and viewing it on television sets or in theaters. In short, there is not one easily identified victim; all humans conspire to spread sin. We victimize each other in a never-ending spiral of evil thoughts and actions. Some people, like Loman, are more deeply caught in the spell of evil; their tragedy is not simply their evil ways but also their inability to recognize the fact that they are locked into self-delusional scapegoating of others for their own problems. Loman mistakenly praises brand-name products as signs of social progress, yet at the same time his own family is disintegrating partly as a result of the new consumer culture that rejects tradition as an important source of meaning.[78]

Communication scholars and media critics who assume a human tendency toward evil could be said to be working more nearly within the biblical metanarrative. Mahan, for instance, decries media criticism that implicitly "ignores the complexity of the narrative use of suspect elements, such as sex and violence, and implicitly denies the need to expose the shadow side of life." He even criticizes liberal and conservative Christians who fail to recognize how media producers and audiences both assume a simplistic approach to identifying evil in the media.[79] Bellah comes close to the metanarrative's position when he declares, "Prejudice, discrimination, and hostility to others arise from this inevitable fact of human personal and social life."[80] Similarly, James A. Aho suggests in *This Thing of Darkness* that it might not be possible for people to struggle against evil without being tainted by it.[81] As we all know from everyday observation, human beings often are fascinated by evil. Sometimes otherwise good people seek to do evil. If media producers are culpable, why are not audiences also culpable?

The idea of indigenous human culpability is generally at odds with liberal and conservative critiques of the mass media. Both ideological camps tend to criticize the media, not the audience. Marxists see the media as cultivating false consciousness in the interest of corporations and at the expense of audiences.[82] Conservatives typically believe that the media liberalize audiences, often as a conspiracy led by media elites. Film critic Michael Medved, for instance, portrays the battle as "Hollywood vs. America," leaving little space for any discourse about audiences' own evil desires.[83] Similarly, Stanley Rothman concludes that moviemakers "have reoriented movies toward the darker side of spiritual belief." Filmmakers, he believes, "abandoned conventional religious stories and began churning out movies exhibiting a fascination with evil."[84] Fair enough, but why are these films fascinating to audiences? Why do viewers desire macabre stories? Rothman concludes that movies are much less likely today to depict "traditional religious figures" positively. Even if his content analysis of the top-grossing films from 1946 to 1990 is accurate, who is responsible for causing such changes? Says Rothman, "The elimination of censorship and other changes within the movie industry and American society in the sixties and seventies resulted in the replacement of these films with much more ambiguous representations of a declining number of religious characters."[85] What social changes does he have in mind? Were these changes caused by the media? The fact is that many of the movies that he criticizes, such as *The Exorcist*, were enormously popular. Audiences seem to desire this religiously "ambiguous" storytelling, to use Rothman's term. Americans apparently seek out narratives that do not necessarily reflect idiosyncratic tribal religious beliefs, creeds, and doctrines.

Clearly a belief in immanent causality, which tends to see audiences overwhelmingly as victims, is cross-ideological. News reporters and columnists from the right and left rely upon it. So do politicians in campaign rhetoric. Immanent causality is a philosophical given in the logic of public life as portrayed in the media. By pointing a finger of causality at the media elite, the market system, entertainment industries, and the like, scholars and ideologues are able to identify various symbolic culprits and thereby support their own preconceived ideas. Since the public expression of alternative, tribal views of evil is understandably deemed intolerant or sectarian, the "doctrine" of immanent causality reigns supreme in the mainstream media.

Researchers and media critics alike read into the media content some of their own fundamental assumptions about human nature, including the scope and impact of evil. They assume quasi-theological convictions—that is, they hold a priori views of the character and spread of evil. Clinging to such assumptions, scholars, critics, and the media make American public discourse about the media particularly "moralistic"—a process of identifying the evil persons who supposedly cause evil. They also assume the culpability of one group or another, thereby reflecting their own penchants and perhaps even their own collective weaknesses. Such moralistic rhetoric of discernment, shaped by the assumption of immanent causality, becomes a form of symbolic finger pointing, not an open discourse about shared culpability or the evil that might reside in all human hearts. Meanwhile the media themselves muddy public discourse about evil even more by attributing evil causes only to particular social groups, from particular religions or nationalities to specific ethnic or socioeconomic sectors. In this sense, popular media criticism, media research, and mass-mediated narratives use remarkably similar rhetorics of discernment predicated on corresponding versions of immanent causality.

The concept of immanent causality evident in the popular victimization motif of public media is clearly at odds with much biblical theology. Human causality is, in one sense, a deeply biblical concept: sin exists in all social institutions and is passed down from generation to generation. Certainly the Hebrew prophets affirm the existence of cross-generational evil that is indeed transmitted from individual to individual.[86] A theological contextualization of this causality, however, challenges the victimization motif in popular theology. Mass-mediated "theology," as expressed in popular subnarratives, attempts to locate evil merely in the actions of victimized people. Christian tradition and biblical theology, on the other hand, generally look also to the inherent human disposition toward evil, sometimes called original sin. The media mythology regarding civil sinners as victims cannot easily accept any universal fallenness, cross-humankind tendency toward evil, or root human imperfection. It focuses instead on

particularly evil people, and then it seeks to rid society of these idiosyncratic carriers of civil sin. A belief in providence—the agency of God—
"gives way to a belief in the efficacy of human agency and will to
determine the direction of events in time."[87] Of course religious tribes still
can bring their own interpretations about evil to their understandings of
news reports, television docudramas, and other narrative forms. As previously suggested, tribal media critics carry some of that responsibility on behalf of the tribe and the broader public.

Purging Civil Sinners from the Media World

Writing in the early years of the Cold War, Hannah Arendt explained how
a divided Europe created rhetorical enemies. "As long as Europe remains
divided," she wrote, Europe "can afford the luxury" of dodging some of the
most "disturbing problems of the modern world."[88] Chief among these
problems was the nature of modern warfare, which could put in jeopardy
the survival of a whole people. What does courage mean in a world where
the alternative between liberty and death may lose its meaning in the face
of threats to the continued existence of humankind on earth? A divided
Europe, Arendt claimed, enabled Europeans to pretend "that the threat to
our civilization comes to her from without, and that she herself is in danger from two outside powers, America and Russia. . . . Both anti-
Americanism and neutralism are, in a sense, clear signs that Europe is not
prepared at this moment to face the consequences and problems of her
own development."[89]

Arendt's interpretation of the state of European thinking about the future during the Cold War mirrored similar rhetorical shifts within the
United States. As she wrote in the essay "The Threat of Conformism," all
European countries except Sweden and Switzerland had experiences with
totalitarianism, either in the form of totalitarian movements or domination. Americans had no such experience; to them, totalitarian movements
and governments seemed strangely "un-American." Americans would
reply to the European victims of Nazism and Bolshevism, "It can't happen
here! To Europeans, McCarthyism appear[ed] to be conclusive proof that it
can."[90] In effect, Americans declared that there was no immanent causality
that could lead the United States to totalitarianism. To Europeans, however, McCarthyism seemed like a sufficient cause.

These examples of political rhetoric suggest that human beings, as both
individuals and groups, define evil from without or within and then live

with the consequences of their definitions. The media generally see evil as an exterior causality—as the product of recent, prior evil acts. Christian and Hebrew theology, on the other hand, sees evil as partly the actions of people who inherited fallenness long ago and must live with evil as a fundamental characteristic of human nature. In the latter view, evil springs at least as much internally from the human heart as it does from external causes. Although institutions can foster collective evil, such manifestations of evil often depend on a prior manifestation of or a tendency toward evil in the individual. Social justice will always be a problem because of the existence of evil in the human heart from generation to generation.

The existence of evil in the world is obvious, even though the particular ways that human beings define it and address it in real time and space vary enormously. But the human tendency is to locate the source of evil outside of the self and even outside of the tribe. It is much easier, probably less painful, and certainly more comforting to believe that the source of evil in the world is not in one's own heart or tribe but rather is confined primarily to others' hearts and tribes. By demonizing others we can rhetorically save ourselves from guilt. Then, by a symbolic slight of hand, we can purge evil by eliminating others. The media "solve" the problem of civil sin by sacrificing perpetrators of evil on the altars of popular narrative. If evil is not entirely universal to humankind and if it is limited largely to particular kinds of individuals and groups, then the obvious solution to the public problem of evil is the elimination of these civil sinners. In this scenario both the problem and the solution rest in human hands. Sin is an immanent problem requiring no transcendent action. Humans cause it, and humans can purge it. All that society needs is a continuous supply of hard-core evildoers who can be sacrificed on behalf of all righteous people for the good of society. The only problem for the purveyors of this popular media theology is correctly anticipating public sentiment about the level of purgatorial action that it will take to justify the sacrifice of civil sinners. "Once we killed bad men: now we liquidate unsocial elements," writes C. S. Lewis.[91]

The everyday purgation of evil in mass-mediated narratives borrows its symbolic power analogously from the Hebrew and Christian metanarratives. In the Hebrew tradition priests made sacrifices to God in order to purge the sin of God's people. According to the Christian Gospel, God sacrificed Jesus Christ for the eternal salvation of sinners. God the Father sacrifices the innocent Jesus Christ as payment for the sins of a guilty humankind. In the media "gospel," heroic or sometimes common people sacrifice guilty evildoers presumably for innocent people. The media locate these evil people in the stereotypes that they use to demonize allegedly wicked persons and groups. These evildoers symbolize the immanent source of evil in the world. Mass media "theology" thus depends on this rhetoric of immanent causality to identify the people who must be purged from society. As a Roman Catholic essay on books and movie thrillers puts it, "Establishing world peace or freeing our neighborhoods of crime requires only the elimination of this one foe. And because these fiends are so irredeemably evil and dangerous, we don't need to bother negotiating with them or exercising any sort of restraint."[92]

Popular dramas, especially television series, probably best illustrate how civil sinners become sacrificial victims. Andrew Greeley and others have suggested that television drama is much like the medieval morality play.[93] JR of *Dallas*, for example, represented "unmitigated, unabashed, pure evil" behind the "disguise of virtue."[94] He is the kind of person audiences love to hate. Melodramatic television programming is predicated largely on such clear moral positions and characters.[95] There is little room for a symbolic ambiguity that would suggest there is both good and bad in all people. As the media affirm existing stereotypes, they help audiences to divide society into "good" and "evil" groups. Such collective stereotyping changes over time as people feel the need to find new individuals and groups to demonize and new forms of evil to purge. The mainstream media in a market system nevertheless find their dramatic power partly by stereotyping and demonizing particular groups.

Popular media produce symbolically charged tales that transform the paradoxes about evil into relatively unambiguous morality plays about guilt and purgation. By connecting their popular stories to the moralistic winds of contemporary culture, media confirm and deepen existing cultural sentiments about good and evil. Murder and rape, for instance, might be good symbolic fodder to define civil sin and to identify specific culprits. Adultery and lying, on the other hand, may be too morally ambiguous unless they are part of a pattern indicating someone's evil character. Civil sin requires a public certainty about what constitutes evil; it assumes a framework for identifying public morality. Comic books, romance novels, and Saturday-morning kids' programming capture this kind of unambiguous morality. A Christian news magazine celebrates *The Mighty Morphin Power Rangers* children's program for its "universe of moral clarity, its sharp boundaries between right and wrong and no ambiguity about what is good and what is evil." The reviewer lauds the program for depicting "absolutes" that "are real and worth fighting for."[96] In the 1920s and 1930s some popular novels, short stories, essays, autobiographies, fan magazines, and periodicals branded Hollywood as a demonic figure that was undermining good social values. Throughout the twentieth century major American media participated in these kinds of moralistic rituals.

The moralistic certainty behind public conceptions of civil sin also extends to nonfictional genres such as news reporting. Convinced in 1993 that General Motors's trucks sometimes burst into flames upon crash impact, *Dateline NBC* apparently wanted to make sure that it purged society of such evil. So the show's producer applied a sparking device to a test case, guaranteeing that the test truck would explode upon impact. The "hue and cry that followed the incident," writes Todd Gitlin, "missed the deep and abiding sin of television news."[97] Popular media theology—the simplistic morality of a mediated world—focuses its simplified aesthetic of evil on the currently fashionable sins, including those of media industries.[98]

Edward W. Said's critique of Western stereotypes of Islam, *Covering Islam: How the Media and the Experts Determine How We See the Rest of the World*, describes the ways that the West simplistically stereotypes and demonizes members of Islam. The West, he argues, has "redivided the world into Orient and Occident . . . the better to blind ourselves not only to the world but to ourselves." Westerners must "fix, personify, stamp the identity of what they feel confounds them collectively or individually." Most Americans, he maintains, learn about Islam through the media, which "constitute a communal core of interpretations providing a certain picture of Islam." Americans see on their television sets, hear on the radios, and read in their periodicals about "chanting 'Islamic' mobs accompanied by commentary about 'anti-Americanism.'" As a result of this simplistic stereotyping, the American news about Islam is "uniform in some ways, reductive, and monochromatic."[99] In effect, popular dramas and news media give the American public what it wants—an unambiguous sense of who its enemies are and who eventually needs to be purged.

American media use caricatures of race, gender, occupation, religion, and the like to identify evildoers, thereby Balkanizing the world into good and evil categories. The media also sensationalize stories and polarize characterizations as a means of rhetorically accentuating the categories. Media demonize religious fundamentalists as intolerant and militant; the very term "fundamentalist" assumes deeply negative connotations.[100] News reports paint pictures of corporate villainy, occasionally even creating some of the villainy in order to make the reports more fully stereotypical and to heighten the apparent evil of the transgressions.[101] Some media also portray rich businesspeople as evil.[102] At times the mass media perpetuate society's prejudices about people with disabilities—a long-standing process with roots in public exhibitions, circus sideshows, and early movies.[103] American media play a role in "framing mutual mistrust and resentment."[104] Early American films portrayed the "fallen women" in Hollywood who "took to the streets or became the mistress of some successful man in order to survive." But audiences wanted to make sure, as did members of the Hays Office, which regulated movie content, that these women "fell" far enough; they wanted clear evil and solid stereotypes.[105] Adolescents may learn from the media the stereotypical ways of solving problems violently.[106] Film thrillers portray a "toxic villain" who can be "blamed, hated, and punished with impunity."[107] The media might even demonize youth and the youth culture, creating "a metaphor for trivializing" adolescents' own resistance to the consumer culture.[108] Media sometimes point to computer technology and information workers as sources of evil.[109] All of these kinds of demonizing help the media to give audiences what they want: a means of identifying external evil for the purpose of freeing themselves from any culpability and purging civil sinners from society.

In a host of different ways print and electronic media pander to people's "suspicion, hostility and conspiracy mania," suggests John Taylor.[110] As social problems grow more complex, people seek simplistic answers—and the media oblige. Politicians infect their campaign rhetoric with subtle racism. Critics demonize the establishment. Concludes Taylor, "While it is an emotional truth for Oliver Stone that an Establishment conspiracy killed Kennedy, for Michael Crichton that Japan is taking over the country, for Susan Faludi that *thirtysomething* helped thwart the feminist agenda, it is an equally emotional truth for David Duke that blacks are lazy and for Bill Cosby that AIDS is a conspiracy."[111] All of these assumptions about the source of evil are what Taylor calls "emotional truths" that play to existing prejudices and fester damaging polarizations among Americans.

In a mass-mediated world, argues Ellul, this process of demonization affects all strata of society, including elites and the well educated.[112] The intellectual, he believes, no longer conceives of anyone else as his or her "neighbor." Instead of truly communicating with others, the intellectual analyzes them, categorizes them, and "scientifically" separates himself or herself from other people. Eventually entire intellectual movements and philosophies serve as a means of subjecting others rather than serving them. The Nazis and the Communists, writes Ellul, concentrate "the whole idea of evil in 'the enemy.' Soon the enemy is the expression of evil itself: on the one hand 'the Jew,' the 'Communist,' the 'plutocrat.' On the other hand, the 'bourgeois,' the 'saboteur,' the 'Trotskyite' incarnates all evil upon earth, and in consequence we have to kill him without pity, for he is no longer a human being, he is a symbol."[113] Ellul suggests that mass society fosters a deep disrespect for anyone who is significantly different from the fashionable norm. Such societies might speak rhetorically of tolerance and freedom, but their media tend toward superficial stereotypes and even intense demonization.

In America the tension between religious tribalism and mass-mediated consensus is probably good for society. Religious pluralism potentially provides a wide range of tribal views of the nature of evil, but no religious norm is institutionally or sociologically forced upon society. Tribal media can maintain common norms for the faith, including shared concepts of evil. Meanwhile the wider society can think differently about evil. As a result, the commercial media become loosely woven tapestries for building a kind of consensus of public opinion about what the nation will deem evil. The media may not seek this rhetorical role of moral agent, but they nevertheless acquire it by virtue of their privileged place in public discourse. In order to gain audiences they must consider at some level the notions of evil that exist in the tribes. Without the countervailing tribal opinions, the media could function autonomously like a moralistic state church for secular society. But just as the tribes can themselves mistakenly look for outsiders to explain evil, the media can prey upon the cross-tribal weaknesses regarding self-admissions of stereotyping and scapegoating.

Clearly the American media's market system, which provides the freedom for mass media to try to find a consensus on morality, tends to move American culture toward shared opinions and even stereotypical assumptions about groups whose culture is not the national norm. As the media address evil in both news and drama, they implicitly define the moral consensus. George Gilder says that in the "absence of God and the good and the true, a culture tends to preoccupy itself with evil and fatality."[114] That kind of preoccupation is part of what Reinhold Niebuhr calls "group pride," which "achieves a certain authority over the individual and results in unconditioned demands by the group upon the individual."[115] As the media identify and facilitate a collective public sense of civil sin, they can fuel the growth of particular varieties of social conformity and shared demonization. "The group is more arrogant, hypocritical, self-centered and more ruthless in the pursuit of its ends than the individual," warns Niebuhr.[116] Americans face this dilemma of national "group think" as they try to build public consensus about evil. The market can be sensitive to society's need for expressions of civil sin that are more or less in tune with cross-tribal recognitions of evil, but the market can also fuel the human urge to victimize and demonize outsiders, dividing the complex world into simplistic categories that simultaneously satiate the audience's desire for evil and lead that audience to reactionary moralism.

Edward T. Oakes reflects on these issues in an insightful essay about human nature. He wonders why American society has become so violent. Are the culprits the media? Parents? The justice system? Americans assume, he says, that the problem of evil comes "from without"; they assume that individuals acquire evil from the society. Oakes suggests that Americans wrongly believe, along with Jean-Jacques Rousseau, that "if only the environment were properly geared toward human fulfillment, the motivation to commit evil would disappear like a bad dream."[117] He highlights the way that Americans frequently point to the media as the eternal causes of evil. The mass media, too, become rhetorical scapegoats, symbolic manifestations of what is actually a broader problem with human nature. While the media frequently deliver the bad news, they also become part of the bad news. Whereas Oakes sees evil as pervasive and human, the media identify evil with easily blamed persons and institutions. In his view, the media focus at best on penultimate rather than ultimate causes of evil. As moralistic storytellers, the popular media unreflectively depict rather than critically investigate human nature.

The ways the media address crime and criminality might best reveal how they misuse the rhetoric of civil sin for their own purposes. Mass-mediated portrayals of crime may have even "displaced the spectacle of public punishment as a vehicle for symbolically affirming moral sentiments and reproving their violation." So-called reality-based TV programs such as *America's Most Wanted* isolate crime to evil fugitives who are presumed guilty.[118] The documentary style of these programs creates the false impression of veracity and objectivity. The show *Cops* similarly "closes off" alternative readings of real-life events by providing "neat ways" and creating an "illusion of certainty."[119] Program editor Debra Seagal describes how the staff of *American Detective* "reduced fifty or sixty hours of mundane and compromising video into short, action-packed segments of tantalizing crack-filled, dope-dealing, junkie-busting cop culture." The show "cleverly breezed past the complexities that cast doubt on the very system that has produced the criminal activity" and smoothed out the "indiscretions of bumper detectives that casually makes them appear as flailing heroes rush-ing across the screen."[120] Media crime stories, suggests Maria Grabe, have replaced public executions as the "vehicle for constructing society's moral-ity and exercising social control."[121] As Lippmann might have put it, the mass-mediated pseudo-environment offers Americans shared ways of knowing and believing about crime and criminals. The media accept and then affirm existing American stereotypes of evil. In a sense, they make us more like we already are, all the while generating profits on the exploita-tion of human weaknesses.

In Westerns, detective shows, action series, and the like the public is similarly treated to a fairly limited assemblage of stock characters who rep-resent unambiguous good and evil.[122] The media concentrate on easily grasped moral symbols and on the characters in the white and black hats. Over the years the evildoers have included scalp-hunters, psychopaths, mobster bosses, hired killers, and rapists. Some ethnic and racial groups have been represented more than others, undoubtedly reflecting various existing stereotypes. Television melodrama also facilitates American no-tions of good and bad.[123] All of these kinds of fictional narratives con-tribute to the ways that Americans perceive and promote particular symbolic expressions of evil in society. In the process, of entertaining themselves with media products, Americans also enact their individual and collective rituals of civil sin and purgation.

Apparently the key to creating truly evil characters, whether in drama or the news, is establishing enough wickedness that the characters seem to merit nothing good and to deserve stiff justice, sometimes even death. These villains thereby "get their due" and through their "sacrifice" presum-ably help make the world safer for the rest of us righteous souls. Obviously this type of sacrifice is not particularly allegorical to either the Christian Gospel or ancient Hebrew animal sacrifice, since in both cases it was the innocent who were killed on behalf of the guilty. See René Girard, *I See Satan Fall Like Lightening*, trans. James G. Williams (Maryknoll, NY: Orbis Books, 2002), 154–60. Media criminals are brought to justice partly as a means of affirming the quasi-theological idea that evil resides principally in evil people, not generically in the human race. These victims' deaths are society's gains—the means of purging humankind of undesirable, danger-ous, and even savage people. Even detective stories "regularly distort or unmask the world so that sociality and crime become the everyday norm, but at the same time charm away the seductive and ominous challenge through the inevitable triumph of order."[124] Mass-mediated storytelling in a market system both expresses popular stereotypes of evil and obfuscates the deeper issues at stake and the more complex "causes" of evil.

In the United States the two most significant dramatic genres in this popular theology of evil have been Westerns and detective shows, first in Saturday movies and network radio, and beginning in the 1940s on network television.[125] *Gunsmoke* and *Wagon Train* used gunslingers, American Indians, bank robbers, cattle thieves and desperados. Occasionally a good person would turn bad, but typically the savage characters were easily contrasted with the civilized townspeople trying to live righteous lives. Detective programs, which largely replaced Westerns on North American television in the 1970s, shifted the battle from the frontier to the city.[126] Detective series were urban Westerns with new savages: mobsters, hired killers, drug kingpins, and the like. Cities thus became new frontiers where good and evil characters battled for control of society.[127] Cattle rustlers and hired killers were sacrificed on thousands of programs—all in the name of vicarious morality. These dramatic genres cultivated deep-seated American notions of evil, while soap operas and sitcoms addressed the more superficial but just as important morality of everyday family life.

Transformations in these genres' formulas over time probably reflect important changes in American culture, including shifts in public conceptions of evil. The major difference between early Westerns and their detective-series successors was the degree of morality required of heroes. Western heroes tended to be remarkably righteous (Matt Dillon would not take advantage of Kitty and repeatedly risked his life by refusing to bushwhack hardened criminals). Detectives were much more likely to use ethically questionable means to accomplish justice; they often lied, for instance, to get information about criminals. The likely explanation for this shift in American popular culture during the 1970s was the nation's own public cynicism about established authority. If evil rested in real heroes, including the president of the United States, who faced impeachment proceedings in the Watergate scandal during the 1970s, then the public needed hard-boiled heroes who might have to use uncivil means to secure justice and stop evil. The sitcom *M*A*S*H*, also popular during the period, reflected similarly ambivalent sentiments about the prospects for eliminating evil; the show institutionalized evil in a way that is rarely present in such a popular medium.[128]

In spite of these infrequent exceptions to the popular American mythology of evil, the morality plays of the media continue to invest tremendous hope in humankind's ability to eliminate civil sin by ridding itself of the evil individuals who represent stereotypical categories of evil people. The media reinforce this doctrine with an endless stream of new tales that are usually nothing more than variations on old ones.[129] Most of the stories are fictional drama, but certainly the news reports and docudramas play their parts in this purgation myth with every new story about captured criminals. An outsider to American culture might be perplexed by this whole scenario: "How can these consumers of popular theology maintain their faith when evil reappears in the media day after day?" The answer of course is that the media require evil in order to eliminate evil. Through a public rhetoric of discernment, Americans agree collectively about who the villains are in society. Then, through a rhetoric of communion, Americans can identify with the forces of good. Finally, in an implicit rhetoric of praise, Americans can share aesthetic and moral delight in the symbolic purgation of evil from society.

Conclusion

In *Uncivil Religion*, Bellah completes his study by asking whether society would be better off without religion. After all, he reminds us, societies have long been encumbered with religious prejudice, discrimination, and hostility. He claims that in the contemporary world only nationalism rivals religious identity as a source of "group belongingness" and therefore as a "source of intergroup hostility and conflict."[130] Along with such power come the misuses of power. But the idea of eliminating religion, Bellah concludes, is simply one more "example of the inveterate human tendency to draw boundaries and then to look down on those on the other side."[131] The Christian and Hebrew metanarratives suggest that even religious tribes, like the wider society, are populated by sinful people. These tribes ought to be the first social institutions to admit so and to hold their own members to a high standard of self-criticism. The tribes similarly should be willing to remind themselves and society that merely demonizing or locking up evildoers, even when right and proper, will not eliminate evil. Finally, the tribes should be responsible enough to help all other tribes keep the media honest in how they portray evil, sin, and the human quest for justice through revenge.

Jay Tolson addresses this benefit in an insightful essay on Americans' responses to the tragic high school shootings at Littleton, Colorado, in 1999. Tolson wonders if Americans have "lost a vocabulary adequate to the enormity of the evil." He posits that early generations of Americans likely "possessed a vocabulary that balanced religious and humanistic traditions in a way that never fully absolved individuals from responsibility for the good or bad they did." Americans need, he suggests, both the religious language of St. Augustine and the humanistic language of the Socratic heritage. From the Augustinian tradition Americans learn that evil results when people abandon God, forsake humility, and turn wickedly "lower."[132] In this tradition people are flawed creatures and creators—even sinners. From the ancient Greek tradition Americans learn that evil results also from human defects of knowledge, from people's errors in knowing and judging. The latter view of the source of evil suggests a degree of human perfectibility as people come to know more about the world. But the former, biblical view is generally understood as more pessimistic about the human condition; it offsets the optimism of scientific thought and progressive ideas with the reality of human rebellion and selfishness. In short, this tribal rhetoric helps Americans to avoid the kinds of sentimental humanism that assumes easy answers and quick fixes to the human condition. It also militates against any rhetorics of praise that might naively place too much hope in the ability of human beings to eliminate civil sin by rituals of symbolic purgation. Aleksandr I. Solzhenitsyn warns that the purely humanistic way of thinking "did not admit the existence of intrinsic evil in man, nor did it see any task higher than the attainment of happiness on earth."[133]

When it comes to the nature and scope of evil, the biblical metanarrative and the subnarratives of mass-media theology are mutually supportive and subversive. Since their fundamental assumptions are incompatible and each one implicitly or explicitly claims authority over the other, the two rhetorics will never be identical. Charles Horton Cooley optimistically suggested in the early years of the twentieth century that "religious formulas" would "henceforth be held with at least a subconsciousness of their provisional status." He also predicted that future creeds would be "simple" and "universal" rather than intellectual and sectarian.[134] He was at least partly wrong, since scientific and other progressive ways of knowing also have become provisional in a postmodern world. The church and media often quibble with each other and sometimes enter rhetorical battle over issues such as the freedom of the press, morality, and the portrayal of religion. In a democratic context, however, these are probably healthy tensions as long as they do not slip into namecalling and demonization. A religious tribe needs to maintain its own distinctive identity in society, without succumbing to mass-mediated mythology. But such tribes need other groups to exist in society in order to get a less self-interested view of themselves. The church, for instance, had better listen to its own rhetoric about the pervasiveness of the Fall from grace, including how that fallenness affects the tribes' views of evil in the contemporary world.

Very likely, given the historical record, the mass media will never serve as a satisfactory substitute for religion for most people. Civil sin is an attractive media theology that seems at least temporarily to give some people a better grip on evil and a firmer hope for a better world. Nevertheless, Christianity's deeper sense of sin, while more frightening, has rung true for millions of people over two millennia. If anything, the Christian tribes' concept of original sin, as opposed to the media's "doctrine" of immanent causality, might lead some people to want the Gospel rather than popular culture all the more. Human hearts still search for the eternal other as a way of dealing with their own evil. Puddefoot suggests that human freedom depends upon the ambiguity of information that we confront when we try to "find ourselves in the other rather than remain centered upon ourselves." If the media world merely interpreted itself, he adds, "there would be no room for misunderstanding or creative participation in the reconstruction of meaning."[135] William Willimon writes, "It is the problem of being human and not being able to do one blessed thing about it except to lynch, kill, blame, accuse, lie and suffer, trapped in our own stupid B-grade movie of a tragedy that we have seen enacted a hundred times before, more victims than villains, caged animals, dying every day, wishing to God it were not so but it is, oh, it is."[136] No media experts, even the noble intellectuals imagined by Lippmann, will be able to clean up the ambiguity and solve the problem of evil once and for all. The best we can do might be to "discover a new language," as Ellul says, a language that helps us "to understand one another, in spite of publicity, a language which permits men to abandon their despairing solitude, and avoids both rational sterility and subjective emotionalism."[137]

7

Discerning Professional Journalism:
Reporters Adopt Fundamentalist Discourse

◪ ◪ ◪

In 1996 *Today* show host Bryant Gumble interviewed former U.S. president Jimmy Carter about his new autobiography. Gumble asked Carter the following question: "You write that you prayed more during your four years in office than basically at any time in your life, and yet I think it's fair to say, and I hope this doesn't sound too harsh . . . you are consistently reviewed as one of the more ineffective Presidents of modern times. What do you think, if anything, that says about the power of prayer?"[1]

Gumble's leading question implicitly addresses the heart of this chapter. Should religious faith, whether personal or collective, be addressed in public discourse? From the early years of the Republic, religion has been one of the largely private passions that influence many Americans' public actions. Alexis de Tocqueville wrote in the 1830s, "The spirit of the journalist in America is to attach coarsely, without preparation and without art, the passions of those whom it addresses, to set aside principles in order to grab men; to follow them into their private lives, and to lay bare their weaknesses and their vices." Nevertheless, adds Tocqueville, "Americans so completely confuse Christianity and freedom in their minds that it is almost impossible to have them conceive of the one without the other." He observed that in the United States religion is not "confined to the manners, but it extends to the intelligence of the people."[2] If Tocqueville's observations about America still hold today, maybe journalists and other chroniclers are obligated as public fiduciaries to illuminate the significance of religion in contemporary society. Perhaps religious ideas and customs are not only the province of religious institutions but also a subject for the news media.

Gumble's question to Carter seems to assume that if the president's religion is valid his prayers should have made him a more effective or even successful president. Gumble implicitly sees religious faith as a kind of instrumental technology whose value depends on its practical power to achieve particular human desires. If prayers do not "work," he implies, why believe in God? Does Gumble's view of prayer represent the agnosticism of the public, the skepticism of journalists, or merely his personal penchant? In addition, did Gumble have an obligation to admit to his viewers any of his own disdain for Carter or for prayer? Inside the journalistic profession, writes Allan R. Andrews, "[w]hen our critical words are turned against ourselves, we tend to speak with a forked tongue. . . . We are told, for example, that objectivity and fairness demands (sic) that reporters who cover religion should take care not to express personal religious views. I've read articles in professional journals debating, 'Can religion reporters be religious?'"[3]

This chapter argues that professional journalism has contributed to the privatization and secularization of religion in the United States. This development has worked to the advantage of professional journalists, who increasingly have taken over some of the social functions and cultural authority formerly held by religious institutions. Like religion, modern news is an epistemology, a way of knowing about the world, and a means of locating ourselves in that world. As Robert E. Park writes, news "performs somewhat the same functions for the public that perception does for the individual man . . . it does not so much inform as orient the public. . . . It does this without any effort of the reporter to interpret the events he reports, except in so far as to make them comprehensible and interesting."[4] News substitutes in America partly for custom and tradition, including religious tradition. Louis Wirth says that such mass communication is a paradox because in "order to communicate with one another we must have common knowledge, but in a mass society it is through communication that we must obtain this common body of knowledge."[5] Either tradition, public opinion, the news, or some other form of cultural transmission must provide the common knowledge that Americans need to participate in a democratic society. News is increasingly the way Americans orient themselves to their shared life as a nation.

The first section of this chapter argues that in early colonies news was largely the province of religious leaders who delivered it to their communities of faith. In Christian churches the Good News contextualized the "common occurrences" of everyday life. As historian David Paul Nord argues, the "origin of American news—its subject matter, style, and method of reporting—is deeply rooted in the religious culture of seventeenth-century New England."[6] But by the time of the American Revolution the colonies were filled with "secular" or general-interest newspapers that focused far more on politics and business than on religion. In the nineteenth century, religious groups in America responded to the growth of the mainstream commercial press by establishing their own religious periodicals, which took up some of the social commentary formerly controlled by pastors. The religious media offered a forum for maintaining social control within tribes through a rhetoric of discernment, which distinguished between the tribe's idiosyncratic beliefs and those of the broader society. The nineteenth-century religious press essentially provided a countervailing moral force to the growth of secular newspapers and eventually magazines.

The second section addresses the ways that mainstream news media replaced many religious media in American society. Over the last 200 years, news reporting became more popular, professional, and secular, attracting a wide range of readers from across the nation's increasingly diverse religious landscape. In order to build such heterogeneous audiences journalists professionalized their reporting and sought to establish a publicly respectable ideology for their craft. Reporters eventually adopted a fundamentalist mode of interpretation—informational fundamentalism—that emphasized fact, event, and conflict rather than context and meaning.[7] This professional hermeneutic provided journalists with a rhetoric of discernment that implicitly questioned any religious claims, often cynically, while simultaneously relying on the opinions of secular experts. Journalists increasingly functioned as secular prophets in American society, dispensing quasi-objective knowledge to the people and acting in society for the people.

The third section examines the power of news reporting as a form of public imagination that symbolically frames citizens' views of social and cultural life. Journalism is not so much a reflection of public opinion, writes Sharan L. Daniel, as it is a form of rhetoric that makes arguments that may or may not serve a community.[8] Journalists do not merely report the facts or simply provide perspective; much more important, they imagine stories. Contemporary journalism is a ritual of imaginative storytelling designed to convince both journalists and their audiences that the world is more or less like the way that they have imagined it.

Certainly in a heterogeneous society like the United States this type of mythmaking is highly problematic because of the conflicting interests and competing metanarratives that Americans bring to their understanding of the news.[9] Lacking their own coherent metanarratives—except for the tale of journalism's own progressive professionalization—and relying largely on a fundamentalist mode of reporting, journalists are unable to integrate the news into a reasonably coherent and meaningful tapestry of American life. A journalist's personal religious convictions sometimes might shape implicitly the "imagination" behind her news storytelling, as John Schmalzbauer contends, but the overarching rhetoric of explicitly secular reporting still dominates mainstream journalism.[10]

The fourth section contends that religious reporting today usually contributes to the ghettoization of religious life, relegating matters of faith and action to the religion page or patronizing them humorously at the end of the nightly news. By defining the religious aspects of life largely in terms of tribal bureaucracies and religious organizations or in terms of religious self-interest and tribal intolerance, the news media effectively squelch the important languages of religious faith and action from the public square. With few exceptions, journalists examine religion only as isolated phenomena, not as a significant part of American cultural and social life. In American reporting practically everything in life has a cause and especially a consequence, but hardly any aspects of human thought and conduct have essential value, transcendent virtue, or even inherent good. By dismissing religious epistemologies, journalists eclipse one of the most significant sources of discourse about the common good in society.

When Gumble put former president Carter on the spot during the live broadcast of the *Today* show, he joined the many media personalities and news reporters who interpret religion with dismissive stereotypes. As an informational fundamentalist, he assumed that commonsense cynicism should guide his inquiry. Today religious tribes often feel like outsiders to the news media—like voyeurs peering out of the window of a tour bus driven by skeptical reporters who are narrating the rapidly changing scenes. As journalists reduce religion to collages of special interests, religious persons wonder if they should fire salvos back at the news media or simply opt out of public life. Focusing on "the specious present," journalists do little to help us understand the broader religious issues within democratic discourse and at the center of human life.[11] Although this is a serious flaw in modern reporting, it is also why religious tribes should support their own journals of comment and opinion about contemporary events.

News As the "Good News"

Former network news anchor John Hart recalls how he was caught in a conflict between a church's mission and a journalist's job.[12] Hart resigned from NBC news in early 1988 and shortly thereafter accepted a journalistic position with *World Monitor*, an international television service launched by the Christian Science Publishing Society, which also publishes the *Christian Science Monitor*. Hart read in the five-year plan for *World Monitor* that the new television service would be "part of the vast mission of Christian Science to the world—a mission that brings redemption and healing to individual man and mankind through the scientific action of the Christ-power in human experience."[13] He wondered how to respond to the apparent conflict between the church's mission and his role as an unbiased reporter.

Hart believed in the "separation of religious interests from the newsroom," but now he found himself facing a news organization that was rewriting news reports for theological reasons—such as refusing to predict natural events without "sourcing" them.[14] Hart and his Christian Scientist colleagues clashed over which news reports to include in broadcasts as well as how to contextualize the selected stories. The church, for instance, did not want Hart to use the term "affliction" to describe leprosy and refused to let Hart give the cause of death in obituaries—both positions resulting from of the church's view of human sickness and death. Recognizing the growing tension between the church's mission and his own professional standards of reporting, Hart drafted a resignation that began, "A reporter can't have a mission. The most we can have is a duty. To be as accurate, fair, and balanced as humanly possible. The purpose is to know. . . . Caring about where the chips fall means one is tempted to meddle. Having a mission means a purpose beyond and in addition to finding knowledge."[15]

We tend today to think of the conflicts between church and state and media, but Tocqueville saw in the 1830s a very different America where "a public opinion in favor of religion is produced" and where the influence of religion is "more lasting." Religion does not directly participate in

government, he wrote, but it "singularly facilitates" the existence of free institutions and holds an "indispensable" role in the "maintenance of republican institutions." The press constitutes "an extraordinary power, so strangely
mixed of goods and evils, without which freedom cannot live and with
which order can hardly be maintained."[16] This role of the press as both
champion of public liberty and molder of public opinion makes sense in the
context of the country's democratic philosophy, which in the First Amendment protects the freedom of religion, as well as speech. History reveals this
close connection between vibrant journalism and lively religion—even
though the modern mind tends to see democracy and religious faith as rivals
if not enemies. As Doug Underwood puts it in his book on the religious roots
of the secular press, journalists still "draw much of their professional inspiration from the Bible's prophetic complaints about moral corruption, as well as
the calls for reform that grew out of the Protestant Reformation, the Progressive and Populist movements, and the muckraker and Social Gospel campaigns in the United States during the late nineteenth century and early
twentieth."[17]

The United States has a long and important tradition of religious media
that contributed to public discourse. In the early years of the nation local
pastors were the major sources of news and the most significant public
voices on social and political affairs. The clergy were the unrivaled, authoritative sources of information and interpretation for most people, the most
believable and trustworthy sources that individuals and communities used
to orient their lives, epistemologically and morally, in the emerging nation.
Even as late as 1740, the clergy constituted 70 percent of all learned professionals in Massachusetts.[18] Educated clergy were the natural intelligentsia—
the professional movers and shakers who had the knowledge, respect,
and moral authority to advise citizens on matters of local and national
importance.

Seventeenth-century American news—distributed by pulpit, press, and
word of mouth—was deeply rooted in Protestant culture. News was what
Nord calls "teleological," reflecting the assumption that "everything happened according to God's perfect plan."[19] Religious news publishers, who
largely controlled news creation and dissemination in the colonies, interpreted public events within the context of a divine order, the Christian
metanarrative, which saw daily events within the larger pattern of God's
work in history. As Nord puts it, "New England generated a kind of news
that was oriented to current events, yet conventional, patterned, and re-
current in subject matter. It was religious and public in importance and

purpose, yet directly accessible to individual people. It was controlled and reported by public authority, yet was simple, plain, and empirical in form."[20] This religiously inspired form of newswriting was certainly journalistic, but it was not highly systematic, objective, or scientific. News was a means publicly to make sense of what Protestants often called the "occurrences of life." The public meaning of news was largely indistinguishable from the religious and theological interpretations of news. News was simultaneously part of God's story and the narrative of the New World.

Early American news was akin to preaching, namely, a means of exegeting events of the day in light of particular religious assumptions. In New England, the home of American news reporting, Americans invented their own religiously inspired approaches to printed news and eventually the newspaper. New Englanders used biblical narratives to interpret the everyday tales of local and to some extent regional life. Of course American Puritans imported this religious worldview from Europe, but they distinguished their form of newsmaking from those of the homeland by using the doctrine of divine providence to frame storytelling in public media.[21] After all, they reasoned, America was to be the City upon a Hill, the center of God's activity on earth. Among these early news publications were printed sermons delivered on official public occasions, at Sunday services, and in response to natural occurrences.[22]

Many seventeenth-century colonial newspapers viewed religion as a vital part of colonial life. These papers framed public life in the most commonly shared language of the time—the language of Protestant faith. They saw providence as the center from which all events derived their cosmic meaning and historical interpretation. Even when the papers did not refer directly to religion, they reported events with a sense of Christian worldview.[23] Historically speaking, colonial news essentially defined human events in the context of God's divine role in biblical history. American newsmaking was a kind of public liturgy for celebrating God's hand in American events and for admonishing those people who were not living up to God's apparent claim on their lives. Sermons and news were two views of the same arena of divine providence.

Since the life of the colonies was far more than religion, however, it was only a matter of time until newspapers addressed the arenas of commerce, politics, and entertainment. Newspaper publishing exploded in the colonies and the new nation, driven by a tremendous public thirst for information, entertainment, and perspective. As Tocqueville reports, by the 1830s every little town seemed to have its own press. The number of periodicals "surpasses belief," he writes, suggesting that "the only way to neutralize the effect of public journals is to multiply them indefinitely."[24] America exploded as a new publishing nation in the years after the revolution. This "tremendous expansion in newspaper publishing," says John Nerone, "was fueled by the consciousness of the implied necessity for effective communication in a nation to be governed by popular consent."[25] In 1730 there were seven newspapers in four colonies; by 1800 there were over 180.[26] Rev. Samuel Miller wrote around 1785 that the "great body of the people" already had "free and constant access to public prints, receiving regular information of every occurrence, attending to the course of political affairs, discussing public measures. . . . Never . . . was the number of political journals so great. . . . Never were they . . . so cheap, so universally diffused, and so easy to access."[27]

George Whitefield, who invented the personality-driven popular religious revival in America, did more than anyone else to fuse pulpit, press, and personality into mainstream American news media. As he awaited travel orders to the new Georgia colony in 1737, Whitefield preached in London a series of enormously popular sermons that attracted the interest of the British press. His dramatic performances convinced the press that there was a large, cross-denominational market for printed copies of his sermons. The flamboyant preacher realized the importance of publicity by the time he arrived in the colonies. His sermons competed in the press with news about government, business, and recreation, and he in turn became a celebrity who vied for publicity with war heroes, politicians, and actors. As historian Harry S. Stout suggests, Whitefield taught American papers "how to make religion *news*, and the press would respond with almost universal acclaim and adulation."[28] The popular preacher gave the mainstream press a new form of news story that sold papers and generated tremendous interest in Whitefield's appearances—which created more news that sold more newspapers. Side-by-side with the distinctly religious press, then, the mainstream press took up religion news as a new narrative commodity. Daniel J. Boorstin writes, "Very early the American newspaper had to justify itself as a commodity rather than as a purveyor of orthodoxy."[29] Religion became a subject for reporting rather than a perspective from which to report.

While the printed news business grew in early-nineteenth-century America, it gradually challenged the privileged role of the clergy and the authority of religious media. Insofar as the clergy represented the only authoritative profession in society, as they had in the seventeenth-century colonies, the secular impact of journalism was not a major social issue. As journalists competed with the clergy as exegetes of daily occurrences, however, disputes over the definition of news became a significant source of social and cultural conflict. Journalists and clergy vied for both social status and authority in the expanding nation—a competition that continues to this day in the public salvos fired back and forth between the two groups. The clergy could no longer expect people to trust only them in matters of historical and cultural interpretation. As Mark Silk writes, "Journalism in America practically began by giving offense to religion."[30]

For many years the rise of secular-journalistic authority was offset partly by the amazing proliferation of religious media, especially religious periodicals. These periodicals provided the means for Christian institutions and movements to combat secular news interpretations by cultivating their own journalistic hermeneutics across geographic space. In fact, religious periodicals represented the first important centrifugal movement of news across the inchoate nation. As one observer puts it, the religious papers "cleansed" the news media and "polished" them into "mirrors which reflect the divine glory to the darkest and most distant parts of the country. . . . In light of these great facts, is not our age a modern Pentecost and our republic a modern Jerusalem?"[31] Both postmillennial and premillennial believers saw in the rise of the many religious periodicals a great increase in knowledge, the advancement of science, and especially the spread of the Gospel.[32] Nathan O. Hatch writes, "Virtually nonexistent in 1800, religious periodicals had by 1830 become the grand engine of the burgeoning religious culture, the primary means of promotion for, and bond of union within, competing religious groups."[33] The Methodist weekly *Christian Advocate and Journal and Zion's Herald*, for example, in 1830 claimed a circulation of 25,000, more than the reported circulation of any other journalistic periodical in the world.[34] During the first three decades of the nineteenth century the number of subscribers to American religious periodicals jumped from 5,000 to about 400,000. In 1790 there were only 14 religious journals; by 1830, 605 had been founded.[35] Some of the nation's religious periodicals were part of the African-American press that sought to liberate slaves. The United States sprouted a range of religious publications that reflected the mosaic of American Christianity.

The explosive dissemination of religious periodicals increasingly put new stresses on the country's social system and public life—the stresses of religious diversity and competition. The formerly coherent Protestant subcultures, previously held together more or less geographically within the structures and by the allegiances of a few major denominations, were running into one another in public life. The sometimes combative groups were promoting their own doctrines and practices with all of the zealousness of mass-media entrepreneurs. By the mid-1830s the increasingly eclectic world of religious publishing probably represented the major competition with mainstream newspapers as a means for citizens to learn about the affairs of the nation beyond their own towns and cities. Nord suggests that when religious groups launched their own periodicals they were "fighting fire with fire, for they viewed the rise of mass printing as perhaps the most precious manifestation of the market revolution."[36] Religious and religion news competed locally and, increasingly, nationally.

Perhaps the most crucial period in the history of the religious press in America was the second half of the nineteenth century. During this era religious and mainstream media competed for public influence, providing countervailing cultural forces. The religious press was able to take up issues that were too controversial for mainstream, commercial media. As Ann Douglas chronicles, religious publishing and writing even provided antebellum women with a vision for professional involvement, leading to the feminization of American culture.[37] But most of all, the western religious press tried to integrate all aspects of life and every part of the public square into one periodical that would likely be the only medium to serve a particular geographic area. Wesley Norton describes the religious papers in the Old Northwest, quoting from various early papers as follows, "The uniqueness of the antebellum religious newspaper was in its blend of secular and religious purposes. For most churchmen, the object involved far more than the proportion of religious material or the mere grafting onto the secular content of newspapers 'religious principles and aims.' The religious newspaper was an organ which gave not 'merely religious intelligence, but a *news* paper, complete in every department of general news, yet upon a religious, instead of a political or literary basis'." This kind of periodical, Norton adds, was to be an agent in the sanctification of the whole vastness and variety of American life, especially the western part of it, as God's domain. "Let theology, law, medicine, politics, literature, art, science, commerce, trade, architecture, agriculture—in time, all questions which concern and secure the welfare of a people—be freely discussed and treated, and this, too, for God, for Jesus Christ, and the advancement of the Redeemer's kingdom among men." The religious newspaper "surveys the world not with the eye of the politician, or the merchant, but condenses, arranges, and reports the events of the day, as connected with the religion of Jesus

Christ." The news itself had its moral and its gospel, the news sheet being nothing less than "the horologe of Providence."[38]

As a horologe of progress—a timekeeper of the events of community life—this type of religious paper combined the early colonial concept of news, which linked divine providence with the everyday matters of people, and the modern daily newspaper, which offered secular reports about public affairs. The western religious press assumed that there was religious meaning and significance even in the everyday occurrences of people in public life, but it also saw the need to open up the public conversation to the more general issues and events of community life. Religious news was crucial as a way of interpreting coherently the events of real people in an actual nation, a kind of contemporary ritual for understanding the cosmic and theological relevance of the "parables" of American culture and society. "Man alone," wrote Tocqueville, "shows a natural disgust for existence and an immense desire to exist. . . . Religion is therefore only a particular form of hope, and it is as natural to the human heart as hope itself. Only by a kind of aberration of the intellect and with the aid of a sort of moral violence exercised on their own nature do men stray from religious beliefs; an invincible inclination leads them back to them."[39] Religious journalism increasingly represented a way for Americans to maintain a religious hope about events without having to subscribe to a sectarian vision of truth.

In spite of the phenomenal popularity of religious periodicals in the nineteenth century, these important media eventually lost much of their influential role in public life to the advancing popularity of the mainstream urban newspaper. By 1900 "the specifically Protestant press was struggling to maintain a distinctive voice in a society that was becoming increasingly pluralistic and secular."[40] Not because of any antireligious movement or secular-humanistic conspiracy but simply because of the changing character of American democratic society, the daily newspaper largely supplanted the religious press as the major carrier of public information, the central means of public discourse, and the necessary vehicle for cultivating a shared perspective on community and national life. Michael Schudson suggests that the nation was "transformed from a liberal mercantilist republic, still cradled in aristocratic values, family, and deference, to an egalitarian market democracy, where money had new power, the individual new standing, and the pursuit of self-interest new honor."[41] Religion could not replace democracy any more than democracy could replace religion. As Tocqueville discovered, the nation derived its moral vitality from religion, but the same country often separated religion from public expressions of political convictions. "Therefore," he writes, "one cannot say that in the United States religion exerts an influence on the laws or on the details of political opinions, but it directs mores, and it is in regulating the family that it works to regulate the state."[42]

The citizens of the land increasingly regarded their religious beliefs and practices as only one part of the new democratic order. As a biographer of *New York Tribune* editor Horace Greeley put it in 1855, "Men have been heard to talk of their Bible, their Shakespeare, and their Tribune, as the three necessities of spiritual life." Greeley's competitor, James Gordon Bennett, claimed that he might make the daily press the "greatest organ of social life" since the "temple of religion has had its day."[43] Bennett even claimed that true religion was not the "dogmas of any church" but merely one's own conviction.[44] In response to such lofty rhetoric the Roman Catholic archbishop of Baltimore, James Cardinal Gibbons, assessed in the first decade of the twentieth century the impact of the newspaper on the person of faith: "One Sunday morning, as he is defamed by the conventionalities of society from going to his place of business, he seizes the morning paper and devours its contents . . . its news of stocks and bonds, pleasures and amusements, or crime and scandal, until his whole being is saturated with this unwholesome diet." Then, concluded Gibbons, "like animals gorged with food, he spends the morning in a comatose condition. . . . without once entering the House of his Heavenly Father or invoking His benediction."[45]

News became a secular commodity as well as a secular epistemology. Newspapers, says Schudson, "were spokesmen for egalitarian ideals in politics, economic life, and social life through their organization of sales, their solicitation of advertising, their emphasis on news, their catering to large audiences, their decreasing concern with the editorial."[46] In this scenario there was no reason to treat religion any differently than any other journalistic subject. As the *New York Christian Advocate and Journal* put it in 1858, "Experience has accustomed us to expect from much of the nonreligious press of all grades, when the subject [of religion] is not systematically ignored, either the most apathetic recognition of vital religion, or sneers of the 'fanaticism' of its professors, or a kind of patronizing or half-way apologetical confession of some of its incidentally beneficial results."[47] Even formerly religious media, such as the *New England Magazine*, hired new journalistic experts who borrowed their reform-minded ideologies from earlier Christian writers.[48]

In short, newsmaking became in the nineteenth century a largely secular profession without the constricting Protestant worldview that once gave clergy and the religious press a more influential and coherent role in public life. As a form of public rhetoric, news reporting was ever more secular in its overall outlook on life and the human condition. As such, mainstream news increasingly adopted its own quasi-scientific epistemology, its own quasi-religious perspective on human affairs in the democratic nation. Moreover, public opinion increasingly replaced implicitly biblical understandings and theological convictions as a basis for adjudicating social issues and resolving cultural tensions within society.[49] News reporters hung on to parabolic and sermonic styles of storytelling, while shedding distinctly religious language and perspective.

By the beginning of the twentieth century the modern daily newspaper emerged as the major public medium alongside new national magazines. This modern news did not inherit the deeply theological perspective of the earlier religious press but instead adopted the secular outlooks of news professionals and media entrepreneurs who together established journalism as a socially respectable profession. While newspapers flourished in the first decades of the twentieth century, the religious press began its steady decline, eventually becoming primarily a servant of church institutions and some charismatic leaders rather than a serious contender for a piece of the increasingly naked public square.[50] Among the few exceptions were the kinds of small-circulation religious journals discussed in Chapter 3. Simply put, religion news beat religious news in the cultural race to see which one could democratize its content and present itself most appealingly to mass audiences. The new form of newswriting owed much to its religious ancestors, but not enough to distinguish news any longer as a distinctly religious form of public interpretation. Reporters developed irreligious rhetorical stances loosely derived from Christian tradition (for example, the value of good works, the importance of tolerance, the evils of hypocrisy), but they stopped short of connecting the events of the day directly to divine providence or sectarian theology.[51] Nonreligious media won by refocusing the public square as a nonsectarian arena.

Today the vast majority of religious periodicals are merely specialty organs of various churches and parachurch organizations. They "concentrate upon the minutiae of church management, the problems of fund-raising, the progress of religious education, and the activities of church officials, in very much the same way that magazines financed by philatelists and numismatists, or doctors and lawyers, properly emphasize specialized topics of concern only to their own constituencies."[52] Certainly there is nothing intrinsically wrong with such publications;

they serve an important professional function within the nation's myriad of centrifugally organized church organizations. But few religious periodicals address the public weal seriously and provocatively; they leave that task largely to the secular or "mainstream" media. Only a handful of religious journals even attempt to "identify the universal relevance of that faith" or endeavor "to place contemporary political, social, and economic issues within a religious context."[53]

Mainstream Journalism As Informational Fundamentalism

In 1994 the *Washington Post* published a notice for the position of "religion reporter." The notice included the following description of the kind of person that the paper hoped to recruit: "The ideal candidate is not necessarily religious nor an expert in religion."[54] It is hard to imagine a similar job posting for a political or business reporter. The *Post*'s job listing captured the profession's sense of uninterest in religion as well as its own skepticism about religious people. Why not require a reporter who writes about religion to know something about the topic—even if he or she is not personally religious? Perhaps knowledge is commitment, and commitment might lead to subjectivity and a lack of balance in reporting. In this case ignorance—religious ignorance—is not bliss, but it certainly can seem professional. Like the image of the cold, dispassionate scientist, the *Post*'s description of a reporter suggests that good journalists should not get too close personally to their subject. According to this popular hermeneutic of reporting, news should focus on what Park calls the "transient and ephemeral" qualities of stories.[55]

Marvin Olasky argues nearly the opposite, calling for engaged, perspectival reporting anchored in the reporter's religious worldview. In *Telling the Truth: How to Revitalize Christian Journalism* he suggests that journalists resuscitate the early colonial style of reporting that grounded daily stories in the divine providence expressed through the Christian metanarrative. A Christian journalist's "news and feature stories should have some implicit Christocentric content," he says, in opposition to the "world's definition of *objectivity*." He defines this as directed reporting that combines biblical direction and detailed reporting. Olasky concludes that the goal of such reporting is "perspective that is grounded in a biblical worldview. If there is insufficient biblical rationale for a story theme, out it should go."[56] If most mainstream reporters favor news that is reported without any accompanying personal or institutional perspective, Olasky seeks the reverse—news reports framed by a tribal vision of truth. Olasky's proposal suggests that news needs an overarching perspective, such as Christianity's worldview. His directed reporting seems to support St. Augustine's idea that true knowledge always stems from the fear of God—that faith precedes knowledge.[57]

Modern journalism, however, rejects such religious assumptions in favor of a commonsense objectivity. Although human objectivity is now contested in most academic fields, journalists strongly defend their ability to be detached truth-tellers. Every profession has its ideology, of course, and in the news business the rhetoric of commonsense objectivity is foundational for journalists' professional integrity. Journalists purport to solve the subject-object dichotomy, the problem of bias, by resorting to their own version of literalism. This hermeneutical paradigm is remarkably close to the interpretive method that many religious fundamentalists use to exegete sacred texts. The worldview of American daily news reporting is a form of informational fundamentalism that emphasizes facts, actions, and conflict with little regard for historical context and motive.

First, the rhetoric of informational fundamentalism emphasizes the facts of a story. In political reporting the public opinion polls provide such exactitude, and much campaign coverage follows the daily changes in the polls like equity brokers follow the stock tickers. Sports reporting focuses on game scores, averages, player trades, and the like. "There are two things American reporters know how to cover well: politics and sports," claims *Los Angeles Times* media critic David Shaw. "So we try to reduce everything to that. We talk about who's ahead rather than looking closely at the issues. When it comes to religion, we try to fit stories into the athletic or political paradigm."[58]

Reporters for mainstream and religious periodicals alike often interpret American religion similarly in terms of the rise and fall of particular religious figures and institutions. In some cases reporters actually create the facts: periodicals' and wire services' annual "top-ten-religion-stories" articles try to create an objective list of religion-related stories either by polling writers or by editorial decision. In 1991, for instance, *Christianity Today* selected its own top-ten list based on its small news staff's ranking. The "War in the Gulf" was number one, while the "Dead Sea Scrolls" came in tenth; the latter entry said simply, "After decades of frustration, scholars finally gained full access to the 2,000 year old documents."[59] The statisticalization of religion news mirrors the simplistic analysis that so many reporters rely on to make objective sense of the complex cultural landscape. News becomes a string of largely unconnected bits and pieces of information. The modern newspaper, says Jacques Barzun, has become a "daily encyclopedia, social register, and business directory."[60]

Time magazine's coverage of the Promise Keepers movement in 1995 is an excellent example of the factual penchant within informational fundamentalism. The periodical emphasized the numerical size of the groups' events—a rate of growth that made the group "one of the century's fastest-growing religious phenomena" and that would soon lead 727,000 men to pay $55 each to "listen to soft Christian rock and hard Christian preaching and weep in one another's arms."[61] The article described a Promise Keeper who helped create a 200-member men's ministry in his church and then recruited thirty-two team leaders as foot soldiers who eventually enlisted 2,500 new members. In spite of two pages of facts about the men's movement, the report failed to offer any explanation for the growth, any historical perspective, any theological interpretation, or even any comparisons or contrasts with other contemporary or historical religious movements. For that matter, the article missed the significance of the parachurch phenomenon in America. Columnist John Leo of *U.S. News and World Report* devoted an entire page to the misreporting about Promise Keepers that tended to jump to conclusions about the effects without first understanding the movement.[62]

Second, reporters' informational fundamentalism emphasizes human actions. In the reporter's paradigm the world is essentially a closed system in which people act and react in an endless chain of causes and effects. The role of the journalist is to take a snapshot of the action at a particular point in time to capture those actions "on the record." Among the most important actions is what someone says. "Sources" are the main actors in this world, since they provide the language of action that will drive the news narrative. Expert sources are the most critical because presumably they carry more value and trustworthiness. A religious miracle, for instance, cannot be reported as a miracle unless an expert on miracles verifies that one occurred. So when Dan Wakefield wrote a book about people who have experienced miracles, he became newsworthy as the author of such a book; authors are, by virtue of their status as authors, experts on the topic of their book.[63] In this case reports of miracles in his book were even more newsworthy because they involved some well-known people—Michael Crichton and Ron Darling—who had their own encounters with miracles. Wakefield's miracle was the fact that he stopped drinking one day after years of living within the "mythology of the drinking writer."[64]

One of the problems for many religion writers is how to tell factually the mysterious stories that challenge commonsense rationalism and seemingly depend on the actions of an unidentifiable God who cannot be interviewed and therefore has no standing within a reportorial plot. Professionally speaking, for journalists to report as if God exists is just as much folly as to report as if aliens exist or as if a UFO is a craft from outer space. Such stories are information by outsiders and for outsiders, with very little attention to the history of faith tribes, to the more human side of the new religions, and to nonexpert sentiment and experience.[65] Minority faiths rarely are covered as good news, presumably because these groups' faith and practice do not fall within the normal standards of moral religious convention.[66]

In addition to emphasizing facts and actions, informational fundamentalists perceive conflict as a crucial aspect of their stories. Just as the religious fundamentalist usually divides the world into two camps—the holy and the apostate—and assumes irreconcilable conflicts between the two, the reporter assumes a social world of conflicting self-interests. Political columnist David Broder admits that it is "conflict—not compromise—that makes news. . . . The media bias is verbal slugging over legislative virtuosity."[67] Religion columnist Terry Mattingly suggests that there is one type of religion story that even "anti-religion editors" always love—a scandal.[68] Scandals often highlight divisions and hypocrisy within religious tribes without requiring reporters to understand doctrinal or cultural nuances. Reporters simply have to find the facts and the actions that pinpoint where the religious world is in peril or where religious tribes are in battle. As an everyday epistemology, news focuses on points of tension in society, on tears in the fabric of relationships among actors in a universe of human contention and struggle. News reporters ignore stories that point to the meaning of and coherence in life because these topics suggest stability and longevity rather than conflict and change. Not surprisingly, even within the journalistic profession reporters see religion news as haphazard, insensitive, and inadequate.[69]

Religion news is a particularly strong example of the importance of conflict in reporting. The network television program *Nightline* largely ignored religion in the 1980s until the PTL televangelism scandal broke—a story of sex, hypocrisy, and money, among other things. The nightly broadcast then devoted eleven programs to televangelism scandals and achieved record audiences. As one assessment of *Nightline*'s coverage concluded, the broadcasts had "little to do with the impact of religion on our society, or the role of religion abroad. Instead, it preferred flashy personalities and sexy scandals."[70] Similarly, a study of television and print coverage of the Roman Catholic Church concluded that journalists tend to portray the church as "oppressive and anachronistic" and favor church critics over defenders.[71] This penchant for novelty and conflict might also explain why in 1994 the network television newscasts reported more stories about New Age spirituality than about all Protestant denominations combined.[72] After all, new religions represent a challenge to traditional ones. The problem, some critics suggest, is that religion writers use the same rules and conventions to cover religion that they use for politics, crime, and the like.[73] Martin E. Marty argues that the growing number and intensity of rifts within religious groups in American during the 1990s might explain why there was apparently an increase in religion reporting during the period.[74]

In 1996 Pope John Paul II sent his personal greetings to the Roman Catholic Church's Pontifical Academy of Sciences, a kind of senate that reviews and interprets scientific developments. The press reported his communication as one or another variation on the theme that the pope and presumably the church finally accepted biological evolution. Journalists interpreted the pope's letter in the context of the conflicts within the ongoing evolution-creation debate. In truth, both the pope's missive and the church's historical documents simply refused to accept a simplistic dichotomy between faith and science. The pope's letter actually affirmed scientific activity while cautioning scientists not to presume knowledge beyond the bounds of what science can know for certain. He rejected, as the church always has, any purely materialistic theory of evolution that failed to identify the divine origin of the human soul. Even the evangelical *Christianity Today* chastised the mainstream news media, writing that "when the media portrayed the Pope as adopting evolution, they left the impression that he was surrendering to . . . anti-God explainers. In actuality, the Pope's main message was that faithful Christians engaged in such science must keep God in the picture."[75] As journalists succumb to the temptation to frame facts and action in terms of social and cultural conflict, they lose grasp on the historical continuities and the conserving traditions that maintain religious communities through time. Reporters thereby contribute to the existing cultural instabilities and historical amnesia that afflict many groups in modern society.

Finally, journalistic fundamentalism essentially decontextualizes religion by failing to see the data, actions, and conflicts of the day in a historical perspective that allows for the possibility of complex motives. As James W.

Carey argues in his essay "The Dark Continent of American Journalism," reporters tend to rely on boilerplate explanations of events and on rational interpretations of motives.[76] Journalists often depend on preconceived notions about the world, on simplistic and stereotypical understandings of human affairs that enable them to make quick judgments about complex historical stories. Reporters see human motives not as mysterious, enigmatic, and even contradictory—which motives often are in the everyday world—but instead as straightforward reflections of self-interest. Rather than interpreting human affairs from the rich complexities of those who are living it, reporters force human life into the "literary and even legal convention" of the news business. In Carey's view, one of the biggest sins of journalism is to assume that people are "driven by self-interest" when in fact "all self-interested action is knotted into and contained by other, larger, and often more memorable motives." As a result, concludes Carey, modern journalism wrongly assumes that there are always "hidden" motives awaiting journalistic uncovering. Reporting becomes the "unmasking and revealing of the 'true' motives behind appearances." Journalism leaves little room for any interpretations that focus on the "content of character or nobility of purpose."[77] Informational fundamentalism relies upon simplistic understandings of complex practices, phenomena, and traditions. Too often reporters assume that religious prelates and laity alike merely "use" religion to "cover up" their true motives.

Mainstream news reporting about the Texas State GOP convention in 1994 reflected such boilerplate coverage of both politics and religion. *USA Today* declared "A 'Crisis' for Texas Republicans as Evangelists Gain Virtual Control," and the *Fort Worth Star-Telegram* exclaimed that "Christian Activists Capture GOP Helm." CBS's Bob MacNamara similarly reported, "Today, here and in many states, they're [religious conservatives] not only on the inside; they're in charge."[78] In fact, Texas Republicans had nominated only one abortion-rights supporter for a seat in the U.S. Senate and another one for governor. The reporters used as evidence for a GOP takeover the convention's choice of a GOP chair, Tom Pauken, hardly a stooge for the so-called religious right. Pauken, a Roman Catholic, considered himself a "Reagan conservative." The problem with news coverage of the convention, lamented Pauken, was that some journalists already had their stories written before arriving at the convention. The reporters "expected the convention was going to turn into chaos," said Pauken. "They interviewed me and everything went on the cutting room floor because I didn't say what they wanted me to say, which is that we are trying to impose a theocracy." The real story was that there were few liberals or moderates left in the party even before the convention.[79] Journalists looked for the short-term conflict and missed the longer-term historical trends in the state. They relied upon the boilerplate motive of right-wing self-interest to explain complex sociological and political changes—changes that were certainly worth explaining but which could not reasonably be reduced to overnight clashes between conservatives and liberals at the state convention.

There are even stranger examples of journalists' simplistic explanations for religious motive. In 1995 news media reported on a sociological study designed to determine if members of the religious right make rational choices to support their political views. "Religious Right Shaped by Reason, Study Finds," read one newspaper headline about the study. "Typically, members of the religious right are conservative, deeply religious individuals who have made rational choices to support their political views," began the article.[80] The "news" was that religious conservatives make rational choices. Amitai Etzioni, president of the American Sociological Society, told the Associated Press that he did not believe that anyone "in his right mind would believe that 40 million evangelicals have a perverted personality. They are like the rest of us."[81] Why would journalists consider such a study to be newsworthy, except for the fact that it challenged their own preconceptions about the intelligence of deeply religious people?

Such superficial, ahistorical reporting about motive reflects the shallow perspectives in much religion reporting. In real life many people's faith is oriented at least as much by tradition and historical convention as by present circumstances or conditions. Contemporary news, by contrast, focuses on present events and their short-term impact almost entirely to the exclusion of historical perspective. "A decision to emphasize consequence over causes and motives," writes Carey, "is a decision to emphasize the future over the past. Consequences are predictions of what will happen rather than a recounting of what has happened."[82] Of course the future is always in doubt until it actually occurs, so journalistic preoccupation with future consequences puts them on interpretive ground that is even more unstable than that of the historical interpretation. The result, says Carey, is that "consequence stories throw journalists into the arms of experts, the futurologists of one kind or another who are able to divine the far horizons of human life."[83] News reporting and religious faith are likely always to be antagonists, says C. John Sommerville, because news recognizes only "change, whereas religion tries to concentrate on eternal questions."[84]

As news moved from the pulpit to the mainstream press in America, it translated a formerly theological and moral vision of reporting into a secular viewpoint that mirrored some of the epistemological assumptions of Enlightenment science. Broder believes that "secularism . . . pervades the journalistic culture."[85] Like the scientist, the journalist wants proof that justifies any faith in anything, including God. In this perspective, faith is largely folly compared with the facts of reporting. "Catholicism is largely a joke in newsrooms," laments one Catholic reporter, "so nobody asks me about [the faith]. I just try to not rant and rave when people carry on about the church."[86] When they report on religion, like everything else, American journalists become highly pragmatic fact collectors who gather information about conflicts and personalities. They seek expert rather than common experience and the latest facts rather than wise counsel. As an information-collecting profession, modern journalism is less interested in coherence and integrity than in factuality. If the facts are right, the story is presumably objective. If opposing experts are interviewed, the story supposedly has balance. Journalism's standard epistemology of informational fundamentalism is precisely why mainstream reporters so frequently botch religion stories. One study of *Time* magazine religion news between 1947 and 1976 found a high degree of "journalistic contagion" in which the periodical "might have narrowed its sources of information" by relying on "generic (or class-bound) rules."[87] Mainstream religion reporting falls into a hermeneutic where one fundamentalist tribe (reporters) describes others (religions).

Peter Hennici tells the story about a European bishop who is interviewed by an aggressive reporter upon arriving in New York City. "'When you come to New York, do you go to a night club? [*sic*]' asked the journalist. The bishop responded with mock naïveté, 'Are there night clubs [*sic*] in New York?' The next morning the headline read, 'Bishop's First Question: Are Their [*sic*] Nightclubs in New York?'"[88] This type of fundamentalist objectivity is what James Wall, former editor of *Christian Century*, hyperbolically calls a "hostility to any genuine religious witness."[89] Lacking a coherent framework for religious understanding, journalists usually fail to perceive the wider religious significance within stories as well as any religious perspectives of stories. Reporters' own professional fundamentalism limits their worldview to narrow-minded immanence.

The inability of many national journalists to identify religious significance even in the major events of the day was clear in their poor coverage of the unusual prayer that Bishop William R. Cannon delivered at the inauguration of President Jimmy Carter in January 1977. Departing from the upbeat tone of previous inaugural prayers, Cannon called the nation "from the arrogant futility of trying to play God: as if our wealth were so great that we could satisfy the needs of people everywhere over the world and buy their favor and support; as if our own power were limitless, so that we could manage and direct the affairs of humankind."[90] The prayer was a beckoning to national humility and even repentance, not a celebration of American might and right. The *Washington Post* and *New York Times* correctly reported facts about the prayer but failed to comprehend "the full significance of the changes in rhetorical form and philosophical content contained in the prayer," says Martin J. Medhurst. Moreover, although news media commented on practically everything else, from dress to the price of postceremony concert tickets, the prayer received only scant attention.[91]

Journalists wrongly assumed that the inaugural prayer was little more than a required formality prior to the real business at hand—running the White House. As Medhurst documents, however, the prayer was not mere ritual or empty tradition; Cannon's prayer challenged the rather benign and self-evident truths spoken ritualistically at previous inaugurations. It was among the first important indications that things might not be entirely business as usual in the Oval Office because Carter was not only born again but a man who carried his faith into the public square. Michael J. Sandel says that Carter's vision "departed from the republican tradition and reflected the public philosophy of his day." Carter's call for "honesty and openness" stood for a "larger ambition—to collapse the distance between government and the governed, to approach a kind of transparence, or immediacy, between the presidency and the people." Sandel describes Carter as a leader for "moralism and managerialism."[92] Cannon's prayer might not have tipped off reporters to Carter's leadership style, but it should have given journalists enough pause to wonder if the White House would be the same kind of place for the next four years.

About a decade earlier than Carter in 1976, presidential candidate George McGovern had similar problems with the press's uninterest in religion. "Many in the working press were unable to deal with the moral categories being used by candidate McGovern," writes columnist Michael McIntyre. "Time after time, he lapsed into the language of morality, judgment and justice, only to see reporters close notebooks, glance at each other in embarrassment or grin indulgently, or look at their watches. It was as though all the refugees from countless Sunday schools had suddenly been trapped back in a lesson from Chronicles and were waiting for the bell to ring."[93] If colonial preachers were immersed in their own religious view of the news of everyday occurrences, contemporary journalists are trapped in their self-imposed informational fundamentalism.

On the surface contemporary news media seem to do a creditible job of locating and reporting religion news, but in actuality religion news generally lacks legitimacy in the newsroom.[94] David Shaw says religion coverage represents a "journalistic ghetto filled with listings of the next day's sermon topics, schedules of church-sponsored rummage sales and potluck dinners and press releases from local ministers." Such religion pages are written by the "oldest over-the-hill reporters . . . the staff alcoholic or . . . the youngest, least-experienced reporters."[95] Journalists generally consider religion a second-class beat to be shunned by talented reporters.[96] Perhaps this attitude toward religion news explains why nearly 40 percent of all religion writers and editors are women in a business where very few women achieve senior positions.[97] One study determined that editors and reporters ranked news of religion last out of eighteen categories of news.[98] A national survey of newspapers discovered that only 25 percent of all religion journalists work full time covering religion news; 60 percent reported spending less than half of their time on the religion beat. Moreover, about half of the religion journalists said that they rely heavily on mailings and news releases from churches for their news. Journalism educators and programs, too, have largely ignored religion in their teaching and research.[99]

Of course journalists might be concerned that religion is too personal and controversial for news coverage. Religious persons often do get upset with the way their tribe's faith and customs are portrayed seemingly unfavorably in news accounts. Warren Breed found in the 1950s that journalists often "screened out" potential religious stories because of their "sensitive" nature.[100] Although religion writers and editors for even the nation's most prestigious papers and wire services are among the journalists most interested in stories that document and examine religious ideas and trends that influence society, they still worry about ensuring that such coverage is not perceived by readers as either pro- or antireligion.[101] One way of dealing with sensitive stories is simply to avoid them.

When journalists themselves are religious, however, they are more bold and less hesitant about religion stories. Don Ranly discovered that editors who are involved in local congregations feel much more strongly than other editors that there should not be a religion page. The churchgoing editors suggested that religious events are bona fide news and should compete with other stories for space on the main news pages. In their view, religion should not be ghettoized as ecclesiastical reports and laundry lists of local church events. Most interesting of all, these editors, though representing a minority of all religion editors (about a fifth), felt most strongly that "church and synagogue people are generally the most difficult of all to deal with" in religious reporting. Unlike their more secular colleagues, these churchgoers sought vigorously to legitimize religion as a respectable part of public life. They were highly dissatisfied with their jobs and very critical of religion writing and writers—much more so than skeptical religion editors.[102]

The underlying cause of this friction between religion reporting and religion is the incompatibility of informational fundamentalism with religious faith and practice. American TV news anchor Peter Jennings touched on this problem one day during a newsroom discussion of a plane crash. "One survivor," Jennings recalls, "was comforted by a reporter who asked, 'How did you manage to get through this alive?' 'God got me through,' answered the passenger. 'Yes but what really happened?,' countered the reporter." Reflecting on that kind of exchange between a religious source and a professional journalist, Jennings concluded, "There is a fundamental difference in the way we as secular journalists see the truth and the definition of truth accepted by many people of religious faith. People of faith believe that what they believe is true. We secular journalists are trained to believe that it is our obligation to put what we encounter to a rational test that we can comprehend." Perhaps, he wrote, the doubting St. Thomas "could well be journalism's patron saint."[103]

Journalists' informational fundamentalism naively assumes that neutrality is possible, including neutrality regarding matters of religious custom and faith. Reporters too uncritically believe their own professional rhetoric. They seek to avoid news bias by gathering facts and relaying them telegraphically to audiences. In this sense, journalism is the "quintessentially Enlightenment profession."[104] The reporter says, "Prove it. Show me. Give me the evidence. Where are the documents? Do you have two sources on the virgin birth?" The news media are "a cousin of the modern social sciences that implicitly use positivist assumptions that are "inhospitable to the 'supernatural' preoccupation of Christianity."[105]As Wall puts it, media coverage of religion is "biased in favor of Enlightenment rationality. Our culture's embrace of scientific rationality as the ultimate measure of all reality has pushed religious faith over into a corner of irrelevancy. Even religion's most informed advocates are reluctant to speak of their faith in public for fear of rejection by their intellectual peers."[106] Journalists' secular-rational "faith" establishes a bias against religion within the profession.

Although reporters would hardly recognize it, they owe their epistemological method to nineteenth-century Enlightenment thought that also shaped American religious fundamentalism. The Scots tried to liberate theology from "the taints of radicalism or skepticism." As Mark A. Noll maintains, this Scottish philosophy held that nature can be known empirically; that detached, natural, scientific inquiry "was the ultimate arbiter of genuine knowledge"; and that by "pursuing a more disciplined inquiry into the experiences opened by the senses, humanity could progress to new heights of glory." The Scots essentially grafted this scientific philosophy into their theology, arguing that such convictions could serve Christianity without altering the faith's basic beliefs. They created a didactic form of Enlightenment thought that linked Christianity with scientific as well as moral and spiritual progress. Many American Protestants had used this philosophy in the revolutionary period both to justify the break with Great Britain and to "establish principles of social order for a new nation that was repudiating autocratic government, hierarchical political assumptions, and automatic deference to tradition." Moreover, such thought had the necessary advantage of maintaining Christianity, especially Protestantism, as the sovereign rule of life in a society that officially denied such authority to any particular religion.[107]

Like many journalists today, the Scots convinced themselves that they had no system of interpretation. They dubbed their philosophy a "commonsense" approach to the interpretation of Scripture. The Scots refused to accept the possibility that their philosophy implicitly accepted particular understandings of history, deference, and tradition.[108] They accepted their quasi-scientific method as a neutral, fact-based common sense, just as reporters eventually claimed to be able to interpret everyday events through a method of empirically based, commonsense reasoning about the "facts" of a story. One Disciples of Christ leader expressed this method in the context of interpreting the Scriptures, "I have endeavored to read the Scriptures as though no one had read them before me."[109] As Noll documents, Scottish Enlightenment thought swept through American Protestantism in the decades before the Civil War, enabling evangelicalism, in particular, to flourish in the United States. Protestants, he concludes, "mastered not just the media of communications but also the dominant interpretive system of the day."[110] Many evangelicals both accepted this commonsense approach to interpreting Scripture and used it to bolster publicly the position of the church's rhetoric of discernment in the growing industrial nation.

The form of theistic Enlightenment thought developed by the Scots spread rapidly from the revolutionary era to the Civil War, shaping American culture in ways that we are yet discovering.[111] As Norman Fiering suggests, the Scottish Enlightenment offered a "moral philosophy" that "was uniquely suited to the needs of an era still strongly committed to traditional religious values and yet searching for alternative modes of justification for those values."[112] The philosophy collapsed moral theology into an everyday understanding of objective interpretation and practical learning. Protestants could retain their romance with the future while embracing the scientism of the Enlightenment; they were able to defuse the threats of modernity by embracing a commonsense variety of modern thought, a mode of everyday reasoning that seemed at the time to be as obvious and irrefutable as science.[113]

Journalists in the early twentieth century forged their own version of this gospel of everyday scientific reasoning. As odd as it seems today, American journalists are methodological and theoretical heirs of the very kind of religious epistemology that so many reporters find antiquarian if not superstitious—fundamentalism. The difference, of course, is that religious fundamentalists face the daunting task of interpreting the world through their Enlightenment understanding of scripture, whereas journalists carry no such weight of a reigning metanarrative. Instead journalists have the luxury of approaching each story without the weight of other stories, except perhaps a quick read of the competing news agencies and a brief look at earlier stories on the same topic. Journalists' antiphilosophical and antimetaphysical biases are increasingly and painfully obvious to some young practitioners who learn about postmodernism in liberal arts courses while studying "objective" reporting in their journalism classes. Informational fundamentalism leads to what Aleksandr I. Solzhenitsyn calls "generally accepted patterns of judgment and maybe common corporate interests, the sum effect being not competition but unification."[114]

The best reporters simply reject such a telegraphic approach to reporting; they use history, philosophy, theology—indeed all fields of study— to help them make imaginative sense of the world. They implicitly break from informational fundamentalism into the wider epistemological horizons of the humanities. But this is not easy for them to do because journalists maintain their fundamentalist theories and methods of reporting by shrouding them in a progressive view of the history of their craft. Journalists use their "Whig" interpretation of the history of reporting to marry the doctrine of progress with the flow of journalistic history. Carey describes this triumphalistic version of journalism history as a tale about "the slow, steady expansion of freedom and knowledge from the political press to the commercial press, the setback into sensationalism and yellow journalism, and the forward thrust into muckraking and social responsibility."[115] This kind of self-serving interpretation of journalism history serves a quasi-religious function within the profession by giving journalists a professional metanarrative in which they can believe and a professional story that harmoniously blends progress, freedom, and objectivity—three of the major myths of the profession as well as of modernity. Not surprisingly, journalists who take this fundamentalist position believe that the way to "de-marginalize" religion in reporting is to seek greater journalistic "professionalism."[116] Of course there is always some truth to such professional mythmaking, but there is also much self-exhortation and self-aggrandizement as well as immense historical oversimplification.

Journalists' informational fundamentalism helps to explain why the *Washington Post* would advertise for a religion writer who might know little or nothing about religious practices, history, and institutions. Strictly speaking, wrote Park, news is "not a story or an anecdote" but rather is for the "person who hears or reads it an interest that is pragmatic rather than appreciative."[117] Park might have said the same thing about the value of news to the media companies that create and distribute news reports. For them, news is as much a way of attracting audiences and selling them to advertisers as it is a mode of cultural interpretation.[118] Facts alone do not make for an interesting or readable story about religion or anything else. The facts even change from one day to the next. The result, says Solzhenitsyn, is "many hasty, immature, superficial, and misleading judgments" that confuse readers and leave them with stereotypes and simplifications.[119] Informational fundamentalism leads to newsrooms where reporters are hopping from one press release to another and filling news holes under tight deadlines, with little sense of obligation to coherence, meaning, transcendent truth, and even the common good. Thomas C. Ogletree even argues that objective reporting cannot produce moral "readings" of human events; such journalism is ethically unimaginative.[120]

The Power of News As
Unimaginative Social Liturgy

Washington Journalism Review editor Ruth Ravenel tells the story of Dick Dabney's attempt in 1980 to write a piece for *Harper's* magazine about Rev. M. G. "Pat" Robertson's *700 Club* religious television program. Dabney had not only watched Robertson's program; he also contributed financially to the program. But along the way Dabney had become increasingly "grossed out by the way that [Robertson] was raising money." Robertson's financial appeals seemed to Dabney to promote a kind of quasi-religious gambling—the more money that viewers sent to the program, said Robertson, "the more cash [God] will give right back to you." According to Dabney, the *700 Club* tried to block publication of his *Harper's* article by offering to pay Dabney more than he would receive from the magazine for the piece. Robertson's attorneys even threatened Dabney ("We'll keep you in court 'til we destroy you!") and questioned his religious faith.[121] Clearly Robertson wanted Dabney's story killed—one way or the other.

Dabney had a great tale to tell, but what was the purpose of publishing it, beyond informing readers about Robertson's questionable fund-raising tactics? As Ravenel says, Dabney's *Harper's* articles and many others published in the late 1970s and early 1980s focused on evangelicalism as if it were a cohesive social movement, a unified play for theocratic power in America. Robertson's pressure to kill Dabney's story fit the stereotype. Ravenel suggests that the real religious story during this period was not the isolated grab for power or even the hints of theocracy but the growing diversity and complexity within evangelicalism. Reporters focused on politics and money—two seemingly crucial themes within evangelicalism. But evangelicals were infighting, not unifying under a common political banner. Some of them were even uniting with Roman Catholics and mainline Protestants on particular social and political issues. In addition, most evangelicals cared more about salvation and family problems than about politics. As one former reporter and member of televangelist Rex Humbard's ministry put it, when "you talk [to reporters] about saving souls or putting homes back together, that doesn't really click." The failure to understand American evangelicals, concludes Ravenel, "may be the press' biggest failure in covering the evangelical movement."[122]

Journalists' reportorial storytelling mediates various social groups' understanding of each other in society. As reporters broker symbols on behalf of their news organizations, they also wield rhetorical power in the public sphere. By letting some voices into the news while turning away others, and by casting some interpretations rather than alternatives, reporters regulate citizens' access to and understanding of the wider society. In the case of evangelicalism, journalists during the twentieth century often focused on the obvious evangelical institutions and popular movements rather than on the grassroots faith and practices within evangelicalism. Journalists relied on the voices of the religious groups' self-appointed leaders and on the perspectives of scholars who, like reporters, usually study evangelicalism from outside the faith. Reporters as public mediators thereby legitimize some versions of religious reality while debunking others. They regulate some of the keys to the public imagination through their own rituals of reporting.

Time essayist Roger Rosenblatt captures journalists' mediation of life in a column titled "Dreaming the News." What would happen, he wonders, if he read the daily newspaper like he reads fiction, as if the news story were "an outline or sketch of a deeper (more crafted and layered) story that was being withheld from the reader and at the same time invited the reader's imagination to fill in the blanks." So he began to charm his way into his reading of the news, imagining elaborate and illuminating background to the everyday events that were reported telegraphically in the morning paper. He "bored into language," "invented" and "expected revelation." He read the news not as "the first draft of history but as the first draft of a work of art." As Rosenblatt slid from fact to fiction, fiction to fact, history to art, and back again to history, he recognized that fiction and the news are more alike than different, joined in an endless chain of narratives. "Everything is news, everything imagined," he concluded.[123] Both journalistic and literary stories can help readers to understand each other as different parts of a shared humanity. History, journalism, and all forms of narrative are "thought experiments" that imaginatively interpret human action and its consequences.[124] No matter how truncated or telegraphic a news report is, it is still a work of human imagination that inherently claims to make sense of a particular state of affairs.

Journalistic storytelling, in particular, is a priestly ritual that can coalesce people around common understandings. Reporters can decide for the public, for instance, which new religious movements are legitimate and which ones are cults—both by what reporters say and how they say it.[125] By interpreting religion through the same reportorial frame of reference that they use for all other telegraphic reporting, journalists unimaginatively reduce most religion coverage to tales about institutional bureaucracy, tribal disputes, and spiritual celebrities. Religion news has come to rely upon the same logic applied to reports about crime and political campaigns. In the worse cases journalists now cast religion news "three notches below flower shows on the priority list for news" reporting, transforming American religious life into an "unending series of stories about picnics, rummage sales, revivals and cryptic ceremonies."[126] In the best cases news gets the facts correct about a religious conflict or movement.

Modern news emphasizes immediate events and immanent facts, not eternal verities or even social or cultural meaning. It embraces the particularity of events and shies away from the universality of meaning. Instead of providing insight or coherence, news becomes isolated reports that have "obtruded" themselves from the surrounding social conditions.[127] Regardless of the rhetoric of the journalistic profession, news is not fundamentally concerned with the "truth"—with right and proper beliefs and standards of conduct, with underlying historical verities, even with the most meaningful or compelling interpretations of daily events and worldwide incidents. Wrote Walter Lippmann, "News and truth are not the same thing, and must be clearly distinguished. The function of news is to signalize an event, the function of truth is to bring to light the hidden facts, to set them into relation with each other, and make a picture of reality on which men can act."[128] Lippmann might have overstated the value of "hidden facts" and undervalued nuance and perspective, but his call for truth rather than mere fact properly broadens the conversation about the necessary role of reporting in society.

One of the long-standing functions of the public square in democratic nations, aside from celebration and simple social intercourse, is to provide a place for truth-seeking and consensus-building discourse aimed at exploring the common good. Over the centuries humans have met in town halls and churches, taverns and inns to discuss the issues of the day in the context of their experiences. Today, however, few Americans enter the public arena except in the limited contexts of work and material consumption, especially at the shopping mall. Boorstin speaks of the United States as a collection of "consumption communities" held together by the goods they purchase and display more than by ideology or religious belief.[129] The formerly geographic public square has shifted to the media, where citizens and organizations face off through the mediation of journalists who largely direct how society tells news stories to itself. Today journalists regulate the various interpretations of the drama of public life, just as preachers did so in the early years of the Republic. As the geographic public square has evaporated, the media have assumed the role of creating largely journalistic fabrications of it. Carey lucidly argues this in the case of newspapers:

> It is in this vein that the newspaper takes itself to be representing the public, or more fashionably these days, the people. This is a noble role but . . . it possesses a fatal weakness: the community to be represented has become remarkably dissolved, is in eclipse. The evidence of this eclipse is that the newspaper has little contact of any direct kind, physical or verbal, with this community. In effect, the entire system of communication has become one of address: that is, the people are spoken to, are informed, are often propagandized but in no sense are their own perceptions, understandings, judgments fed back into the process. Certainly the letters-to-the-editor column does represent some kind of community return to the source of information, but this column, often the best column in the newspaper, is radically underutilized and constitutes a thin trickle of return to an outpouring of information.[130]

As a result, much of public life is now in the hands of priestly media professionals who naturally attend to their own interests and devise their own professional rhetoric as much as they serve the phantom public.

By trying to remove journalists' personal, presumably subjective convictions from the interpretive process, modern reporting systematically narrows the scope of public life. As our primary square for addressing the issues, concerns, and interests of the public, the media have created a marvelous means of delivering audiences to advertisers and providing citizens with particular kinds of human-interest material and telegraphic reports about people and conflicts. Meanwhile, the rest of what is significant in public life, indeed the most important issues that the public faces—from boredom and euthanasia to human rights, and from social justice to joy and curiosity—evaporate from the news record and hence from the public imagination. When these broader, deeply subjective topics do manage to capture the interest of journalists, it is usually because people with interests at stake have brought them to reporters' attention. Religion, too, becomes just another collection of interest groups clamoring for media attention and represented through "official" spokespersons. The mystery of faith and the possibility of shared moral discourse seem ever more implausible to citizens; all of life is reduced to the politics of rights and interests.

Certainly limiting expressions of the religious imagination in the news media can enhance public life in a democratic nation. To the extent that religious beliefs promote intolerance or self-interest, they can indeed squelch public conversation and further polarize social groups. In theory, limiting the expression of sectarian voices in the media ensures that all extant views of truth are open for discussion. No particular religious tribe or institution, such as a state church, should be able to dominate media discourse. Theocratic religious expressions, for instance, are typically antidemocratic and inherently denigrate other tribal cultures as well as nonreligious ones. For democracy to work, religion must be more or less just another voice in the cacophony of voices and the myriad of subcultures. Stewart M. Hoover argues, for instance, for a kind of news reporting that "does not advocate for any single position" and "attempts to make clear to an idealized general audience the essence of religious issues, trends, and conflicts in a general language that is accessible to them."[131] Journalistic discourse can inform the public about religion without advocating for any particular religious positions. Perhaps news reports can even reveal cross-tribal truths that seem to undergird the religious facts or events of the day.

On the other hand, fully separating religion journalism from religious journalism wrongly asserts that people—newsmakers, reporters, and news "consumers" alike—can or should separate their public and private lives. This type of subject-object distinction mistakenly assumes that a journalist can be religious in private without appealing to the resulting religious sensibilities when he or she is in the newsroom or interviewing someone in person. Religiously informed news, in this view, is both too biased and too sectarian for public expression. To put it in Park's language, journalists should be free only to express "knowledge about" but not "acquaintance with" religious faith and practice—unless the journalist is merely reporting someone else's acquaintance with religious faith.[132] Here again the separation of public and private worlds seems to rest on Enlightenment assumptions about truth and objectivity. By removing personal religious expression from the work of reporting, the journalist is presumably better able to find and disseminate truth. By practicing informational fundamentalism, the reporter is, in theory, also nonsectarian. Of course this kind of journalistic bifurcation is simply inadequate for developing a form of reporting that is hermeneutically robust enough to make sense of religious yearnings, customs, and traditions.

The problem with this type of Enlightenment rhetoric is that it is biased against religion and all other ways of knowing that are not modernist. *America* magazine observes, for instance, that journalists sometimes unconsciously hold to a liberal orthodoxy that actually disrespects reason and freedom.[133] Journalists can turn on and off their fundamentalistic grids of interpretation as needed to support their own preexisting biases. Even journalists' views of the so-called religion beat manifest such underlying biases. Reporter Julia Duin calls religion the "Rodney Dangerfield of beats," a wry comment upon the professions' own assumptions about the importance of subjective religion in news.[134] Enlightenment-driven professionalism in journalism is hardly objective when it addresses ideas and practices that are outside of the quasi-scientific paradigm, including religious beliefs and traditions. In its own way journalistic fundamentalism is a deeply biased hermeneutic that closes the public square to nonsecular-rational ways of knowing and experiencing.

One way of trying to solve this dilemma is to accept the artificial dichotomy between objective and subjective reporting and then embrace both forms of imaginative storytelling in the public arena. Perhaps the public square needs both religious news and religion news—both the facts about religion and expressions of religion. Maybe journalists have an obligation to contribute to local and national religious discourse by listening both to the supposedly disinterested experts and to the religious people and institutions. "Religion's protean place in American culture deserves to be open to public view," says Marty, not shrouded in the telegraphic language of the modern news report.[135] For example, when actress Shirley MacLaine addressed the American Society of Newspaper Editors convention in 1993 on the topic of religion, attendees should have listened carefully to her message even if her belief in reincarnation seemed to many journalists to be irrational or subjective. In fact, parts of her speech were insightful critiques of media coverage of religion. "We are seeing, hearing and learning of these religious conflicts," said MacLaine, "through exploitative headlines, glib sound bites and tabloid-style journalism which predictably sensationalize the craziness, but rarely undertake investigation of themes which resonate with *man's* deeper nature."[136] There was plenty to think about in her speech, partly because of her own spiritual quest, partly because of what her quest reflects about American spirituality, and partly because we all ought to ponder the media's own role in publicly mediating our understanding of America's religious tribes.

The most damaging and perhaps damning aspect of journalists' informational fundamentalism is the way that it elevates reportorial storytelling over people's own everyday understandings of life. Journalistic "professionalism" leads reporters to see their role in society as informing the relatively ignorant public that merely consumes the news. Reporters become both priests and prophets, heralders of the "official" truth and prognosticators of what is likely to happen in the near future. In the newspaper business, writes Park, the serious editorial writer "is likely to conceive of himself as a minor prophet, or at any rate as a leader and inspirer of public opinion." Priestly journalists believe that it is "their business to get and print the news, and make the public read it. Most newspaper men have a poor opinion of the public." As one journalist puts it, the public is "like a baby in the bath. You have to drum on the bathtub to keep it amused while you labor to improve its condition."[137] With such an elitist view of themselves, journalists can scarcely do more than imaginatively entertain the mindless public that they disdain in the course of doing their priestly work. The rhetorical voice of the priest is in some sense "extra-human" and "always originating within a certain elite substratum of society and represents a religion that the audience can only superficially hope to approach."[138] The quasi-scientific approach to reporting reduces the scope of a journalist's imaginative storytelling, trading the fundamentals of good interpretation for the fundamentalism of lifeless fact-finding, market-driven sensationalism, and recurring cynicism about everything, including faith.

Christian News in the Public Square

In 1995 *New York Times* media critic Walter Goodman reviewed Bill Moyers's short news commentaries that were being aired on NBC *Nightly News*. "Mr. Moyers," wrote Goodman, "who claims a certain cachet and attracts a loyal congregation, can make his point and get away fast before God can respond and unimpressed viewers have a chance to click over to ABC." Staying with his religious metaphor, Goodman said that Moyers's "mini-sermons are amiably delivered" and described one commentary as a "homily or community briefing on affirmative action." Goodman concluded his review, "Mr. Moyers, representing the unrepentant middle-left, will not let the opportunity dissolve into sanctimony."[139]

Goodman's tongue-in-cheek critique of Moyers's commentaries highlights the media's own holier-than-thou attitude, which grants journalists of all political stripes the public space to trivialize and sometimes even satirize religion. To the extent that religion and journalism compete in America, reporters are likely to protect their own social standing by expressing implicitly or explicitly their distrust of religious leaders and institutions. In the United States, one of the most religious of the industrialized nations, religion is an awkward part of public life. Religion seems too intolerant, divisive, and parochial to be in public space; its truth claims appear so deeply absolutistic and inflexible. The First Amendment nevertheless guarantees religion a place in public life precisely because, of all public claims, religion's are sometimes the most divisive. So the news media more or less reflect society's ill-at-ease attitude about public religion. Journalists even take over words such as "fundamentalist" and "born again," reframing them in secular terms. Columnist Jane Bryant Quinn refers in 1993 to Americans' "born-again belief in stocks."[140] *Premiere* magazine's cover trumpets the "Born Again" career of actor Christian Slater.[141] A reporter in *Newsweek* writes of politician Pat Buchanan's "born-again isolationism."[142] Goodman's review of Moyers's commentaries reduces the language and rituals of faith to pithy plays on pietistic words.

The decline of public life and the related rise of journalistic professionalism have accelerated the eclipse of religion from public discourse and the trivialization of religion in journalism. Over 150 years ago Tocqueville described the United States as the most Christian nation in the world: America is "the place in the world where the Christian religion has most preserved genuine powers over souls; and nothing shows better how useful and natural to man it is in our day, since the country in which it exercises the greatest empire is at the same time the most enlightened and most free."[143] Today, however, the media largely ignore the ways that any religions—let alone Christianity—address the most perplexing questions about life, the human condition, and human nature. As Rev. Thomas McSweeney writes, religion is "in danger of being driven out of the public debate because it is not being treated as seriously as it should be."[144] Journalists instead display an infatuation with religious scandals, a trendy reporting about a globetrotting pope, and a penchant for listening to people who make extreme claims about religion. Richard Harwood rightly wondered in 1990 if the news media were missing one of the greatest religious stories of all, namely, the many Moslems who were settling on American soil partly to secure religious freedom. "There are obvious stories in these people," writes Harwood. "Who are they? Where have they come from and why? What are their emotions—and their politics—as the world's leading Christian nation poises for war with Iraq."[145] When the World Trade Center and the Pentagon were terrorized in 2001, it became painfully clear that in the previous ten years American citizens had learned little about their Islamic neighbors. Stereotyping and misunderstanding were rife. Many Americans had to remind themselves repeatedly that Islam is a diverse faith rather than a tribe of vengeful Arabs.

Moreover, the public square is still being secularized in America, not in the narrow sense of a lack of public information about denominations and other church organizations, but in the broader sense of a growing uninterest in the major questions and issues that religion has addressed throughout history. Wall calls this a "language gap" between religion and journalism, a gap between two modes of understanding that are like different languages.[146] The more universal and broadly human concerns of religion—from the nature of the good life to righteous living and social justice—are simply too far removed from the daily agenda of the news. Religion has much to offer the public and the media in America—if only journalists will listen, observe, examine, and report intelligently. Even some of the most contentious squabbles over public policies are at root theological debates about moral responsibilities, the value of human life, and the capacity of human beings to control the future and guarantee progress. "Knowledge carries with it certain theological imperatives," writes Jonathan Kozol in response to various media reports of the horrible evil that some Americans have inflicted upon others. "The more we know, the harder it becomes to grant ourselves redemption."[147] Public expressions of faith and its implications are always potentially divisive. But at the same time religious faith and serious religious reporting can enliven the public square with greater moral insight and less pragmatic exigency. Journalism in America does not need more objectivity and greater professionalism as much as it needs a much broader and more culturally sensitive hermeneutic that is open to religious thought, practice, and tradition as modes of public imagining and understanding that can complement democracy.

According to the modern and perhaps the postmodern worldview, religion threatens public life with its dogmatic, intolerant, and sectarian ideas. In this scenario religious faiths can weaken public life by stopping conversation with talk of absolutes and undemocratic ideas. This is partly why an influential philosopher such as Richard Rorty would suggest that "we shall not be able to keep a democratic political community going unless the religious believers remain willing to trade privatization for a guarantee of religious liberty."[148] According to this concern about religion's hegemonic tendencies, news should not concern itself seriously with faith, except as stories about the misguided attempts by religionists to shape public policy, create theocracies, or legislate morality in tune with their own assumptions. In the absence of such concerns reporters should normally be silent about religion, just as citizens should hold their religious convictions in private and frame their public discourse in nonreligious terms.[149]

Religious faith can become a dynamic source of negative cultural and social transformation that brings injustice and other evil to greater might in the world. When faith lacks humility, it becomes ripe for some of the worst imaginable exploitation. Fanaticism can take religionists over the edge of civility into rhetorical manipulation, cultic control, and horrendous oppression. Fundamentalist theocracies continue to emerge around the globe, destroying hobbled democracies and often pitting one ethnic group against another. Human history reminds us of all manner of religious crusades that tried to settle religious and political differences once and for all with weapons of murder and destruction.

Certainly faith in God, whenever it is deeply rooted in the human heart, is potentially explosive for society and culture. In its strongest forms faith springs from deep and even eternal commitments, not merely from transitory feelings and sentiments. Faith cannot be explained away as the product of social forces or psychological variables. In a very real sense religion is still a significant challenge to all worldly institutions, from government to the press. Theologian Dietrich Bonhoeffer and other Lutherans organized an underground seminary as the Third Reich gained control of the German nation and much of the state church, and Bonhoeffer eventually was executed for his group's attempt to assassinate *the Führer*. Bonhoeffer could have stayed safely in America during the travails of his native land, but as he wrote, "I will have no right to participate in the reconstruction of Christian life in Germany after the war if I do not share the trial of this time with my people."[150] Similarly, the civil rights movement in the United States was religious as well as political.[151] Reports in the 1980s eventually confirmed that in the former Soviet Union and the Eastern Bloc countries religious faith helped galvanize the antitotalitarian sentiment that eventually brought down the Iron Curtain. Yet today in China pockets of Christian faith still challenge, however weakly and silently, the Communist leadership. In the 1980s strong grassroots religious movements confronted the centers of authoritarian control in Poland and Tibet. Religious faith continues to play a very significant role in the political and economic struggles in Central America; indeed there is considerable evidence that Protestantization is transforming countries such as Guatemala into vibrant market economies.[152] Garry Wills says that religion "has been at the center of major political crises, which are always moral crises."[153] "You can scarcely point to a progressive change in America . . . where there weren't religion voices openly in the leadership and happily accepted by people," claims Yale law professor Stephen Carter.[154]

Journalism errs when it assumes that religious faith necessarily closes the gate to the public square. Religious faith and customs survive in the modern world precisely because they frequently resonate with some of the deepest yearning of the human heart for intimacy, community, and virtue.[155] Living in a purely secular world is like "living in an astrodome with a roof over the top," says Roy Larson. "The temperature is always 70 degrees and the grass is always green. Even in a place that holds 70,000 people, you feel claustrophobic. You need to breathe some fresh air."[156] Journalists have a legitimate responsibility to investigate and to expose religious intolerance and extremism, but they also have an obligation to address the goodness that faith instills in many persons and institutions. "Part of journalism's function is to examine the political conflict and gamesmanship," says James Fallows, former editor of *U.S. News and World Report.* But he rightly adds, "The other part is to say what it means."[157] Religion has the potential to cause evil, but so does any other system of belief, political ideology, or professional dogma. Like all of the other aspects of what it means to be human, the religious journey is a two-edged sword. A blanket silencing of religion in public life is neither prudent nor good because, as philosopher Nicholas Wolterstorff argues, political discourse in the liberal democratic tradition is best governed by a "respect for certain peculiarities of one's fellow citizens."[158]

The principal effect of opening the public square to religion is not an unleashing of religious intolerance and fanaticism, but rather more public discourse to the wide-ranging concerns of religion throughout the ages, particularly truth, freedom, justice, and love. As Solzhenitsyn has told Western audiences repeatedly through his speeches and novels, faith can help a people maintain a moral vision rather than a purely ideological or instrumental one.[159] At its best, religion can keep us alert to the transcendent and universal aspects of polity, power, and meaning. Without a vibrant democracy open to the obligations of stewardship and humility before the Creator, we are more likely to become mere pragmatists or ideologues. By contemplating eternal rather than merely immediate concerns, we can better gain senses of proportion and patience in the public sphere. "Hastiness and superficiality," says Solzhenitsyn, "are the psychic diseases of the twentieth century and more than anywhere else manifested in the press." The media have "become the greatest power within the Western communities excluding that of the legislature, the executive and the judiciary."[160] Religious faith is often the best antidote to excessively pragmatic politics and unchecked power-mongering precisely because it concedes the existence of transcendent truths, humbles itself to a deity, and challenges the goodness of selfish motives. Czech Republic president Václav Havel says, "The relativization of all moral norms, the crisis of authority, the reduction of life to the pursuit of immediate material gain without regard for its general consequences—the very things Western democracy is most criticized for—originate not in democracy but in that which modern man lost: his transcendental anchor, and along with it the only genuine source of his responsibility and self-respect."[161]

Just as religious faith and accompanying customs can humble us, they can help us to discern important decisions. Neuhaus argues that without a "transcendent or religious point of reference, conflicts of values cannot be resolved; there can only be procedures for their temporary accommodation."[162] One of the major responsibilities of the news media should be to keep alive public discourse about the commitments and obligations that should inform our public policy and should influence our public actions. Instead of advancing secularism through selfish claims to their own professionalism, journalists should open their reporting to the broadest possible discussion and conversation about matters of public interest. Some religious periodicals with rather small circulations already do relate the issues of the day to enduring values and transcendent beliefs.[163] Indeed journalists ought to read those journals as much as they read other newspapers. In other words, reporters need to listen less to journalists and more to nonjournalists. Criticizing the rhetorical antics of the host and guests of CNN's lively but superficial talk show *The McLaughlin Group*, columnist Charley Reese suggests that McLaughlin ought to give the show's guests "absolution after each show. Some of [McLaughlin's] panel members are quick to parrot the propaganda."[164] What Reese sees as a problem with one talk show is actually a problem endemic to the news media, namely, a stubborn, priestly arrogance that panders to audiences while berating the opposition with rhetorical cleverness. Television talk-show journalists are particularly good at articulating ritualistic appeals to the public's right to know and journalistic objectivity, while providing little or no insight of enduring value. Television news reporting is becoming a form of show business, like sports broadcasts.[165]

In a pluralistic republic such as the United States no religious group has the right to conform the nation theocratically to its own beliefs. Nevertheless, the Constitution opens the public square to religion, guaranteeing the freedom of religion not just as a matter of personal practice but also as a mode of public expression. As Carey argues the case, religious freedom was perhaps "the most difficult liberty for Americans to adjust to. Compared with other forms of speech, religious heresy was the one most likely to be viewed as both a personal and a community assault."[166] The press could too easily use religion to demonize particular groups for political purposes, just as the press of North Carolina and Virginia depicted spiritualism in the decade preceding the Civil War as an example of the irrationality in Northern reform and in "fermenting" reform movements.[167] According to the First Amendment, Carey continues, "[n]o one could be excluded from the public realm on the basis of religion, the one basis upon which people were likely to exclude one another."[168] The Constitution imagined a nation that was made up of people who would agree that the use of power in democratic institutions must be leavened by a combination of religious values and public reason. The only alternatives are government by ideology and by pragmatism.

Ideology often leads to government control of public discourse because a purely ideologically driven government becomes a de facto religion. True freedom of speech threatens established power and authority. This is precisely why so many totalitarian nations attempt either to eliminate religious belief or, more likely, to co-opt it for the purposes of the state. There is usually more open public discourse in nations with strong religious traditions than there is in those with highly ideological governments. Religion often permits and frequently encourages various kinds of ideology, while ideology without religion tends to advance its own philosophical assumptions as the only legitimate ones. "Like conventional religion," contends Alvin W. Gouldner, "ideology too seeks to shape men's behavior." Whereas religion is concerned with the "round of daily existence," ideologies "assemble scarce *energies* for focused concentrated discharge in the public sphere. . . . Ideology seeks earthly reaction, reform, or revolution, not transcendental reconciliation. Religions . . . see men as limited, created, or other-grounded beings and foster a sense of men's limitedness; ideologies focus on men as sources of authority and as sites of energy and power."[169] Havel concludes that ideology is a "specious way of relating to the world" because it "offers human beings the illusion of an identity, of dignity, and of morality while making it easier for them to part with them."[170]

In this respect religious fundamentalism, at least in its most dogmatic forms, is sometimes more like ideology than authentic religion, which recognizes doubt and embraces humility before God. Protestant fundamentalism in the United States, for example, frequently is premised on a particular attitude about culture—namely, the reactionary rejection of modern culture—than it is on the historical tenets and beliefs of the Christian faith.[171] Similarly, the views of some fundamentalists about the proper American policy in the Middle East appears to be governed more by ideology than religion; they interpret Middle East Bible prophecy in the context of ideological assumptions about the historical role of the United States, as a special nation under God, in the affairs of the world.[172] If fundamentalists hope to contribute to democratic life, they, too, must adopt "democratic predispositions," such as a desire to work with people of no or little faith toward common ends, and be open to compromises in the interest of the greater good.[173] Apart from some forms of religious fundamentalism, Christianity in America largely challenges dogmatic ideologies and promotes democratic and republican ideals, as Tocqueville discovered back in the 1830s. Journalists are obligated as public fiduciaries to take religion seriously as part of the discourse that makes democracy possible, not to promote one or another religion any more than government does.

The media-saturated United States probably faces the problem of political pragmatism more than the problem of ideology. The lack of vibrant public discourse has led to highly pragmatic forms of political action that focus on manufacturing votes and persuasively promoting candidates' images. Political principles, if they exist at all, typically are grounded in politicians' and parties' self-interest more than in ideology. The news media nurture this pragmatic self-interestedness in society by their overreliance on expert opinions and the "spin doctors" who chant words right off the pages of carefully crafted press releases and standardized "talking points." The news becomes primarily the stories of battling interest groups who "leak" information to reporters instead of addressing it openly and honestly. After the experts, unnamed sources, and reporters and columnists all have had their say, there is little space left for "the public"—indeed, the public disappears from the news grid as the professionals' special interests take over the limelight. No wonder citizens get cynical about the news and even about their society. We all become tired and disbelieving members of a vacuous public represented abstractly in the opinion polls.

Unless it engages religiously grounded values and perspectives, contemporary news reporting will find that journalists, too, are ever more mocked and dismissed by the citizens whom news media supposedly serve. Informational fundamentalism shifts power not to the public but to journalists and special interests. It serves the interests of expert sources and the news profession, which seeks ways of gathering and disseminating the news as a commodity. Special-interest politics and the media in the United States have become birds of a pragmatic feather. In spite of their occasional antagonisms and conflicts, special-interest politics and the media in America synergistically rely upon each other to accomplish their own ends.

Politicians need positive public exposure, while the news media need stories that will garner audiences and sell papers. After all, the rise and fall of colorful politicians is the next best thing to a juicy sex-and-religion scandal.

Conclusion

The contemporary news media are quite secular, not so much in their reporting about churches and ecclesiastical matters but in their overall uninterest in the human condition, in the substance of virtue, and in the transcendental aspects of the human responsibility to care justly for the world. News reporting is grounded in the secular faith that there is no transcendent purpose to life and therefore no ultimate responsibilities. The prevailing hermeneutic of informational fundamentalism implicitly feeds a naturalistic view of society as a collection of groups and individuals advancing their own interests as they battle for survival. In Carey's view, Marxism has implicitly "become the ideology of late bourgeois America because our vocabulary of motives pretty much comes down to whose ox gets gored."[174] The news media, in particular, seem to lack a language of good and noble action, a way of identifying and expressing virtuous character or the common good. Journalists also seem uninterested in news as one vehicle by which citizens can join public discourse in the collective search for the common good. Reporters reduce society to a feuding collection of losers and winners, with no overarching purpose or teleological direction. Citizens must go on, but why they must go on in life is never clear. In this journalistic paradigm life is an elaborate but dismal scenario of contentious groups and ambitious persons. The only thing left to praise is liberty, which in the form of the freedom of the press becomes the core of journalists' rhetoric of praise, the god of their own values.

Contemporary journalists have created a professional identity that ties reporters to a quasi-religious quest for truth and justice. Reporters position themselves like prophets, supposedly unearthing misdeeds while proclaiming the truth. Herbert J. Gans identifies this attitude as a latter-day version of early-twentieth-century Progressivism.[175] Progressivism had a religious fervor with a moral tone, but it also carried some notions of social justice rather than today's journalistic obsession with experts and facts. Now political news pundits, in particular, dispense their own brands of truth while netting five-figure speaking engagements and authoring politically vacuous but anecdote-rich best sellers.[176] Yet very little reporting actually does seek to explore the broader truth and bigger picture, as contrasted with the mere "facts." The informational fundamentalism that undergirds the journalistic enterprise is epistemologically too narrow to oblige a greater and more noble purpose. Reporters as priests and prophets paradoxically wring the spiritual life out of democratic discourse.

One of the great problems facing the United States and other democracies is how to reestablish the public square as a legitimate and friendly arena for civil dialogue and consensus building. Within that project, the nation needs to reassess the proper role of religion, the only type of conviction explicitly protected by the First Amendment. As Tocqueville recognized, rhetoric, reason, and religion are at the heart of the American experiment with liberal democracy. Religious convictions, among other commitments and interest, often drive Americans into public life, where they associate civilly with others for the purpose of pursuing the good society. At its best, religion nurtures the shared sense of responsibility and the elements of the common moral framework that help maintain civil discourse, foster a respect for all individuals, and keep alive basic issues of social justice. Once in the public arena, religious people, like all others, use reason and rhetoric to make sense of our common predicaments and to pursue with all people a better world. They do not have to act religiously or to make distinctly religious arguments once they enter public discourse. Recognizing the distinction between private and public life, the religious citizen must make the same tough judgments about how to present himself or herself to others as every citizen must make. Losing any sense of the public-private distinction is a recipe for disaster, because then one can gobble up the other to the point where freedom and responsibility no longer make any sense; freedom requires choices, and responsibilities require distinct areas of obligation. Journalists, too, do not have to wear their religious convictions or lack thereof on their sleeves, but neither should they be uncivil or even unfriendly to citizens who seek to be true to their faith as well as their calling to journalism.

At its worst, religious conviction nurtures theocratic desires and produces gaggles of moralistic self-interest groups honking their demands in the marketplace of ideas. To the extent that journalists focus too much on these religious groups, however, they make us all more cynical about the value of religion in the public square. Religion's major contribution to the formation of a public, as Tocqueville recognized, is to give citizens and the democratic process a moral basis and thereby to guide the civility of responsible participants in public discourse. Americans are able to think less selfishly about democratic ideals partly because of their shared moral dispositions, which often are cultivated by underlying religious faith and religious community.

Often missing from the public square today is a language of public faith— not a shared faith in a particular religious dogma or tribe but a language of faith that enables us as a people to lay claim to common, transcendent values in which we can believe. We hear in public life some "God talk" about the personal faith of politicians and the activities of religious special-interest groups, but we seem unable to sustain the more crucial language of "one nation under God." Contemporary journalists, taken captive by their quest for informational fundamentalism and caught up in their own privileged place in public discourse, merely remind us of our religious tribalism, with no overarching respect for the deeper matters of the heart, of justice, of responsibility, and of a deep respect for the value of persons.

The news media are crucial to rebuilding this kind of open public life in the United States. Tribal media can help each tribe to articulate to itself how it can serve the general public as well as its own interests. Meanwhile the mainstream media provide forums where, as Park and the others put forth, we can pursue shared understanding and consensus in spite of our tribal differences.[177] Much of national public life must of necessity be conducted via the media. This makes journalists the principal public storytellers who narrate society, just as preachers did in the early colonies. Reporters carry a deep responsibility for promoting the kinds of public dialogue that will help us transcend our tribalism while simultaneously recognizing our dependence on the tribes for many of the moral and philosophical resources that will continue to nurture democratic sensibilities and habits.

The news media in a democracy have a higher calling than informing the public. They should help the nation to be a public instead of merely an audience, a circulation, or a collection of tribes of citizens who are mad as hell or as self-interested as animals. More reporting is not the answer. Better analysis and interpretation, interviews, and invited columns are beginnings. But citizens in general, including people of religious faith in particular, must themselves participate in the making of the public narratives that we call "news." Journalistic storytelling is one of the imaginative liturgies of democratic conversation. "To regain our sight for the coherence of the public world," says philosopher Albert Borgmann, "we must be able to count on our chroniclers—the journalists, essayists, and historians—and we must allow their work to come to rest and attention for a day at least, or a month, or some years."[178]

Most citizens do not expect religion news to focus only on their own faith or merely to puppet their own agendas, but they do rightly expect the media "to represent the underlying contributions of religion to daily life in the culture of the nation."[179] This is a perfectly reasonable expectation, because the drama of democracy is "about permanent contestation between conservation and change, between tradition and transformation. To jettison one side is to live in either a sterile present-mindedness or an equally sterile reaction."[180] Political institutions and the news media should take religion seriously. America needs religious news, not just religion news, but the time and place for each type of news are critical. The mainstream media need to balance religious and religion news, using the former to help the public understand the tribe, the tribe to understand the broader public, and all citizens to understand their shared responsibilities for the health of the Republic. Religiously informed and committed columnists and commentators are vitally important, but no one should be excluded because they lack faith.

The burden for nurturing religious news, however, falls first on the shoulders of the distinctly religious media that are centrifugally organized for particular faith communities. As chapter 2 documents, these media can converse and imagine with the freedom of sectarian voices in the spirit of intratribal communion. The religious news in these speech communities can help individual members of the tribe find their way morally and civilly in the wider public sphere. Lynn says that the church does "not need more radio commentaries on 'religious' news." Rather the church needs "more radio commentaries which see the news from a religious point of view. Our greatest need is not for more slick church journals which will defend and promote the activities of the denomination. Our need is for newspapers and magazines that will make the impact of the Gospel felt in interpreting the East-West struggle or in the crucial issues of domestic politics."[181]

In a satirical essay entitled "Let Us Prey," former U.S. senator Eugene McCarthy charges that the Fourth Estate is "dangerously close to becoming a new religion." While church members are challenging the special knowledge of the clergy, writes McCarthy, "journalists continue to pronounce absolute judgment on the most complex social, political, and moral issues." He argues that journalists have their own "Index," an official list of people and organizations that merit coverage and those that do not. Journalists even engage in a kind of "Inquisition," deciding "who is to be sustained, who is to be elevated, who is to be rejected, who is to live and die in the public eye." And like many religious groups, the media refuse to reveal the "failing of their own kind." McCarthy concludes that if the news media continue to assume the "powers and privileges traditionally associated with religion, they must be prepared to demonstrate the purity, detachment, and moral superiority of their agents and officials."[182] Perhaps vows of chastity, poverty, and obedience are not proper for journalists, but as McCarthy suggests, refusing honoraria and publicizing their sources of income might be good places to start.[183] I would add at least two oaths: communicating with humble honesty and listening with gracious appreciation. If Bryant Gumble had a deeper sense of the limitations of informational fundamentalism and a greater sense of obligation to the public weal, he might have been able to sustain a meaningful dialogue about matters of faith with former president Carter.

8

Praising Democracy: Embracing Religion in a Mass-Mediated Society

◪ ◪ ◪

In his classic sociology textbook published in 1909, Charles Horton Cooley assessed the relationship between democracy and religion. "The democratic movement," he wrote, "insomuch as it feels a common spirit in all men, is of the same nature as Christianity; and it is said with truth that while the world was never so careless as now of the mechanism of religion, it was never so Christian in feeling." Comparing the "higher spirit of democracy" to the "teaching of Jesus Christ," Cooley claimed that Jesus "calls the mind out of the narrow and transient self of sensual appetites and visible appurtenances, which all of us in our awakened moments feel to be inferior, and fills it with the incorrupt good of higher sentiment." The human mind, he concluded, in its "best moments" is "naturally Christian."[1]

Cooley's generous assessment of the universal value of general Christian teachings prefigured the moralistic rhetoric of American Progressivism. Like later journalists and social reformers, including a growing number of social scientists and mainline Protestant clergy, Cooley hoped to stretch the canvas of Christian faith broadly over a nonsectarian frame of universal love and common good. As the twentieth century opened, many social thinkers and political activists sought to leverage the moral language of Christianity for the service of democratic reform, without succumbing to what they viewed as the narrow-minded tribal allegiances and contentious dogmas of particular faith traditions. Expressing this generic Christianity, Cooley rhapsodized that the Golden Rule, in particular, offered a means of reconciling the "sympathetic" and the "rational" in life, for "what is good for you is good for me because I share your life; and I need no urging to do by you as I would have you do by me."[2] Echoing Alexis de Tocqueville's sentiments, Cooley and other reformers imagined the moral base of Christianity as the overarching paradigm for social justice and cultural progress in America.[3]

Nearly a century after Cooley's sanguine writing, such sanguine rhetoric about the value of the Christian faith for liberal-democratic reform seems like the wishful thinking of a bygone era. Yet it is difficult to comprehend the moral fervor of American optimism without also understanding its religious roots in the nation's public imagination—especially its roots in Christianity. The history of the United States is partly the story of a democratic dance with oddly yoked partners, including the tribe and the public, the church and society, and technology and culture. As a democratic people generally in favor of inviting newcomers to the dance, Americans embrace seemingly irreconcilable ideas, beliefs, and sentiments. Such tensions are part of the genius of American democratic life; as they love moderation, Americans are able to call upon resources that go dry only when such democratic sentiments are yoked to fanaticism. This concluding chapter argues that Americans perform this dance repeatedly as a ritual of public hope. The mainstream media are one of the major dance floors where Americans address the resulting tensions between popular democracy and sectarian religions.

The easiest way of making the dance popular is to imagine religion itself as democratic—in effect, to invite everyone to the church liturgy and to baptize the nation as a Christian land. Cooley and other Progressives did this by claiming that the essence of Christianity was universally inclusive. Other groups did so by locating the nation's democratic legacy in its "Judeo-Christian" roots. These two rhetorics of communion emphasized the nation's cross-tribal continuities, but neither one is adequate for the twenty-first century, when the United States is becoming an even more heterogeneous nation of religious tribes from outside the Hebrew and Christian folds.

A more inclusive means of reconciling political and religious pursuits is to respect the vital role of tribal faith in establishing and maintaining the moral base upon which democracy depends for civil discourse. According to this rhetoric of communion, all faiths more or less share some of the same moral values and virtues that sustain democracy—such as truth-telling and respect for others. Tribes package these tenets differently, but they all adhere to some of the same social mores—what Tocqueville called "habits of the heart."[4] By democratizing religious practice within the nation, we also could foster a moral framework that nurtures civility, responsibility, and neighborliness. In Tocqueville's language, the religiously inspired habits of the heart will leaven society as individuals practice a softer self-interest that is "well understood."[5] Whether the media will embrace this type of open dance is unclear, since the Fourth Estate often pursues its own interests instead.

In short, religion and democracy need each other, but along the way they have to give way to each other as well. The media and Christianity, for instance, have had to interact, not just react to each other. Among the many remarkable stories behind the American experiment is not just the prohibition against a state church but also the guarantee of religious rights, including the right to religious practice. Freedom of religion was built into the Bill of Rights because religion was the most likely reason for someone to be excluded from public life in early America.[6] As a result of this religious freedom, designed apparently to protect the rights of all religious believers in public life as well as to provide a moral base for democracy, religious customs significantly shaped and reflected public life, including the rituals of mass communication. In far more oblique ways the same mass media, even the most seemingly secular and purely amusing ones, both shaped and reflected religious life in the nation. Although the points of tension between religion and the media are sometimes painfully obvious, the two are also so deeply and synergistically interconnected that it is impossible to completely untangle the mutual webs of culture, rhetoric, and economics that they share. The dance goes on in twenty-first-century America, even when neither side feels like entering the dance floor with the other one.

This final chapter reflects upon the meaning and significance of the previous case studies illustrating the relationship between Christianity and the mass media in the United States. It argues that democratic America needs to nurture four kinds of tension in society: tensions between time and space, tribal and public interests, religious and secular cultures, and technology and culture. It also suggests that these points of tension are necessarily played out partly in and through the media. The tensions produce inelegant and sometimes damnable alliances among various parties, and they occasionally seem to subvert both democracy and religion. These tensions are still crucial parts of the American experiment, just as each branch of government must check the power of the others. Moderation, one of the great virtues on which democracy depends, is crucial for maintaining the balance that holds together each pair of tensions. Democracy is partly a balancing act.

The mass media, as consensus-building as well as conflict-producing avenues for public discourse, at their best can help the sacred and secular dimensions of modern life interact for the benefit of both. Among other things, the secular media can help to ensure that religious tribes avoid acting upon any theocratic aspirations. To accomplish this feat the mainstream media must foster lively public discourse that empowers and ennobles civil conversation among the nation's many religious and nonreligious tribes, thereby fostering a real public that transcends opinion polls and publicity campaigns. Meanwhile the religious tribes, including their own media, can help not only to maintain a moral base for the civil functioning of democracy but also to provide a check upon the quasi-religious powers of consumerism and media professionalism—including journalism—that sometimes aim to thwart democracy by redirecting and controlling public life in their own interests.

Democracy needs both media and churches that take seriously their responsibilities as public communicators in a democratic land. Responsible communication is crucial not just for the mainstream media but also for tribal media, since religious groups typically make claims about the rest of society, not just about their own group. As Robert E. Park argues, human communication is "indispensable" to the cultural process; communication is the very means in and through which human beings become a "cultural unit" by spinning webs of "custom and mutual expectation."[7] As Americans approach a world of digital communication held together partly by computer networks, the mutual obligations are crucially important for the maintenance of democratic life. In Cooley's day the press was the major mass medium for maintaining national solidarity amid ethnic and religious tribalism. Today we must consider every medium of communication, from conversation to cyberspace, as a potential vehicle for healthy social conflict as well as for pursuing together the good life.

Balancing Culture in Time and Space

If we listen to American advertisers, the great evangelists of our age, practically every new product and service is revolutionary. Or if we believe the popular press and television news programs, it seems that each day brings revolutions in fashion, politics, and economics. More than anything else, such hyperbolic rhetoric about technology and culture reflects Americans' lack of historical insight. One writer in a new media periodical in 1998 claimed, for instance, that the Internet is "helping us become *multitemporal*" and has "released us from the tyranny of space and time."[8] Cultural and social changes occur continuously, but revolutions are hardly everyday occurrences. There is undoubtedly far more continuity than discontinuity in history, and few events or new technologies should properly be called a revolution. Enchanted with the rhetoric of conversion, Americans are obsessed with superficial novelty. This is not good for religion or democracy.

In spite of all of the rhetoric about how media technologies are supposedly changing the world, human life is still fundamentally limited by space and time. Culture is always situated historically in time and geographically in space. Human beings are not eternal; in fact, they are constantly losing culture to forgetfulness. Optimistic Americans still tend to imagine new media technologies as space-conquering, time-dominating gods. Our rhetoric of technological conversion wishes a world in which human beings were more like God and less like people, more like apolitical champions of omnipresent democracy and less like vehicles for interest groups to ply us with their wares, and more like time machines that magically connect us to the past, present, and future than like stupefying technologies that induce retrograde amnesia. "The greatest danger to freedom," argues Stephen Bertman, "lies in freedom itself: the freedom to ignore, the freedom to forget."[9] While public rhetoric about the media tends to slip into a veneration of new technologies, religious tribes stubbornly maintain allegiances to the past—and rightly so. The two social institutions—media and tribe—clash on matters of how culture should be imagined and formed in the past, present, and future. Without such tension, America could become either a self-immolating culture of hell-bent innovation or a stagnant culture of traditionalism. The media are not neutral conduits for messages but instead are always biased toward what Harold Adams Innis called space-binding or time-binding communication.[10] They tend either to promote messaging across geographic space or to foster communication through generational time. Balancing these two biases is crucial for the good of the democracy as well as its many religious tribes.

Religious institutions generally rely upon traditional, proximate practices such as prayer, worship, and fellowship that stabilize culture from generation to generation. Such practices slow down the rate of cultural evolution by maintaining time-honoring habits and long-standing virtues. As Michael Warren suggests, religious meaning must perdure as "an achievement of human intentionality and resulting care."[11] Similarly, democracy must be cultivated over time in social institutions such as governments and the press that help transmit democratic practices and republican responsibilities from generation to generation. There is no quick route to religious community or to enduring democracy. Human language can foster communication only where it is rooted.[12] Just as tribal faith requires patient training and character formation, democracy requires discussion, conversation, and civil dialogue over time, in addition to the particular institutions that maintain such venerable practices. Ultimately the tribal adherent who is also a democratic citizen is a member of two traditions—one religious and one political—and is therefore responsible for carrying on the practices required for nurturing both social institutions.[13]

This type of political and religious solidarity over time is maintained primarily through oral communication, not through the mass media. Traditional religious customs and democratic habits are cultivated mostly at the local level in communities of moral discourse. Oral communication is crucial in religious institutions, for instance, as a means of nurturing faith among people who know each other well enough that they can empathize with and love one another as neighbors in the biblical sense. We should not let our own infatuation with new media lure us away from our local and particular cultures, where democratic participation and neighborly religiosity are grown over time and maintained from generation to generation.

Strong oral communication, anchored in proximate communities, is vital for religion and government in the democratic tradition. Local communities of faith, directed by particular traditional beliefs and participatory actions, are the most tenacious means of maintaining religions even in mass society. Any media that weaken local congregational life will tend over time to make the religious speech community much more vulnerable to changes induced by external shifts in society, especially the growth of mass-mediated consumption communities and nonparticipatory media usage. Similarly, authentic democracy cannot be sustained by plebiscite technologies like cyberspace that promise instant voting from home and perfect ballot counting. In short, religious tribes and local governance need time-honoring media for their own survival. When we nurture strong local communities, we can better provide some of the cross-generational continuity that is vital for the maintenance of a good and participatory society over time. As Michael J. Sandel suggests, "At their best, local solidarities gesture beyond themselves toward broader horizons of moral concern, including the horizon of our common humanity."[14]

The interaction of Christianity and the media in modern America, then, is partly a struggle between traditional and contemporary agents of socialization. On the one side are largely local and tribal institutions, and on the other are most mainstream media institutions, such as Hollywood film companies, radio and television networks, and Internet portals. The mainstream media have depended primarily on the power of print, electronic, and now digital communication to extend their cultural influence across space into every nook and cranny of American society. They understandably are uninterested in the problem of cultural continuity over time. Although these mainstream media may compete among themselves for audiences and advertising revenues, collectively they represent a relatively homogenous, market-oriented system aimed at meeting mass audiences' desires for amusement and diversion. For all of their parochialism, religious tribes have always been among the most important means of counterbalancing the cultural superficiality and homogeneity spread by space-biased media. Strong local communities of faith and democracy can help us protect the habits of the heart from the consumerist onslaughts championed by increasingly international media conglomerates.

The history of the United States during the twentieth century is partly a gradual shift from local and ethnic ways of life to national, cosmopolitan cultures established in and through the mass media. Cooley wrote already in the early 1900s that "location itself—to begin with man's attachment to the soil—has been so widely disturbed that possibly a majority of the people of the civilized world are of recent migratory origin."[15] Partly because of the impact of electronic media, local ways of life founded on traditional institutions such as the church and the family are generally weaker today than in the past. Oral communication is still important, but it now must compete with many printed and electronic messages that enter Americans' private spaces, including living rooms and bedrooms. Parish pastors feel the tug of the electronic church on the religious sensibilities of their congregants, just as public school teachers recognize that movies and popular music compete for the hearts and minds of their students. We cannot and should not aim merely to return to past ways of life, but we still need to strengthen the time-biased institutions that can stabilize culture and nurture noninstrumental practices that have moral and political rather than merely pecuniary value.

Oral, proximate communication is crucial to maintaining all forms of intergenerational continuity in modern society. As James W. Carey puts it, the framers of the Constitution assumed the existence of independent "frameworks of communication and memory" that would help balance stability and change.[16] The electronic and perhaps the digital media tend to promote excessive communication within each generation, stratifying society according to rapidly changing lifestyles defined largely by professional communicators with vested interests in marketing particular products or championing self-interested causes. Margaret Mead observed decades ago that North Americans had created the first society where young people learn more about life from other young people than from older members of society.[17] Elders often seem increasingly irrelevant to youth, who yearn to connect "personally" with the national and international cultural fads found in teen-oriented music, video, film, and the like. Teenagers understandably feel that they have more in common with their peers than with their own parents, pastors, and teachers. Instead they join church "youth groups" that, for all of their benefits in ministering to teens, can also become merely a means of assimilating young people into consumer-oriented, quasi-religious culture—the "teen curriculum" and "contemporary Christian music" and other potential fads that sometimes exacerbate the very generational discontinuities that they claim to be solving. Similarly, old and young alike are less apt to know more about state or especially national political issues than they are likely to be aware of the needs of their own towns and cities. Today most people do not participate in the religious life of the mind cultivated through tribal journals of comment and opinion—and understandably so, since those media too often are forums for church elites, not the laity. We orient our lives to distant, mediated worlds without considering the everyday world in which we actually live.

Even tribal mass media find it difficult to create discourse that transcends the generational divides. Most evangelical radio stations have given up on trying to find a common culture within the church, preferring instead to imitate the mainstream media by segmenting the church into demographic breakouts and abstracted market categories that serve program directors and advertising salespeople but worsen the generational gaps within the church. As tribal media have created new national webs of popular culture, they, too, often have weakened local, intergenerational communication that was the basis for maintaining traditions over time.[18] If religious practices are to be passed from generation to generation, oral communication will have to be strengthened locally. Digital and printed materials can be part of the process of bringing up young people in the faith, but nothing is as powerful and effective as personal, dialogic communication grounded in real relationships among equals in the community of faith. Tribal criticism of mainstream culture is not a substitute within the tribe for strong oral communication and culture in the task of assimilating young people so that they will eventually accept responsibility for future faith communities.[19]

Both democracy and religion depend on discourse about the past. In his study *How Societies Remember*, Paul Connerton suggests that a people's experience of the past depends upon their knowledge of the past. Moreover, he argues that communication across generations is "impeded by different sets of memories," and the "different generations may remain mentally and emotionally insulated, the memories of one generation locked irretrievably, as it were, in the brains and bodies of that generation." He believes that cultural memory requires two things—recollection and bodies. Unlike written or printed texts, he contends, bodies enable human beings to perform meaningful commemorative ceremonies that are passed along generationally as social habits and enacted as bodily automatisms. Connerton believes that in ancient rural societies, before the rise of the mass media and even organized schools, the oldest generation of the family generally educated the youngest members of the tribe; such oral, embodied communication "must surely have contributed to a very substantial extent to the traditionalism inherent in so many peasant societies."[20]

If Connerton is right, oral forms of communication, anchored in local democratic and religious habits of mind and heart and requiring personal, bodily participation, might be among the most powerful means of communicating spiritual and political culture from generation to generation. It should not surprise us, then, that both the Greek city-state and the early church were largely proximate institutions that relied on participatory human discourse. The ancient church did not expand throughout the Roman world via mass communication as much as via an extension of bodily communion, supplemented by written texts, such as letters circulated from one community to the next. Believers literally carried memory from place to place—in their minds and through their embodied practices. In order to remember the major aspects of the faith, they instituted rituals and rites based largely on the earlier performative practices of the Jews. The mythos of the electronic church, like a rhetoric about cyber-democracy, glosses over this fundamental aspect of bodily communion and oral communication. In America rhetorics of conversion easily slip into rhetorics of praise for the latest technology; Americans are apt to forget the crucial role of rhetorics of discernment and communion as countervailing ways of thinking, imagining, and performing life in the world. "Culture changes through the ongoing engagement between tradition and transfor-mation," writes Jean Bethke Elshtain. "If we lose tradition, there will be no transformation. Only the abyss."[21]

We face a time when tremendous advances in communication technol-ogy have actually made empathy, understanding, and cultural continuity more difficult.[22] We are so out of balance, weighed heavily toward one-way, distant messaging as against participatory discourse, that we might lose the connections to the past that make democracy morally and politi-cally possible. "There are public idiots," writes John Lukacs, "who proclaim this flood of communications as a 'knowledge explosion.'" We are confus-ing the "speed of communication" with real understanding, because the "availability of communications from a distance" is accompanied by the "deteriorating receptivity of minds." The result is the "devolution of liberal democracies into bureaucracies" and a democracy where more people speak but fewer listen.[23] Addressing the same issues, Carey warns that modern media are widening the range of reception while narrowing the range of distribution. "Large audiences receive but are unable to make di-rect response or participate otherwise in vigorous discussion."[24]

Christianity and democracy both depend on cultural innovation as well. While seriously embracing their idiosyncratic pasts, they also have to be open to new, unforeseen cultural challenges and opportunities. Eighteenth-century Christians developed lively religious newspapers that were the fore-runners of today's religious journals of comment and opinion. Christians in the 1920s rightly considered how the new medium of radio might supple-ment their other media ventures and even serve local congregations. But the rhetoric of technological praise is so strong and persistent in American society that it seems always to threaten cultural traditions and institutional memories with the latest versions of revolutionary progress. One of the most "revolutionary" aspects of both Christianity and democracy in con-temporary America should be their tenacious interests in their own histo-ries, traditions, and rituals of embodied communication. A task of religious tribes in a technological world, suggests William F. Fore, is "to provide an alternative environment to the media environment, namely, face-to-face community."[25] The "function of communication," writes Park, "seems to be to maintain the unity and integrity of the social group in its two dimensions—space and time."[26] Faith communities and democratic institutions depend on a balance of space-binding and time-binding media to maintain their traditions in the midst of cultural changes. Today the space-binding media are threatening the maintenance of culture over time. To borrow some language from Walker Percy, ten boring Hail Marys are now worth more than ten hours of Joseph Campbell on television.[27]

Balancing Tribal and Public Interests

In his essay "Reflections On Communication and Culture," Park argues that human beings live in symbiotic as well as social relationships. Outside of their "little tribal and familiar units," he suggests, people inhabit a wider social and economic order that is "enforced and maintained by competition, but competition modified and controlled to an ever-increasing degree by custom, convention, and law." He concludes that American citizens live in two worlds—the intimate world of the family and the more impersonal world of commerce and politics. In the larger orbit of life the individual is free to pursue personal interests relatively "uninhibited by the expectations and claims which, in a more intimate social order, the interests of others might impose upon him." Park describes this larger arena of politics and commerce as "competition," a sublimated form of conflict and rivalry.[28] Between these intimate and impersonal social worlds are mediating organizations, including mass media and religious tribes. Some tribes are simply acculturated over time by the wider culture, while others maintain their distinctive ways of life in the face of assimilatory competition from the mainstream mass media and other secular social institutions. As tribes try to socialize their own members, they also face assimilation by external cultural trends and movements that might be outside of the tribes' immediate control. The assimilated tribes count themselves more or less as society's natives, whereas the unassimilated tribes typically see themselves as exiled aliens in society.[29] As agents of cultural assimilation, the mainstream mass media implicitly regulate much of the inclusion of ethnic and religious tribes into America society. They also publicly define what constitutes mainstream culture as the shared life of a democratic nation.

Television, for instance, probably contributes significantly to our self-identities as both spiritual and political creatures. Robert N. Bellah imagines television as an agent of moral discourse that affirms Americans' shared belief "that the one firm reality is the individual self. Everything else, even marriage and family and certainly the more distant social attachments, are seen as the fragile product of the individual will, constantly in need of individual effort to maintain, and frequently collapsing because of such effort."[30] If Bellah is correct about television, the medium probably reflects the crucially important role of individual freedom in the nation's own rhetoric of communion. Louis Wirth identifies the roots of this kind of individualism in secularism, the "increasing skepticism toward all dogmas and ideologies." He says that Americans are "reluctant to accept things on the old authority" and often "unable to sustain a reasoned belief in its faith." As a result, Wirth continues, "secular man cultivates his personal tastes and elevates his right to choose as a faith in itself."[31] Today we even equate our democratic liberties with our ability to select from products and services created by others whom we generally do not know.

This type of radical individualism actually makes persons vulnerable to forms of social control and mass persuasion that appeal to their desire for personal freedom.[32] Americans may feel liberated from tradition, but in a mass-mediated world they might also feel increasingly shackled to therapists, professionals, and managers who offer pragmatic means for individual victory over unhappiness, depression, meaninglessness, and the like. Seeking autonomy without shared virtue, Americans find themselves vulnerable to the rhetorics of social movements and professional communicators who claim to offer freedom from anxiety and loneliness. Quick pathways to the American Dream are hardly capable of delivering us to long-term happiness and personal fulfillment. Mainstream media tend to champion individualism at a cost to tribal solidarity. People find themselves privately consuming media or "bowling alone" with minimal participation in public life.[33]

We can overcome such individualism by our tribal associations and by our broader participation in public life. Sharing our lives with others and contributing our talents to amelioration of the problems in our communities and our nation inherently build the common good. Such activities help us to overcome one of the primary tensions in American society, the struggle between special and general interests. Contemporary news and entertainment programming exacerbate these tensions by portraying the nation as a land of competing lifestyles, expert opinions, and social roles. The "language of opposition" tells us repeatedly that we have less in common with each other than we have exclusively.[34] We make ourselves into the image of competing clans and tribes, religious and secular. Even traditional religions are succumbing to this kind of self-interested retribalization, creating public relations offices, lobbying politicians, and forming the nonprofit equivalents of trade associations. If such special-interest pursuits are not offset by countervailing movements toward a shared public life, democracy will become little more than a collection of competing groups with no shared vision of the good life and ultimately no way of working together toward such a vision.

Tribal mass media can easily assume the centrifugal function of serving only particular interests of the tribe, with no respect for the larger picture of society. They can and should help groups to maintain distinct identities and to work toward tribal causes. American religious groups, including many denominations, pararchurch organizations, and movements, are partly media-maintained tribes within the broader society. So are many political, ethnic, and lifestyle groups organized online or through print and broadcast media. Using a rhetoric of discernment to distinguish between themselves and the rest of society, and a rhetoric of communion to articulate their common beliefs and sentiments, these tribes often identify themselves more or less as exiled outsiders to mainstream American culture. They then work to combat the broader political and cultural trends that they believe threaten their own ways of life. Meanwhile the large, centrifugal media become the primary public stages in and through which the various clans speak to each other as well as to the broader society. In order to gain a voice, however, the tribal spokespersons typically must speak through news reporters, documentarians, and other media professionals—unless the tribe can afford program time or advertising costs to speak directly to audiences. Most members of mediated tribes participate in both centripetal and centrifugal media, living in the tension between the tribal culture and the broader American culture, between tribal interests and public interests. In the best circumstances such tribes create "pockets of community where a moral language is kept alive, nurtured by religious praxis and compassion, where speaking about the common good is not met with befuddlement and confusion."[35] In the worst ones, however, tribalism eclipses any concern for public interests. To some extent modern democratic liberalism was born out of the attempt to tame tribalism by accommodating particularly religious tribalism within the political system.[36]

America's national rhetoric of democratic republicanism and personal liberty sometimes conflicts with tribal rhetoric. Strident religious tribes might support their own interests over those of the wider society. In addition, tribes occasionally use their own media to organize attempts to change mainstream society, as the religious press discussed in the early days of broadcasting. In some cases tribal media critics call for television or film boycotts, greater government regulation of the media, and stronger industry self-regulation. Generally speaking, this tension between democratic and tribal rhetorics is good for the nation. The health of the Republic is partly a function of the dynamism and energy of its competing groups, as James Madison argued.[37] Contemporary theologian George Lindbeck suggests that even a sectarian community of faith "is likely to contribute more to the future of humanity if it preserves its own distinctiveness and integrity than if it yields to the homogenizing tendencies" associated with the postliberal age.[38] Democracy depends on strong, vibrant, and meaningful rhetorics of inclusion and exclusion, communion and exile. In the best scenario the moral voices of tribes are moderate and charitable, blending with other voices to the good of the nation.

But without a countervailing sense of public interest, religious tribes can become too exclusivistic and moralistic. When their commitment to the commonweal wanes, they might call for quasi-theocratic politics or reforms that merely match their own self-interests. This is why America must continually identify and articulate a meaningful democratic metanarrative as an umbrella for the nation's increasingly disparate factions and special interests. Tribes need to know the shared public rules and common obligations that should limit their efforts to fashion society solely in tune with their own desires. Although tribes are free to believe as they wish, they are not free to impose their tribal convictions on the rest of society. Nor is society free to limit or control tribal beliefs, practices, and sentiments—as long as they are not a threat to the freedoms of others or to the Republic. After all, both tribes and governments are to be made up of individuals who are also members of the public, the common group of all citizens who agree both to disagree civilly and to work toward a shared good.

Benjamin Franklin spoke in 1749 of the need for a "Publick Religion" that could cultivate religious character among private persons and help to counter "the mischiefs of superstition." He even thought that such a public faith would show the "Excellency of the CHRISTIAN RELIGION above all others, ancient and modern." But Franklin added that what really mattered were "the essentials of every religion"—hardly an unreserved endorsement of sectarian exclusivism as the basis for an American public religion.[39] In his own way Franklin articulated the kind of liberal thought that would characterize American Progressivism in the twentieth century. Liberal currents have always pushed American democratic rhetoric beyond the boundaries of sectarian faith to the wider good. Cooley wrote, "At the present time all finality in religious formulas is discredited philosophically by the idea of evolution and of the consequent relativity of all higher truth, while, practically, free discussion has so accustomed people to conflicting views that the exclusive and intolerant advocacy of dogma is scarcely possible to the intelligent." He concluded that "the formulas of religion will henceforward be held with at least a subconsciousness of their provisional character." Cooley called for a more generic form of religion that would offer people "social salvation" and would engender a "moral awakening and leadership of the public mind."[40] He sought a broad religious consensus as a substitute for religious tribalism in the United States.

Striving for such religious consensus, however, could diminish the vibrancy and dynamism of tribal life. Democracy gains from both a public language of the common good and underlying religious tribalism. In fact, Franklin's "Publick Religion" probably could never adequately satisfy the spiritual desires of most people. Generic religious beliefs can help people navigate the public sphere, since such beliefs are least likely to offend others and most likely to engender common efforts and a collective will. But the real flames of religious conviction seem to burn only in the context of highly particular practices nurtured within identifiable religious traditions and communities. Religion seems to be naturally tribalistic, whereas democracy is naturally accommodating and consensual as well as competitive. Overly zealous tribalism is one of the necessary costs for strong voluntary religious associations that richly nurture the habits of the heart and leaven public life.

Unbridled tribalism contributes to a postmodernist image of democratic society in which the nation perceives itself merely as a collection of self-interested groups, without a national metanarrative to coalesce public interest. Tribes sometimes assess major historical claims about the nation on the basis of how well they comport with tribal mythology. Issues such as prayer in public schools and posting the Ten Commandments in public places become hotly contested and strongly polarized struggles among contending groups to legitimize their own readings of social reality. This kind of Balkanization of the United States, true to Cooley's argument about the "provisional character" of religious claims, makes it increasingly difficult to adjudicate cross-tribal wars. The resulting politicization of American Christianity, as Robert Wuthnow points out, is transforming religious institutions and rearranging the social and cultural strata of the church along ideological lines.[41] Certainly debates about the entertainment industry are among the most highly charged expressions of tribalism. Mainstream media content, whether news reports or television drama, can stir controversy and elicit strong tribal reactions. The perennial debates over sex, violence, and profanity now focus on particularly charged social issues, from the portrayal of gay sexuality to violence against women. The media both elicit tribalistic reactions and become the arena in which competing tribes seek to legitimize their own view of reality.

Democracy requires, in the face of potentially excessive tribalization, a public sense of the value and importance of the common good as the public interest. Democratic institutions cannot survive in a society that is little more than a heterogeneous collection of feuding tribes. Nor can democracy artificially impose one theological metanarrative on society as the only cultural and ideological scheme for all groups. Bellah speculates about the possibilities for "a world civil religion [that] could be accepted as a fulfillment and not a denial of American civil religion."[42] But such parareligious rhetoric would surely elicit strong theological and biblical critiques from many tribes. In fact, many American religious tribes derive much of their distinctive identity from the rhetorics of discernment and exile that they use to distinguish themselves from the broader society. To them, civil religion might be apostasy, not democracy. The public interest is not so much a civil religion as a cross-tribal consensus nurtured through dialogue and informed by both reason and moral suasion. This is partly why, as Carey puts it, "the public" is the "God term" of the press, the very justification for the existence of the news media in society.[43] In order to legitimize itself, each tribe wants to say it represents the real public, the silent majority or the moral majority. As definitions of the public become politicized among competing tribes, the public becomes a mere symbol leveraged for utilitarian purposes. "Only when there is no strong communal life to give substance to the concretion," writes Søren Kierkegaard, "will the press create this abstraction 'the public,' made up of unsubstantial individuals who are never united or never can be united in the simultaneity of any situation or organization and yet are claimed to be a whole."[44]

The health of the Republic depends on a strong, common will and on the dynamism among the various tribes that constitute the nation. Democracy values both tribal diversity and public unity. Park rightly calls for "common public existence in which every individual, to greater or less extent, participates and is himself a part."[45] More recently, Michael Ignatieff contends that Americans naively believe that they can "establish the meaningfulness" of their "private existence in the absence of any collective cosmology or teleology."[46] But such a common cosmology is not a substitute for our tribal existence. Instead it provides the social cohesion that enables democracy to risk freedom for the tribe and individual alike. Peter Mann says that "our understanding of the common good becomes itself 'mediated,' enlarged or narrowed by the images, symbols and stories of the media."[47] As mainstream media foster a genuine public, they simultaneously protect liberty. Only a vibrant public sphere can harbor the liberties that the tribes need to maintain their own identities through time and across geographic space. Similarly, tribal media that point the tribe to its public responsibilities as well as to its idiosyncratic interests are crucially important for maintaining democratic ideals in society. Clearly tribal journals of comment and opinion did this in their internal discourse about broadcast regulation. Perhaps they were even more faithful in this regard than were mainstream news media during the same period.

The rise of media elites in tribal and mainstream media, however, can hinder the nurturing of a public sphere in America. Religious broadcasting, for example, is increasingly characterized by a cadre of gurus and experts whom audiences look to for advice. The resulting personality cults lend power to a few individuals. As the mainstream media use these public figures as sources, they elevate the stature of free-standing broadcast leaders who may not be under the purview of any religious tribe. Christian media are increasingly dominated by these tribal personas, who in some cases establish fund-raising organizations and political-interest groups to further their interests. But mainstream media are just as celebrity oriented and fully as dependent on expert opinions from ideologues who use cable programs, syndicated columns, and the speaking circuit to build their flocks of followers. Journalists' dependence upon informational fundamentalism exacerbates this situation, since reporters become so dependent on expert opinions, official sources, and conflict-oriented stories. Much of contemporary reporting continuously recycles the opinions held by the same people from the same religious or secular-professional tribes.

Mainstream news media, in particular, carry an enormous obligation to facilitate cross-tribal discourse about the public's shared interests. The fundamental responsibility of journalists is not to "get the facts"—there are always more and other and arguable facts—but rather to provide a forum for citizens to converse intelligently about common interests and to forge meaningful expressions of those interests for public action. News media should not merely report to or for the public but should report with and from within the public. Addressing the need for such cross-tribal interests in American news reporting, Jay Rosen argues for a "public journalism" that would help communities understand and organize themselves coherently in the face of cultural fragmentation and the media's own professionalization. Whereas modern journalism is largely the province of professional reporters who rely upon the opinions of expert sources, public journalism locates reporting in the conversational life of the community and its citizens. Rosen suggests that journalists "1) address people as citizens, potential participants in public affairs, rather than victims or spectators, 2) help the political community act upon, rather than just learn about, its problems, 3) improve the climate of public discussion, rather than simply watch it deteriorate, and 4) help make public life go well, so that it earns its claim on our attention."[48]

Rosen's argument rightly assumes that we need a cross-tribal, suprapro-fessional language for public discourse. We must be able to talk about tribal conflicts, for instance, without resorting to tribal salvos, or about religion without advocating tribal language. Religion is not a topic that journalists should avoid or that citizens should ignore, since it is often a crucially important part of community life as well as a personal belief. Rosen's case rests on the importance of community, particularly geographic community. In effect, he equates "the public" with the geographic community as the general and common interests of the collective body of people within range of a given medium's distribution. He argues that news media must become part of the life of the community rather than merely a business endeavor or a group of professionals with its own agenda and with its own privileged epistemology. Presumably even tribal media have an obligation to point members to the broader life of the community and the nation as well as to their own prophetic and priestly voices on behalf of the tribe.

Both the tribe and the public, then, need their own distinct rhetorics of communion that define who the believers are, what they need to believe, and how they should relate to those with whom they disagree. Tribal rhetorics of communion help establish identity by articulating who is included in the group or nation. If there is not some bottom-line agreement about what one must believe or do in order to join the group, there is no group. Religious journals, for instance, frequently articulate a distinctive understanding of the wider world. Similarly, "being a United States citizen" must include a commitment to the U.S. Constitution and to the kind of republican ideals that such a document is meant to serve. That commitment, in turn, maintains shared values and beliefs about human nature, government, the importance of laws and justice, and even the value of the individual in society. All of these types of political-philosophical assumptions are like religious dogmas that Americans profess and share as a national community of democratic belief. The Constitution, in particular, is America's Bible, its "sacred" document that articulates the nation's shared public philosophy as a basis for law and politics. Religious tribes will often have much to say about how the Constitution should be interpreted and applied in a changing world, but they, too, must accept and use the language of the Constitution as a means of sharing a national rhetoric of communion. A tribe that merely transposes its rhetoric of discernment with the nation's rhetoric of communion ceases to be part of the public life of the country.

When the U.S. Congress formed the Federal Radio Commission (FRC) in the 1920s to regulate the new broadcast frequency spectrum, it rightly assumed that public as well as tribal interests were at stake. The FRC and its successor, the Federal Communications Commission (FCC), attempted to regulate the airways in the "public interest, convenience and necessity." But when the FRC applied this congressional phraseology to early radio broadcasting, it essentially equated commercial broadcasting with the public interest. In historical hindsight it seems absurd that the FRC would call early religious stations "propaganda broadcasters." Was not commercial radio also a form of propaganda? Of course the FRC and FCC partly overcame this kind of objection by requiring commercial radio stations to broadcast a variety of "public affairs" programming, including, ironically, religious broadcasting. But the inclusion of such specialized programming requirements essentially granted licensees a Balkanized view of American society as a collection of disparate interests and irreconcilable categories, such as "political affairs" and "religion." In short, the government and federal regulators were ill-equipped to articulate a rhetoric of communion that would support a notion of public-oriented broadcasting as more than a hodgepodge of specialized fare. Calling commercial stations "general" broadcasters did not make them any more public oriented than were religious broadcasters. Years later Congress created "public broadcasting" as an alternative to purely commercial broadcasting.[49] It also officially opened the radio and television channels to religiously oriented licensees, thereby transplanting tribalism from categories of programming to institutions of broadcasting.

One of the rhetorical strokes of genius in the development of American democratic philosophy was the assumption of at least some continuity between public and tribal interests. The "self-evident" truths expressed in the Declaration of Independence assent to ideas that are not merely matters of self-interest or tribal opinion, but statements of revealed truth that pertain to all people and express the rights and inherent value of every citizen regardless of her or his tribal loyalties. "A thing can be sectarian only in the climate of establishment," writes Leonard Verduin.[50] Yet at the same time the Bill of Rights guarantees personal and therefore tribal rights to assemble, speak, and believe as one likes. One tribe need not agree with every other tribe or even with the government on any given issue. Tribes will be tribes; indeed, they should be tribes. Nevertheless, somehow, out of the free and dynamic interplay of the tribes, the public itself—the general interests of all people—should also be served. In an editorial in 2000 about the vice-presidential nomination of Senator Joseph Lieberman as the first Jew ever selected to run for national office, *The New Republic* appropriately called the United States "a country that does not demand an erasure of self or an erasure of tradition as a condition of citizenship; that does not recoil before the particular as the enemy of the universal; that assumes the rights of individuals and groups, and does not condescend to grant them; that defeats tribalism with pluralism; that prefers equality to tolerance."[51] Tribal and public interests are never fully identical, but they sometimes do support each other when citizens are willing to look empathetically beyond their backyards to the good of the neighborhood, and beyond that seemingly parochial neighborhood to the more cosmopolitan cities, and even beyond that urban area to the entire nation. As human beings created from the same cloth of life, members of all tribes will see that they share much with members of other tribes and that those commonalities provide the basis for public life. Here I agree with Nicholas Wolterstorff's "consocial" argument that the ethic of a citizen in a liberal democracy should not be bound to a secular basis for his decisions and actions even in public life.[52] But here again citizens depend upon mass media and media professionals to support this type of public view of the yard, neighborhood, city, and nation.

Balancing Religious and Secular Culture

One of the more remarkable of Tocqueville's assessments of American society during the 1830s was his strong endorsement of religion. Whereas some Americans today often see religion as a political theocratic threat to the nation's democracy, Tocqueville saw voluntary faith communities as a crucial prerequisite to maintaining liberty in the nation. "Religion is much more necessary in the republic . . . than in the monarchy," he wrote. "How could society fail to perish if, while the political bond is relaxed, the moral bond were not tightened?" He concluded that the American style of democratic republicanism, which champions the liberty of the individual over the rule of elites and monarchies, depended on religious faith as a means of providing adequate cultural order and social control. "And what makes a people a master of itself if it has not submitted to God?" he wondered.[53] Without citizens' personal belief in God, they might revert to immoral conduct and deeply uncivil political actions that would destroy the Republic. In Tocqueville's view, Americans' personal fear of God was crucial for maintaining the moral fiber and civil discourse necessary for democracy. He imagined the secular realm of politics as directly dependent on the sacred domain of religion.

Tocqueville's observations still rang true into the twentieth century as new communication technologies expanded the geographic and cultural boundaries across which political and religious life occurred. The United States juggled spiritual and civil freedoms, often using the mass media to discuss the proper relationships between church and state. By all measures the United States continued to be a nation of religious believers and church members, and traditional religion continued expanding into new popular media forms.[54] Americans occasionally attacked the mass media for their alleged role in promoting immoral conduct and for being indifferent to the role of religion in society. In a poll conducted in 2000, Americans embraced freedom of religion more than freedom of the press; 53 percent of Americans said that the press had too much freedom. "The majority of Americans would restrict public speech that is offensive to racial or religious groups and would ban art shows that offend some members of a community," concluded one report about the survey. "At the same time, they would allow prayers at school-sponsored events and let schools post the Ten Commandments in classrooms. They would applaud government involvement in rating TV entertainment shows, and they would ban TV networks from projecting election winners while the polls were still open."[55] Tocqueville seemed to hold prescient knowledge: 170 years later Americans were deeply religious people who firmly believed that the religious life should help guard public as well as private morality and should

even influence mass media practices. Sacred beliefs and practices could—
and should—influence secular ones.

Yet Americans were also uncomfortable about bringing their religious
faith and practices into the public arenas of work and politics. When Jewish immigrant Otto Ochs acquired the bankrupt *New York Times* in 1896, he
had to figure out how to relate his religious tradition to the daily task of
running a metropolitan newspaper and serving a heterogeneous public
made up largely of Protestants and a growing percentage of Roman
Catholics. How should his ethnic religion influence the decisions that he
would have to make on behalf of the readers who lived in New York City?
After conducting a lengthy study of the extended family that ran the *New
York Times* throughout the twentieth century, Susan E. Tifft and Alex S.
Jones conclude that "the family's self-image as Jews has profoundly shaped
the paper." Hoping to live the American Dream and to avoid appearing too
Jewish in a Gentile world, Ochs's relatives "shed the habits and customs of
their Old World religion, embracing a Reform Judaism that largely replaced
Hebrew with English in synagogues, and they often looked with embarrassment at the later-arriving Jews from Eastern Europe who retained
vivid evidence of their Jewishness." In place of seemingly sectarian ethnicity, the Ochs clan adopted the cultural values and personal qualities that
helped many German Jews rise to social prominence and economic success
in American culture—"pride, caution, ambition, and energetic patriotism."
The Ochs families' desires to separate their traditional Jewish faith from
their professional endeavors elicited criticism from some Jews who thought
that the paper was simply not adequately tribal.[56] But Ochs and his kin decided to approach the task of running a major newspaper on a secular basis
as the way of best serving a heterogeneous city and the paper's diverse
readership. They felt a tension between two goods—the calling to be faithful Jews and the desire to publish a newspaper respected by the citizens of
New York.

The tension between secular and religious culture in the United States is
a major part of the history of the nation and a crucial aspect of the story of
mass communication. Americans' self-identities typically are forged out of
their religious commitments to a tribe and out of their more general, civic
commitments to the nation's democratic freedoms and institutions. This
tension frequently surfaces on the media stage as people both celebrate
and lament the conflicts. Americans have long complained about immoral
media content partly because of their personal and collective commitments
to a moral vision of the goodness of the nation and its people. From at least

Tocqueville's visit to America in the 1830s to the present, the media have been lightning rods that attract expressions of pent-up moral outrage and even serve as a means for particular religious tribes to communicate their frustration about broader cultural trends and movements. Tribal media mobilize rhetorics of discernment as a way of framing and expressing these in-house concerns. Mainstream media thereby become symbols of right-eousness and corruption, morality and depravity, heaven and hell. As tribes express their concerns publicly, public opinion, the market, and tradition often vie for legitimacy.

In a section on the "trend of sentiment" in his early-twentieth-century sociology textbook, Cooley argued that unfettered cultural competition in democratic America would lead to a disordered nation characterized by chaos and immorality. "In the lack of clear notions of right and duty the orderly test of strength degenerates into a scuffle," he wrote, "in which the worst passions are released and low forms of power tend to prevail—just as brutal and tricky methods prevail in ill-regulated sports." He suggested that America needed to foster two seemingly contradictory but actually code-pendent "attitudes of mind"—the active and the contemplative. Cooley associated contemplation with the "ideal of science and speculative philosophy" in which a person declines to take moral stands on issues; contemplation imagines the world as a picture to be viewed, not a moral universe to be shaped in the name of right and wrong, duty, responsibility, blame, and praise. In his view, such contemplation was simply inadequate for the development of society. Even crime, Cooley argued, is a "moral disease" that calls for "moral remedies, among which is effective resentment."[57] The citizen of a democratic nation cannot merely ponder, speculate, or theorize about society. A citizen must also be able to act wisely and specifically in society, applying a practical moral framework to the problems of the day.

Americans have addressed the moral tension between the media and religion using both secular and sacred languages. The secular language is often ideological and focuses on the interests at stake and the forms of power available through the use of mass media in contemporary society. It is, to use Cooley's terms, more contemplative and seeks to explain social relations and cultural processes so well that it can predict and presumably even eventually control the outcome of media campaigns and media regulation. Social scientists, in particular, often adopt the secular, detached language of pure contemplation. Religious language, on the other hand, tends to focus much more directly on the immediate moral implications of the media and to see far less value in careful description and analysis; frequently it has little patience for paradoxes, ambiguities, and uncertainties. Religious rhetors want change, action, improvement—not studies, reports, and analyses. Tribal critiques of the media often even focus on immediate action without a clear sense of the purpose of such action, as evidenced in much of the media watchdog rhetoric expressed by some Christian groups. The best tribal critics combine contemplation and action in formulating their understandings of the role and impact of the media in American society.

But the history of Christian critiques of the media in twentieth-century America suggests that churches tend to rely primarily upon moral and religious language rather than on ideological and secular language. In other words, the church has tended to counter the prevailing rhetoric of scientific description and objective critique with contrasting forms of moral understanding. On the one hand, the nation is served by scientific analyses of the mass media that try to accumulate data about the impact of mass communication and to build theories around those data—theories predicated largely on studies of media effects and functions. On the other hand, these social-scientific studies are also ideological in the sense that they represent the understanding and interests of a particular priestly class of experts, not necessarily the understandings of common citizens or even thoughtful media critics. So the tribe enters public discussion about the media not so much as a formal institution with a prescribed theory of communication and culture but as a faith community with some moral and theological convictions as well as social concerns. Christian tribes generally rely upon language that is informed epistemologically by particular religious, biblical, and theological understandings. Tribal critics are more like engaged exegetes than detached social scientists. The psychologists and sociologists speak in scientific language such as variables, demographics, and inferred causality, whereas the religious tribes might communicate instead in moral and theological terms such as social justice, mythology, ethics, salvation, and sin. In the best situations tribal critics thereby supplement the secular rhetoric of scholars with the more humanistic rhetoric of religion and theology.

Park distinguished between "referential" and "expressive" forms of language and communication. He associated the former with scientific understanding and the latter with the more interpretive cultural domains such as literature and the fine arts.[58] Broadly speaking, the churches and their tribal media critics have tried to sustain expressive forms of cultural understanding by using theologically informed language instead of scientific and referential symbols. Referential language, under the influence of such scientific ideals of objectivity and empiricism, has tended to remove moral, theological, and even political forms of expression from public discourse about the mass media. Social-scientific interpretations of the media have emphasized messages' particular, isolatable, measurable effects on individuals and groups. As religious understandings strive for the larger moral picture, scientific understandings aim for the pieces of various narrowly conceived puzzles—summarized wonderfully by Harold D. Lasswell's famous dictum about the proper research agenda for communication research: "Who says what, to whom, and with what channel, with what effect?"[59] The tribe's understanding of mass communication typically is much more interested in the moral sentiments expressed through the media, the apparent theological and biblical assumptions and worldviews presented in the media, the practical consequences of these assumptions, and the relationships between such mass-mediated messaging and both the interests of the media and the desires of Americans. Tribal criticism is often richly expressive rather than deeply referential.

Tribal media criticism, then, is one way that Americans try to maintain epistemological and moral integrity in their understanding of the role of the media in public life. Secular criticism, represented primarily by social-scientific understandings of media effects on individuals and society, eschews any clear moral universe or theological constructs in favor of empirical verification. Of course such social-scientific studies are bound to contradict one another or at least to be so theoretically and methodologically divergent that the average person can neither reconcile them nor integrate them into a meaningful paradigm—a situation that is likely exacerbated by scattered and inept journalistic reporting about social-scientific studies. It is hard for the average person to believe in such reports unless they happen on face value to support a tribe's or person's preexisting preconceptions about the news media. Scientific reports might connote validity and legitimacy, but they lack an overarching context in tune with everyday tribal beliefs. As Wirth suggests, secularism "carries with it the disintegration of unitary faiths and doctrines."[60] Tribal media criticism often tries to reclaim such unity. Religious language may in some cases be no more exact or precise than scientific or other secular language, but within the context of tribal belief it can provide a kind of coherence that resonates with tribal sentiment, and beyond the tribe it can provide expressive language that better equips critics to grasp the media's mythological aspects.

Tribal epistemologies still may be limited by a narrow traditionalism—
expressed ways of thinking that produce foregone conclusions, regardless
of empirical reality. Tribal media criticism carries its own biases, penchants,
and idiosyncrasies. Theological unity, which serves as a kind of aesthetic
coherence as well as moral integrity, can itself lead to oversimplifications.
Tribal critics can even use such unity to boost the impact of their rhetoric
within the tribe. Parachurch critics who depend on tribal financial donations regularly dilute the value of tribal criticism with their own attention-
getting, contribution-eliciting rhetoric. They corrupt tribal rhetorics of
discernment for their own purposes. Karl Mannheim saw the transformation of religion into ideology as an important aspect of the secularization of
modern society. He viewed it not as a liberalizing of religion but rather as
modernization of tradition into worldly ideology.[61] When this happens, religious criticism of the media loses much of the epistemological divine.

Perhaps it makes sense to consider tribal criticism as a paradigm akin to
Marxism, feminism, or structuralism. Faith-based criticism enables tribes to
contextualize particular case studies in the light of an overarching paradigm. It provides another way of interpreting the significance of the media
in secular society. As Carey suggests, "Reality cannot be exhausted by any
one symbolic form, be it scientific, religious, or aesthetic. Consequently,
the true human genius and necessity is to build up models of reality by the
agency of different types of symbols—verbal, written, mathematical, ges-
tural, kinesthetic—and by differing symbolic forms—art, science, journalism, ideology, ordinary speech, religion, mythology—to state only part of
the catalogue."[62] In other words, democratic life offers us the freedom to
think in sacred as well as secular terms, to select from a remarkably broad
spectrum of interpretive modes, all of which might have a role in helping
us to make sense out of complex and sometimes deeply mysterious human
phenomena. "As a life force operative within a people," writes Warren,
"religion offers new perceptions, new commitments, new patterns of social
relations, as well as a series of new freedoms—from fear, from external
pressures, even from certain civic laws."[63] In Kenneth Burke's language,
we then have many rhetorics of motive.[64] Tribal language of media criticism, at its best, swings open the gates of discourse to include not just
questions of interest and effects—as secular ideologies love to examine—
but also issues of ultimate meaning and purpose as well as practical concerns of moral suasion.

In the end, however, the "cosmic" theories of particular tribes are not
incontestable or even necessarily more accurate than other understandings

of social reality. Religiously conceived and theologically honed understandings of the media are an important part of the record of the ways that human beings have tried to make sense of their world, build better societies, and provide a moral base for the good functioning of democracy. As Alvin W. Gouldner puts it, religions and ideologies are disposed to contrary ontologies of human beings and correspondingly different epistemologies. Religion makes knowledge "a phenomenon that is *bestowed* on men and vouchsafed by higher powers and authorities, while ideologies give greater emphasis to the self-groundedness of men's knowledge, involving his reason and his experience: *cogito ergo sum.*"[65] We gain as a democracy when we consider the role and impact of the media from religious perspectives, but we lose when we become too dependent on particular tribal wisdom.

Tribal rhetoric can challenge secular ideologies' purely market-based understandings of the relationship between religion and the mass media. Historically speaking, the market and tradition are two of the most significant and often competitive forms of social control. Rabbi Jonathan Sacks argues that a tradition "might be undermined not by anti-market ideologies but by the very power of the market itself. For the market is not only an institution of exchange. It is also a highly anti-traditional force, at least in advanced consumer societies." The market's "cult of the new" tends to "encourage a view of human life itself as a series of consumer choices rather than as set of inherited ways of doing things."[66] The market can thereby displace human identity, eclipse tradition, and baptize both market mechanisms and market interests as godlike forces to which people feel compelled to give their time, talent, and money. Sacks concludes, "The idea that human happiness can be exhaustively accounted for in terms of things we can buy, exchange, and replace is one of the great corrosive acids that eat away the foundations on which society rests; and by the time we have discovered this, it is already too late."[67]

Perhaps no arena of public discourse better illustrates the impact of the market on the tribe than the American media. The twentieth-century discourse about media regulation in the United States has focused on the role of the market as means of identifying, organizing, and distributing cultural resources across geographic space. As the tribal debates over broadcast regulation suggest, media markets can become de facto arbiters of public taste, silencing some forms of expression and emphasizing others. Religious tribes have become some of the greatest supporters of mass-media deregulation even though they are also among the most outspoken critics of the mainstream media. Too often the concept of deregulation is a rationale for turning decision-making over to abstract and imperfect market mechanisms that are increasingly controlled by international media conglomerates. Deregulation will not itself produce media that represent the public interest. As in the case of religious radio, deregulation favored particular religious traditions whose messages and rhetorical styles functioned most effectively in an open market. Religious journals show that tribal rhetoric can contribute to democratic public discourse some of the critical language of social justice, social responsibility, and human rights. Tribal rhetoric can nurture forms of moral discourse that enable the public to talk about more than whether to support "free-market media." By contrast, most market-driven television will be only remotely religious. "On popular culture," says Thomas S. Gibbs, "we are children of this lesser God."[68]

Turned loose in network television, market mechanisms produce programming that takes little account of any ethnic or religious traditions. Popularity, as measured in audience ratings, becomes the de facto means of assessing the merits of a particular mythological system. Cooley suggested years ago that competition is the "very heart" of the economic process in market systems.[69] Competitive media discount traditional cultures in favor of abstract notions of the "market," thereby negating the value of ideas, sentiments, and beliefs that might reflect any minority tastes or perspectives in society. The Christian Gospel, for example, becomes an "unpopular opinion," a rather scandalous and highly particular system of belief that will supposedly divide audiences. Markets tend to generate secular culture, because expressions of sacred belief are always particular and frequently divisive. This is likely why religion is the only area of thought protected by the First Amendment. The only sustained type of religious face on American television has been the televangelists, who in the footsteps of earlier evangelical radio personalities learned how to create and market programming.

The case studies in this book suggest a number of crucial relationships between markets and religion in American democratic culture. First, the mythos of the electronic media, derived from secularized Christian ideals, leads Americans rather uncritically to adopt market metaphors as positive ways of evaluating new media technologies. Second, tribal journals of comment and opinion have provided some insightful critiques of market rhetoric, but they have also become some of its major advocates, particularly among evangelicals. Third, market-oriented discourse tends to lead to regulatory policies aimed at eclipsing traditional religious fare from the media while embracing consumerism. Fourth, market forces can flatten religious cultures and eclipse religious traditions. Fifth, mainstream mass media use their own market measurements to create quasi-religious mythologies that resonate with widespread "spiritual" sentiments that are only vaguely connected to particular religious traditions. Sixth, the role of tribal critics in making sense of mass-media markets is important for the life of the tribe. Without such critics, individual tribes will have an ever more difficult time differentiating their traditional beliefs and practices from those of the generic popular culture—although even tribal critics can be co-opted by the market as they seek to expand their status and influence within the tribe. Finally, journalists' secular hermeneutic is geared toward a mass market that transcends political and religious groups with a vacuous faith in informational fundamentalism. This is partly why Carey views the act of "reading a newspaper less as sending or gaining information and more as attending a mass, a situation in which nothing new is learned but in which a particular view of the world is portrayed and confirmed."[70] In each of these ways markets shape as well as reflect broader, secular cultural currents that usually challenge traditional religious cultures.

In the United States religious cultures represent crucially important centers of both conservative tradition and liberal dissent. As Cooley argues, most religious sentiment is more or less distinctly traditional.[71] Religious faith is collective and historical, anchored in specific faith traditions that have existed over time and that are expressed through relatively unchanging practices and sentiments. If democracy tends to "make every man forget his ancestors," as Tocqueville argues, religious traditions reassociate individuals with the people, practices, and precepts of a historic faith. "We cannot hold our minds to the higher life without a form of thought," writes Cooley, "and forms of thought come by traditions and usages which are apt to enchain the spirit." He adds that the "iconoclastic fervor against formalism that usefully breaks out from time to time should not make us imagine that religion can dispense with institutions."[72] But out of traditional faith and relatively static institutions human beings gain not just preexisting beliefs and practices but also ever-changing critical stances with respect to the wider world. Faith communities typically provide forms of speech and ways of understanding that assume a gap between the way the world is and the way that it should be. Using revelation and reason, tribes challenge secular ideologies and market-based logic with their own traditional rhetorics of discernment. Tribes thereby become countercultural and even sometimes revolutionary.

Religious tribes bring to media markets alternative ways of understanding and interpreting the significance of commodities. Lloyd Eby suggests that one way of thinking religiously about human cultural productions as more than mere commodities is to imagine them as "thought experiments." Films and other dramas, for instance, provide people with a public means of considering the "consequences and outcomes of human arrangements— moral stances and choices, various ways of life, political and economic views and systems."[73] Advertising "works" rhetorically in the market by boosting product awareness and strengthening market share, but it still is a kind of experiment that posits a particular, future-oriented, nontraditional view of social reality and personal happiness or success—various means toward self-realization or secular well-being.[74] The market simply says to the audience, "Here it is. It's great. It will improve your life, entertain you, impress you." Viewed as humanly devised thought experiments, market productions are mere states of affairs or particular renderings of reality. The market itself places little value on religious reflection, whereas a religious community might wonder how particular cultural productions relate to the life of the tribe—the version of reality that the productions serve. Markets are unable to place moral or even cultural value on their products— only pecuniary value. Religious rhetoric, however, can exegete and evaluate such market-based products from the standpoint of a tribe and its traditions.

The tension in the United States between religious and secular culture also exists in conflicts between prophetic and priestly rhetorics. Like all nation-states, America must somehow balance innovation and change in order to provide a means for cultural stability in the midst of social and economic changes resulting from technological, political, and economic developments. Secular cultures infuse the nation with all kinds of ideologies and markets, while religious cultures offer their own prophetic and priestly rhetorics that flow from various traditional beliefs, sentiments, and practices. These tensions are generally healthy for democratic life because they implicitly provide rhetorical checks and balances on public life by preventing either secular or sacred modes of communication from dictating reality and controlling shared culture within the nation.

Prophetic discourse, much of it derived from tribal traditions and communities, can serve the nation by challenging the goodness of secular powers. Religious newspapers in the antebellum period fought for abolition, sometimes taking radical stances that even many abolitionists could not yet support. As Carol Sue Humphrey documents, many religious newspapers during this period "provided the ideas and language that permeated the abolitionist litany."[75] Pope John Paul II repeatedly addressed the need for mass-media reform around the world during the 1980s and 1990s, calling humankind to "a stance of active resistance to those elements of the wider culture which they judge to be false" and encouraging media producers to "apply norms of human goodness to every proposed rendition of life's meaning."[76] Avery Dulles directs Christians to "take a resolute stand against the commonly accepted axioms of the world" and calls on the Roman Catholic Church to "perpetuate itself . . . through a long chain of discipleship."[77] Lukacs asks us to consider whether the perception of the sinful nature of humankind is not realistic, borne out not just by religious revelation but also through the evidence of history.[78] From early American religious agitators to nineteenth-century abolitionists, and from the civil rights rhetoric of Martin Luther King Jr. to the pronouncements of a pope, religious rhetoric has a long history of using countercultural images and prophetic language to make the case publicly for truth and justice.

Obviously in a democratic nation prophetic discourse is a strange and often intimidating form of public communication that on the surface challenges the very democratic spirit of equality. A prophet claims to be "above" the crowd, to have special revelation from "on high," and to understand the human condition better than others. Within a democratic milieu, prophetic discourse seems terribly arrogant if not hegemonic. Yet all democratic institutions and movements depend upon it, even in secular forms. The rhetorical motifs of repentance, reform, and renewal help democracies identify the difference between what they claim and how they actually operate. For instance, democracy never lives up fully to its claims of inclusiveness and its charge of respect for all people. This is why in democratic nations both tribal and secular prophets are likely to expose hypocrisy, hubris, and pride—as some of the religious journals of comment and opinion tried to do with respect to broadcast regulation. Prophetic rhetoric also calls for reform as a means of changing the particular states of affairs in society and culture; repentance without change is itself often hypocritical.

The rhetorics of conversion, communion, exile, discernment, and praise are equipment for religious rhetoric within and beyond the tribe. Communion holds the tribe to the faith tradition as a shared, covenantal agreement between God and the tribe as well as among members of the tribe. Discernment reveals the gap between the way things ought to be and the way they really are—the difference between the two cities. Exile expresses for the tribe its cultural and spiritual location in a world that fails to meet the standards of peace and justice articulated within the religious tradition.

Praise orients the tribes to what is ultimately good and right rather than merely to what is efficacious, efficient, or evil. Vibrant democracies create analogous secular language that serves the public rather than merely the tribe, but the form of such rhetoric nearly always comes originally from tribal sources, just as the writers of the Constitution relied upon the theistic and deistic language of the day. The integration of religious language and perspectives into democratic life is always a danger, however, it is also an important source of moral vision and a means of softening private and group egoism.[79]

Without the countervailing forces of democracy, tribal language is more likely to become self-serving and dangerously oppressive. In theocratic contexts prophetic rhetoric can uphold autocratic institutions that serve the interests of tribal leaders and arrogantly plunder the rest of society. In biblical history false prophets repeatedly contorted God's revealed truth for the purposes of establishing their own kingdoms on earth. Democracy both provides the freedom for religious groups to act faithfully within their traditions and establishes forums for public discourse in which particular religiously derived claims can be evaluated against those of the market, ideology, and competing religious traditions. Secular public discourse should not be able to dictate tribal beliefs and sentiments, but it should be used to assess religious rhetoric in the larger court of public reason. Democracy opens up the public square to the claims of social scientists, secular ideologues, and religious critics, among others. Religious tribes need that kind of open discourse as much as does the rest of society. In the Hebrew and Christian traditions God's truth often comes from the most unexpected quarters, particularly from those on the margins of society. Democratic discourse serves the tribe as well as society—as long as the religious tribes maintain their own prophets who can keep the tribe from ignoring or abandoning its history and community.

Balancing Technology and Culture

The tension between technology and culture is also healthy for democracy. Liberal-democratic societies depend both on technological systems of communication and on geographically grounded communities and traditions. Particularly in the developed West, technological developments tend to advance according to instrumental logic and market dynamics that can threaten organic ways of life that nurture habits of the heart and cultivate noninstrumental practices such as friendship, neighborliness, and hospitality.

The future of democracies depends significantly on their ability to maintain both national systems of communication and agonistic ways of life that oppose the wholesale adoption of technique. Historically speaking, Christianity has provided one of the most vital sources for moral, nontechnological culture. As Michael L. Budde suggests, "The cultural environment associated with the latest era of capitalism, dominated as that environment is by the global culture industries, presents new and imposing barriers . . . to the formation of deep religious convictions." He concludes that such technological developments threaten not just particular religious tribes "but the capacity to think, imagine, feel, and experience in ways formed by the Christian story."[80] At its best, religiously shaped culture challenges the dominance of purely technological worldviews, retards the standardization and homogenization of culture brought about by advanced industrialization, and provides some of the moral-rhetorical equipment that a democratic society needs in order to pursue the common good.

Mass communication technologies are not neutral tools for conveying messages but instead are value-laden combinations of social institutions, cultural forms, and technical machines. In Carey's words, "Technology, the hardest of material artifacts, is thoroughly cultural from the outset: an expression and creation of the very outlooks and aspirations we pretend it merely demonstrates."[81] Media technologies in particular amplify humankind's capacity to create "pseudo-environments" that mediate between local and distant cultures, among tribes, and between special-interest groups and the general public. In contemporary America, media technologies are so integrated into the very fabric of daily life that we rarely think about how they have fundamentally altered many of our habits, practices, and customs. Although we use communication technologies extensively, we do not easily perceive how value laden they really are.

Tribal critics are among those who see most clearly that mass-media technologies often compete with nontechnological cultures. They are apt to recognize that the ideals of technological society—such as unfettered innovation, geographic expansion, greater efficiency, and tighter control—are frequently at odds with the moral fabric of organic cultures. Communication technologies and religious traditions often compete in the sense that they both express frameworks for understanding who people are and how they should live. Fore argues that the "technological era" brings with it "its own world view—one that challenges the world views of all historic religions." In his perspective, the technological era is functional, pragmatic, utilitarian, and relativistic; its worldview is "thoroughly secular, demanding rationality and personal autonomy," and it "rejects metaphysical claims and demands that religion deal with the here and now."[82] In opposition to this kind of instrumental vision of life, religious culture generally embraces such ideals as stewardship, goodness, and intimacy. By balancing such contrasting practices and ideals we can better leaven technological progress with humane values. A vibrant democracy not only needs technology; it also depends on cultures that will inspire citizens to seek venerable purposes, humane institutions, and intrinsically good customs.

Jacques Ellul summarizes the technological worldview as *la technique*, a state of mind that focuses narrowly on instrumental means of efficiency and control.[83] He argues that contemporary ideologies and market structures tend to idolize the apparent power of technique. Totalitarian systems, for instance, rely increasingly on technique to create effective bureaucracy and propaganda, whereas democratic nations depend on experts and other professionals who master efficiency and control especially for the exploitation of markets. In a market system television and radio compete to deliver audiences to advertisers as cheaply and effectively as possible. The means of technique lead to media that are "messaging" technologies capable of transmitting large quantities of messages to enormous audiences of consumers; broadcasting is one of the most efficient means ever devised for delivering audiences to advertisers. The instrumental worldview anchored to mass-messaging technologies is so attractive that even some religious tribes get caught up in the magic of the technological sublime, hoping to convert large audiences of solitary viewers and listeners into fervent "believers." Technique offers the hope for mass conversion—a hope that is at the heart of the mythos of the electronic church, consumerism, and Communism. Marilynne Robinson suggests that "we cherish a myth of conversion in which we throw off the character our society gives us and put on a new one in all ways vastly superior."[84] Technology tends to run roughshod over culture in democratic societies unless citizens pay as much attention to the quality of life as they do to the quantity and nature of their communication.

Although Americans easily integrate technique with religious culture, tribal traditions within Christianity usually are somewhat at odds with the values of technique. Technology is grounded in its own ultimate "givens," fundamental assumptions about the nature of human cultural activity and the value of efficiency and control for the advancement of the human race. This is why so much popular American rhetoric about technology is deeply salvific. Martin Heidegger imagines the nature of technological activity as an art that echoes the creative acts of God. In his view, human beings use *techne* to fashion the world in their own image; they "bring forth" poetic versions of technological life that in turn become part of life itself. Humans do not simply "use" technology; they "become" technological people whose character reflects the technologies that they adopt. Heidegger even suggests that behind such poetic *techne* is the human desire to overpower death, the most fundamental of all human problems.[85] The cultural frameworks that we produce with technologies can expand or constrict our understanding of technology itself. As the mythos of the electronic church shows, religious tribes' own understanding of technology can be co-opted by broader, extratribal ideas and practices. Theologian James M. Houston warns that today the power of technique is magical for many people, just as technocrats are today's magicians.[86]

Technology offers clear-cut and attractive means, but it never questions its own ends. Democracies, by contrast, require good ends as well as civil means. The common good has to be framed in terms of a worthy telos, such as peace and justice. The good ends of the common life are certainly debatable in a democracy, but clearly they should not be collapsed within technique. Too often technology takes on a life of its own, fed by social institutions that benefit from technique and fostered by experts who exercise their technological know-how on behalf of self-interested organizations. The church, too, tends to restructure tribal culture to make it more compatible with the demands of media technologies; it technologizes worship, dilutes community life, transforms prayer into a self-help technique, replaces sermons and homilies with multimedia presentations, accedes to demands to put congregations "on the air," and replaces its dialogue with the wider society with monologic media evangelism campaigns. If they are not judicious in their technological decisions, religious tribes will find themselves reforming their traditions in the images of efficiency and control. Technique tends to invade every aspect of society, turning technological means into unquestioned and often inhumane ends.

By refusing to become appendages to purely technological means, tribal cultures can help society maintain moral forms of thought and virtuous habits of the heart. Paul Tillich argues that the revolt against industrial society began in the seventeenth century in response to the machinelike worldview of Newtonian physics.[87] From at least Pascal (1623–1662) until the present, Christian tribes from a broad range of traditions have been among those groups protesting the demeaning aspects of overly technological ways of life. They have also courted visions of community and notions of justice that point to virtue rather than technique. Ellul's critique of technological-mindedness is one of the latest and most trenchant theological assessments of new technological invention and expansion. Ellul acted both as a tribal critic speaking candidly to the church and as a general critic committed to speaking to the public about the common good. His goal was not just to reveal our growing reliance on technique, but also to illuminate how unbalanced approaches to technological "progress" lead to moral and religious impoverishment. Ellul became a gadfly, challenging both tribe and public to reconsider the widespread myth that communication technologies are neutral "tools."[88]

Yet the naïve view of media technologies as neutral tools continues to obstruct tribal attempts to establish a full-fledged alternative to simplistic and nonreflective adoption of each new technology.[89] Christians, too, have been among the most unreflective early adopters of new media. Within the broader Christian tradition, however, there are significant assessments of the limitations of technology for improving the quality of life. The Anabaptist emphasis on local community, the Reformed focus on cultural stewardship, and the Catholic commitment to the common good are a few of the Christian traditions that have nurtured some important critiques of technology's impact on venerable ways of life.[90] These habits of the religious heart are more than tribal penchants; they are rhetorical motifs that can help both tribe and public make moral sense of the new technological world and maintain more humane ways of life.

Tribal cultures frequently foster rhetorical strategies for questioning the nearly automatic distribution of new technologies in developed nations. Governmental regulators, communications companies, and some educators wax eloquent about the prospects for "universal" access to new technologies, but they rarely ask the tough questions about the implications of such widespread distribution. What do we lose if everyone is equally plugged in, networked, and wired? Perhaps the critical social issue is not merely equal public access to all media and all types of information, but rather the maintenance of a plurality of cultures that are free to wisely adopt, adapt, or reject technology in tune with their own noninstrumental customs and good ends. After all, humans lose as well as gain whenever they import technology into existing culture. For example, sometimes we acquire a new form of entertainment or information but also give up some intimacy with family and friends. Each religious tradition tends to be sensitive to some of the gains and losses. The pope's pronouncements about the dehumanizing effects of unbridled technological innovation shed different light on technology than we can gain from Ellul's critiques of technique or those of the Shakers, the Amish, and the Mennonites. The range of tribal assessments of communication technologies is itself a rich tapestry of ideas about nurturing time-bound ways of life, promoting the local community, orienting culture to virtue, and maintaining a spiritual quality of life.

Universal technology without cultural diversity will invariably lead to even greater cultural homogeneity. Unless we ask tough questions about the impact of technique, we will threaten the viability of older, more particular modes of oral discourse and time-intensive rituals that frame religious life. Carey reminds us that nontechnological traditions claim "interests in time—history, continuity, permanence, contraction; whose symbols were fiduciary—oral, mythopoetic, religious, ritualistic; and whose communities were rooted in place—intimate ties and a shared historical culture."[91] Before mindlessly adopting new media forms we need to figure out how they can be used in the service of venerable traditions rather than merely for instrumental purposes or narrow self-interests. In technological societies the connection between human means and ends otherwise tends to be lost in the sheer experience of instrumental work and play. Arnold Pacey describes this as "the experience of those who get wrapped up in solving puzzles or building ever more elaborate machines, or who seek esoteric knowledge, and who feel that these things are ends in themselves. Their work often seems imbued with dedication and purposiveness, but without any definable social purpose." Pacey favorably compares this kind of technological "play" to "musical experience" but fails to address the fact that most of the enduring music in the Western world emerged from the efforts of people who worked within communities of faith that held to strong religious and social purposes.[92]

Canada has tried much more self-consciously than the United States to use communication technologies to maintain cultural pluralism. But there, too, technological culture is weakening the nation's traditional ways of life. Canadian journalist George W. Grant, author of *Lament for a Nation: The Defeat of Canadian Nationalism*, suggests that technology is becoming the new Canadian god, the implicit arbiter of culture, and the prime mover of Canadian politics.[93] According to his argument, technology is claiming the very soul of Canadian public life. Coupled with the state, another highly secular force, technology is reformulating and distributing a new, thoroughly secular Canadian identity that reduces cultural pluralism to little more than a formal policy of "multiculturalism." But not one of the cultures included within that easily coined rubric is able any longer to shape Canadian identity politics or to arrest the nation's technological development. The government subsidizes Canadian filmmaking and puts restrictions on the amount of non-Canadian content that can be included in Canadian media, but meanwhile satellites, cable television, and the Internet continue to deliver American popular culture to Canadian tribes. As Innis argued over half a century ago, Canadians ship their natural resources down to the United States, only to receive American culture in return—the very popular culture that weakens traditional cultures within Canada and makes it increasingly unlikely that Canadians will be able to chart their own multicultural future.[94] As goes Canada, so goes the United States, except with greater speed and apparently fewer second thoughts.

The tension between technology and culture is crucially important in contemporary nations that claim to respect and even to value religio-ethnic traditions as a crucial means of preserving moral life. When technology and the state marry, the new entity rationalizes and bureaucratizes culture. Such techno-democratic nations pursue what Carey calls a "high" communication policy "aimed solely at spreading messages further in space and reducing the cost of transmission." Modern states thereby create what Innis dubs "monopolies of knowledge" that centralize decision-making and foster highly rational ways of life.[95] Describing the effects of this kind of technological-mindedness in Canada, Jonathan Mills writes, "The soul has no place in politics: everything psychic (ethnicity, religion, art, the family) exists in the framework provided by the state. Ethnic-religious groups enter this future by being obliterated."[96] Technology and state have reduced traditional, nonrationalized cultures to mere "heritages" and "backgrounds" that have meaning only in the past and offer nothing for the future. Multiculturalism, says Mills, has become "homogenization's hood ornament." Affirming Grant's critique, Mills writes that technology is an "equal-opportunity negator of all ethnic groups," insensitive to the claims of religions and ethnicity. Technology becomes, in Heidegger's phrase, the "ontology of our age."[97] There is then only one major tribe left—the techno-tribe that venerates technique and is fascinated with its own power to manipulate data, compile information, and distribute messages with ever greater speed.

Even if the critics overstate the case against the mindless adoption of technique in modern forms of communication, they raise important questions about our technological pursuits. Religious culture provides not merely an alternative to technological culture but also a variety of tribal rhetorics that might help us to gain coherent insights into the technological milieu. Media technologies unleash torrents of data, information, entertainment, stories, and song that overload our senses and make it increasingly difficult to interpret our existence and value noninstrumental ways of life. The so-called information age is also the era of enormous confusion and anxiety, a time of cultural machinations and social upheavals that are compressing more and more change into ever-shorter periods of time. It no longer makes sense to measure such change by generations. Even siblings live in different cultures, consuming different media products and wearing different clothing. Now the flood of mediated images, words, and sounds is being accelerated by digital technologies that promise to increase bandwidth and expand the smorgasbord of available messages. The Internet is just the most obvious example of this process: digitalization—the computerization of communication—promises to expand audio, video, and text "content" to every available means of instant delivery, from satellites to cable and fiber optics. This is not just information overload; it is a recipe for social entropy and cultural chaos.

Learning how to balance technology and culture will require journalists and other storytellers who are capable of translating tribal understandings of communication technologies into a broader, public language. We need their help discerning what Americans should learn about communication technologies from religious and other traditions. Documentarians can explore the tribal rhetorics of technological discernment, thereby providing an arena for traditional voices to speak to the wider culture. Journalists must get beyond the reporting of facts and the imparting of expert information; in a technological society they need the skill of adding a wider range of voices to public discourse. In Park's language, the journalist needs "not only the ability to feel and empathize" but also "the ability to think and reason with others."[98] A wise and virtuous public emerges in democratic life not as a result of opinion polls, expert testimony, or instantaneous messaging, but instead when the many voices find civil expression and when people then engage in dialogue with the desire to find the common good and work toward it. We need journalists and other communicators who will bring the tribal wisdom into the public sphere so we can understand it and act upon it when it seems good and right to do so. The "essence of culture is understanding," writes Park, and the principal means of producing such understanding is maintaining "the unity and integrity of the social group in its two dimensions—space and time."[99]

The irony is clear: America's primary rhetoric of and for technological discourse, the mythos of the technological sublime, is also a major stumbling block to producing coherent public rhetorics of technological discernment. In

fact, this mythos now is essentially the only national rhetoric of technological understanding, the sole commonly shared set of symbols that Americans
use to make sense of their instrumental pursuits in the twenty-first century.
As I suggested earlier, Wirth perceptively concludes that in order to communicate effectively with one another we must have common knowledge, but
in a mass society it is through communication that we must obtain this common body of knowledge."[100] We are trapped by our own self-referencing le-
gitimization of the very media technologies that we need to assess. For all of
our technical expertise in the United States, we simply do not know what
kind of people we are becoming as a result of our love affair with technique.
Wirth suggests that we must be "content to grope haltingly for such elemen-
tary understandings as can be supplied on the basis of the scanty and superficial common experiences that even the most casual and superficial contact
supplies."[101] We need to hunt for such common experiences within the
tribes as well as across the entire society, monitoring our own personal and
community lives for evidence of what communication technologies mean,
how they shape our cultures, how their values support or undermine our
hopes for a civil and just society, and how we might cultivate rhetorics of
both communion and discernment in a high-tech world.

Edmund V. Sullivan suggests that "critical-commonsense" modes of
thinking cannot come from within a technological system that is enchanted by its own ways of knowing and built upon self-interested means
of discovering truth.[102] Religious cultures are particularly important
sources of commonsense wisdom that has been nurtured over generations
and for the purpose of helping people find their ways wisely in confusing
times. Technological language, by contrast, is too morally vacuous and
nonreflective. Commonsense discourse, seeking simple but profoundly
good virtues, offers society a means of opening up public rhetoric about
media technologies, revealing to us all, in Cooley's words, that "society is
not a machine" but an "expression of human nature, capable of reflecting
whatever good human nature can rise to."[103] Gouldner argues that religion differs from ideology in that people's religious sentiments focus not
merely on discharging political energies but more fundamentally on *everyday life* and its proper conduct." Technological rhetoric, he claims, is
premised on the power of the presented sermon rather than on the authority of the participatory Mass.[104] Freed from its own sermonic, salvific,
and monologic tendencies, religious rhetoric can enable and even ennoble
public participation in discourse about communication technologies, both
by welcoming nonelite persons to the discussion and by broadening the

scope of such discourse from mythos and technics to the central issues of the human condition.

.

Conclusion

In his remarkable study of the social aspects of memory, Connerton contrasts "the storage of present-day information technologies" with the "commemorative ceremonies" of tribal life. Our experience of the present, he contends, always depends upon our knowledge of the past. Moreover, our collective memory of the times gone by is not merely a technical issue of digital storage space or brain chemistry but instead a question of "legitimation, the question of the control and ownership of information being a crucial political issue."[105] Our memories are not blank computer disks but rather recollections negotiated through various media forms and among many different communicators, from media professionals to teachers and pastors. Human communication both depends on memory and creates new memories in an endless process from generation to generation and increasingly from place to place around the world. More than anything else, however, memory is a living cultural repository that can leverage the wisdom of the past creatively on behalf of the present and future. Religious traditions, for instance, sanctify particular memories, noting their particular meaning and relevance and highlighting their value as sources of virtue. We all communicate memorably partly as a means of reminding ourselves who we are, from where we came, and where we should be headed. Religious narratives are among the most powerful forms of shared recollection. Much of our hopeful thinking is retrospective; we remember and thereby believe, as Jesus Christ said at the last meal before his crucifixion.[106]

Democratic nations provide a fertile environment for hope because they transform memories of past revolutions into resources for building the future. Americans use rhetoric not just to converse and to dissect, to entertain and to inform, but also to refashion hopes for new contexts. In short, we use the past to wrap our public rhetoric around a future that we cannot see fully but that we believe to be good and therefore that we wish to make real. All five of the rhetorics addressed in this book—conversion, communion, praise, discernment, and exile—can support the broadly American hopes for a good future. These rhetorics are dynamic ways of continuously reorganizing our lives in order to keep them in line with the much-anticipated future. Taken from the biblical narratives, they enable us to discover the meaning of our otherwise senseless actions and to use our collective memories to work toward the fulfillment of our hopeful desires. In other words, these rhetorical topoi help us to think wisely even when present circumstances would suggest that hope is naively salvific or apocalyptic. The problem is that when we anchor ourselves too tightly to only one of them, we lose the checks and balances that we need to avoid folly.

The rhetoric of conversion is the center of the pentad of hope. The heart of American rhetorical vernacular is a faith in our ability to effect change, especially progress. Such optimism drives the mythos of the electronic revolution, encourages tribal excursions into new media, entices tribal columnists to fight for justice and freedom in American broadcast regulation, motivates tribal media critics to carry out their work for the kingdom of God, and even produces a remarkable tradition of religious journalism that is the precursor to modern news reporting. Taken to an extreme, however, the American drive for change clouds our memories, diminishes our critical faculties, and even produces fanaticism about both religion and technology.

The rhetoric of discernment highlights the gap between what is and what should be in the world. Conversion without discernment is foolhardy. We need to seek good change, not just any change. Discernment can keep us true to ourselves, to a shared vision of the good life, and to the moral customs that keep it good. Discernment without practical reasoning, however, makes conversion impossible. Stagnation is no better than unbridled innovation.

The rhetoric of exile illuminates the conditional character of tribal belief within the larger, heterogeneous world of conflicting cultures. On the one hand, exile seems like the ultimate oppression—a people cast out of the larger society, isolated and then dismissed. Exiled people no longer have a voice in the greater society. On the other hand, exile reminds the tribe that existence is conditional; every tribe faces the possibility of being assimilated by popular culture, converted by the rhetoric of other tribes, or simply subsumed by the monolithic combine of uncontrolled technique. Exile is also a call to self-conversion, a reminder that tribes come and go, that cultural as well as literal death is a reality in a world with more than one tribe. Only in exile can a tribe gain a clear sense of who it is and who it should be.

The rhetoric of communion is a call to faithful community among members of the tribe. It recognizes that no one is an island, that we all depend on others in the journey to be good and faithful people. In liberal-democratic society, however, the tribe shares a broader communion with the public. It must be able to live harmoniously in both the "City of God" and the "City of Man."

When the tribe is being faithful to God and to neighbor, it has a basis for expressing a rhetoric of praise. Praise is the most natural human response to genuinely good rhetorics of conversion, discernment, exile, and communion. To praise the right things requires discernment. Perhaps nothing more authentically defines a people than the objects of its praise.

Biblical metaphors can help us to establish a rhetorical theory of the dynamic relationship between Christianity and the media in democratic America. The interaction of the mass media and Christianity taking place in the United States is not mirrored anywhere else in the world—even in other democracies with Christian tribes. Tocqueville's great work, *Democracy in America*, includes marvelous sections on the interaction of the press and religion. The Frenchman recognized that such interaction was crucial to the functioning of democracy. Park and his colleagues in Chicago rediscovered that fact in the early years of the twentieth century and sought to revitalize the public sphere as a place of shared moral as well as rational discourse. Neither Tocqueville nor Park could have predicted that Americans would eventually squander much of the public life in a race to create a "republic of technology."[107]

The historical sequencing of the case studies in this book is intended to demonstrate that although religion is still a central part of the American experience, it is increasingly serving the purposes of media technology, not the purposes of a just and good republic. Wuthnow rightly argues that "our freedom as a people may ultimately depend more on maintaining a critical perspective toward technology than on accepting it completely as our guiding myth."[108] This is why tribal communities of critical moral discourse are so fundamentally important for the future of democracy, not just for the health of America's religious tribes. Religious criticism of the media provides one means for tribes to maintain a clear sense of their own rhetorical location in the confusion of national, regional, and local cultures. But religious criticism also can serve the wider public with moral vision and theological insight that transcend tribal interests.

Perhaps the greatest challenge the United States faces is cultural continuity. We repeatedly have to remind ourselves who we are as both democratic and tribal people. Mass media tend to abrogate cultural continuity over time, replacing venerable customs and meaningful metanarratives with pecuniary storytelling. Tribal traditions of cultural exegesis and praxis can still provide continuity through generational time as well as across space. It is one thing to create a tribally inspired theory of rhetoric or rhetorical criticism; it is something else altogether to establish a tribal rhetoric that might simultaneously illuminate the dangers of technological mythology, affirm the value of noninstrumental faith amid mainstream secular culture, celebrate democracy as an open form of political life, and nurture the kind of public discourse that recognizes the historical and future value of religion for the common good. Yet that is the kind of tribal rhetoric that we need in the media-saturated America. Oddly enough, the media and Christianity need each other to accomplish this feat.

Notes

Introduction

1. I use the term "America" to refer to the United States of America, although I realize that many other residents of the "Americas" rightly call themselves Americans as well.
2. James W. Carey, *Communication As Culture: Essays on Media and Society* (Boston: Unwin Hyman, 1989).
3. Ibid.
4. Nathan O. Hatch, *The Democratization of American Christianity* (New Haven, Conn.: Yale University Press, 1989); James W. Carey and John J. Quirk, "The Mythos of the Electronic Revolution," in *Communication As Culture*, 113–41.
5. Carey and Quirk, "The Mythos of the Electronic Revolution," 113–41.
6. Two books that supposedly revealed the truth about the entertainment industry in the United States were Kenneth Anger, *Hollywood Babylon* (New York: Dell, 1975); and Anger, *Hollywood Babylon II* (New York: E. P. Dutton, 1984).
7. "Resistance Is Futile," *Business 2.0* (January 1999): 21.
8. Ray Kurzweil, "Pattern Recognition," interview by Daniel P. Dern, *Computerworld* (18 January 1999): 71.
9. Carey, "The Mythos of the Electronic Revolution."
10. Morris Janowitz, preface to *Introduction to the Science of Sociology*, by Robert E. Park and Ernest W. Burgess (Chicago: University of Chicago Press, 1969), xii.
11. Gregor Goethals, *TV Ritual: Worship at the Video Altar* (Boston: Beacon Press, 1981).
12. Daniel J. Czitrom, *Media and the American Mind: From Morse to McLuhan* (Chapel Hill: University of North Carolina Press, 1982).
13. Martin E. Marty, "Denominations near the Century's End," *Stob Lectures of Calvin College and Seminary* (Grand Rapids, Mich.: Calvin College and Seminary, 1991).

Chapter 1

1. Alexis de Tocqueville, *Democracy in America*, ed. and trans. Harvey C. Mansfield and Delba Winthrop (Chicago: University of Chicago Press, 2000), 280.
2. Ibid., 275, 278.
3. Ibid, 355.
4. James Carey, "'A Republic, If You Can Keep It': Liberty and Public Life in the Age of Glasnost," in *James Carey: A Critical Reader*, ed. Eve Stryker Munson and Catherine A. Warren (Minneapolis: University of Minnesota Press, 1997), 216, 217.
5. The Chicago School saw communication as the glue of society, the means of transforming what Dewey called the "Great Community" into the "Great Society." John Dewey, *The Public and Its Problems* (New York: Henry Holt, 1927); see also Jean B. Quandt, *From the Small Town to the Great Community: The Social Thought of Progressive Intellectuals* (New Brunswick, N.J.: Rutgers University Press, 1970). As Park put it, communication is, "if not identical with, at least indispensable to, the cultural process." Wrote Park, "Family group or labor organization, every form of society except the most transient has a life-history and a tradition. It is by communication that this tradition is transmitted. . . . Thus the function of communication seems to be to maintain the unity and integrity of the social group in its two dimensions—space and time." "Communication As Culture," in *Robert E. Park: The Crowd and the Public and Other Essays*, ed. Henry Elsner Jr. (Chicago: University of Chicago Press, 1972), 101, 102. Throughout this chapter and the rest of the book I address the ways that Americans used the media to communicate in space and time their conversations *about* and *for* religion.
6. Martin J. Medhurst and Thomas W. Benson, *Rhetorical Dimensions in Media: A Critical Casebook* (Dubuque, Iowa: Kendall/Hunt, 1984), ix–xxiii.
7. Tocqueville, *Democracy*, 177, 176, 172.
8. Alvin W. Gouldner, *The Dialectic of Ideology and Technology: The Origins, Grammar, and Future of Ideology* (New York: Seabury Press, 1976), 27.
9. As I suggest in Chapter 2, Christian broadcasters and "secular" broadcasters in America are two sides of the same rhetoric of technological hope, what Carey calls the "mythos of the electronic sublime." See James W. Carey, *Communication As Culture: Essays on Media and Society* (Boston: Unwin Hyman, 1989). The term "consumption community"

is from Daniel J. Boorstin, *The Americans: The Democratic Experience* (New York: Random house, 1973), 89–90.

10. For brief summaries of evangelical and mainline approaches to broadcasting, see Quentin J. Schultze, "Keeping the Faith: American Evangelicals and the Media," in *American Evangelicals and the Mass Media*, ed. Quentin J. Schultze (Grand Rapids, Mich.: Zondervan/Academie, 1990), 23–46; Dennis N. Voskuil, "Reaching Out: Mainline Protestantism and the Media," in *Between the Times: The Travail of the Protestant Establishment in America 1900–1960*, ed. William R. Hutchinson (Cambridge: Cambridge University Press, 1989), 72–92; and William F. Fore, "A Short History of Religious Broadcasting," in *Religious Television Programs*, ed. A. William Bleum (New York: Hastings House, 1969), 203–11.

11. On the importance of Sheen, see J. Harold Ellens, *Models of Religious Broadcasting* (Grand Rapids, Mich.: William B. Eerdmans, 1974), 38–44; and Daniel P. Noonan, *The Catholic Communicators: Portraits of Father Charles E. Coughlin, Archbishop Fulton J. Sheen, Pope John Paul II, Mother Angelica, Father Patrick Peyton, Mother Teresa* (Huntington, Ind.: Our Sunday Visitor, 1990).

12. For information on Mother Angelica, see Lou Jacquet, "Mother Angelica: Can Anyone This Nice Be for Real?" *Our Sunday Visitor* (14 August 1988): 8–9; and Noonan, *The Catholic Communicators*.

13. Stephen J. Pullum, "Common Sense Religion for America: The Rhetoric of the Jewish Televangelist Jan Bresky," *Journal of Communication and Religion* 15 (March 1992): 43–54. One could argue that Jewish involvement in American media was primarily ownership and management. See, e.g., Neal Gabler, *An Empire of Their Own: How the Jews Invented Hollywood* (New York: Crown, 1988).

14. For an interesting review of Mennonite use of technology, see Sharon Hartin Iorio, "How Mennonites Use Media in Everyday Life: Preserving Identity in a Changing World," in *Religion and Mass Media: Audiences and Adaptations*, ed. Daniel A. Stout and Judith M. Buddenbaum (Thousand Oaks, Calif.: Sage, 1996), 211–27.

15. David Paul Nord, "The Evangelical Origins of Mass Media in America," *Journalism Monographs* 88 (1984): 1–30.

16. Religious discourse often provides the moral discourse that a political philosophy requires. See Michael J. Sandel, *Democracy's Discontent: America in Search of Public Policy* (Cambridge: The Belknap Press of Harvard University Press, 1996), 323.

17. Harry S. Stout, *The New England Soul: Preaching and Religious Culture in Colonial New England* (New York: Oxford University Press, 1986).
18. Nathan O. Hatch, *The Democratization of American Christianity* (New Haven, Conn.: Yale University Press, 1989).
19. Schultze, "Keeping the Faith"; Voskuil, "Reaching Out"; and Fore, "A Short History of Religious Broadcasting."
20. Carey, *Communication As Culture*, 16–17.
21. Jacques Ellul, *The Technological Society* (New York: Alfred A. Knopf, 1964).
22. Allan Nevins, "The Tradition of the Future," in *Now and Tomorrow*, ed. Tom E. Kakonis and James C. Wilcox (Lexington, Mass.: D. C. Heath, 1971), 396–404.
23. Louis Wirth, "Consensus and Mass Communication," in *On Cities and Social Life*, ed. Albert J. Reiss Jr. (Chicago: University of Chicago Press, 1964), 22, 35.
24. See Daniel J. Czitrom, *Media and the American Mind: From Morse to McLuhan* (Chapel Hill: University of North Carolina Press, 1982), 91–121; Jean B. Quandt, *From the Small Town to the Great Community: The Social Thought of Progressive Intellectuals* (New Brunswick, N.J.: Rutgers University Press, 1970); Fred H. Matthews, *Quest for an American Sociology: Robert E. Park and the Chicago School* (Montreal: McGill-Queen's University Press, 1977); Winifred Raushenbush, *Robert E. Park: A Biography of a Sociologist* (Durham, N.C.: Duke University Press, 1979); and especially James W. Carey, "The Chicago School and the History of Mass Communication Research," in *A Critical Reader*, ed. Stryker and Warren, 14–33.
25. Wirth, "Consensus and Mass Communication," 35.
26. Quoted in Edward M. Berckman, "The Changing Attitudes of Protestant Churches to Movies and Television," *Encounter* 41, no. 3 (summer 1980): 297, 298.
27. Wirth, "Consensus," 38.
28. Paul Greenberg, "A Jewish Boy at Catholic High," *Grand Rapids (Michigan) Press*, 16 December 1997.
29. Carey, "A Republic," 217.
30. Robert E. Park, *Race and Culture* (Glencoe, Ill.: Free Press, 1950), 338.
31. Robert Wuthnow, *The Restructuring of American Religion: Society and Faith since World War II* (Princeton, N.J.: Princeton University Press, 1988).
32. Wirth, "Consensus," 31.
33. Ibid.

34. James W. Carey, "The Communications Revolution and the Professional Communicator," in *A Critical Reader*, ed. Stryker and Warren, 131; and Harold Adams Innis, *The Bias of Communication* (Toronto: University of Toronto Press, 1951).

35. Carey, "The Communications Revolution," 130.

36. Ibid.

37. Joel Carpenter, *Revive Us Again: The Reawakening of American Fundamentalism* (New York: Oxford University Press, 1997).

38. Charles Horton Cooley, *Social Organization: A Study of the Larger Mind* (New York: Schocken Books, 1962), 24.

39. Ibid., 375.

40. Ibid., 376.

41. John Dewey, "Liberating the Social Scientist: A Plea to Unshackle the Study of Man," *Commentary* 4, no. 4 (October 1947): 382.

42. Cooley, *Social Organization*, 377, 379, 381.

43. Robert E. Park, "New As a Form of Knowledge," in *On Social Control and Collective Behavior*, ed. Ralph H. Turner (Chicago: University of Chicago Press, 1967), 33–38.

44. Walter Lippmann, *Public Opinion* (New York: Macmillan, 1922).

45. Carey, "A Republic," 218.

46. See William R. Hutchinson, ed., *American Protestant Thought in the Liberal Era* (New York: University Press of America, 1984).

47. George M. Marsden, *The Soul of the American University: From Protestant Established to Establishment Nonbelief* (New York: Oxford University Press, 2000).

48. For an excellent summary of Williams's thoughts on this issue, see Michael Warren, *Communications and Cultural Analysis: A Religious View* (Westport, Conn.: Bergin and Garvey, 1992), 11–13.

49. See Hanno Hardt, *Social Theories of the Press: Early German and American Perspectives* (Beverly Hills, Calif.: Sage, 1979), 144–45.

50. Carey, "A Republic," 218.

51. St. Augustine, *City of God* (New York: Modern Library, 2000).

52. Carey, "Communications Revolution," 129.

53. Wirth, "Consensus," 35.

54. Ibid.

55. Carey, "A Republic," 218.

56. Barna Research, *Media and Technology* [cited 17 July 2000]. Online: http://www.barna.org/cgi-bin/PageCategory.asp?CategoryID=27.

57. Robert E. Park, "Reflections on Communication and Culture," in *The Crowd*, ed. Elsner, 100.

58. Ibid., 102.

59. Peter Fornatale and Joshua E. Mills, *Radio in the Television Age* (Woodstock, N.Y.: Overlook Press, 1980), 61–91.

60. Czitrom, *Media and the American Mind*, 88.

61. Quentin J. Schultze et al., "Rocking to Images: The Music Television Revolution," in *Dancing in the Dark: Youth, Popular Culture and the Electronic Media* (Grand Rapids, Mich.: William B. Eerdmans, 1991), 178–210.

62. Daniel J. Boorstin, *The Americans: The Democratic Experience* (New York: Random House, 1973), 89–164.

63. Park, "Communication and Culture," 103.

64. See, e.g., David G. Meyer, *The American Paradox: Spiritual Hunger in an Age of Plenty* (New Haven, Conn.: Yale University Press, 2000).

65. Donald B. Rogers, "Maintaining Faith Identity in a Television Culture: Strategies of Response for a People in Exile," in *Changing Channels: The Church and the Television Revolution*, ed. Tyron Inbody (Dayton, Ohio: Whaleprints, 1990), 147.

66. Ibid., 153.

67. Arthur W. H. Adkins, "Myth, Philosophy, and Religion in Ancient Greece," in *Myth and Philosophy*, ed. Frank Reynolds and David Tracy (Albany: State University of New York Press, 1990), 96.

68. Ibid.

69. Richard J. Neuhaus, *The Naked Public Square*, 2nd ed. (Grand Rapids, Mich.: William B. Eerdmans, 1984).

70. Quentin J. Schultze and William D. Romanowski, "Praising God in Opryland," *Reformed Journal* 39, no. 11 (November 1989): 10–14; also see William D. Romanowski, "Contemporary Christian Music: The Business of Music Ministry," in *American Evangelicals*, ed. Schultze, 143–70; and Charlie Peacock, *At the Crossroads: An Insider's Look at the Past, Present, and Future of the Contemporary Christian Music* (Nashville, Tenn.: Broadman and Holman, 1999).

71. David Paul Nord, "Religious Publishing and the Marketplace," in *Communication and Change in American Religious History*, ed. Leonard I. Sweet (Grand Rapids, Mich.: William B. Eerdmans, 1993), 269.

72. R. Laurence Moore, *Religious Outsiders and the Making of Americans* (New York: Oxford University Press, 1986).

73. For analysis of Jerry Falwell and the Christian Coalition, see Gabriel Fackre, *The Religious Right and Christian Faith* (Grand Rapids, Mich.: William B. Eerdmans, 1982).

74. Wendy Murray Zoba, "Daring to Discipline America," *Christianity Today* (1 March 1999): 31–38.

75. Wirth, "Consensus," 25.

76. Ibid., 18–43.

77. Amish and Mennonite rejection of some communication technologies, for instance, is based on the desire to maintain distinctive identities rather than be fully co-opted by mainstream culture. See Wendell Berry, *The Unsettling of America: Culture and Agriculture* (San Francisco: Sierra Club Books, 1977); Howard Rheingold, "Look Who's Talking," *Wired* (January 1999): 128–31, 160–63; and Jamie Sharp, *The Amish: Technology Practice and Technological Change* [cited 24 May 2001]. Online: http://www.loyola.edu/dept/philosophy/techne/sharp.html.

78. Sandel, *Democracy's Discontent*, 66.

79. Rogers, "Maintaining Faith," 153.

80. Jean Bethke Elshtain, *Who Are We?: Critical Reflections and Hopeful Possibilities* (Grand Rapids, Mich.: William B. Eerdmans, 2000), 63.

81. Quentin J. Schultze, *Televangelism and American Culture: The Business of Popular Religion* (Grand Rapids, Mich.: Baker Book House, 1991), 39–41.

82. Wendell Berry sounds like a radical when he writes, "I do not see that computers are bringing us one step nearer to anything that does matter to me: peace, economic justice, ecological health, political honesty, family and community stability, good work." *What Are People For?* (New York: North Point Press, 1990), 172.

83. John Lukacs, introduction to *Confessions of an Original Sinner* (South Bend, Ind.: St. Augustine's Press, 2000), xiv.

84. For an excellent review of the changing meanings of the word "popular" in the English language, see Raymond Williams, *Keywords: A Vocabulary of Culture and Society*, rev. ed. (New York: Oxford University Press, 1983), 237–38.

85. Schultze and Romanowski, "Praising God," 11.

86. This is discussed cogently in Raymond Williams, "On High and Popular Culture," *The New Republic* 23 (November 1974): 13–16; see also William D. Romanowski, *Pop Culture Wars: Religion and the Role of Entertainment in American Life* (Downers Grove, Ill.: InterVarsity Press, 1996).

87. Park, "Communication and Culture," 101.

88. See, e.g., Horace Newcomb, ed., *Television: The Critical View*, 4th ed. (New York: Oxford University Press, 1987); E. Ann Kaplan, ed., *Regarding Television: Critical Approaches: An Anthology* (Frederick, Md.:

University Publications of America, 1983); John Fiske and John Hartley, *Reading Television* (London: Methuen, 1978); and Todd Gitlin, ed., *Watching Television* (New York: Pantheon, 1986).

89. I suggest three reasons for this. First, much television criticism is done by people who like to watch a lot of television rather than study television. Second, art criticism in general today is under the shadow of modern subjectivism, which holds that there really are no standards for criticism; one critic's views are as "accurate" as any other critic's views. Third, the field of communication produces many researchers who are methodologically sophisticated but theoretically uneducated.

90. Wirth, "Consensus," 19–20.

91. Park, "Communication and Culture," 102.

92. James Carey, "The Chicago School and the History of Mass Communication Research," in *A Critical Reader*, ed. Munson and Warren, 14–33.

93. Many of these historical developments are addressed in a special issue of the *Journal of Communication* 33 (summer 1983) entitled "Ferment in the Field."

94. Quoted in Park, "Communication and Culture," 103.

95. See Hardt, *Social Theories of the Press*, 144.

96. Leonard I. Sweet, "Communication and Change in American Religious History: A Historiographical Probe," in *Communication and Change*, ed. Sweet, 30.

97. Tocqueville, *Democracy*, 275.

98. For a contrast of the bardic versus the priestly functions of rhetoric, see Thomas M. Lessl, "The Priestly Voice," *Quarterly Journal of Speech* 75 (1989): 183–97.

99. Romanowski, *Pop Culture Wars*.

100. Louis Wirth, *Louis Wirth on Cities and Social Life* (Chicago: University of Chicago Press, 1982), 35.

101. James W. Carey and John J. Quirk, "The Mythos of the Electronic Revolution," in *Communication As Culture*, 113–41.

102. Quoted in Eugene H. Peterson, *The Wisdom of Each Other* (Grand Rapids, Mich.: Zondervan, 1998), 96.

103. William F. Fore, "A Short History of Religious Broadcasting," in *Religious Television Programs*, ed. A. William Bleum (New York: Hastings House, 1969), 209.

104. See Romanowski, *Pop Culture Wars*.

105. Peterson, *Wisdom*, 43, 37.

106. Carey, "A Republic," 217.

Chapter 2

1. *CNN Today,* "Viewers Call In with Comments on Hubble Sightings" (aired 3 November 1995).

2. Kenneth Burke, *The Philosophy of Literary Form* (Berkeley: University of California Press, 1973), 4.

3. Kenneth Burke, *Permanence and Change* (Indianapolis: Bobbs-Merrill, 1965), 74.

4. Ibid.

5. James W. Carey and John J. Quirk, "The Mythos of the Electronic Revolution," *American Scholar* 39 (1970): 220.

6. Robert E. Park and Ernest W. Burgess, *Introduction to the Science of Sociology* (Chicago: University of Chicago Press, 1969), 30, 35.

7. Darrell J. Fasching, "Technology As Utopian Technique of the Human," *Soundings* 63 (1980): 138.

8. Ibid.

9. Robert E. Park, "Social Planning and Human Nature," in *Robert E. Park: The Crowd and the Public and Other Essays,* ed. Henry Elsner Jr. (Chicago: University of Chicago Press, 1972), 91.

10. Carl L. Becker, *The Idea of Progress since the Renaissance,* ed. Warren W. Wagar (New York: John Wiley and Sons, 1969), 12.

11. Ibid.; Ernst Benz, *Evolution and the Christian Hope* (New York: Doubleday, 1966); Fred L. Polak, *The Image of the Future* (New York: Braziller, 1971); T. H. Van Leeuwen, *Christianity in World History* (New York: Charles Scribner and Sons, 1960); and Kenneth Vaux, *To Create a Different Future: Religious Hope and Technological Planning* (New York: Friendship Press, 1972).

12. Kenneth Vaux, *Subduing the Cosmos: Cybernetics and Man's Future* (Richmond, Va.: John Knox Press, 1970), 126.

13. Genesis 1:28–29.

14. Paul Marshall, "Is Technology Out of Control?," *Crux* 20, no. 3 (September 1984): 5.

15. Ibid.

16. Genesis 11.

17. Robert A. Wauzzinski, "Technological Optimism," *Perspectives on Science and Christian Faith* 48, no. 3 (September 1996): 145.

18. David F. Noble, *The Religion of Technology: The Divinity of Man and the Spirit of Invention* (New York: Alfred A. Knopf, 1997), 29.

19. Ibid.

20. Pauline Moffitt Watts, "Prophecy and Discovery: On the Spiritual Origins of Christopher Columbus's 'Enterprise of the Indies,'" *American Historical Review* 90 (1985): 73–102.

21. Howard P. Segal, *Technological Utopianism in American Culture* (Chicago: University of Chicago Press, 1985).

22. Quoted in ibid., 59.

23. Wauzzinski, "Technological Optimism," 144–45.

24. Segal, *Technological Utopianism*, 74–75.

25. For a review of the history of the idea of progress in Western thought, see Carl L. Becker, "Definitions and Origins," in *The Idea of Progress*, ed. Wagar, 9–18.

26. Howard Mumford Jones, *O Strange New World* (New York: Viking Press, 1965), 36–37.

27. David Copeland, "Religion and Colonial Newspapers," in *Media and Religion in American History*, ed. William David Sloan (Northport, Ala.: Vision Press, 2000), 55.

28. Vernon L. Parrington, *American Dreams: A Study of American Utopias*, 2nd ed. (New York: Russell and Russell, 1964).

29. Henry Nash Smith, *Virgin Land* (New York: Vintage Books, 1950); and Leo Marx, *The Machine in the Garden* (New York: Oxford University Press, 1964).

30. Otto F. Kraushaar, "America, Symbol of a Fresh Start," in *Utopias: The American Experience*, ed. Gairdner B. Moment and Otto F. Kraushaar (Metuchen, N.J.: Scarecrow Press, 1980), 11–29.

31. Quoted in Lois Rose and Stephen Rose, *The Shattered Ring: Science Fiction and the Quest for Meaning* (Richmond, Va.: John Knox Press, 1970), 18.

32. Ernst Tuveson, *Redeemer Nation: The Idea of America's Millennial Role* (Chicago: University of Chicago Press, 1968).

33. Noble, *Religion of Technology*, 5.

34. Perry Miller, *The Life of the Mind in America: From the Revolution to the Civil War* (New York: Harcourt, Brace and World, 1965), 275.

35. Wendell Berry, *The Unsettling of America: Culture and Agriculture* (San Francisco: Sierra Club Books, 1977), 56.

36. Miller, *Life of the Mind*, 52.

37. Kenneth M. Roemer, *The Obsolete Necessity: America in Utopian Writings, 1888–1900* (Kent, Ohio: Kent State University Press, 1976), 172.

38. Wauzzinski, "Technological Optimism," 145, 146.

39. Miller, *Life of the Mind*, 52.

40. Carolyn Marvin, *When Old Technologies Were New: Thinking About Electric Communication in the Late Nineteenth Century* (New York: Oxford University Press, 1988), 232, 233.

41. Ibid., 64.

42. Daniel J. Czitrom, *Media and the American Mind: From Morse to McLuhan* (Chapel Hill: University of North Carolina Press, 1982).

43. Quoted in Frank A. Reel, *The Networks* (New York: Charles Scribner and Sons, 1979), 96.

44. H. Richard Niebuhr, *The Kingdom of God in America* (Chicago: Willett, Clark, 1937), 179.

45. David Paul Nord, "Systematic Benevolence: Religious Publishing and the Marketplace in Early Nineteenth-Century America," in *Communication and Change in American Religious History*, ed. Leonard I. Sweet (Grand Rapids, Mich.: William B. Eerdmans, 1993), 242.

46. David Paul Nord, "The Evangelical Origins of Mass Media in America: 1815–1835," in *Media and Religion*, ed. Sloan, 69.

47. Quoted in James H. Moorhead, "The Millennium and the Media," in *Communication and Change*, ed. Sweet, 221.

48. David Paul Nord, "The Evangelical Origins of the Mass Media in America," *Journalism Monographs* 88 (1984); see also Nord, "Systematic Benevolence."

49. Nord, "Systematic Benevolence," 246.

50. Ibid., 241.

51. Ibid., 247.

52. Jean B. Quandt, "Religion and Social Thought: The Secularization of Postmillennialism," *American Quarterly* 25 (October 1973): 391.

53. Quoted in ibid., 404, 409.

54. Moorhead, "Millennium and the Media," 223.

55. Quoted in ibid., 224.

56. Ibid., 225.

57. Leonard I. Sweet, "Communication and Change in American Religious History," in *Communication and Change*, ed. Sweet, 48.

58. Quoted in Carol Sue Humphrey, "Religious Newspapers and Antebellum Reform," in *Media and Religion*, ed. Sloan, 109.

59. Leonard I. Sweet, "'A Nation Born Again': The Union Prayer Meeting Revival and Cultural Revitalization," in *The Great Tradition*, ed. Joseph D. Ban and Paul R. Dekar (Valley Forge, Pa.: Judson Press, 1982), 206.

60. Quoted in ibid.

61. Robert S. Fortner, "The Church and the Debate over Radio: 1919–1949," in *Media and Religion*, ed. Sloan, 235.

62. For more on evangelicalism as an integral part of the modernization process in America, see Grant Wacker, "Uneasy in Zion: Evangelicals in Postmodern Society," in *Evangelicalism and Modern America*, ed. George M. Marsden (Grand Rapids, Mich.: William B. Eerdmans, 1984), 17–28.

63. For an analysis of Catholic views of the media, see Robert White, "Mass Media and Culture in Contemporary Catholicism," in *Vatican II: Assessment and Perspectives: Twenty-Five Years After (1962–1987)*, ed. René Latourelle (New York: Paulist Press, 1989).

64. Douglas Frank, *Less Than Conquerors: How Evangelicals Entered the Twentieth Century* (Grand Rapids, Mich.: William B. Eerdmans, 1986), 27.

65. James W. Carey, *Communication As Culture: Essays on Media and Society* (Boston: Unwin Hyman, 1989), 15.

66. Ibid., 34.

67. Ben Armstrong, "Christian Broadcasting Produces Fast-Growing Churches," *Religious Broadcasting* (March 1988): 22.

68. George M. Marsden, *Reforming Fundamentalism* (Grand Rapids, Mich.: William B. Eerdmans, 1987), 2.

69. For instance, see James Engel, *What's Gone Wrong with the Harvest?: A Communication Strategy for the Church and World Evangelism* (Grand Rapids, Mich.: Zondervan, 1995); and Engel, *How Can I Get Them to Listen?* (Grand Rapids, Mich.: Zondervan, 1977).

70. John Bachman, "The Next Age and Stage of BFC" (address delivered at the meeting of the Broadcasting and Film Commission Board of Managers of the National Council of Churches of Christ in the USA, New York, 7 February 1964).

71. "Big Churches Learn Radio 'Savvy' to Counter Revivalist Racket," *Newsweek* (22 January 1945): 74, 76; and Wilbur M. Smith, *The Life of Charles E. Fuller* (Boston: W. A. Wilde, 1949).

72. George M. Marsden, *Fundamentalism and American Culture: The Shaping of Twentieth-Century Evangelicalism, 1870–1925* (New York: Oxford University Press, 1980), 224–5.

73. Eugene Bertermann, "The Radio for Christ," *United Evangelical Action* (March 1949): 3.

74. Quoted in Glenwood Blackmore, "NRB Sees Great Gains in Radio-TV Cooperation," *United Evangelical Action* (March 1957): 3.

75. Edward Berckman, "The Changing Attitudes of Protestant Churches to Movies and Television," *Encounter* 41 (summer 1980): 293–306.

76. Quoted in "Two Analyses of Religious Broadcasting," *Christianity Today* (August 1960): 33, 38.

77. Jerry Falwell and Elmer Towns, *The Church Aflame* (Nashville, Tenn.: Impact Books, 1971), 75.

78. Jerry Falwell and Elmer Towns, *Capturing a Town for Christ* (Old Tappan, N.J.: Fleming H. Revell, 1973), 7.

79. William H. Foulkes, *The Message and Method of the New Evangelism*, ed. J. M. Bader (New York: Round Table Press, 1937), 230, 233.

80. Falwell and Towns, *Capturing a Town*, 74.

81. Jimmy Swaggart, "Divine Imperatives for Broadcast Ministry," *Religious Broadcasting* (November 1984): 14.

82. Quoted in Robert Walker, "The Rising Tide," *Christian Life* (January 1984): 35.

83. "Outreach to the Masses," *Christianity Today* (September 1968): 35.

84. Evangelicals cite as a biblical basis for this commission Matthew 28:19, "Therefore go and make disciples of all nations, baptizing them in the name of the Father and of the Son and of the Holy Spirit" (New International Version).

85. Taken from author's notes on a 1986 broadcast of *Jimmy Swaggart Ministries.*

86. For an understanding of fundamentalist beliefs and practices, including their views about the Second Coming, see Marsden, *Fundamentalism and American Culture.*

87. John Lippman, "Global Village Is Characterized by a Television in Every Home," *Grand Rapids (Michigan) Press*, 25 October 1992, F9.

88. James W. Carey and John J. Quirk, "The Mythos of the Electronic Revolution," in *Communication As Culture*, 113–41.

89. I mean by "evangelical" those Christians, from whatever denominations or religious background, who emphasize (1) the Reformation doctrine of the final authority of Scripture; (2) the real, historical character of God's saving work recorded in Scripture; (3) eternal salvation only through personal trust in Christ; (4) the importance of evangelism (proclaiming the gospel of Christ to others) and missions; and (5) the importance of a spiritually transformed life. Marsden, introduction to *Evangelicalism and Modern America*, ix–x. Mainline Christian churches are typically members of the large, well-known denominations—Presbyterians, Lutherans, Methodists, and so forth. There are, however, evangelical members of all of the mainline denominations, and some local churches within these denominations are evangelical. In this study mainline American Protestantism is

associated generally with the Federal Council of Churches and its successor, the National Council of Churches, both instruments of these large denominations.

90. The critics included Bruce Edwards, "The Mission and the Medium," *Mission Journal* (May 1981): 4–9; Malcolm Muggeridge, *Christ and the Media* (Grand Rapids, Mich.: William B. Eerdmans, 1971); Virginia Stem Owens, *The Total Image: Or Selling Jesus in the Modern Age* (Grand Rapids, Mich.: William B. Eerdmans, 1980); and C. Schalk, "Religion in America and the Churches' Use of the Mass Media," *Concordia Theological Monthly* 33 (June 1962): 337–49.

91. Ben Armstrong, "The Electric Church at 65," *Religious Broadcasting* (February 1986): 78–80.

92. "New Era for Christian Communication," *Christianity Today* (October 1966): 3.

93. George N. Patterson, "The Communications Revolution and the Christian Gospel," *Christianity Today* (22 November 1968): 3–6.

94. Theodore H. Elsner, "NRB-Ever-Present Help in Evangelical Radio," *United Evangelical Action* (March 1949): 5–6.

95. Armstrong, "Electric Church at 65," 80.

96. Eugene R. Bertermann, "Mass Media: Opportunity and Obligation," *United Evangelical Action* (February 1967): 13, 31.

97. Ben Armstrong, "The Year of Evangelism," *Religious Broadcasting* (June/July 1974): 2.

98. Ben Armstrong, *The Electric Church* (Nashville, Tenn.: Thomas Nelson, 1979), 8–9.

99. Ibid., 10–11, 171.

100. Revelation 14:6, quoted in ibid., 172–73.

101. "McLuhan on Religion," *Christianity Today* (13 February 1970): 34.

102. Armstrong, *Electric Church*, 12.

103. Allen Nevins, "The Tradition of the Future," in *The Tradition of the Future: Now and Tomorrow*, ed. Tom E. Kakonis and James C. Wilcox (Lexington, Mass.: D. C. Heath, 1971).

104. Robert Walker, "The Rising Tide," *Christian Life* (January 1984): 31–33.

105. Robert G. Clouse, "The New Christian Right, America, and the Kingdom of God," *Christian Scholar's Review* 12 (1983): 3–16.

106. Robertson even ran unsuccessfully for the Republican presidential nomination in 1992.

107. See Pat Robertson, *The End of the Age* (Waco, Tex.: Word Books, 1998); and Jerry Falwell, *Falwell: An Autobiography* (Billings, Mont.: Liberty House Press, 1997).

108. See Harry S. Stout, *The Divine Dramatist: George Whitefield and the Rise of Modern Evangelicalism* (Grand Rapids, Mich.: William B. Eerdmans, 1991).

109. Nord, "Systematic Benevolence," 239–69.

110. See Leigh Brackett, *The Long Tomorrow* (Garden City, N.Y.: Doubleday, 1955).

111. For an analysis of the novel by a Mennonite critic, see Elmer F. Suderman, "Mennonite Culture in a Science Fiction Novel," *Mennonite Quarterly Review* 49 (1975): 53–56.

112. Quoted in Ermine Huntress Lantero, "What Is Time?: More Theological Aspects of Science Fiction," *Religion in Life* 40 (1971): 424.

113. James Blish, "The Tale That Wags the God: The Function of Science Fiction," *American Libraries* 1 (1970): 1029–33; Blish's books include *A Case of Conscience* (New York: Ballantine Books, 2000) and *Dusk of Idols* (New York: Severn House, 1996).

114. Win Arn, "A Church Growth Look at 'Here's Life America,'" *Church Growth: America* (January/February 1978); J. Harold Ellens, *Models of Religious Broadcasting* (Grand Rapids, Mich.: William B. Eerdmans, 1974); Peter Horsfield, *Religious Television* (New York: Longman, 1984); David Paul Oberdorfer, *Electronic Christianity: Myth or Ministry* (Taylor Falls, Minn.: John L. Brekke and Sons, 1982); Tim Stafford, "Evangelism: The New Wave Is a Tidal Wave," *Christianity Today* (18 May 1984): 42–43; and Peter C. Wagner, "Who Found It?" *Eternity* (September 1977): 13–19.

115. Nathan O. Hatch, "Evangelicalism As a Democratic Movement," in *Evangelicalism and Modern America*, ed. Marsden, 82.

116. For background on televangelism as a poltical movement, see Jeffrey K. Hadden and Charles E. Swann, *Prime Time for Preachers: The Rising Power of Televangelism* (Reading, Mass.: Addison-Wesley, 1981).

117. Robert Galbreath, "Fantastic Literature As Gnosis," *Extrapolation* 29 (1988): 331.

118. Stephen May, "Salvation, Culture and Science Fiction," in *Christ in Our Place: The Humanity of God in Christ for the Reconciliation of the World*, ed. Trevor A. Hart and Daniel P. Thimell (Exeter, England: Paternoster Press, 1989), 337–38.

119. Arend Theodoor Van Leeuwen, *Prophecy in a Technocratic Era* (New York: Charles Scribner and Sons, 1968).

120. Jerry Falwell, "Church and Media: The Vital Partnership," *Religious Broadcasting* (January 1981): 55.

121. Peter M. Lowentrout, "Religion and Speculative Fiction," *Extrapolation* 29 (1988): 319.

122. Van Leeuwen, *Prophesy*, 41.

123. Matthew 28:19–20.

124. James W. Carey and John J. Quirk, "The History of the Future," in *Communication Technology and Social Policy*, ed. George Gerbner, Larry Gross, and William H. Melody (New York: John Wiley and Sons, 1975): 502.

125. Theodore Sturgeon, "Science Fiction, Morals and Religion," in *Science Fiction, Today and Tomorrow: A Discursive Symposium*, ed. Reginald Bretnor (New York: Harper and Row, 1974), 100, 101, 112. For a contrary view, namely, that science fiction writers understand science more than religion, see Ermine Huntress Lantero, "What Is Man? Theological Aspects of Contemporary Science Fiction," *Religion in Life* 38 (summer 1969): 242–55.

126. Peter M. Lowentrout, "The Meta-Aesthetic of Popular Science Fiction Film," *Extrapolation* 29 (1988): 363.

127. Carol Murphy, "The Theology of Science Fiction," *Approach* 23 (spring 1957): 2, 7.

128. Polak, *Image*.

129. For my arguments about evangelicals' lack of interest in tradition, see Quentin J. Schultze, "Keeping the Faith: American Evangelicals and the Mass Media," in *American Evangelicals and the Mass Media*, ed. Quentin J. Schultze (Grand Rapids, Mich.: Zondervan, 1990), 23–29.

130. Willis E. McNelly, "Science Fiction and Religion," *America* (10 May 1980): 397.

131. J. Norman King, "Theology, Science Fiction, and Man's Future Orientation," in *Many Futures Many Worlds: Theme and Form in Science Fiction*, ed. Thomas D. Clareson (Kent, Ohio: Kent State University Press, 1977), 238.

132. Ibid., 257.

133. Frederick A. Kreuziger, *The Religion of Science Fiction* (Bowling Green, Ohio: Bowling Green State University Popular Press, 1986), 2. See also Kreuziger, *Apocalypse and Science Fiction: A Dialectic of Religious and Secular Soteriologies* (Chico, Calif.: Scholars Press, 1982).

134. See, e.g., Robert Galbreath, "Ambiguous Apocalypse: Transcendental Versions of the End," in *The End of the World*, ed. Eric S. Rabkin,

Martin H. Greenberg, and Joseph D. Olander (Carbondale: Southern Illinois University Press, 1983), 53.

135. C. Wright Mills, "The Social Role of the Intellectual," in *Power, Politics and People: The Collected Essays of C. Wright Mills*, ed. Irving L. Horowitz (New York: Ballantine, 1963), 302.

136. R. Laurence Moore, *Religious Outsiders and the Making of Americans* (New York: Oxford University Press, 1986), 302, 6.

137. Kenneth M. Roemer, *The Obsolete Necessity: America in Utopian Writings, 1888–1900* (Kent, Ohio: Kent State University Press, 1976).

138. Irving Hexham, "Science Fiction, Christianity, and Technical Civilization," *Word and World: Theology for Christian Ministry* 4 (winter 1984): 41.

139. Ibid.

140. C. W. Sprinks, "Prophecy, Pulp or Punt: Science Fiction, Scenarios, and Values" (paper presented at the annual conference of the World Future Education Society, Dallas, 13–16 February 1983), 3.

141. Harvey Cox and Anne Foerst, "Religion and Technology: A New Phase," *Bulletin of Science, Technology and Society* 17 (1997): 53, 54–55.

142. Louis Wirth, "Preface to *Ideology and Utopia*," in *On Cities and Social Life*, ed. Albert J. Reiss Jr. (Chicago: University of Chicago Press, 1964), 139.

143. Neil P. Hurley, "Hollywood's New Mythology," *Theology Today* 39 (January 1983): 402–8.

144. H. McKennie Goodpasture, *Cross and Sword: An Eyewitness History of Christianity in Latin America* (New York: Orbis Books, 1989); David Martin, *Tongues of Fire: The Explosion of Protestantism in Latin America* (Oxford: Basil Blackwell, 1990); David Stoll, *Is Latin America Turning Protestant?: The Politics of Evangelical Growth* (Berkeley: University of California Press, 1990); and Carlos Alberto Torres, *The Church, Society, and Hegemony: A Critical Sociology of Religion in Latin America* (Westport, Conn.: Praeger, 1992).

145. Timothy George, "Apocalyptic Fever: After Repeated End-Times Embarrassments, How Can the Church Rightly Read the Signs of the Times?" *Christianity Today* (14 December 1992): 12.

146. See Sandeep Junnarker and Jim Hu, "AOL Buys Time Warner in Historic Merger," *CNet*, 10 January 2000 [cited 23 November 2001]. Online: http://news.cnet.com/news/0–1001–202–1518888.html.

147. Phyllis Mather Rice, "Interview with Pat Robertson," *Your Church* (May/June): 1979, 5.

148. For background on Robertson's media endeavors, see Alec Foege, *The Empire God Built: Inside Pat Robertson's Media Machine* (New York: John Wiley and Sons, 1996). For background on Murdoch's media empire and his acquisition of the Family Channel, see Marc Gunther, "The Rules According to Rupert," *Fortune*, October 1998 [cited 23 November 2001]. Online: http://www.business2.com/articles/mag/print/ 0,1643,4303,FF.html. For information on Murdoch's sale to Disney, see Jonathan Stemple, "Disney Sells Debt to Buy Back Stock," *Reuters*, 17 September 2001 [cited 23 November 2001]. Online: http://biz.yahoo.com/rb/010917/business_leisure_disney_goldman_d c_1.html.

149. Alan Trachtenberg, *The Incorporation of America* (New York: Hill and Wang, 1982).

150. Jamie Buckingham, "Interview with Pat Robertson," *Charisma* (April 1983): 28.

151. John Kasson, *Civilizing the Machine: Technology and Republican Values in America 1776–1900* (New York: Penguin, 1977), 233.

152. Razelle Frankl, *Televangelism: The Marketing of Religion* (Carbondale: Southern Illinois University Press, 1987); and Owens, *Total Image.*

153. Jimmy Swaggart, "Divine Imperatives for Broadcast Ministry," *Religious Broadcasting* (November 1984): 14.

154. Quentin J. Schultze, "Vindicating the Electronic Church? An Assessment of the Annenberg/Gallup Study," *Critical Studies in Mass Communication* 2, no. 3 (1985): 283–90.

155. Daniel J. Boorstin, *The Republic of Technology: Reflections on Our Future Community* (New York: Harper and Row, 1978), 11.

156. Harold Adams Innis, *The Bias of Communication* (Toronto: University of Toronto Press, 1951).

157. "Training the World's Evangelists," *Christianity Today* (5 September 1986): 40–43.

158. Frederic Elkin, *Rebels and Colleagues: Advertising and Social Change in French Canada* (Montreal: McGill-Queen's University Press, 1973), part 3.

159. William F. Fore, "A New World Order in Communication," *Christian Century* 14 (April 1982): 442.

160. Paul Robinson, "Should Canada Allow Christian Radio and Television Stations?" *Christianity Today* (5 March 1982): 81–84.

161. Robert E. Park, "Reflections On Communication and Culture," in *The Crowd*, ed. Elsner, 98.

162. John G. Cawelti, "With the Benefit of Hindsight: Popular Culture Criticism," *Critical Studies in Mass Communication* 2 (December 1985): 363.
163. Reinhold Niebuhr, *Faith and History* (New York: Charles Scribner and Sons, 1949).
164. O. B. Hardison Jr., *Disappearing through the Skylight: Culture and Technology in the 20th Century* (New York: Viking, 1989).
165. Wagar, *Idea of Progress*, 192.

Chapter 3

1. J. David Valaik, "American Catholic Dissenters and the Spanish Civil War," *Catholic Historical Review* 53, no. 4 (January 1968): 537, 538–39, 540, 541.
2. Ibid., 542–44, 547, 548, 552.
3. James W. Carey, "The Problem of Journalism History," in *James Carey: A Critical Reader*, ed. Eve Stryker Munson and Catherine A. Warren (Minneapolis: University of Minnesota Press, 1997), 88.
4. Robert E. Park, "Human Migration and the Marginal Man," in *Robert E. Park: On Social Control and Collective Behavior*, ed. Ralph H. Turner (Chicago: University of Chicago Press, 1967), 194–206.
5. Robert E. Park, "The Urban Community as a Spatial Pattern and Moral Order," in *On Social Control*, ed. Turner, 65.
6. I take the term "natural history" from Robert E. Park, "The Natural History of the Newspaper," in *On Social Control*, ed. Turner, 97–113.
7. Although I do not address in this chapter all of the relevant articles from these periodicals over the fifty-year period, I try to be as even-handed as possible with the examples used. Before writing this chapter I reviewed every article on the subject of broadcasting published between 1920 and 1970 in these five religious periodicals—and a few other periodicals that I did not have the space to include. I decided not to include articles appearing after 1970 because of the subsequent growth of new communication technologies, such as cable and satellites, which are used more for narrowcasting than for broadcasting. Carey argues that from about 1970 through the end of the century the mass media in America increasingly specialized and diversified audiences into all kinds of demographic categories, lifestyles, and special-interest groups. James W. Carey, "Afterword: The Culture in Question," in *A Critical Reader*, ed. Munson and Warren, 323–4. I also selected for this chapter religious journals that I believed would represent identifiable groups or movements within Catholicism and

Protestantism. I was particularly interested in the unofficial, nondenominational periodicals because they often have the freedom to develop a more independent and perhaps even a more prophetic voice in public conversations about religion and religious issues. While the periodicals used in this research are arguably not representative of all of American Christendom, perhaps they do represent the major streams of thought. Unfortunately, the periodical that I chose to illustrate the evangelical position, *Christianity Today*, did not begin publication until 1956. Thus this chapter does not include an examination of evangelical interpretations of the early development of radio, although it is arguable as to whether there even existed a modern evangelical movement or identity prior to World War II, after which evangelicals established numerous nonsectarian publications, seminaries, and parachurch organizations largely as alternatives to both fundamentalist and mainline Protestant institutions.

8. Sister Mary Patrice Thaman, *Manners and Morals of the 1920's: A Survey of the Religious Press* (New York: Bookman, 1954), 167, 168, 169.

9. Mediation is discussed in Stewart M. Hoover and Knut Lundby, "Summary Remarks: Mediated Religion," in *Rethinking Media*, ed. Hoover and Lundby, 308.

10. Clifford G. Christians, "Technology and Triadic Theories of Mediation," in *Rethinking Media*, ed. Hoover and Lundby, 73.

11. Stewart M. Hoover, *Religion in the News* (Thousand Oaks, Calif.: Sage, 1998), 151.

12. Ibid.

13. Mark Silk, *Unsecular Media: Making News of Religion in America* (Urbana: University of Illinois Press, 1995), 25.

14. Quoted in Dennis N. Voskuil, "Reaching Out: Mainline Protestantism and the Media," in *Between the Times: The Travail of the Protestant Establishment in America 1900–1960*, ed. William R. Hutchinson (Cambridge: Cambridge University Press, 1989), 73.

15. Ibid.

16. Robert E. Park, "Spatial Pattern and a Moral Order," in *On Social Control*, ed. Turner, 65.

17. Voskuil, "Reaching Out," 75, 74.

18. Martin E. Marty, "Fragile Starts," *Christian Century* (in this chapter hereafter referred to as *CC*) 101 (4–11 July 1984): 695.

19. Michael R. Real, "Trends in Structure and Policy in the American Catholic Press," *Journalism Quarterly* 52 (1975): 265–71.

20. Ibid., 271.

21. Ibid.
22. Mary Biggs, "Small Publishing: A Review Article," *Library Quarterly* 52, no. 1 (1982): 59–65.
23. Walter Brueggemann, *The Prophetic Imagination* (Philadelphia: Fortress, 1978), 67.
24. Hannah Arendt, *The Human Condition* (Chicago: University of Chicago Press, 1958), 55.
25. Rita J. Simon, "Public Opinion and the Immigrant: Print Media Coverage, 1880–1980" (Ph.D. diss., American University, 1985).
26. J. Daniel Hess, "The Religious Journals' Image of Mass Media," *Journalism Quarterly* 41 (1964): 106–8.
27. Alexis de Tocqueville, *Democracy in America*, ed. and trans. Harvey C. Mansfield and Delba Winthrop (Chicago: University of Chicago Press, 2000), 177.
28. Louis Wirth, "Consensus and Mass Communication," in *On Cities and Social Life*, ed. Albert J. Reiss Jr. (Chicago: University of Chicago Press, 1964), 29.
29. Ibid., 30.
30. For historical background, see Esther Josephine MacCarthy, "The Catholic Periodical Press and Issues of War and Peace: 1914–1946" (Ph.D. diss., Stanford University, 1977); Martin James Bredec, S.J., "The Role of the Catholic Layman in the Church and American Society As Seen in the Editorials of *Commonweal* Magazine" (Ph.D. diss., Catholic University of America, 1977); Paul Edward Czuchlewski, "The Commonweal Catholic: 1924–1960" (Ph.D. diss., Yale University, 1972); and Rodger Van Allen, *Being Catholic: Commonweal from the 1970s to the 1990s* (Chicago: Loyola University Press, 1993).
31. Deborah E. Lipstadt, "Pious Sympathies and Sincere Regrets: The American News Media and the Holocaust from Krystalnacht to Bermuda, 1938–1943," *Modern Judaism* 2 (February 1982): 53–72.
32. Historian John Lukacs, who wrote for the journal, comments, "The important matter about *Commonweal* was not its liberalism, that it was more liberal than the ideology of most American Catholics; the important matter was its intellectual standards." *Confessions of an Original Sinner* (South Bend, Ind.: St. Augustine's Press, 2000), 170.
33. Rodger Van Allen, *The Commonweal and American Catholicism: The Magazine, the Movement, the Meaning* (Philadelphia: Fortress Press, 1993), 5.
34. Ibid., 191.
35. "A Commonweal Catholic," *America* (in this chapter hereafter referred to as *A*) (7 April 1984): 252.

36. "Twenty-Five Years Later," *First Things* 16 (October 1991): 67.
37. Jaroslav Pelikan, *The Vindication of Tradition* (New Haven, Conn.: Yale University Press, 1986), 65.
38. "The New Immoralism," *Commonweal* (in this chapter hereafter referred to as *C*) (9 February 1927): 365.
39. "Views and Reviews," *C* (11 November 1938): 72.
40. "Radio and Free Speech," *C* (24 February 1939): 489–91.
41. "Should Radio Be As Free As the Press?" *C* (20 February 1948): 467.
42. "The NAB Code and Father Coughlin," *C* (24 November 1939): 114, 116. Historians are unsure as to why Coughlin was taken off the air. Some argue that it was in response to a directive from the pope. Others believe that his removal was necessitated by Catholic lay pressure on the network and its stations.
43. "To Clarify and Reassure," *C* (15 September 1939): 486.
44. See Garth Jowett, *Film: The Democratic Art* (Boston: Little, Brown, 1976), 246–56.
45. Clifton M. Utley, "How Illiterate Can Television Make Us?" *C* (19 November 1948): 139.
46. "Now Political Qualifications," *C* (6 October 1950): 622.
47. "The March of TV," *C* (4 August 1950): 406.
48. "Coast to Coast TV," *C* (14 September 1995): 541.
49. "Few Complaints," *C* (6 July 1951): 300.
50. "Two Systems for TV," *C* (2 February 1951): 414.
51. John Dewey, *The Public and Its Problems* (New York: Henry Holt, 1927).
52. "Martin Luther in Chicago," *C* (15 February 1957): 499.
53. "The 'Martin Luther' Controversy," *C* (15 March 1957): 603–5.
54. "Controversy, No Soap," *C* (22 March 1957): 635.
55. George W. Hunt, "America: How Did It Happen?" *A* (9 April 1994): 8–9, 10; and "Anniversaries," *A* (16 April 1983): 289.
56. See, e.g., their contrasting views on education as interpreted in Francis James Sullivan, "A Study of Controversial Educational Issues as Treated in America and The Commonweal, 1947–1962" (Ph.D. diss., New York University, 1965); and their mutual perspectives on Catholic renewal in the years before the Second Vatican Council in Michael John Tori, "The Roman Catholic Church on the Eve of Renewal: Editorial Perspectives from 'The Commonweal' and 'America' Magazines, 1958–1963" (Ph.D. diss., St. Louis University, 1996).
57. Tori, "Roman Catholic Church."

58. Tocqueville, *Democracy*, 275. John Lukacs has argued persuasively that Tocqueville was a believing Catholic and that the Frenchman's religious convictions were an important part of his intellectual work. Lukacs reviews the evidence in "The Last Days of Alexis de Tocqueville," *Catholic Historical Review* 50, no. 2 (July 1964): 155–70.

59. "Radio Censorship," *A* (8 July 1933): 317.

60. "Radio Censorship," *A* (24 February 1934): 486.

61. "Federal Radio Control," *A* (28 May 1938): 181.

62. "Free Speech and the Radio," *A* (19 November 1938): 157.

63. "Radio Free Speech," *A* (5 December 1931): 199.

64. "Federal Radio Censorship," *A* (6 February 1932): 42.

65. John LaFarge, "The Threat of World Censorship," *A* (9 December 1933): 223.

66. "The Shuler Case," *A* (28 January 1933): 397.

67. "Nuisance and Also a Menace," *A* (8 July 1933): 317.

68. George Henry Payne, "Our Newest Monopoly," *A* (16 March 1935): 534, 535.

69. "Radio Programs Throttle the Spiritual," *A* (16 October 1937): 29.

70. "Why Radio Needs an 'Angel,'" *A* (27 April 1940): 76.

71. "Religion and Radio," *A* (20 January 1923): 327.

72. Ibid.

73. "Laudetur Jesus Christus," *A* (9 April 1932): 47.

74. "Microphoned Religion," *A* (14 March 1931): 541.

75. Leslie Rumble, "Many Become Catholics by Listening to the Radio," *A* (25 January 1941): 430.

76. "Radio Censorship," *A* (17 September 1938): 566.

77. "Censorship of the Radio," *A* (4 November 1939): 99; see also "Free Speech," *A* (28 January 1939): 397.

78. "Father Coughlin," *A* (20 November 1937): 156.

79. "Radio Writes a Code That Claims to Be Fair," *A* (25 November 1939): 176.

80. "Censorship of the Radio."

81. "A Production Code for Radio," *A* (1 June 1935): 173.

82. "Dead Giveaway," *A* (28 August 1948): 460.

83. "Radio Pots of Gold Doomed?" *A* (3 September 1949): 571.

84. "Get-Rich-Quick-It Is," *A* (7 April 1951): 8.

85. "Power and Challenge of the Coming Television," *A* (13 May 1944): 152.

86. "Education on TV," *A* (10 February 1951): 542.

87. "Education on TV," *A* (23 June 1951): 303.

88. "TV 'Thaw' Looses Lots of Problems," *A* (3 May 1952): 123.
89. "Free Air for Commie Stooges," *A* (30 August 1952): 513.
90. "The Dilemma of a Home," *A* (22 September 1951): 588.
91. "TV Agrees to Censor Itself," *A* (3 November 1931): 114.
92. Dennis N. Voskuil, "American Protestant Neo-orthodoxy and Its Search for Realism, 1925–1939," *Ultimate Reality and Meaning* 8 (1985): 277–87.
93. James M. Wall, "Integration and Imperialism: The Century 1953–1961," *CC* (21 November 1984): 1091.
94. Quoted in ibid., 1094.
95. Linda-Marie Delloff, "C. C. Morrison: Shaping a Journal's Identity," *CC* (18 January 1984): 44, 43.
96. Ibid., 45, 47, 43; see also Linda-Marie Delloff, "The Century on the Arts," *CC* (21–28 March 1984): 291–92.
97. Linda-Marie Delloff, "The Century in Transition: 1916–1922," *CC* (7 March 1984): 243.
98. See, e.g., Martin E. Marty, "War's Dilemmas: The Century 1938–1945," *CC* (26 December 1984): 867–71; Dean Peerman, "Forward on Many Fronts: The Century 1923–1929," *CC* (6–13 June 1984): 595–600; Peerman, "Breadlines and Storm Clouds: The Century 1930–1937," *CC* (29 August-5 September 1984): 795–99; and Marty, "Peace and Pluralism: The Century 1946–1952," *CC* (24 October 1984): 979–83. For an examination of the journal's role in the civil rights movement, see Michael Shermis, "Interreligious and Interdenominational Cooperation in the Civil Rights Movement" (master's thesis, Indiana University, 1990); for a review of the magazine's strong stand on civil liberties issues, see J. Theodore Hefley, "Freedom Upheld: The Civil Liberties Stance of *The Christian Century* between the Wars," *Church History* 37, no. 2 (June 1968): 174–94.
99. "One Hundred Years of Pot-Banging," *CC* (4–11 July 1984): 651–52.
100. James M. Wall, "Adopting Realism: The Century 1962–1971," *CC* (12 December 1984): 1171.
101. "The Radiophone and Preaching," *CC* (22 March 1923): 355.
102. "Widening Dr. Cadman's Radio Ministry," *CC* (11 October 1928): 1216.
103. "The Radio an Inconvenience to Religious Narrowness," *CC* (16 August 1923): 1029.
104. "Radio Preaching and Its Problems," *CC* (25 December 1924): 1654.
105. "Religious Radio Programs Need Much Improvement," *CC* (16 February 1944): 197.

106. "Religion and the Radio," *CC* (12 March 1941): 349.

107. "Workshop Defines Policies for Religious Radio," *CC* (11 September 1946): 1084.

108. "Is the United Radio Program Out of the Question?" *CC* (18 October 1944): 1189.

109. "A New Chance for Church Radio," *CC* (28 November 1945): 1308.

110. Alfred Grant Walton, "Reconsider Religious Radio!" *CC* (10 September 1947): 1079.

111. Charles S. Macfarland, *Christian Unity in the Making* (New York: Federal Council of the Churches of Christ in America, 1948), 300. See also Louis Gasper, *The Fundamentalist Movement* (Paris: Mouton, 1936), 76–85; and Charles M. Crowe, "Religion on the Air," *CC* (23 August 1944): 973–75.

112. Charles M. Crowe, "Television Needs Religion," *CC* (10 August 1949): 938. See also "Church Television," *CC* (12 October 1949): 1202.

113. J. Edward Carothers, "A Television Ministry," *CC* (11 May 1949): 591–92; and Carothers, "Why Church Television Is Stalled," *CC* (21 September 1949): 1104–5.

114. "The Churches and the Radio," *CC* (20 March 1924): 355.

115. "Freedom for the Radio Pulpit," *CC* (27 January 1932): 113.

116. "'Bob' Shuler Is off the Air," *CC* (22 February 1923): 245.

117. "Less Bigotry Needed, Not More," *CC* (20 August 1930): 1104, 1105.

118. "Radio Writes a Code for Itself," *CC* (26 July 1939): 917.

119. "One Radio Chain Cleans House," *CC* (29 May 1935): 716.

120. "New Developments in the World of Radio," *CC* (15 April 1931): 502.

121. "Why Not a Hearer's Chain?" *CC* (3 May 1933): 580; see also "Uneasy Days for the Radio Chains," *CC* (3 May 1933): 579–80.

122. "New Developments in the World of Radio," 503.

123. "People's Air Lanes Need Scrubbing," *CC* (12 April 1950): 453; and "Has a New Type of Political Campaign Arrived?" *CC* (22 November 1950): 1381.

124. "What Should Be Done About TV Programs?" *CC* (28 May 1952): 637.

125. A. Gordon Nasby, "Television and the Church," *CC* (2 February 1949): 143.

126. "Bible Belt Broadcasting," *CC* (28 June 1961): 801.

127. "Christian TV Series Gets Big Mail," *CC* (17 December 1952): 1462.

128. "Demand License Hearing on Chicago TV Station," *CC* (20 February 1957): 220.

129. "Censorship in Chicago," *CC* (23 January 1957): 102.

130. Billy Graham, "In the Beginning," interview in *Christianity Today* (17 July 1981): 26–27.

131. Quoted in Mark G. Toulouse, "*Christianity Today* and American Public Life: A Case Study," *Journal of Church and State* 35 (1993): 242.

132. Cynthia Schaible Boyll, "Evangelicals, American Culture and *Christianity Today* Magazine" (master's thesis, Calvin College, 1989), 55.

133. Toulouse, "A Case Study," 266, 276–77, 282.

134. For a study of the contrasting views of *Christianity Today* and *Christian Century* on the Vietnam War and the Cold War, see David E. Settje, "The Vietnam War, the Cold War, and Protestants: How *The Christian Century* and *Christianity Today* Reflected American Society in the 1960s" (London, Ontario: American Journalism Historians Association Annual Convention, 3–5 October 1996), part 2; for an analysis of the role of *Christianity Today* in the development of a "mainstream" evangelical movement in the years after World War II, see David Harrington Watt, "A Transforming Faith: Essays on the History of American Evangelicalism in the Middle Decades of the Twentieth Century" (Ph.D. diss., Harvard University, 1987).

135. "Improving the Quality of Religious Radio-TV," *Christianity Today* (in this chapter hereafter referred to as *CT*) (1 April 1957): 22.

136. "The Scramble for Radio-TV," *CT* (18 February 1957): 20, 22, 23.

137. "New Era for Christian Communication," *CT* (14 October 1966): 3.

138. "The Communications Revolution and the Christian Gospel," *CT* (22 November 1968): 3–4.

139. The campaign is described in Bill Bright, *A Movement of Miracles* (San Bernardino, Calif.: Campus Crusade for Christ International, 1977).

140. "Evangelical Visibility in TV Programming," *CT* (16 January 1970): 24.

141. "Can Churches Break the Prime-Time Barrier?" *CT* (16 January 1970): 4.

142. "In the Beginning," 27.

143. Toulouse, "A Case Study," 279–80.

144. "Broadcasting, National and International," *Catholic World* (in this chapter hereafter referred to as *CW*) (August 1926): 619, 623.

145. "Editorial Comment," *CW* (May 1934): 134–36.

146. Ibid., 136.

147. Ibid., 137.

148. John J. McMahon, "Buffalo Is on the Air," *CW* (May 1941): 225, 226, 227.

149. "The Catholic Hour," *CW* (February 1934): 611. See also Edward D. Wroblewski, "The Catholic Hour: An Historical Survey of the Church's First Official Use of Radio and Television in America" (master's thesis, St. Paul's College, 1962).

150. "Tenth Anniversary of Catholic Radio Hour," *CW* (March 1940): 748.

151. "Editorial Comment," *CW* (October 1930): 99–100, 104.

152. "I Believe in Television," *CW* (March 1950): 402.

153. Ibid., 401.

154. "Down with Aunt Minnie," *CW* (October 1948): 51.

155. "Radio and Television," *CW* (July 1950): 302.

156. "Radio and Television," *CW* (April 1951): 64.

157. Fortner, "The Church and the Debate over Radio: 1919–1949," in *Media and Religion in American History*, ed. William David Sloan (Northport, Ala.: Vision Press, 2000), 241–42.

158. Edward A. Purcell Jr., *Crisis of Democratic Theory* (Lexington: University Press of Kentucky, 1973).

159. Evidence suggests that American "faith" in communication technologies dates at least to the development of the telegraph. See James W. Carey and John J. Quirk, "The Mythos of the Electronic Revolution," *American Scholar* 39 (spring 1970): 219–41.

160. "The more the antagonisms of the present must be suffered, the more the future is drawn upon as a source of pseudo-unity and synthetic morale," writes sociologist C. Wright Mills. *Mills, Power, Politics, and People: The Collected Essays of C. Wright Mills*, ed. Irving L. Horowitz (New York: Ballantine, 1963), 302. James W. Carey and John J. Quirk write, "The future becomes a time zone in which the human condition is somehow transcended, politics evaporated, and a blessed stage of peace and democratic harmony achieved." "The History of the Future," in *Communication Technology and Social Policy*, ed. George Gerbner et al. (New York: John Wiley and Sons, 1973), 489. See also Daniel J. Czitrom, *Media and the American Mind: From Morse to McLuhan* (Chapel Hill: University of North Carolina Press, 1982).

161. Note how many of the current "success stories" in religious broadcasting are depicted in the media as the product of pluck and luck.

Chapter 4

1. Everett C. Parker and Fred Eastman, "Religion on the Air in Chicago: A Study of Religious Programs on the Commercial Radio Stations of

Chicago," *Chicago Theological Seminary Register* 22, no. 1 (January 1942): 12–22.

2. Ibid., 12.

3. Communications Act of 1934, 73rd Cong., 2d sess., 1934, *House Committee Report,* 1850.

4. Parker, "Religion on the Air," 12.

5. For a similar argument, see Robert S. Fortner, "The Church and the Debate over Radio: 1919–1949," in *Media and Religion in American History,* ed. William David Sloan (Northport, Ala.: Vision Press, 2000), 243.

6. Quoted in Dave Berkman, "Long before Falwell: Early Radio and Religion—As Reported by the Nation's Periodical Press," *Journal of Popular Culture* 21, no. 4 (spring 1988): 3.

7. R. Laurence Moore, *Selling God: American Religion in the Marketplace of Culture* (New York: Oxford University Press, 1994), 233.

8. Quentin J. Schultze, "The Mythos of the Electronic Church," *Critical Studies in Mass Communication* 4 (1987): 245–61.

9. Spencer Miller, "Radio and Religion," *Annals of the American Academy of Political and Social Science* 177 (January 1935): 140.

10. W. H. Ferrin, "Greater Providence: A Great Opportunity," *Radio Caroller Announcer* (April 1929): 19.

11. Nathan O. Hatch, "Evangelicalism as a Democratic Movement," in *Evangelicalism and Modern America,* ed. George M. Marsden (Grand Rapids, Mich.: William B. Eerdmans, 1984), 72.

12. Joel A. Carpenter, "Fundamentalist Institutions and the Rise of Evangelical Protestantism: 1929–1942," *Church History* 49 (1980): 62–75.

13. George M. Marsden, "Fundamentalism As an American Phenomenon: A Comparison with English Evangelicalism," *Church History* 46 (1977): 226.

14. Joel A. Carpenter, "From Fundamentalism to the New Evangelical Coalition," in *Evangelicalism and Modern America,* ed. Marsden, 4.

15. Quoted in Jack Kuney, "'Dat ole' time religion': Broadcasting and the Pulpit," *Television Quarterly* 27, no. 1 (1994): 70.

16. J. Fred MacDonald, *Don't Touch That Dial: Radio Programming in American Life 1920–1960* (Chicago: Nelson-Hall, 1979), 106.

17. George M. Marsden, *Fundamentalism and American Culture: The Shaping of Twentieth-Century Evangelicalism, 1870–1925* (New York: Oxford University Press, 1980), 184–88.

18. E. M. Berckman, "The Changing Attitudes of Protestant Churches to Movies and Television," *Encounter* 41 (1980): 293–306.

19. Vincent Edwards, "The First Church Broadcast," *Christian Advocate* (14 November 1968): 12.
20. "Religious Radio: 1921–1971," *Christianity Today* (1 January 1971): 6.
21. Robert H. Wiebe, *The Search for Order: 1877–1920* (New York: Hill and Wang, 1967).
22. Alfred Grant Walton, "Reconsider Religious Radio!" *Christian Century* (10 September 1947): 1079.
23. R. Laurence Moore, *Religious Outsiders and the Making of Americans* (New York: Oxford University Press, 1986).
24. In spite of the significant role of religious tribes in early radio, none of the broadcast histories and only a few religious histories addressed the subject. Among the historians of U.S. broadcasting, Francis S. Chase dedicates only three paragraphs to all religious programming. *Sound and Fury: An Informal History of Broadcasting* (New York: Harper, 1942). The first two volumes in Erik Barnouw's history include incidental references to religious broadcasting, except for an extended discussion of Father Coughlin's political sermons of the 1930s. *A Tower of Babel: A History of Broadcasting in the United States to 1933* (New York: Oxford University Press, 1966); and *The Golden Web: A History of Broadcasting in the United States* (New York: Oxford University Press, 1968), 44–47. Gleason L. Archer's triumphalistic history of early radio summarizes the development of religious programming in less than two pages. *History of Radio to 1926* (New York: American Historical Society, 1938). Edward P. J. Shurick devotes a brief chapter to religious broadcasting but without a cultural or historical context. *The First Quarter-Century of American Broadcasting* (Kansas City, Mo.: Midland, 1946). Christopher H. Sterling and John M. Kittross similarly pay scant attention to religious radio broadcasting. *Stay Tuned: A Concise History of American Broadcasting* (Belmont, Calif.: Wadsworth, 1978). A few studies of American religion, however, have addressed the subject of religious broadcasting. Studies by George H. Hill and by Jeffrey K. Hadden describe early evangelical broadcasting but largely fail to elucidate its historical importance. Hill, *Airwaves to the Soul: The Influence and Growth of Religious Broadcasting in America* (Saratoga, Calif.: R and E, 1983); and Hadden, *Prime Time Preachers: The Rising Power of Televangelism* (Reading, Mass.: Addison-Wesley, 1981). Joel Carpenter and Razelle Frankl examine the historical role of religious broadcasting in shaping American Protestantism. Carpenter persuasively argues the significance of fundamentalist broadcasting in the development of modern American

Evangelicalism. "From Fundamentalism"; "Fundamentalist Institutions." Frankl leaps from turn-of-the-century urban revivalism to contemporary televangelism, a jump that largely overlooks the role of religious radio in American religion. *Televangelism.* Studies of contemporary religious broadcasting erroneously assume that the so-called electronic church was a new phenomenon in the 1970s, while broadcast histories wrongly imply that evangelical radio was a minor aspect of early American broadcasting and American culture. In early 1923 religious organizations owned at least twelve stations, about 2 percent of the existing licensees. William Peck Banning, *Commercial Broadcasting Pioneer: The WEAF Experiment 1922–1926* (Cambridge: Harvard University Press, 1946), 132. By 1924, three years after the first radio station began broadcasts, local churches held one out of every fourteen licenses, and many additional "special" stations were owned and operated by educational institutions associated with religious bodies such as the Roman Catholic Church, the Knights of Columbus, and the YMCA. "The air is filling up with propaganders," protested *Popular Radio*, a magazine for radio buffs in 1925. Armstrong Perry, "Religion's Raid on Radio," *Popular Radio* (25 January 1925): 5. Twenty-nine stations were operated by churches and other religious organizations in 1924, and by 1925 the number increased to seventy-one. William H. Leach, "The Church Takes the Air," *Homiletic Review* 90 (October 1925): 300–302; and Robert E. Summers and Herbert B. Summers, *Broadcasting and the Public* (Belmont, Calif.: Wadsworth, 1966), 35.

25. Martin J. Neeb, "An Historical Study of American Non-Commercial AM Broadcast Stations Owned and Operated by Religious Groups, 1920–1966" (Ph.D. diss. Northwestern University, 1967), abstract in *Dissertation Abstracts International* 28 (1968): 2368A-69A.

26. Quoted in Barry C. Siedell, *Gospel Radio* (Lincoln, Nebr.: Back to the Bible Broadcast, 1971), 64–65.

27. Quentin J. Schultze and Carolyn Marvin, "CB: The First Thirty Years," *Journal of Communication* 27 (summer 1977): 104–17.

28. Summers and Summers, *Broadcasting*, 39.

29. Neeb, "An Historical Study," 8.

30. *United States v Zenith Radio Corporation*, 12 F.2nd 614 (N.D. Ill. 1926).

31. George H. Gibson, *Public Broadcasting: The Role of the Federal Government, 1912–1916* (New York: Praeger, 1977), 7.

32. Federal Radio Act of 1927, Public Law 632, 69th Cong., (23 February 1927).

33. Summers and Summers, *Broadcasting*, 39.

34. C. B. Rose, *National Policy for Radio Broadcasting: Report of a Committee of the National Economic and Social Planning Association* (New York: Harper, 1940), 170.

35. Robert W. McChesney, *Telecommunications, Mass Media, and Democracy: The Battle for Control of U.S. Broadcasting, 1928–1935* (New York: Oxford University Press, 1993), 27.

36. Gibson, *Public Broadcasting*, 9; and Werner J. Severin, "Commercial vs. Non-Commercial Radio during Broadcasting's Early Years," *Journal of Broadcasting* 22 (1978): 491–504.

37. David F. Noble, *America by Design: Technology and the Rise of Corporate Capitalism* (New York: Oxford University Press, 1979), 97.

38. Federal Radio Commission, *Third Annual Report* (Washington, D.C.: GPO, 1929), 34.

39. Quoted in McChesney, *Telecommunications, Mass Media, and Democracy*, 27.

40. Royston Pike, *Jehovah's Witnesses: Who They Are, What They Teach, What They Do* (New York: Philosophical Society, 1954), 21; and Joseph Franklin Rutherford, *Religion: Origin, Influence upon Men and Nations, and the Result* (Brooklyn, N.Y.: Watchtower Bible and Tract Society, 1940), 65, 320.

41. Neeb, "A Historical Study," 177.

42. Joseph Franklin Rutherford, *Prophecy: Many Mysteries of the Bible Made Plain and Understandable* (Brooklyn, N.Y.: International Bible Students Association, Watch Tower Bible and Tract Society, 1929), 233.

43. Charley Orbison, "'Fighting Bob,' Early Radio Crusader," *Journal of Broadcasting* 21 (fall 1977): 459–72.

44. Federal Radio Commission, *Third Annual Report*, 35.

45. Gene A. Getz, *MBI: The Story of Moody Bible Institute* (Chicago: Moody Press, 1969), 283.

46. Stewart M. Hoover and Douglas K. Wagner, "History and Policy in American Broadcast Treatment of Religion," *Media, Culture and Society* 19 (1997): 17.

47. Getz, *MBI*, 290.

48. Joel A. Carpenter, *Revive Us Again: The Reawakening of American Fundamentalism* (New York: Oxford University Press, 1997), 133–4.

49. W. L. Muncy, *A History of Evangelism in the United States* (Kansas City: Kansas Central Seminary Press, 1945), 171; and Neeb, "A Historical Study," 448–63.

50. Carpenter, "Fundamentalist Institutions."

51. Paul L. Maier, *A Man Spoke, a World Listened: The Story of Walter A. Maier and The Lutheran Hour* (New York: McGraw-Hill, 1963), 72.

52. Alan Graebner, "KFUO's Beginnings," *Concordia Historical Institute Quarterly* 37 (1964): 91.

53. Maier, *A Man Spoke*, 73.

54. Graebner, "KFUO's Beginnings," 92.

55. Maier, *A Man Spoke*, 72.

56. Paul L. Maier, "He Preached, the World Listened," *Christian Herald* (October 1980): 44–52; William F. McDermott, "Old Time Religion Goes Global," *Collier's* (6 May 1944): 50; and "Religion: Lutherans," *Time* (18 October 1943): 46–49.

57. Graebner, "KFUO'S Beginnings," 90.

58. David L. Clark, "Miracles for a Dime: From Chautauqua Tent to Radio Station with Sister Aimee," *California History* 57 (1978/1979): 354–63.

59. Barnouw, *A Tower of Babel*, 180; and Neeb, "A Historical Study," 128.

60. J. L. Hood, "The Old-Time Religion: Aimee Semple McPherson and the Original Electronic Church" (master's thesis, Wheaton College, n.d.), 74.

61. Neeb, "A Historical Study," 156.

62. Clark, "Miracles for a Dime."

63. Robert E. Park, "Reflections On Communication and Culture," in *Robert E. Park: The Crowd and the Public and Other Essays*, ed. Henry Elsner Jr. (Chicago: University of Chicago Press, 1967), 102.

64. Federal Communications Commission, *Public Service Responsibility of Broadcast Licensees* (Washington, D.C.: GPO, 7 May 1946), 10; and Lee Loevinger, "Religious Liberty and Broadcasting," *George Washington Law Review* 33 (1965), 631–59.

65. George C. Ericson, "Swedish Radio Services in Chicago," *Swedish Pioneer Historical Quarterly* 24 (1973): 157–62.

66. William Albig, *Public Opinion* (New York: McGraw-Hill, 1939), 347; Sterling and Kittross, *Stay Tuned*, 73.

67. Leon Whipple, "Letters and Life: The Heavens Declare," *Survey* (1 July 1926): 432.

68. "Tuning In on Religion," *Literary Digest* (30 July 1927): 30.

69. Banning, *Commercial Broadcasting Pioneer*, 151.

70. William James DuBourdieu, "Religious Broadcasting in the United States" (Ph.D. diss., Northwestern University, 1933).

71. "Sending Out the Good News over the Air," *Sunday School Times* (28 March 1931): 184.

72. "Notes on Open Letters: Do People Want Gospel Radio Broadcasts?" *Sunday School Times* (23 January 1932): 42.

73. Siedell, *Gospel Radio*, 63.

74. DuBourdieu, "Religious Broadcasting," 164.

75. Federal Council of the Churches of Christ in America, Department of Research and Education, *Broadcasting and the Public* (New York: Abingdon Press, 1938), 133.

76. George H. Betts, "Radio's Contribution to Religion," in *Education on the Air*, ed. Josephine MacLatchy (Columbus: Ohio State University, 1932), 37–51.

77. Judith C. Waller, *Radio: The Fifth Estate*, 2nd ed. (Boston: Houghton Mifflin, 1950), 234.

78. Federal Council of the Churches of Christ in America, *Broadcasting and the Public*, 138–39; and Parker and Eastman, "Religion on the Air in Chicago."

79. Quoted in Federal Council of the Churches of Christ in America, *Broadcasting and the Public*, 137.

80. Edgar E. Willis, *Foundations in Broadcasting: Radio and Television* (New York: Oxford University Press, 1951), 100.

81. Kenneth Baker, "An Analysis of Radio's Programming," in *Communications Research 1948–1949*, ed. Paul F. Lazarsfeld and Frank N. Stanton (New York: Harper, 1949), 65.

82. Betts, "Radio's Contribution to Religion," 46.

83. Federal Council of the Churches of Christ in America, *Broadcasting and the Public*, 141.

84. Parker and Eastman, "Religion on the Air."

85. "Radio Log of Evangelical Broadcasts," *Christian Life* (August 1948): 17; and "The Radio Preacher," *Newsweek* (4 April 1967): 88–89.

86. Federal Council of the Churches of Christ in America, *Broadcasting and the Public*, 141.

87. Ibid., 141, 147.

88. Chase, *Sound and Fury*, 248.

89. Cameron Shipp and Frank J. Taylor, "California's New-Fashioned Religion," *Collier's* (15 January 1949): 145, 52–53.

90. J. Leonard Reinsch, *Radio Station Management* (New York: Harper, 1948), 38.

91. Paul F. Lazarsfeld and Patricia L. Kendall, *Radio Listening in America: The People Look at Radio* (New York: Prentice-Hall, 1948), 21.

92. Ibid., 123.

93. Paul F. Lazarsfeld, *The People Look at Radio* (Chapel Hill: University of North Carolina Press, 1946), 63–64.

94. "Religious Programs Popular in Kentucky," *United Evangelical Action* (1 August 1946): 10–11.

95. Quoted in Moore, *Selling God*, 235.

96. Alexis de Tocqueville, *Democracy in America*, ed. and trans. Harvey C. Mansfield and Delba Winthrop (Chicago: University of Chicago Press, 2000), 284.

97. Ibid., 210.

98. Elizabeth Benneche Peterson, "Religion in the Armchair," *Radio Stars* (August 1938): 22.

99. Robert Moats Miller, *Harry Emerson Fosdick: Preacher, Pastor, Prophet* (New York: Oxford University Press, 1985), 379.

100. Quoted in Ernst B. Gordon, *An Ecclesiastical Octopus: A Factual Report on the Federal Council of the Churches of Christ in America* (Boston: Fellowship Press, 1948), 88.

101. Orbison, "'Fighting Bob,'" 459–72; "The Preacher on the Air," *Atlantic Monthly* (December 1943): 123–24; Samuel L. Rothafel and Raymond Francis Yates, *Broadcasting, Its New Day* (New York: Century, 1925); and Lowell Saunders, "The National Religious Broadcasters and the Availability of Commercial Radio Time" (Ph.D. diss., University of Illinois, 1968).

102. Charles Crowe, "Religion on the Air," *Christian Century* (23 August 1944): 973.

103. James A. Brown, "Selling Airtime for Controversy: NAB Self Regulation and Father Coughlin," *Journal of Broadcasting* 24 (spring 1980): 199–224.

104. Federal Council of the Churches of Christ in America, *Broadcasting and the Public*, 136–37.

105. Moore, *Selling God*, 234.

106. Ibid.; Thomas Porter Robinson, *Radio Networks and the Federal Government* (New York: Columbia Press, 1943), 79; and Charles H. Schmitz, "Religious Radio in the United States," *Crozer Quarterly* 24 (October 1947): 289–315.

107. Brown, "Selling Airtime," 211.

108. National Association of Broadcasters, *The Code of the National Association of Broadcasters* (Washington, D.C.: National Association of Broadcasters, 1939), 5.

109. Brown, "Selling Airtime," 215–16.

110. Ibid, 218.

111. Dennis N. Voskuil, "Reaching Out: Mainline Protestantism and the Media," in *Between the Times: The Travail of the Protestant Establishment in America, 1900–1960*, ed. William R. Hutchinson (Cambridge: Cambridge University Press, 1989), 72–92.

112. Spencer Miller Jr., "Radio and Religion," *Annals of the American Academy of Political and Social Science* 177 (January 1935): 137.

113. Saunders, "National Religious Broadcasters," 137–44; Siedell, *Gospel Radio*, 71.

114. Daniel P. Fuller, *Give the Winds a Mighty Voice* (Waco, Tex.: Word Books, 1972), 156; and Saunders, "National Religious Broadcasters," 106.

115. Schultze, "Religious Radio."

116. Saunders, "National Religious Broadcasters," 38–39.

117. Llewellyn White, *The American Radio: A Report on the Broadcasting Industry in the United States from the Commission on Freedom of the Press* (Chicago: University of Chicago Press, 1947), 66.

118. John Bachman, "The Next Age and Stage of the BFC" (address delivered at the meeting of the Broadcasting and Film Commission Board of Managers of the National Council of Churches of Christ in the USA, New York, 7 February 1964); and "Religion and the Radio," *Christian Century* (12 March 1941): 349.

119. Maier, *A Man Spoke*, 113; and Kenneth Hartley Sulston, "A Rhetorical Criticism of the Radio Preaching of Walter Arthur Maier" (Ph.D. diss., Northwestern University, 1958).

120. Graham Mark, "The Word in 56 Languages," *Coronet* (February 1956): 141–44; and Siedell, *Gospel Radio*, 73.

121. Maier, "He Preached," 46.

122. Sulston, "Rhetorical Criticism," 37.

123. Maier, "He Preached," 46; and "Religion: Maier vs. Council," *Time* (11 April 1938): 47–48.

124. Gordon, *An Ecclesiastical Octopus*, 88.

125. Sulston, "Rhetorical Criticism," 56; and Sterling and Kittross, *Stay Tuned*, 511.

126. "Religion: Lutherans," *Time* (18 October 1943): 46–49.

127. Maier, "He Preached," 51.

128. Fuller, *Give the Winds*, 75, 103–4.

129. Ibid., 140.

130. "Big Churches Learn Radio 'Savvy.'"

131. "The Radio Preacher," *Newsweek* (24 April 1967): 88–89; and Hadden and Swann, *Prime Time Preachers*, 81.

132. "The Radio Preacher," 88.

133. Saunders, "National Religious Broadcasters," 210–11.

134. "Spirit of Revival Marks NAE at Indianapolis," *United Evangelical Action* (1 May 1950): 3–8, 14–18.

135. Fuller, *Give the Winds*, 176; James DeForest Murch, "Fuller Revival Hour Goes on ABC Network," *United Evangelical Action* (1 June 1949): 13; and "Lutheran Hour Now on ABC Network," *United Evangelical Action* (1 October 1949): 12.

136. Robert A. White, "Religion and Media in the Construction of Cultures," in *Rethinking Media, Religion, and Culture*, ed. Stewart M. Hoover and Knut Lundby (London: Sage, 1997), 38.

137. Ibid.

138. Park, "On Communication," 102.

139. Ibid., 104.

140. Moore, *Selling God*, 234.

141. Ibid.

142. Louis Wirth, "Consensus and Mass Communication," in *Louis Wirth: On Cities and Social Life*, ed. Albert J. Reiss Jr. (Chicago: University of Chicago Press, 1964), 31.

143. Quoted in Moore, *Selling God*, 234.

144. Peter Fornatale and Joshua E. Mills, *Radio in the Television Age* (Woodstock, N.Y.: Overlook Press, 1980), 90.

145. Susan Smulyan, *Selling Radio: The Commercialization of American Broadcasting* (Washington, D.C.: Smithsonian Institution Press, 1994), 160.

146. Carl Douglas Windsor, "Religious Radio in the 1970's: Uses and Gratifications Analysis" (Ph.D. diss., Ohio State University, 1981), 69.

147. *Broadcasting Cablecasting Yearbook* (Washington, D.C.: Broadcasting Publications, 1989), F88, F93–95.

148. Gary Crossland, "The Changing Face of Christian Radio," *Religious Broadcasting* (September 1988): 13.

149. James B. Keller, "Christian Radio Stations Riding a Wave of Change, Keep Their Popularity," *New York Times*, 1 January 1994, sec D, p. 6.

150. James W. Carey, "Afterword: The Culture in Question," in *James Carey: A Critical Reader*, ed. Eve Stryker Munson and Catherine A. Warren (Minneapolis: University of Minnesota Press, 1997), 323–25.

151. Ibid., 34.

152. Robyn Wells, "Listener Habits Are Outlined by Survey," *Billboard* (30 January 1982): 57.

153. Crossland, "The Changing Face," 35.

154. Gary Crossland, "Vital Signs Improve for Christian Radio," *Religious Broadcasting* (February 1986): 45.

155. William D. Romanowski, "Contemporary Christian Music: The Business of Music Ministry," in *American Evangelicals and the Mass Media*, ed. Quentin J. Schultze (Grand Rapids, Mich.: Zondervan/Academie, 1990), 143–69.

156. Windsor, "Religious Radio," 134.

157. Stuart Philip Johnson, "Contemporary Communication Theory and the Distribution Patterns of Evangelical Radio Programs" (Ph.D. diss., Northwestern University, 1978), 213.

158. Paul H. Virts, "Surprising Findings in Christian Radio," *Religious Broadcasting* (February 1986): 42.

159. Quentin J. Schultze and William D. Romanowski, "Praising God in Opryland," *Reformed Journal* (November 1989): 13.

160. Jim Pennington, "Christian Radio: Breaking Out of the Gospel Ghetto," *Christianity Today* (29 June 1979): 32.

161. Quentin J. Schultze, "Evangelical Radio and the Rise of the Electronic Church, 1921–1948," *Journal of Broadcasting and the Electronic Media* 32 (summer 1988): 301.

162. Johnson, "Contemporary Communication," 124.

163. J. Thomas Bisset, "Religious Broadcasting: Assessing the State of the Art," *Christianity Today* (12 December 1980): 28.

164. Gary Crossland, "How Do Various Christian Formats Compare?" *Religious Broadcasting* (December 1988): 16.

165. As Stewart M. Hoover found with religious television, the supporters of evangelical radio programs were not necessarily the listeners. See Hoover, "The Meaning of Religious Television: The '700 Club' in the Lives of its Viewers," in *American Evangelicals*, ed. Schultze, 215–49.

166. "The Petition against God," *Channels* (September/October 1984): 10–14.

167. Kenneth A. Briggs, "Evangelicals in America," *Gallup Report* (April 1987): 3.

168. Crossland, "How Do Various," 16.

169. Schultze and Romanowski, "Praising God," 11.

170. Rupert R. Ridgeway, "Reflecting on Radio, Ratings and Religion," *Religious Broadcasting* (April 1982): 37; and Crossland, "Vital Signs," 43.

171. Research Department of Christianity Today, "Christian and Secular Radio and Music Listening Habits among Leading Christian Music Buyers" (unpublished research report, 1988).

172. George Bailey, "Radio's Changing Environment. Info. Packets NO. 22," (Washington, D.C.: Corporation for Public Broadcasting, October 1995). The only major study that challenged these low listenership data concluded that in 1998, 39 percent of U.S. adults listened to some Christian radio programming during a typical week, a net audience of seventy-five million to eighty million. These astonishing data are ultimately implausible.

173. Robert E. Park, "Racial Assimilation in Secondary Groups," in *On Social Control*, ed. Turner, 114.

174. Luke 12:13–21. When social critic T. W. Adorno studied the radio speeches of religious broadcaster Martin Luther Thomas in 1935, he concluded that Thomas's rhetorical strategies paralleled those of advertising. Paul Apostolidis, "Culture Industry or Social Physiognomy: Adorno's Critique of Christian Right Radio," *Philosophy and Social Criticism* 24, no. 5 (1998): 53–84.

175. Gary Crossland, "Religious Audiences: More Upscale?" *Religious Broadcasting* (March 1985): 28, 30.

176. Gary Crossland, "Advertising Opportunities on Christian Radio," *Religious Broadcasting* (April 1985): 20, 25.

177. Gustav Niebuhr, "Niche Demographics to Radio Advertisers," *New York Times*, 2 December 1996.

178. Crossland, "The Changing Face," 35.

179. Louis Wirth, "The Limitations of Regionalism," in *On Cities*, ed, Reiss, 210.

180. Jay D. Green, "'Nothing to Advertise Except God': Christian Radio and the Creation of an Evangelical Subculture in Northeast Ohio, 1958–1972," *Ohio History* 106 (1997): 171–91.

181. Ibid., 175.

182. Ibid.

183. Ibid., 176.

184. Ibid., 191.

Chapter 5

1. Jean Shepherd, *A Fistful of Fig Newtons* (New York: Doubleday, 1981), 162.

2. Michael Novak, "Television Shapes the Soul," in *Television As a Social Force: New Approaches to TV Criticism*, ed. Douglass Cater and Richard Adler (New York: Praeger, 1975), 10.

3. Robert E. Park, "Reflections On Communication and Culture," in *Robert E. Park: The Crowd and the Public and Other Essays*, ed. Henry Elsner Jr. (Chicago: University of Chicago Press, 1972), 101.

4. Ronald C. Arnett, *Communication and Community: Implications of Martin Buber's Dialogue* (Carbondale: Southern Illinois University Press, 1986), 125.

5. Louis Wirth, "Consensus and Mass Communication," in *Louis Wirth: On Cities and Social Life*, ed. Albert J. Reiss Jr. (Chicago: University of Chicago Press, 1964), 28.

6. Northrop Frye, *The Great Code: The Bible and Literature* (New York: Harcourt Brace Jovanovich, 1982), ch. 7.

7. James W. Carey, *Communication As Culture: Essays on Media and Society* (Boston: Unwin Hyman, 1989), 20–21.

8. Wirth, "Consensus," 29.

9. Ibid.

10. Stanley Hauerwas, "Story and Theology," *Religion in Life* 45 (fall 1976): 343.

11. Johann Baptist Metz and Jean-Pierre Jossua, eds., *The Crisis of Religious Language* (New York: Herder and Herder, 1973), 86.

12. Quoted in ibid.

13. Erich Auerbach, *Mimesis* (Princeton, N.J.: Princeton University Press, 1953), 168.

14. Metz and Jossua, *The Crisis of Religious Language*, 95.

15. Niels C. Nielsen Jr., *Fundamentalism, Mythos, and World Religions* (Albany: State University of New York Press, 1993), 36, 37.

16. J. J. Bachofen, *Myth, Religion, and Mother Right: Selected Writings of J. J. Bachofen*, trans. Ralph Manheim (Princeton, N.J.: Princeton University Press), 49.

17. Frye, *The Great Code*, 55.

18. Galileo attributes this quote to Cardinal Baronius. See Olaf Pedersen, "Galileo and the Council of Trent: The Galileo Affair Revisited," *Journal for the History of Astronomy* 14 (1983): 18.

19. Alan Schreck, *The Essential Catholic Catechism* (Ann Arbor, Mich.: Servant, 1999), 25; see also Gerald O'Collins, S.J., "Dei Verbum and Exegesis," in *Retrieving Fundamental Theology* (New York: Paulist Press, 1993), 136–49.

20. Joseph Sittler, *The Ecology of Faith* (Philadelphia: Muhlenberg Press, 1961), 39.

21. Indeed the ecumenical creeds of the church, such as the Apostle's and Nicene Creeds, essentially summarize the Gospel.

22. Hannah Arendt, *The Human Condition* (Chicago: University of Chicago Press, 1958), 181.

23. Quoted in Hauerwas, "Story and Theology," 348.

24. William Stringfellow, *A Simplicity of Faith* (Nashville, Tenn.: Abingdon, 1982), 20.

25. Michael Edwards, "Story: Towards a Christian Theory of Narrative," in *Images of Belief in Literature*, ed. David Jasper (New York: St. Martin's Press, 1984), 180.

26. Ibid., 183, 189.

27. Michael Roemer, *Telling Stories: Postmodernism and the Invalidation of Traditional Narrative* (Lanham, Md.: Rowman and Littlefield, 1995), 179.

28. John C. Puddefoot, "Information and Creation," in *The Science and Theology of Information*, ed. Christopher Wassermann et al. (Geneva, Switzerland: Labor et Fides, 1990), 17.

29. T. S. Eliot says that a culture is a "whole way of life." *Notes toward the Definition of Culture* (Reinbek bei Hamburg: Rowohlt, 1961), 29.

30. For an extended discussion of the rise of the professional communicator as a symbol broker, see James W. Carey, "The Communications Revolution and the Professional Communicator," in *A Critical Reader*, ed. Munson and Warren, 128–43.

31. Michael Warren, *Communications and Cultural Analysis* (Westport, Conn.: Bergin and Garvey, 1992), 11.

32. St. Augustine, *City of God*, trans. Marcus Dods (New York: Modern Library, 2000).

33. Anri Vartanov, "Television As Spectacle and Myth," *Journal of Communication* 41, no. 2 (spring 1991): 168.

34. Ibid.

35. Wirth, "Consensus," 29.

36. Carey, *Communication As Culture*, 66.

37. Clifford G. Christians, "Redemptive Popular Art: Television and the Cultural Mandate," *Reformed Journal* 30 (August 1980): 16.

38. Frank D. McConnell, "It's Time to Take Sides," *Commonweal* (22 September 1993): 23.

39. Hugh Dalziel Duncan, *Language and Literature in Society* (New York: Bedminster Press, 1953), ch. 2.

40. Raymond Williams, "The Magic System," *New Left Review* 1, no. 4 (July/August 1960): 27–32; also reprinted in Raymond Williams, *Problems in Materialism and Culture* (London: Verso, 1980), 170–195.

41. Quoted in Johann Baptist Metz, "A Short Apology of Narrative," in *The Crisis of Religious Language*, ed. Metz and Jossua, 86.

42. Wesley A. Kort, *Narrative Elements and Religious Meanings* (Philadelphia: Fortress Press, 1975), 5.

43. James W. Carey, "A Cultural Approach to Communication," *Communication* 2 (1975): 5.

44. Stanley Hauerwas, *Vision and Virtue* (Notre Dame, Ind.: Fides, 1974), 71, 74.

45. Walker Percy, *Signposts in a Strange Land* (New York: Farrar, Straus and Giroux, 1991), 208, 217.

46. See Ephesians 6:12; and Colossians 2:15 KJV.

47. Percy, *Signposts in a Strange Land*, 218.

48. James Carey, "The Communications Revolution," 141.

49. Kenneth L. Woodward, "The Spiritual Surfer," *Newsweek* (1 April 1996): 68.

50. Carey, "The Communications Revolution," 129.

51. Novak, "Television Shapes the Soul," 13.

52. Martin Esslin, *The Age of Television* (San Francisco: Freeman, 1982), 44.

53. See Thomas Skill et al., "The Portrayals of Religion and Spirituality on Fictional Network Television," *Review of Religious Research* 35, no. 3 (March 1994): 251–76; and John P. Ferré, "Prime-Time Piety? It Hardly Exists," *The Banner* 127 (16 March 1992): 14–15.

54. Joel Stein, "The God Squad," *Time* (22 September 1997) [cited 28 November 2001]. Online: http://www.time.com/time/magazine/1997/dom/970922/atele.the_god_squad.html.

55. David Marc, *Demographic Vistas: Television in American Culture* (Philadelphia: University of Pennsylvania Press, 1984), 7.

56. Neil Postman, *Amusing Ourselves to Death: Public Discourse in the Age of Show Business* (New York: Viking, 1985), 6.

57. Genesis 17:17 NIV.

58. Writer and minister Frederick Buechner says that the biblical parables "can be read as high and holy jokes about God and about man and about the Gospel itself as the highest and holiest joke of them all." *Telling the Truth: The Bible as Tragedy, Comedy and Fairy Tale* (San Francisco: HarperSanFrancisco, 1977), 63. The Jewish tradition has produced some biblical exegesis that is not nearly so comedic. See David R. Blumenthal, *Facing the Abusing God: A Theology of Protest* (Louisville, Ky.: Westminster/John Knox Press, 1993); and Todd Linafelt, *Surviving*

Lamentations: Catastrophe, Lament, and Protest in the Afterlife of a Biblical Book (Chicago: University of Chicago Press, 2000).

59. Bachofen, *Myth,* 180.

60. Nelvin Vos, *For God's Sake Laugh!* (Richmond, Va.: J. Knox Press, 1967).

61. Quoted in Nancy McCann, "Freestyle Religion," *Sojourners* (July 1980): 35.

62. I have discussed this at some length in "Popular Culture and Life-Style Politics," *Journal of Communication Inquiry* 6 (spring 1981): 87–96.

63. Joel Achenbach et al., quoted in James Bowman, "Religion or the Merely Kooky?" *New Criterion* 15 (May 1997): 61.

64. Ibid., 63.

65. Harold M. Foster, "The New Literacy: Television, Purveyor of Modern Myth," *English Journal* 75, no. 2 (1984): 27.

66. James Carey, "The Press, Public Opinion, and Public Discourse: On the Edge of Postmodernism," in *A Critical Reader*, ed. Munson and Warren, 230.

67. John J. Navone, *The Jesus Story: Our Life As Story in Christ* (Collegeville, Minn.: Liturgical Press, 1979), 71.

68. G. Thomas, "Providing Order and Escape: Mass Media As Ritualized Communication in Modern Societies," in *The Science and Theology of Information*, ed. Wassermann et al., 281, 282, 285.

69. Thomas Boomershine, "Doing Theology in the Electronic Age: The Meeting of Orality and Electricity," *Journal of Theology* 95 (1991): 285.

70. Sallie TeSelle, "The Experience of Coming to Belief," *Theology Today* 22 (July 1975): 160.

71. Quoted in James M. Wall, "Language Gap," *Christian Century* 111 (20 June-6 July 1994): 627.

72. Ibid.

73. "Introduction to Part Three—Ideological Criticism," in *Screening the Sacred: Religion, Myth, and Ideology in Popular American Film*, ed. Joel W. Martin and Conrad E. Ostwalt Jr. (Boulder, Colo.: Westview Press, 1995), 120.

74. Jeffrey L. Sheller, "Spiritual America," *U.S. News and World Report* (4 April 1994): 54.

75. Warren, *Communications*, 3.

76. The producer probably maintains the most control over the production process. See, e.g., Horace Newcomb and Robert S. Alley, *The Producer's Medium* (New York: Oxford University Press, 1983). However,

power and resources are still dispersed, though unequally, among many people and organizations. See Joseph Turow, *Media Industries: The Production of News and Entertainment* (New York: Longman, 1984).

77. Novak, "Television Shapes the Soul," 13.

78. Among the more interesting attempts are Benjamin Stein, *The View from Sunset Boulevard* (Garden City, N.Y.: Doubleday, Anchor Books, 1980); and S. Robert Lichter, Stanley Rothman, and Linda S. Lichter, *The Media Elite* (Bethesda, Md.: Adler and Adler, 1986).

79. Warren, *Communications*, 3.

80. Raymond Williams, *Keywords: A Vocabulary of Culture and Society*, rev. ed. (New York: Oxford University Press, 1983), 319.

81. John Pilger, "The Brave New Media World," *New Statesman and Society* 6 (June 1993): 14.

82. P. van Dijk, "Revelation," in *The Science and Theology of Information*, ed. Wasserman et al., 94.

83. Ibid.

84. Michael Walzer, *Interpretation and Social Criticism* (Cambridge: Harvard University Press, 1987), 39.

85. Puddefoot, "Information and Creation," in *The Science and Theology of Information*, ed. Wasserman et al., 7.

86. Nicholas Wolterstorff, *Reason within the Bounds of Religion*, 2nd ed. (Grand Rapids, Mich.: William B. Eerdmans, 1984), 15–21.

87. David Thorburn, "Television As an Aesthetic Medium," *Critical Studies in Mass Communication* 4 (June 1987): 172.

88. Frank D. McConnell, "It's Time to Take Sides," *Commonweal* (22 September 1995): 23.

89. The "most hip, the most clever, and the most humorous films and television series are laced with references to pop culture itself, as if there were no world beyond that culture." Thomas S. Hibbs, *Shows about Nothing: Nihilism in Popular Culture from* The Exorcist *to* Seinfeld (Dallas: Spence, 1999), 183.

90. Leszek Kolakowski, *The Presence of Myth*, trans. Adam Czerniawski (Chicago: University of Chicago Press, 1972), 95.

91. For an excellent discussion of the role of myth in fundamentalism, see Nielsen, *Fundamentalism*, 37–41.

92. Eugene H. Peterson, *Five Smooth Stones for Pastoral Work* (Grand Rapids, Mich.: William B. Eerdmans, 1994), 85.

93. See Larry W. Poland, *The Last Temptation of Hollywood* (Highland, Calif.: Mastermedia International, 1988); and Charles Lyons, *The New*

Censors, Movies and the Culture Wars (Philadelphia: Temple University Press, 1997), ch. 5.

94. Julian N. Hartt, *A Christian Critique of American Culture* (New York: Harper and Row, 1967), 405–6.

95. Peterson, *Five Smooth Stones*, 86–87.

96. Andrew M. Greeley, *God in Popular Culture* (Chicago: Thomas Moore Press, 1988); and Richard J. Mouw, *Consulting the Faithful: What Christian Intellectuals Can Learn from Popular Religion* (Grand Rapids, Mich.: William B. Eerdmans, 1994).

97. William D. Romanowski, "John Calvin Meets the Creature from the Black Lagoon: The Christian Reformed Church and the Movies 1928–1966," *Christian Scholars Review* 25, no. 1 (September 1995): 47–62.

98. I adapted this argument from Peterson, *Five Smooth Stones*, 85–87.

99. Mouw, *Consulting the Faithful*.

100. Patrick O'Heffernan, "The L.A. Riots: A Story Made for and by TV," *Television Quarterly* 26, no. 1 (1992): 5, 9, 10.

101. See Romanowski, "John Calvin."

102. Paul Schrader, interview by John Brady, *The Craft of the Screenwriter: Interviews with Six Celebrated Screenwriters* (New York: Simon and Schuster, 1981), 269.

103. Edward J. Carnell, *Television: Servant or Master?* (Grand Rapids, Mich.: William B. Eerdmans, 1950), 6.

104. Ibid., 113.

105. Ibid., referencing Matthew 4:1–11.

106. Carnell, *Television*, 115.

107. Ibid., 116, 117, 120, 136, 165.

108. Ibid., 192–93.

109. William F. Fore, *Mythmakers: Gospel, Culture, and the Media* (New York: Friendship Press, 1990); Fore, *Image and Impact: How Man Comes Through in the Mass Media* (New York: Friendship Press, 1970); and Fore, *Television and Religion: The Shaping of Faith, Values, and Culture* (Minneapolis, Minn.: Augsburg, 1987).

110. Fore, *Image and Impact*, 6–8.

111. Fore, *Mythmakers*, 3.

112. Ibid., 53–54.

113. Ibid., 55.

114. Ibid., 61–71, 11, 12, 13.

115. Ibid., 56.

116. Ibid., 57–58.

117. Ibid., 58–59.

118. Ibid., 137.

119. John Wiley Nelson, *Your God Is Alive and Well and Appearing in Popular Culture* (Philadelphia: Westminster Press, 1976), 21–23.

120. Ibid., 20.

121. Ibid., 19.

122. Ibid., 22–25.

123. Ibid., 17, 16.

124. Ibid., 199, 202, 203.

125. Ibid., 206.

126. Andrew M. Greeley, *God in Popular Culture* (Chicago: Thomas More Press, 1988) 9.

127. For another analysis of a Catholic understanding of popular culture, see Ingrid Shafer, "The Catholic Imagination in Popular Film and Television," *Journal of Popular Film and Television* 19 (summer 1991): 50–57.

128. Greeley, *God in Popular Culture*, 17, 22–23, 27, 30, 63.

129. Ibid., 76, 125, 137, 178–79, 212, 218.

130. Ibid., 246, 252, 261, 263, 253, 268, 272.

131. Ibid., 293, 296.

132. Ibid., 198.

133. Quoted in Evan Gahr, "Tuning Out Religion," *National Review* (27 October 1997): 44.

134. Alexis de Tocqueville, *Democracy in America*, ed. and trans. Harvey C. Mansfield and Delba Winthrop (Chicago: University of Chicago Press, 2000), 176.

135. Park, "Reflections," 115.

136. Jean Bethke Elshtain, *Who Are We?: Critical Reflections and Hopeful Possibilities* (Grand Rapids, Mich.: William B. Eerdmans, 2000), 154.

137. Eugene H. Petersen, *Subversive Spirituality* (Grand Rapids, Mich.: William B. Eerdmans, 1994), 6.

138. Thomas, "Providing Order," 282.

139. Raymond Williams, *Problems in Materialism and Culture* (London: Verso, 1980), 43.

140. Arnett, *Communication and Community*, 125.

Chapter 6

1. Walter Lippmann, *Public Opinion* (New York: Free Press, 1922), 10, 11.

2. James W. Carey, "The Chicago School and the History of Mass Communication Research," in *James Carey: A Critical Reader*, ed. Eve Stryker Munson and Catherine A. Warren (Minneapolis: University of Minnesota Press, 1997), 23.

3. Jacques Ellul, *Propaganda: The Formation of Men's Attitudes* (New York: Alfred A. Knopf, 1971).

4. Jacques Ellul, *The Presence of the Kingdom* (New York: Seabury Press, 1948), 37–38.

5. See especially Pierre Babin, *The New Era in Religious Communication* (Minneapolis, Minn.: Fortress Press, 1991).

6. There is an enormous amount of literature on the nature of popular culture. I have tried to summarize some of the issues involved and to provide a critical perspective in "Popular Culture and Life-Style Politics," *Journal of Communication Inquiry* 6 (winter 1981): 87–96. For a more lengthy examination of popular culture, see Herbert J. Gans, *Popular Culture and High Culture: An Analysis and Evaluation of Taste* (New York: Basic Books, 1975).

7. Jeremy Tunstall, *The Media Are American: Anglo-American Media in the World* (New York: Columbia University Press, 1977).

8. Karl Menninger, *Whatever Became of Sin?* (New York: Hawthorn Books, 1973), 209.

9. Robert Wood Lynn, "The Mass Media and the Kingdom of Evil," *Religion in Life* 21 (spring 1952): 229–40.

10. Kenneth Burke, *The Rhetoric of Religion: Studies in Logology* (Berkeley: University of California Press, 1970), 235.

11. Ibid.

12. Harry Boonstra, "Can Satire Be Religious?" in *The Christian Imagination: Essays on Literature and the Arts*, ed. Leland Ryken (Grand Rapids, Mich.: Baker Book House, 1981), 227–39.

13. See Matthew McCann Fenton, "Jimmy Staggered: Twelve Years Ago, Jimmy Swaggart Confessed His Sins of the Flesh on TV," *Entertainment Weekly* (25 February 2000): 92; see also Joanne Kaufman, "The Fall of Jimmy Swaggart," *People Weekly* (7 March 1988): 35–36.

14. Cornelius Plantinga Jr., *Not the Way It's Supposed to Be: A Breviary of Sin* (Grand Rapids, Mich.: William B. Eerdmans, 1995), 12.

15. Gail Pennington, "MTV's Seven Deadly Sins: Illuminating, Entertaining," *Everyday Magazine* (11 August 1993): 3.

16. Chris Willman, "MTV's 'Seven Deadly Sins' Examines Traps of Humanity," *Los Angeles Times*, 11 August 1993.

17. John Leo, "The Seven Video Sins," *U.S. News and World Report* (23 August 1993): 19.

18. Ibid.

19. Jean Bethke Elshtain, "The Trials of a Public Intellectual," *University of Chicago Magazine*, June 1996 [cited 8 August, 2001]. Online: http://www2.uchicago.edu/alumni/alumni.mag/9606/9606Elshtain2.html

20. Leo, "The Seven Video Sins."

21. Ibid.

22. "Sin," *People Weekly* (10 February 1986): 106–13.

23. Since most religious broadcasting reaches a small number of people, I do not consider it "popular." Even the American televangelists with the largest Sunday-morning audiences reach only about one or two million Americans, less than 1 percent of the population. By contrast, a prime-time TV series might reach 20 percent, and the combined prime-time audience for secular fare is somewhere around 65 percent of American homes every night.

24. Cliff Vaughn, "The Rhetoric of Terrorism: Pray, Combat Evil," *Ethics Report* 9, no. 5 (2001), n.p. Online: http://www.baptists4ethics.com/article_detail.cfm?AID=1266. (29 March 2003).

25. For historical insight into this phenomenon, see Marvin Olasky, *Prodigal Press: The Anti-Christian Bias of the American News Media* (Westchester, Ill.: Crossway Books, 1988), 17–30. The turning point seems to have been the early to mid-nineteenth century, when the periodicals of the day became market-driven enterprises catering to the masses.

26. See, e.g., the films of Claude Berri (*Jean de Florette* and *Manon of the Spring*) and the novels of Aleksandr I. Solzhenitsyn. Edward E. Ericson, *Solzhenitsyn: The Moral Vision* (Grand Rapids, Mich.: William B. Eerdmans, 1980).

27. Martin E. Marty, *The Improper Opinion: Mass Media and the Christian Faith* (Philadelphia: Westminster Press, 1961).

28. Alvin W. Gouldner, *The Dialectic of Ideology and Technology: The Origins, Grammar, and Future of Ideology* (New York: Seabury Press, 1976), 26.

29. Wendy Kaminer, *Sleeping with Extra-Terrestrials: The Rise of Irrationalism and the Perils of Piety* (New York: Pantheon Books, 1999).

30. Neil Gilman, "Authenticity without Demonization," *Journal of Ecumenical Studies* 34, no. 3 (summer 1997): 346, 347.

31. Martin Kaplan, "Can a Postmodern Nation Write a Good-vs.-Evil Tale?" *USA Today,* 29 November 2001, sec. A, p. 17.

32. Os Guinness, foreword to *The Revenge of Failure: The Culture of Envy and Rage* (Burke, Va.: Trinity Forum, 1994), 3.

33. Michael Warren, *Communications and Cultural Analysis: A Religious View* (Westport, Conn.: Bergin and Garvey, 1992), 12.

34. Raymond Williams, *Keywords: A Vocabulary of Culture and Society*, rev. ed. (New York: Oxford University Press, 1983), 174.

35. Quoted in David H. Kelsey, "Whatever Happened to the Doctrine of Sin," *Theology Today* 50, no. 2 (July 1993): 221.

36. John Lukacs, introduction to *Confessions of an Original Sinner* (South Bend, Ind.: St. Augustine's Press, 2000), xiii.

37. Reinhold Niebuhr, *The Nature and Destiny of Man* (New York: Charles Scribner and Sons, 1941), 208.

38. Quoted in Lynn, "Mass Media," 230.

39. St. Augustine, *Confessions*, trans. Henry Chadwick (New York: Oxford University Press, 1991), 146.

40. Charles Krauthammer, "Looking Evil Dead in the Eye," *Time* (15 July 1985): 80.

41. Jeffrey H. Mahan, "Once upon a Time in the West," *Explor* 7 (fall 1984): 81, 82, 91.

42. Reinhold Zwick, "The Problem of Evil in Contemporary Film," in *New Image of Religious Film*, ed. John R. May (Mission, Kans.: Sheed and Ward, 1997), 72, 73, 74.

43. My argument is not exactly the same as Bellah's formulation of "civil religion." I do not see civil sin as a form of civil religion as much as a mass-mediated version of underlying (or overarching) tribal beliefs in America. See Robert N. Bellah, "Civil Religion in America," *Daedalus* 96 (winter/spring 1967): 1–21.

44. Vaughn, "The Rhetoric of Terrorism."

45. Anson Shupe, "Constructing Evil As a Social Process," in *Uncivil Religion: Interreligious Hostility in America*, ed. Robert N. Bellah and Frederick E. Greenspahn (New York: Crossroad, 1987), 214.

46. Paul Ricoeur, *The Symbolism of Evil*, trans. Emerson Buchanan (New York: Harper and Row, 1967), 170, 172–74, 168–69.

47. Neil P. Hurley, "Hollywood's New Mythology," *Theology Today* 39 (January 1983): 402.

48. Ibid., 407.

49. Patrick O'Heffernan, "The L.A. Riots: A Story Made for and by TV," *Television Quarterly* 26, no. 1 (1992): 9, 10.

50. Hurley, "New Mythology," 402, 408.

51. Coleman Luck, "Touched by a Fallen Angel," *Tongue*, 14 February 1999 [cited 14 February 1999]. Online: http://www.thetongue.com/columnist/luck/luck1.html.

52. Ibid.

53. Ibid.

54. Ibid.

55. Guinness, *Revenge of Failure*, 6.

56. Ibid., 3.

57. Paddy Chayefsky, *The Collected Works of Paddy Chayefsky: The Screenplays*, vol. 2 (New York: Applause Books, 1995), 175–76.

58. For examples of media reaction to these events see "Nightmare in Iran: Seizure of the United States Embassy and Its American Staff," *U.S. News and World Report* (19 November 1979): 23–25; Ray Vicker, "U.S. Embassy Siege Has a Carnival Despite the Tension: Iranians Seem to Be Enjoying Publicity from Seizure; But Danger Still Lurks," *Wall Street Journal*, 20 November 1979; "Half a Million Stranded in the Sand," *UN Chronicle* 27, no. 4 (December 1990): 8; Jacob Weisberg, "Choice Cuts," *The New Republic* 205, nos. 8–9 (19 August 1991): 43; and Alex Prud'homme, "Did They All Have to Die? Chagrined Milwaukeeans Learn How the Police Let a Serial Killer Slip through Their Hands to Kill Again," *Time* (12 August 1991): 28.

59. See Pam Lambert, "Out of Sight, Out of Mind," *People Weekly* (18 January 1993); "Kid's Rights Walk Out with the Schools," *Daily Illinois Online*, 27 April 1993 [cited 19 June 2000]. Online: http://www.illinimedia.com/di/archives/1993/April.27/theedit2.html.

60. Shupe, "Constructing Evil."

61. Robert N. Bellah, "Conclusion: Competing Visions of the Role of Religion in American Society," in *Uncivil Religion*, ed. Bellah and Greenspahn, 219–32.

62. Shupe, "Constructing Evil," 215.

63. C. S. Lewis, *Mere Christianity* (New York: Simon and Schuster, 1996), 75.

64. As quoted in Robert Lynn, "The Mass Media and the Kingdom of Evil," *Religion in Life* 21, no. 2 (spring 1952): 237.

65. Elayne Rapping, "What Evil Lurks in the Hearts of Men," *Progressive* 58 (November 1994): 36.

66. James R. Keller, "Like to a Chaos: Deformity and Depravity," *Journal of Pop Film and Television* 23 (spring 1995): 8.

67. Ibid.

68. Ibid., 9.

69. Ibid., 14.

70. For a review of the docudrama, see Ken Tucker, "Overkill: The Aileen Wuornos Story," *Entertainment Weekly* (13 November 1992): 70–71.

71. Jean Bethke Elshtain, *Who Are We?: Critical Reflections and Hopeful Possibilities* (Grand Rapids, Mich.: William B. Eerdmans, 2000), 7–35.

72. For an excellent overview of the pop-culture wars, see William D. Romanowski, *Pop Culture Wars: Religion and the Role of Entertainment in American Life* (Downers Grove, Ill.: InterVarsity Press, 1996); for a review of TV watchdog groups, see Mark Fackler, "Religious Watchdog Groups and Prime-Time Programming," in *Channels of Belief: Religion and American Commercial Television*, ed. John P. Ferré (Ames: Iowa State University Press, 1990), 99–116; and Robert S. Alley, "Television, Religion, and Fundamentalist Distortions," in *Religious Television: Controversies and Conclusions*, ed. Robert Abelman and Steward M. Hoover (Norwood, N.J.: Ablex, 1990), 265–74.

73. Wilbur Schramm, "The Nature of Communication between Humans," in *The Process and Effects of Mass Communication*, ed. Wilbur Schramm and Donald F. Roberts, rev. ed. (Urbana: University of Illinois Press, 1971).

74. Raymond Bauer, "The Obstinate Audience: The Influence Process from the Point of View of Social Communication," *American Psychologist* 19 (1964): 319–28.

75. Fred Molitor and Barry S. Sapolsky, "Sex, Violence, and Victimization in Slasher Films," *Journal of Broadcasting and Electronic Media* 37 (1993): 233, 240.

76. Ibid., 241.

77. Lynn, "Mass Media," 234.

78. Arthur Miller, *Death of a Salesman* (New York: Penguin, 1988). See, e.g., the dialogue on 23.

79. Mahan, "Once Upon a Time," 90.

80. Robert N. Bellah, "Conclusion: Competing Visions of the Role of Religion in American Society," in *Uncivil Religion*, ed. Bellah and Greenspahn, 219.

81. James A. Aho, *This Thing of Darkness: A Sociology of the Enemy* (Seattle: University of Washington Press, 1994).

82. For an introduction to Marxist approaches to studying the media, see Barry Brummett, *Rhetoric in Popular Culture* (New York: St. Martin's Press, 1994), 111–20.

83. See Michael Medved, *Hollywood vs. America: Popular Culture and the War on Traditional Values* (New York: HarperCollins, 1992). For a

critique of conspiratorial views of television, especially among evangelicals, see Quentin J. Schultze, *Redeeming Television* (Downers Grove, Ill.: InterVarsity Press, 1992), 149–55.

84. Stanley Rothman, "Is God Really Dead in Beverly Hills? Religion and the Movies," *American Scholar* 64 (spring 1996): 273.

85. Ibid., 277.

86. Says Jeremiah, "The fathers have eaten sour grapes, and the children's teeth are set on edge." Jeremiah 31:29 (New International Version).

87. Colin E. Gunton, *The One, the Three and the Many: God, Creation and the Culture of Modernity* (Cambridge: Cambridge University Press, 1993), 75.

88. Hannah Arendt, "The Threat of Conformism," in *Essays in Understanding 1930–1954*, ed. Jerome Kohn (New York: Harcourt Brace, 1994), 422.

89. Ibid.

90. Ibid., 423.

91. C. S. Lewis, *The Abolition of Man: Or Reflections on Education with Special Reference to the Teaching of English in the Upper Forms of Schools* (New York: Simon and Schuster, 1996), 81.

92. Patrick McCormick, "The Really Scary Thing about Thrillers," *U.S. Catholic* 59 (August 1994): 47.

93. Andrew M. Greeley, *God in Popular Culture* (Chicago: Thomas More Press, 1988), 9, 13, 123; Gregor T. Goethals, *The Electronic Golden Calf: Images, Religion, and the Making of Meaning* (Cambridge, Mass.: Cowley, 1990); and Goethals, *The TV Ritual: Worship at the Video Alter* (Boston: Beacon, 1981).

94. Harold Fickett, "'Who Killed JR': Images of Evil Brought Back into Focus," *Christianity Today* (24 October 1980): 52.

95. See David Thorburn, "Television Melodrama," in *Television*, 5th ed. Horace Newcomb (New York: Oxford University Press, 1994), 537–50.

96. Gene Edward Veith, "Good against Evil; Television: At Least the Power Rangers Aren't Relativists," *World* 9 (11 February 1995): 23.

97. Todd Gitlin, "Hyping the News," *The Nation* 256 (15 March 1993): 328.

98. John Parris Springer, "Hollywood Fictions: The Cultural Construction of Hollywood in American Literature, 1916–1939" (Ph.D. diss., University of Iowa, 1994).

99. Edward W. Said, *Covering Islam: How the Media and the Experts Determine How We See the Rest of the World* (New York: Pantheon, 1981), 40, 41, 43, 44, 45.

100. Susan J. Douglas, "The Framing of Race," *Progressive* 59 (December 1995): 19; see also George M. Marsden, *Fundamentalism and American Culture: The Shaping of Twentieth Century Evangelicalism, 1870–1925* (New York: Oxford University Press, 1982).

101. Gitlin, "Hyping the News."

102. Sari Thomas and Steven V. LeShay, "Bad Business? A Reexamination of Television's Portrayal of Businesspersons," *Journal of Communication* 42, no. 1 (winter 1992): 95–105.

103. Robert Bogdan et al., "The Disabled: Media's Monster," *Social Policy* 13 (summer 1982-spring 1983): 32–33.

104. Douglas, "The Framing of Race," 19.

105. Frank Walsh, *Sin and Censorship* (New Haven, Conn.: Yale University Press, 1996), 72.

106. Guy Lyon Playfair, *The Evil Eye: The Unacceptable Face of Television* (London: Jonathan Cape, 1990), 124.

107. McCormick, "The Really Scary Thing," 48.

108. Henry A. Giroux, "Hollywood, Race, and the Demonization of Youth: The 'Kids' Are Not 'Alright,'" *Educational Researcher* 25, no. 2 (March 1996): 31.

109. Vic S. Sussman, "Who's the Bad Guy," *U.S. News and World Report* (25 September 1995): 76–77.

110. John Taylor, "The Demon Gap," *New York* (24 February 1992): 50.

111. Ibid., 52, 55.

112. Ellul, *The Presence of the Kingdom*, 89.

113. Ibid., 104.

114. George Gilder, interview in *New Perspectives Quarterly* 12 (spring 1995): 20–21.

115. Reinhold Niebuhr, *The Nature and Destiny of Man* (New York: Charles Scribner and Sons, 1941), 208.

116. Ibid.

117. Edward T. Oakes, "Why Has American Society Become So Violent?" *America* (5 September 1992): 106.

118. Gray Cavender, "In the Shadow of Shadows," in *Entertaining Crime: Television Reality Programs*, ed. Mark Fishman and Gray Cavender (New York: Aldine de Gruyter, 1998), 81, 86.

119. Aaron Doyle, "'Cops': Television Policing as Policing Reality," in *Entertaining Crime*, ed. Fishman and Cavender, 103–4.

120. Quoted in Paul G. Kooistra et al., "The World of Crime According to 'Cops,'" in *Entertaining Crime*, ed. Fishman and Cavender, 154.

121. Maria Grabe, "Does Crime Pay? Tabloid vs. Highbrow News" (Ph.D. diss., Temple University, 1996).

122. The traditional situation comedy, as a form of public amusement, does not depict evil. It is based on mere complication and confusion, not immoral conflict. Consequently, the standard genre does not offer many real villains. Moreover, as Fickett has suggested, sitcoms are largely a "humanist suburb where the characters have been abandoned by heaven and hell to their psychotherapists. In these cramped dwellings of the human spirit Good and Evil have been replaced by Self-esteem and Desire." "'Who Killed JR,'" 52.

123. David Thorburn, "Television Melodrama," in *Television*, ed. Newcomb, 595–604.

124. Theodor W. Adorno, *Prisms* (London: Neville Spearman, 1967), 32.

125. For an introduction to the mythology/history of Westerns, see John G. Cawelti, *The Six-Gun Mystique* (Bowling Green, Ohio: Bowling Green University Press, 1975).

126. I cover this in greater detail in *Television: Manna from Hollywood?* (Grand Rapids, Mich.: Zondervan, 1986), 82–113.

127. One of the most interesting books on this topic is Richard Sparks, *Television and the Drama of Crime: Moral Tales and the Place of Crime in Public Life* (Buckingham: Open University Press, 1992).

128. Horace Newcomb, *TV: The Most Popular Art* (New York: Anchor, 1974), 226–27.

129. For views on the standardization of mass-media formulas, see Herbert J. Gans, *Popular Culture and High Culture: An Analysis and Evaluation of Taste* (New York: Basic Books, 1974), 21–23.

130. Bellah, "Competing Visions," 220.

131. Ibid.

132. Jay Tolson, "The Vocabulary of Evil," *U.S. News and World Report* (10 May 1999): 22.

133. Aleksandr I. Solzhenitsyn, *A World Split Apart: Commencement Address Delivered at Harvard University June 8, 1978* (New York: Harper and Row, 1978), 49.

134. Charles Horton Cooley, *Social Organization: A Study of the Larger Mind* (New York: Schocken Books, 1909), 378–79.

135. John C. Puddefoot, "Information and Creation," in *The Science and Theology of Information*, ed. Christoph Wassermann et al. (Geneva, Switzerland: Labor et Fides, 1990), 22.

136. William Willimon, *Sighing for Eden: Sin, Evil and the Christian Faith* (Nashville, Tenn.: Abingdon Press, 1985), 27.

137. Ellul, *The Presence of the Kingdom*, 125.

Chapter 7

1. Edward Sorel, "Unanswered Prayers," *Nation* 268, no. 21 (7 June 1999): 8.

2. Alexis de Tocqueville, *Democracy in America*, ed. and trans. Harvey C. Mansfield and Delba Winthrop (Chicago: University of Chicago Press, 2000), 177, 280, 279.

3. Allan R. Andrews, "Too Devout, or Not Devout Enough, to Cover Religion," *Editor and Publisher* 132, no. 6 (6 February 1999): 54.

4. Robert E. Park, "New As a Form of Knowledge," in *On Social Control and Collective Behavior*, ed. Ralph H. Turner (Chicago: University of Chicago Press, 1967), 41–42.

5. Louis Wirth, "Consensus and Mass Communication," in *On Cities and Social Life*, ed. Albert J. Reiss Jr. (Chicago: University of Chicago Press, 1964), 25.

6. David Paul Nord, "Teleology and News: The Religious Roots of American Journalism," *Journal of American History* 77 (June 1990): 10.

7. As Park suggests, "the importance of news has grown consistently with the expansion of the means of communication and with the growth of science." "New As a Form of Knowledge," 50.

8. Sharan L. Daniel, "Integrating Rhetoric and Journalism to Realize Publics," *Rhetoric & Public Affairs* 5 (2002): 515.

9. News portrays what Park calls the "freedom of the city" that "magnifies, spreads out, and advertises human nature in all its variations and manifestations." Park. "News as a Form of Knowledge," 18.

10. John Schmalzbauer, "Telling Catholic and Evangelical Stories in American Journalism: The Impact of Religious Imagination," *U.S. Catholic Historian* 20 (spring 2002): 25-44.

11. Ibid., 40.

12. John Hart, "An Account of the Conflict between a Church's Mission and a Journalist's Job," *Columbia Journalism Review* 31, no. 3 (September/October 1992): 44–50.

13. Ibid., 44.

14. Ibid., 45.

15. Ibid., 48.

16. Tocqueville, *Democracy*, 287, 386, 280, 174.

17. Doug Underwood, *From Yahweh to Yahoo! The Religious Roots of the Secular Press* (Urbana: University of Illinois Press, 2002), 5.
18. Richard D. Brown, "Spreading the Word: Rural Clergymen and the Communication Network of 18th Century New England," *Proceedings of the Massachusetts Historical Society* 94 (1982): 10.
19. Nord, "Teleology and News," 10.
20. Ibid.
21. Ibid., 12.
22. Ibid., 19.
23. David Alan Copeland, "The Freshest Advice Foreign and Domestic: The Character and Content of Nonpolitical News in Colonial Newspapers, 1690–1775" (Ph.D. diss., University of North Carolina, 1994).
24. Tocqueville, *Democracy*, 176.
25. John C. Nerone, "The Mythology of the Penny Press," *Critical Studies in Mass Communication* 4, no. 4 (1987): 387.
26. Daniel J. Boorstin, *The Americans: The Colonial Experience* (New York: Random House, 1958), 326.
27. Quoted in ibid., 327.
28. Harry S. Stout, "Religion, Communications, and George Whitefield," in *Communication and Change in American Religious History*, ed. Leonard I. Sweet (Grand Rapids, Mich.: William B. Eerdmans, 1993), 111, 112, 113, 116.
29. Boorstin, *The Americans*, 328.
30. Mark Silk, *Unsecular Media: Making News of Religion in America* (Urbana: University of Illinois Press, 1995), 15.
31. J. M. Leavitt, "The Relation of Our Republic to Other Nations," *Ladies' Repository* 18 (November 1858): 660.
32. "At a time when the United States had few national institutions, virtually no national communications network . . . , and no national corporations," writes Anne M. Boylan, "the American Sunday school union established the framework for . . . a national Evangelical corporation" that distributed Sunday school materials across the country. *Sunday School: The Formation of an American Institution* (New Haven, Conn.: Yale University Press, 1988), 73.
33. Nathan O. Hatch, *The Democratization of American Christianity* (New Haven, Conn.: Yale University Press, 1989), 125–6.
34. Gaylord P. Albaugh, "The Role of the Religious Press in the Development of American Christianity, 1730–1830" (unpublished manuscript, 1984), 6–7. Cited in ibid.

35. Ibid.; Allen W. Palmer and Hyrum Laturner, "Free at Last? Religious Contradictions in the Origins of the Black Press in America" (paper presented at the annual meeting of the Association for Education in Journalism and Mass Communication, Chicago, July 1996).

36. David Paul Nord, "Systematic Benevolence: Religious Publishing and the Marketplace in Early Nineteenth-Century America," in *Communication and Change*, ed. Sweet, 241.

37. Ann Douglas, *The Feminization of American Culture* (New York: Farrar, Straus and Giroux, 1977).

38. Wesley Norton, *Religious Newspapers in the Old Northwest to 1861* (Athens: Ohio University Press, 1977), 2.

39. Tocqueville, *Democracy*, 284.

40. Dennis N. Voskuil, "Reaching Out: Mainline Protestantism and the Media," in *Between the Times: The Travail of the Protestant Establishment in America, 1900–1960*, ed. William R. Hutchinson (Cambridge: Cambridge University Press, 1989), 73.

41. Michael Schudson, *Discovering the News: A Social History of American Newspapers* (New York: Basic Books, 1978), 44.

42. Tocqueville, *Democracy*, 278.

43. James Parton, *The Life of Horace Greeley* (New York: Mason Brothers, 1855), 383.

44. Quoted in Isaac C. Pray, *Memoirs of James Gordon Bennett and His Times* (Manchester, N.H.: Ayer, 1855; reprint, New York: 1970): 276–77.

45. James Cardinal Gibbons, *Discourses and Sermons for Every Sunday and the Principle [sic] Festivals of the Year* (Baltimore: John Murphy, 1908), 400.

46. Schudson, *Discovering the News*, 60.

47. Quoted in Wayne Joubert, "Newspaper Coverage of the American Revival of 1858" (unpublished paper, University of Texas, Austin), 18–19.

48. Mary M. Cronin, "Brother's Keeper: The Reform Journalism of the *New England Magazine*," *Journalism History* 22 (spring 1996): 15–23.

49. See Hanno Hardt, *Social Theories of the Press: Early German and American Perspectives* (Beverly Hills, Calif.: Sage, 1979).

50. I get the term "naked public square" from Richard John Neuhaus, *The Naked Public Square: Religion and Democracy in America* (Grand Rapids, Mich.: William B. Eerdmans, 1984).

51. Mark Silk, "Journalists with Attitude: A Response to Richardson and van Driel," *Review of Religious Research* 39, no. 2 (December 1997): 137; see also Silk, *Unsecular Media*.

52. Robert Lekachman, "The Secular Uses of the Religious Press," in *The Religious Press in America*, ed. Martin E. Marty et al. (New York: Greenwood, 1963), 175.

53. Ibid., 176.

54. John McCaslin, "Inside the Beltway," *Washington Times*, 11 November 1994, sec. A, p. 5.

55. Park, "New As a Form of Knowledge," 41.

56. Marvin Olasky, *Telling the Truth: How to Revitalize Christian Journalism* (Wheaton, Ill.: Crossway Books, 1996): 31, 32, 33.

57. St. Augustine, *The Enchiridion on Faith Hope and Love*, trans. J.F. Shaw (A.D. 421). [cited 28 November 2001]. Online: http://www.newadvent.org/fathers/1302.htm.

58. Quoted in Alicia C. Shepard, "The Media Get Religion," *American Journalism Review* 18 (December 1995) [cited 12 July 1999]. Online: http://ajr.newslink.org/ajrshep2.html.

59. "1991's Top Ten Stories," *Christianity Today* (16 December 1991): 54.

60. Jacques Barzun, "The Press and the Prose," *Occasional Paper* (Freedom Forum Media Studies Center) (10 March 1992): 7.

61. David Van Biema, "Full of Promise," *Time* (6 November 1995): 62.

62. John Leo, "Fairness? Promises, Promises," *U.S. News and World Report* (28 July 1997): 18.

63. See Dan Wakefield, *Expect a Miracle: The Miraculous Things That Happen to Ordinary People* (San Francisco: HarperCollins, 1998).

64. Quoted in Bill Broadway, "Miracles: If You're Awake Enough to See 'Em, Nice Things Await You, Author Says," *Grand Rapids (Michigan) Press*, 15 July 1995, Sec. B, p 6.

65. Barend van Driel and James T. Richardson, "Print Media Coverage of New Religious Movements: A Longitudinal Study," *Journal of Communication* 38, no. 3 (summer 1988): 37–61.

66. Stuart A. Wright, "Media Coverage of Unconventional Religion: Any 'Good News' for Minority Faiths?" *Review of Religious Research* 39, no. 2 (December 1997): 101–15.

67. Quoted in William Raspberry, "When There Is No Fight, Is There News?" *Grand Rapids (Michigan) Press*, 3 November 1995, sec. A, p. 10.

68. Terry Mattingly, "The Religion Beat," *Quill* (January 1983): 17.

69. Ernest C. Hynds, "Large Daily Newspapers Have Improved Coverage of Religion," *Journalism Quarterly* 64 (summer/fall 1987): 447.

70. Thomas Fox, "Who Speaks for Religion in the U.S.," *National Catholic Reporter* (17 February 1989): 2. At least one study concluded that viewers of news reports about the scandals became far more critical

and negative about religious broadcasters. Robert Abelman, "Influence of News Coverage of the 'Scandal' on PTL Viewers," *Journalism Quarterly* 68, nos. 1/2 (spring/summer 1991): 101–10.

71. Kenneth L. Woodward, "Libels in the Cathedral," *Newsweek* (1 April 1991): 59.

72. "Religion on TV News: Still Scarce," *Mediawatch* (April 1995): 6.

73. Ibid.

74. Martin E. Marty, "The Increase of Religion Coverage," *Sightings* (E-mail newsletter), 20 October 1998.

75. David Neff, "The Pope, the Press, and Evolution," *Christianity Today* (6 January 1997): 19.

76. James W. Carey, "The Dark Continent of American Journalism," in *James Carey: A Critical Reader*, ed. Eve Stryker Munson and Catherine A. Warren (Minneapolis: University of Minnesota Press, 1997), 178–79.

77. Ibid., 179, 180, 181.

78. Peter A. Brown, "The Real Story," *MediaCritic* (winter 1995): 76.

79. Ibid.

80. "Religious Right Shaped by Reason, Study Finds," *Grand Rapids (Michigan) Press*, 18 March 1995, sec. B, p. 2.

81. Ibid.; See Clyde Wilcox et al., "Rethinking the Reasonableness of the Religious Right," *Review of Religious Research* 36, no. 3 (March 1995): 263–76.

82. Carey, "Dark Continent," 183.

83. Ibid.

84. C. John Sommerville, "Why the News Makes Us Dumb," *First Things* (October 1991): 24.

85. David S. Broder, *Behind the Front Page* (New York: Simon and Schuster, 1987), 335.

86. Jim Dwyer, quoted in Christopher D. Ringwald, *Faith in Words: Ten Writers Reflect on the Spirituality of Their Profession* (Chicago: ACTA, 1997), 35.

87. Roderick P. Hart et al., "A Rhetorical Profile of Religious News: *Time*, 1947–1976," in *Rhetorical Dimensions in Media*, ed. Martin J. Medhurst (Dubuque, Iowa: Kendall/Hunt, 1984), 262–63.

88. Quoted in Avery Robert Dulles, "Religion and the News Media: A Theologian Reflects," *America* (1 October 1994): 6.

89. Quoted in Broder, *Behind the Front Page*, 335.

90. Quoted in Martin J. Medhurst, "American Cosmology and the Rhetoric of Inaugural Prayer," *Central States Speech Journal* 28 (winter 1977): 277–78.

91. Ibid., 272.

92. Michael J. Sandel, *Democracy's Discontent: America in Search of Public Policy* (Cambridge: The Belknap Press of Harvard University Press, 1996), 304–5.

93. Michael McIntyre, "Religionists on the Campaign Trail," *Christian Century* (27 December 1972): 1319–20.

94. During the 1990s a growing number of papers and even one broadcast TV network hired full-time religion reporters. Shepard, "Media Get Religion."

95. Quoted in Broder, *Behind the Front Page*, 335.

96. Mattingly, "The Religion Beat," 12–19.

97. Don Ranly, "How Religion Editors of Newspapers View Their Jobs and Religion," *Journalism Quarterly* 56 (1979): 845.

98. Charles K. Atkin et al., "How Journalists Perceive the Reading Audience," *Newspaper Research Journal* 4 (winter 1983): 51–63.

99. Judith M. Buddenbaum, "Covering Religion News at Daily Newspapers" (paper presented to the Newspaper Division of the Association for Education in Journalism and Mass Communication Annual Convention, San Antonio, Tex., August 1987), 14, 1.

100. Warren Breed, "Mass Communication and Sociocultural Integration," in *People, Society, and Mass Communications*, ed. Lewis A. Dexter and David Manning White (London: Free Press, 1964), 195.

101. Mattingly, "The Religion Beat"; see also Hart, et al., "A Theoretical Profile," 58–68.

102. Ranly, "Religion Editors," 848.

103. Peter Jennings, "The Media's Challenge in Covering Religion," *Religious Studies News* (November 1996): 15.

104. E. J. Dionne, "Keynote Address," *Commonweal* (24 February 1995), 28.

105. Paul David Baumann, "Epistemological Muddles: Religion and the Media," *Commonweal* (7 October 1994): 5.

106. James M. Wall, "Speaking of Religion," *Christian Century* 113 (24 April 1996): 443.

107. Mark A. Noll, "The Evangelical Enlightenment and the Task of Theological Education," in *Communication and Change*, ed. Sweet, 277, 278, 279.

108. Ibid., 280.

109. Quoted in ibid., 289.

110. Ibid.

111. Tocqueville was puzzled about how pragmatic yet principled Americans were in the 1830s. He wrote that "in their doubt of opinions, men in the end attach themselves solely to instincts and material interests, which are much more visible, more tangible, and more permanent in their nature than opinions." *Democracy*, 180.

112. Norman Fiering, *Moral Philosophy at Seventeenth-Century Harvard: A Discipline in Transition* (Chapel Hill: University of North Carolina Press, 1981), 300.

113. After the Civil War the ideals of theistic Enlightenment quickly faded in mainstream Protestantism but then reemerged during the fundamentalist-modernist disputes in the twentieth century. As George M. Marsden shows, American fundamentalists hung on to Scottish commonsense philosophy, using it both to forge their own approach to interpreting Scripture and, ironically, to battle the incursions of scientific thought into Christianity via higher criticism, including critiques of the veracity of the biblical accounts of human history. *Fundamentalism and American Culture* (New York: Oxford University Press, 1980), 14–16.

114. Aleksandr I. Solzhenitsyn, *A World Split Apart: Commencement Address Delivered at Harvard University June 8, 1978* (New York: Harper and Row, 1978), 27.

115. James W. Carey, "The Problem of Journalism History," in *A Critical Reader*, ed. Stryker and Warren, 88.

116. Stewart M. Hoover, *Final Report: The RNS-Lilly Study of Religion Reporting and Readership in the Daily Press* (Philadelphia: School of Communications and Theater Temple University), 102.

117. Park, "New As a Form of Knowledge," 46.

118. In 1993 the nation spent $4 billion on professional baseball, football, and basketball, compared with a whopping $56.7 billion that was contributed to religious causes; in the same year, however, religion received scant attention in the news compared with the voluminous coverage of sports. "Religion Draws Dollars but Not Media Coverage," *Grand Rapids (Michigan) Press*, 23 April 1994, sec. B, p. 6.

119. Solzhenitsyn, *A World Split Apart*, 25.

120. Thomas C. Ogletree, *Dimensions of Moral Understanding: Hospitality to the Stranger* (Philadelphia: Fortress, 1985), 101.

121. Ruth Ravenel, "The Thee Decade," *Washington Journalism Review* (December 1980): 38.

122. Ibid., 40.

123. Roger Rosenblatt, "Dreaming the News," *Time* (14 April 1997): 14.

124. Lloyd Eby, "Dramatic Art and Religion: An Uneasy Relation," *Dialogue and Alliance* 2, no. 1 (1988): 79.

125. Barend van Driel and James T. Richardson, "Categorization of New Religious Movements in American Print Media," *Sociological Analysis* 49, no. 2 (1988): 171–83.

126. Vincent F. A. Golphin, "Writer's Goal: Make Readers Think about Belief—Their and the Beliefs of Others," *Grand Rapids (Michigan) Press*, 8 September 1990, sec. B, p. 5.

127. Walter Lippmann, *Public Opinion* (New York: Free Press, 1922), 341.

128. Ibid., 358.

129. Boorstin, *The Americans*, 89–164.

130. James W. Carey, "Journalism and Criticism: The Case of an Underdeveloped Profession," *Review of Politics* 36 (April 1974): 241.

131. Stewart M. Hoover, *Religion in the News: Faith and Journalism in American Public Discourse* (Thousand Oaks, Calif.: Sage, 1998), 217.

132. Park, "New As a Form of Knowledge," 33.

133. "The Church in the Media's Mirrors," *America* (20 April 1991), 437.

134. Julia Duin, "Religion Beat Unpopular with Editors," *Editor and Publisher* (14 November 1992): 42.

135. Martin E. Marty, "Covering Religion," *Christian Century* 113 (June 1996): 646.

136. Quoted in David R. Boldt, "Press' Failure to Recognize Important Role of Religion," *Indianapolis Star*, 15 April 1992, sec. A, p. 15.

137. Robert E. Park, "Social Planning and Human Nature," in *Robert E. Park: The Crowd and the Public and Other Essays*, ed. Henry Elsner Jr. (Chicago: University of Chicago Press, 1972), 86–87.

138. Thomas Lessl, "The Priestly Voice," *Quarterly Journal of Speech* 75 (May 1989): 183.

139. Walter Goodman, "4 Minutes a Week: A Liberal on NBC," *New York Times*, 9 March 1995, sec. B , p. 4.

140. Jane Bryant Quinn, "Stocks: Everything but the Kitchen Sink," *Newsweek* (28 December 1993): 37.

141. "Born Again Christian Slater," *Premiere Magazine* (April 1994): cover.

142. Eleanor Clift, "Buchanan: Thunder of the Right," *Newsweek* (25 November 1991): 20.

143. Tocqueville, *Democracy*, 278.

144. Rev. Thomas McSweeney, "Religion Deserves Smart Coverage," *Electronic Media* (31 August 1998): 9.

145. Richard Harwood, "Religious Evasion," *Washington Post* (16 December 1990), sec. K, p. 5.

146. James M. Wall, "Language Gap," *Christian Century* (29 June-6 July 1994): 627–28.

147. Jonathan Kozol, "Spare Us the Cheap Grace," *Time* (11 December 1995): 96.

148. Richard Rorty, *Philosophy and Social Hope* (New York: Penguin, 1999). For a ore recent articulation of Rorty's position, see "Religion in the Public Square: A Reconsideration," *Journal of Religious Ethics* 31, no. 1 (2003): 141–9.

149. For an excellent "debate" on the issue of bringing personal religious convictions into public discourse, see Robert Audi and Nicholas Wolterstorff, *Religion in the Public Square: The Place of Religious Convictions in Political Debate* (Lanham, Md.: Rowman and Littlefield, 1997). Another excellent volume addressing the topic is Paul J. Weithman, ed., *Religion and Contemporary Liberalism* (Notre Dame, Ind.: University of Notre Dame Press, 1997).

150. Quoted in Gustav Niebuhr, "Remembering a Theologian Executed for Trying to Oust the Nazis," *New York Times,* 8 April 1995, sec. Y, p. 7; see also Dietrich Bonhoeffer, *The Cost of Discipleship*, rev. ed. (New York: Macmillan, 1970), 116.

151. See, e.g., Sandel, *Democracy's Discontent*, 60–61.

152. See David Martin, *Tongues of Fire: The Explosion of Protestantism in Latin America* (Oxford: Blackwell, 1993).

153. Garry Wills, *Under God: Religion and American Politics* (New York: Simon and Schuster, 1990), 25.

154. Quoted in Charles Honey, "Yale Professor Believes Religious Conviction Has Its Place in Politics," *Grand Rapids (Michigan) Press*, 13 January 1994, sec. A, p. 7.

155. James M. Houston, *The Heart's Desire: Satisfying the Hunger of the Soul* (Colorado Springs, Colo.: NavPress, 1996).

156. Quoted in Barbara Kantrowitz et al., "In Search of the Sacred," *Newsweek* (30 November 1994): 53.

157. Quoted in Ed Golder, "Magazine Editor Seeks to Root Out Cynicism from Media," *Grand Rapids (Michigan) Press*, 22 January 1997.

158. Nicholas Wolterstorff, "The Role of Religion in Decision and Discussion of Political Issues," in Robert Audi and Nicholas Wolterstorff, *Religion in the Public Square*, 113.

159. Edward E. Ericson, *Solzhenitsyn: The Moral Vision* (Grand Rapids, Mich.: William B. Eerdmans, 1980).

160. Solzhenitsyn, *A World Split Apart*, 27.

161. Václav Havel, *The Art of the Impossible: Politics As Morality in Practice, Speeches and Writings, 1990–1996*, trans. Paul Wilson (New York: Fromm International, 1998), 180.

162. Neuhaus, *The Naked Public Square*, 110.

163. Among the better ones were *Commentary, Christianity and Crisis, Christian Century, Reformed Journal, Commonweal*, and *America.*

164. Charley Reese, "When Journalists Parrot Propaganda," *Grand Rapids (Michigan) Press*, 9 March 1995, sec. A, p. 16.

165. See James Fallows, *Breaking the News: How the Media Undermine American Democracy* (New York: Random House, 1996), 159–81.

166. James Carey, "'A Republic, If You Can Keep It': Liberty and Public Life in the Age of Glasnost," in *James Carey: A Critical Reader,* ed. Eve Stryker Munson and Catherine A. Warren (Minneapolis: University of Minnesota Press, 1997), 217.

167. Robert W. Delp, "The Southern Press and the Rise of American Spiritualism, 1847–1860," *Journal of American Culture* 7, no. 3 (fall 1984): 94.

168. Carey, "'A Republic,'" 217.

169. Alvin W. Gouldner, *The Dialectic of Ideology and Technology: The Origins, Grammar, and Future of Ideology* (New York: Seabury Press, 1976), 26.

170. Václav Havel, *Open Letters: Selected Writings, 1965–1990*, ed. Paul Wilson (New York: Vintage, 1992), 133.

171. Marsden, *Fundamentalism.*

172. Grace Halsell, *Prophecy and Politics: Militant Evangelists on the Road to Nuclear War* (Westport, Conn.: Lawrence Hill, 1986).

173. On the democratic predispositions, see Jean Bethke Elshtain, *Democracy on Trial* (New York: Basic Books, 1995), 2.

174. Carey, "Dark Continent," 180.

175. Herbert J. Gans, *Deciding What's News* (New York: Vintage Books, 1979), 68–69.

176. Dan Nimmo and James E. Combs, *The Political Pundits* (New York: Praeger, 1992), 60.

177. Robert E. Park, "Reflections On Communication and Culture," in *The Crowd*, ed. Elsner, 102.

178. Albert Borgmann, *Holding On to Reality: The Nature of Information at the Turn of the Millennium* (Chicago: University of Chicago Press, 1999), 231.

179. Hoover, *Religion in the News*, 137.

180. Elshtain, *Democracy on Trial*, 136.

181. Robert Lynn, "The Mass Media and the Kingdom of Evil," *Religion in Life* 21, no. 2 (spring 1952): 240.

182. Eugene McCarthy, "Let Us Prey," *Washingtonian* (October 1989): 119, 120.

183. For an excellent assessment of the "sins" of journalists, see Fallows, *Breaking the News: How the Media Undermine American Democracy* (New York: Random House, 1996).

Chapter 8

1. Charles Horton Cooley, *Social Organization: A Study of the Larger Mind* (New York: Schocken Books, 1909), 203.

2. Ibid.

3. One of Tocqueville's hopes for religion was that "it may serve as a reminder of what transcends the mediocrity of democratic public life, and thus of a greatness not usually within its scope." Harvey C. Mansfield and Delba Winthrop, introduction to *Democracy in America*, by Alexis de Tocqueville, ed. and trans. Mansfield and Winthrop (Chicago: University of Chicago Press, 2000), xxxiii.

4. Tocqueville, *Democracy*, 275.

5. Ibid., 500. For a discussion of this concept, see Mansfield and Winthrop, introduction to *Democracy*, lxvi-lxx.

6. See especially James W. Carey, "The Press, Public Opinion, and Public Discourse," in *James Carey: A Critical Reader*, ed. Eve Stryker Munson and Catherine A. Warren (Minneapolis: University of Minnesota Press, 1997), 238–39.

7. Robert E. Park, "Reflections On Communication and Culture," in *Robert E. Park: The Crowd and the Public and Other Essays*, ed. Henry Elsner Jr. (Chicago: University of Chicago Press, 1972), 101–2.

8. Nat Goldhaber, "About Time," *newmedia.com* (September 1998): 22.

9. Stephen Bertman, *Cultural Amnesia: America's Future and the Crisis of Memory* (Westport, Conn.: Praeger, 2000), 117.

10. Perhaps the best explanation of Innis's theories can be found in James W. Carey, *Communication As Culture: Essays on Media and Society* (Boston: Unwin Hyman, 1989), 142–72.

11. Michael Warren, *Communications and Cultural Analysis: A Religious View* (Westport, Conn.: Bergin and Garvey, 1992), 38.

12. James M. Houston, *I Believe in the Creator* (Grand Rapids, Mich.: William B. Eerdmans, 1980), 122.

13. For an interesting study of this within the church, see Avery Dulles, *A Church to Believe In: Discipleship and the Dynamics of Freedom* (New York: Crossroads, 1982).

14. Michael J. Sandel, *Democracy's Discontent: America in Search of Public Policy* (Cambridge: The Belknap Press of Harvard University Press, 1996), 343.

15. Cooley, *Social Organization*, 383.

16. Carey, "'A Republic, if You Can Keep It,'" in *A Critical Reader*, ed. Munson and Warren, 216.

17. Margaret Mead, *Culture and Commitment: A Study of the Generation Gap* (Garden City, N.J.: Natural History Press/Doubleday, 1970).

18. My colleagues and I have addressed this issue with respect to the youth culture in the United States. See Quentin J. Schultze et al., *Dancing in the Dark: Youth, Popular Culture and the Electronic Media* (Grand Rapids, Mich.: William B. Eerdmans, 1991), 46–75.

19. I am skeptical of any approaches to integrating youth in the religious tribe primarily through electronic and digital communication. It seems to me that these approaches might actually be weakening the very tradition that they are trying to extend to the next generation. For an alternative view, argued persuasively from the context of the Roman Catholic Church, see Pierre Babin, *The New Era in Religious Communication* (Minneapolis, Minn.: Fortress Press, 1991).

20. Paul Connerton, *How Societies Remember* (Cambridge: Cambridge University Press, 1989), 2, 4–5, 39.

21. Jean Bethke Elshtain, preface to *Democracy on Trial* (New York: Basic Books, 1995), xv.

22. Harold Adams Innis, *Empire and Communications* (Toronto: University of Toronto Press, 1972).

23. John Lukacs, *Confessions of an Original Sinner* (South Bend, Ind.: St. Augustine's Press, 2000), 270.

24. Carey, *Communication As Culture*, 136.

25. William F. Fore, "The Church and Communication in the Technological Era," *Christian Century* 103 (September 24, 1986): 810.

26. Park, "Reflections," 102.

27. Walker Percy, *Signposts in a Strange Land* (New York: Farrar, Straus and Giroux, 1991), 370.

28. Park, "Reflections," 105.

29. Ibid., 113.

30. Robert N. Bellah, "The Sociological Implications of the Electronic Media," in *The Electronic Media, Popular Culture and Family Values*, ed.

Mary Lou Schropp (New York: United States Catholic Conference, 1985), 15.

31. Louis Wirth, "Consensus and Mass Communication," in *On Cities and Social Life*, ed. Albert J. Reiss Jr. (Chicago: University of Chicago Press, 1964), 29.

32. Alasdair MacIntyre, *After Virtue: A Study in Moral Theory* (South Bend, Ind.: Notre Dame University Press, 1981).

33. Robert D. Putnam, *Bowling Alone: The Collapse and Revival of American Community* (New York: Simon and Schuster, 2000).

34. Elshtain, preface to *Democracy on Trial*, xii.

35. Bette Jean Bullert, "Television and the Vision of the Common Good," in *The Common Good and U.S. Capitalism*, ed. Oliver F. Williams and John W. Houck (Lanham, Md.: University Press of America, 1987), 377.

36. Nancy L. Rosenblum, ed., *Liberalism and the Moral Life* (Cambridge: Harvard University Press, 1989), 139.

37. In this sense, Madison and the others who composed the Constitution in 1787 seemed to agree with the Hobbesian and Calvinistic notion that individuals are contentious and selfish. See Richard Hofstadter, *The American Political Tradition* (New York: Alfred A. Knopf, 1948), 3.

38. George Lindbeck, *The Nature of Doctrine: Religion and Theology in a Postliberal Age* (Philadelphia: Westminster, 1984), 128.

39. Quoted in Martin E. Marty, "Teaching Children about Religion," *Sightings* (E-mail newsletter), 14 September 1998.

40. Cooley, *Social Organization*, 378, 380.

41. Robert Wuthnow, *The Restructuring of American Religion: Society and Faith since World War II* (Princeton, N.J.: Princeton University Press, 1988).

42. Robert N. Bellah, "Civil Religion in America," *Daedalus* 96 (winter/spring 1967): 18.

43. Carey, "A Republic," 218.

44. Søren Kierkegaard, *Two Ages. The Age of Revolution and the Present Age: A Literary Review*, *Kierkegaard's Writings*, vol. 15, ed. and trans. H. V. Hong and E. H. Hong (Princeton, N.J.: Princeton University Press, 1978), 90–91.

45. Robert E. Park and Ernest W. Burgess, *Introduction to the Science of Sociology* (Chicago: University of Chicago Press, 1970), 37.

46. Michael Ignatieff, *The Needs of Strangers* (NY: Picador, 1984), 78.

47. Peter Mann, "Visual Media and the Common Good: Two Experiences," in *The Common Good*, ed. Williams and Houck, 364.

48. Jay Rosen, *What Are Journalists For?* (New Haven, Conn.: Yale University Press, 1999), 262.

49. Ralph Engelman, *Public Radio and Television in America: A Political History* (Thousand Oaks, Calif.: Sage, 1996).

50. Leonard Verduin, *The Reformers and Their Stepchildren* (Grand Rapids, Mich.: Eerdmans, 1964), 279.

51. "Lieberman," *The New Republic* (21 August 2000): 9.

52. Nicholas Wolterstorff, "The Role of Religion in Decision and Discussion of Political Issues," in Robert Audi and Nicholas Wolterstorff, *Religion in the Public Square: The Place of Religious Convictions in Political Debate* (Lanham, Md: Rowman & Littlefield, 1997), 147.

53. Tocqueville, *Democracy*.

54. For an interesting treatment of the expansion of American Christianity into virtually every popular medium and cultural form, see Colleen McDannell, *Material Christianity: Religion and Popular Culture in Modern America* (New Haven, Conn.: Yale University Press, 1995).

55. "Survey Shows Public Would Restrict Speech," *Freedom Forum and Newseum News* 7 (summer 2000): 2, 1.

56. Susan E. Tifft and Alex S. Jones, "The Family: How Being Jewish Shaped the Dynasty that Runs the Times," *New Yorker* (19 April 1999): 45.

57. Cooley, *Social Organization*, 201, 202.

58. Park, "Reflections," 116.

59. Harold D. Lasswell, "The Structure and Function of Communication in Society," in *The Processes and Effects of Mass Communication*, ed. Wilbur Schramm and Donald F. Roberts (Urbana: University of Illinois Press, 1971), 84.

60. Wirth, "Consensus and Mass Communication," 29.

61. See Alvin W. Gouldner, *The Dialectic of Ideology and Technology: The Origins, Grammar, and Future of Ideology* (New York: Seabury Press, 1976), 26.

62. Carey, *Communication As Culture*, 63.

63. Warren, *Communications and Cultural Analysis*, 33.

64. Kenneth Burke, *A Rhetoric of Motives* (Berkeley, Calif.: University of California Press, 1969).

65. Gouldner, *The Dialectic of Ideology*, 26.

66. Jonathan Sacks, "Markets and Morals," *First Things* (August/September 2000): 22, 23.

67. Ibid., 28.

68. Thomas S. Hibbs, *Shows About Nothing: Nihilism in Popular Culture from The Exorcist to Seinfeld* (Dallas: Spence Publishing, 1999), 178.

69. See especially the discussion of Cooley's ideas in Park, "Reflections," 103.

70. Carey, *Communication As Culture*, 20.

71. Cooley, *Social Organization*, 373.

72. Ibid., 374.

73. Lloyd Eby, "Dramatic Art and Religion: An Uneasy Relation," *Dialogue and Alliance* 2 (1988): 79.

74. See T. J. Jackson Lears, "From Salvation to Self-Realization: Advertising and the Therapeutic Roots of the Consumer Culture, 1880–1930," in *The Culture of Consumption: Critical Essays in American History 1880–1980*, ed. Richard Wightman Fox and T. J. Jackson Lears (New York: Pantheon Books, 1983), 3–37.

75. Carol Sue Humphrey, "Religious Newspapers and Antebellum Reform," in *Media and Religion in American History*, ed. William David Sloan (Northport, Ala.: Vision Press, 2000), 118.

76. Warren, *Communications and Cultural Analysis*, 34.

77. Dulles, *A Church to Believe In*, 11.

78. Lukacs, introduction to *Confessions*, xiii.

79. See Nicholas Wolterstorff, "Why We Should Reject What Liberalism Tells Us About Speaking and Acting in Public for Religious Reasons," in *Religion and Contemporary Liberalism*, ed. Paul J. Weithman (Notre Dame, Ind.: University of Notre Dame Press, 1997), 178.

80. Michael L. Budde, *The (Magic) Kingdom of God: Christianity and Global Culture Industries* (New York: Westview Press, 1997), 14, 15.

81. Carey, *Communication As Culture*, 9.

82. Fore, "The Church and Communication," 810.

83. Ellul, *The Technological Society*, xxv.

84. Marilynne Robinson, *The Death of Adam: Essays on Modern Thought* (New York: Houghton Mifflin, 1998), 167.

85. See Clifford G. Christians, "Technology and Triadic Theories of Mediation," in *Rethinking Media, Religion, and Culture*, ed. Stewart M. Hoover and Knut Lundby (Thousand Oaks, Calif.: Sage, 1997), 69.

86. Houston, *I Believe*, 49.

87. Paul Tillich, "Existentialist Aspects of Modern Art," in *Christianity and the Existentialists*, ed. Carl Michalson (New York: Charles Scribner and Sons, 1956), 130.

88. Oddly enough, many scholars are not aware of Ellul's strong Christian faith and deep theological interests. For background on his work, see Jacques Ellul, *In Season Out of Season: An Introduction to the Thought of Jacques Ellul*, trans. Lani K. Niles, based on interviews by Madeleine Garrigou-Lagrange (San Francisco: Harper and Row, 1982).

89. See, e.g., Judo Poerwowidagdo and Dafne Sabanes Plou, "Workshop IV: Media and Information Technology," *Ministerial Formation* 75 (October 1996): 26–29. Plou says, "But we must not demonize the media, nor communications nor information technology. They are tools. They are a product of human culture and as such have positive and negative aspects, and their use can be channeled in the search of common good if we let human values take priority over technology." Ibid., 27.

90. See, e.g., Richard R. Gaillardetz, *Transforming Our Days: Spirituality, Community and Liturgy in a Technological Culture* (New York: Crossroad Publishing, 2000); Ruth Conway, *Choices at the Heart of Technology: A Christian Perspective* (Harrisburg, Pa.: Trinity Press International, 1999); Craig M. Gay, *The Way of the (Modern) World: On Why It's Tempting to Live As If God Doesn't Exist* (Grand Rapids, Mich.: William B. Eerdmans, 1998); and Quentin J. Schultze, *Habits of the High-Tech Heart: Living Virtuously in the Information Age* (Grand Rapids, Mich.: Baker Academic, 2002).

91. Carey, *Communication As Culture*, 160.

92. Arnold Pacey, *Meaning in Technology* (Cambridge, Mass: MIT Press, 1999), 98.

93. George Grant, *Lament for a Nation: The Defeat of Canadian Nationalism* (Toronto: McClelland and Stewart, 1965). See also Grant, *Technology and Empire: Perspectives on North America* (Toronto: Anansi, 1969).

94. Carey, *Communication As Culture*, 159.

95. Ibid., 155, 150.

96. Jonathan Mills, "Technology, Eh?" *Crux* 20 (September 1984): 11.

97. Ibid., 12, 13.

98. Robert E. Park, "The Crowd and the Public," in *The Crowd*, ed. Elsner, 80.

99. Park, "Reflections," 102.

100. Wirth, "Consensus and Communication," 25.

101. Ibid., 25.

102. Edmund V. Sullivan, "Commonsense and Valuing," *Religious Education* 78, no. 1 (winter 1983): 10.

103. Cooley, *Social Organization*, 205.

104. Gouldner, *The Dialectic of Ideology*, 26, 27, 1.
105. Connerton, *How Societies Remember*, 3, 5.
106. Luke 22:19.
107. Daniel J. Boorstin, *Republic of Technology: Reflections on Our Future Community* (New York: Harper and Row, 1978).
108. Wuthnow, *The Restructuring of American Religion*, 294.

Index